STONE PRAYERS

STONE PRAYERS

Native American Stone Constructions of
the Eastern Seaboard

CURTISS HOFFMAN

America Through Time is an imprint of Fonthill Media LLC
www.through-time.com
office@through-time.com

Published by America Through Time / Fonthill Media LLC

First published 2018
Reprinted 2024

ISBN 978-1-63499-049-3

Typeset in Mrs Eaves XL Serif Narrow
Printed and bound in England

PREFACE

Qussuck Qanash
(by Black-Eagle Sun)

The indigenous New England natives have long been buried under a mass of indifference, prejudices, hearsay, and Victorian ideas about "the noble red-men" and guilt complexes of the racially downtrodden. Our television and movies have given the impression that the only American Indian was the Western Indian.

For years, archaeologists have been quietly working behind the scenes, trying to flesh out the prehistoric Indian and his way of life. Since the prehistoric antedates written history, the excavated artifacts of stone must speak for themselves. Interpreting these finds is all-important, and one has little patience with interpretations and museum designs that were developed from intellectual guess-work and not from the "Affective Interpretations" that would have occurred using the indigenous life-ways of attitudinal relationship expressed in the Ojibway term: *"Nakana-Gnaa"*—"We are all related." Plants, animals, the Earth, and all the forces of nature that surround us are part of us. The knowledge of Indigenous people about their environment is a testimonial to the ingenuity, creativity, resourcefulness, and ability of people to learn and to teach harmonious ways of existence with nature. Indigenous people have demonstrated a way of knowing and relating that must be regained and adapted to a contemporary setting— not only for the benefit of those cultures themselves, but for all humankind.

In spite of the importance of connecting to the natural world and the indigenous models available for doing this, much of what Indian people have to offer has been ignored or trivialized. Western culture, through its unique play of history, disconnected itself from the natural world in order to conquer it. In doing so, Western culture also disconnected from the well-spring of the unconscious and ancient primal orientations to spiritual ecology and a deeply internalized sense of place.

Nature is a Sacred Reality for the Indigenous people of North America. Guided by these metaphysical principles, indigenous people acknowledged that all living and non-living entities of nature have important inherent meanings within the context of human life. Based on this understanding, indigenous Native Americans symbolically recognized their relationship to plants, animals, stones, trees, mountains, rivers, lakes, streams, and a host of other living entities.

With this awareness, tempered by intimate relationships with various environments over a thousand or more generations, indigenous people accumulated and applied their ecological knowledge—and still do. It seems that a collective dialogue is due, and right in step with this here and now that calls for the collective wisdom of all to act as one. The reader lives and feels this happening in the space in between the lines. The author is willing the collective wisdom to all who read this offering to join us and create love, peace, harmony, and collective oneness in the service to a higher power or spirit.

In our Nipmuc language, we say: *Moh-Tompan Wunni*—"Greetings."

Nenuko, Wompsikuk Nepauz Othai

I am Eagle Sun Heart, Nipmuc Turtle Clan Medicine Doctor. I am honored to have been asked to offer comment on this archaeologist's venture excursion into the archaeological history of our indigenous relations, who experienced their lives in this southern New England place.

Although those ancient relations have crossed over to the spirit world, those spirits are here contributing. As a valid commentator for a project that I deem necessary to remind the refined technologies of today of the basic technologies in our ancient cultures that, if not practiced, we would not have had the established foundations that support the more advanced technologies in this day and age. The understanding and how the use of "Stone People Knowledge" affected me and guided me to the "Place of Heart" follows.

During the Paleo-Indian period, North American peoples hunted large mammals using Clovis and other stone weapons during this epoch, which is also known as the Stone Age in Europe. From that time until now, the "Stone People" have played an important role and directed our indigenous cultures in their continually refining, spiritual, natural way of existence.

The accumulated knowledge of the remaining indigenous groups around the world represents a body of ancient thought, experience, and action that must be honored and preserved as a vital storehouse of environmental wisdom. This environmental understanding can form the basis for evolving the cosmological reorientation so desperately needed. Modern societies must recapture the ecologically sustainable orientation that has long been absent from their psychological, social, and spiritual consciousness.

Gregory Cajete says:

Indigenous people have preserved ways of ecologically-based living that have evolved over 40,000 years of continuous relationship with special environments. Their understanding and application of relating to their land represent models for the "art of relationship" that must be re-taught through modern education, modern understanding, and reapplication of indigenous relationships to the land that are keys to creating social and economic structures that may mean the survival of modern societies.

Indigenous knowledge bases evolved over thousands of years and hundreds of generations. With the loss of that knowledge one loses access to the approaches and techniques that may become life-saving as we move into the new century. These modes will become essential as we try to deal with the mega-environmental, social and cultural problems, the result of the mindset that modern people have evolved within the last century, particularly their disregard for establishing a viable relationship to the natural world.

Indigenous people have demonstrated a way of knowing and relating that must be regained and adapted to a contemporary setting. Not only for the benefit of those cultures themselves, but for all humankind.[1]

Qussuck Qanash

"A Tribute to the Stone People" is a tribute to our ancient "Grandfather Stones," the oldest living beings in our world, who helped me to quiet my mind, to listen, to see positive visions of a better me, and how to be a better me, in each succeeding breath, an enduring guide that guided me to the Place of Heart, the Place Where All Healing Begins, the Place Where All Answers Emanate For You—Your Heart!

From the womb of Mother Earth, in ceremony, the "Hot-Hearts" of the ancient grandfather stone people were the "tuners" for my human heart, regulated by our seasonal ceremonies dedicated to living a purified, clean life, endurance, cleanliness, strength, and purity. A way of life that kept their lives straight, doing purposeful good acts, and speaking words of truth—all divined from the hissing, steaming, singing "stones." Water represents the lifeblood of the Earth and universe. During the purification ceremonies, the hot stones cause the water to purify and open the spiritual doors to communication. The glowing redness gives messages, how spirit and knowledge make the world well. Our oldest living relations on this earth, the cooled molten core of our mother, who knows best, and puts you to the test! To hear requires that you listen:

1. The grandfathers speak through the stones.
2. The grandmothers speak through the moon.
3. The father speaks through the sun.
4. The mother speaks through the earth.

Are you listening?…
They all have something to say.
Are you listening?…

To truly listen requires that you "quiet" the mind. And the way of life used by our ancient indigenous relations was ritual and ceremony. Ceremony was used to maintain the balanced awareness perspectives required to survive in actual reality, with all aspects of life. The animals (two-legged and four-legged), the birds, the creepy-crawlers, the fish, the vegetables, trees, bushes, minerals, and stones, all aspects of life were considered vibrantly alive, sacred and related. And here now is no different. We are all related as one, and needing that understanding to be felt by all of humanity.

Once again, the silent private moments of here pervades our awareness, drawing us into our inner-reality, the Place of Heart. It offers us the space to co-design vision, and already to see yourself doing what has to be done, with the higher power spirit's creative spirit in union with yours and others who choose to draw that inspirational support from their own Places of Heart.

Every aspect of life, in the animal and in the mineral and the vegetable, all guidance to live properly comes from each individual's heart. Your heart force feeds your life force. Your life force creates your living feeling energy that holds us each together in our highly creative individuations attempting to align with your true self.

> "You cannot know that which you have not first established an experiential relationship." They established relationships with nature on an equal footing … a family relation attitude with all of creation. That attitudinal loss has now brought us to the brink of extinction. Our misuse of technology has mesmerized a majority of society to the point of "mass-loss" and disconnection to our natural surroundings; a "Nature Deficit Disorder."[2]

The misuse of the "thinking process" that thinks a solution, without first having done the personal experiences, to create their personal validity and their basis of knowing, requires addressing.

The rites of passage ceremonies that facilitated the smooth transitions between the different levels of awareness and realizations required in the ageing process are no longer in vogue. The higher power spirit lives in each of our hearts. It is each of our responsibilities to establish that communicative connection within ourselves.

Down through the millennia to this moment now, the stone people have given themselves to the two-leggeds to use as they will, in a sacred manner of service, to insure humanity's survival. To those who are hierolithically inclined, the divined words of stone await your personal divinations in ceremonial silence.

Many tribes saw rocks as medicine and used them in many ways. All rocks were considered sacred and some were holy. The stones that were seen in dreams and visions were considered holy. The sacred pipe was, and still is, the central instrument and manifestation of sacredness for indigenous people. The pipe, and the traditions surrounding it, has become the spiritual legacy of the people who still own it and celebrate the significance of all that it is. For our indigenous ancient relations, the sacred pipe was, and is, the axis mundi, the central axis of the world. For the indigenous cultures, it was the very means by which that mysterious, yet divine relationship is re-established between man and the sun, the earth and the winds, and more profoundly among themselves and other living things, and that which creates and causes motion. As in many ancient cultures, in Algonquian spiritual teachings, the ceremonies with our ancient stone people help us to reconnect to the lifeblood of the universe.

The sacred stone people were utilitarian servants in the hands of the Indigenous, as well as having the sacred qualities of medicines, the sacred pipestone (carved into sacred pipes), all the stone utensils used in ceremonial preparation and ceremony, all sacred relations, all used in the sacred natural way of enduring maintenance with our higher power spirit, who guides us in our service to humanity.

To truly understand indigenous culture, one must live the natural way of life that indigenous cultures lived. To know anything about Mother Earth and her inner and outer inhabitants, one must learn to walk in balance on the earth. This walk includes that attitudinal understanding that we are all related.

Nakana-Gnaa

The Animal, two-legged and four-legged.
The Mineral which includes all of our stone relations…
The Vegetable, the grasses, bushes, trees.

No understanding of a relation can happen until a "communicating-relationship" with that relation is established.

Algonquian spiritual teachings

If archaeologists and indigenous people are to work together, a full and equal acceptance of the sacred spiritual way of life of the indigenous cultures must be achieved. This knowledge cannot be understood by one looking from the "outside" in. You can only know the "stone people" by seeing from your inside out, and doing the ceremonies that let their inside guidance out for us to use. Only man speaks with words. All other beings speak non-verbally. It also should be added that being and living the natural way has nothing to do with "blood." It is living a spiritual way of life, an effective approach to living archaeology—"Bringing Then up to date with Now!"

To all the Sacred Medicine Teachers, who have guided and given me the Spiritual Teachings of Peace, *Kuttabottomish*—I thank you.

Kesuckquand, ohke-okaas…
  Taubotne … "Manito-oo Manito-oo"

Acknowledgments

A vast number of individuals have contributed their knowledge of local sites to this study. Without their information, the collection of information would have been much less productive. They are listed below alphabetically by last name, along with the abbreviations for the states and provinces in which the sites they have reported are located.

Thanks to Richard Adverbly (PA), Peter Anick (CT, MA, NH, RI, VA), Robert Austin (MA), Peter Backes (NY), Ted Ballard (MA, NH, RI), Lockwood Barr (NY), Karen Bartnicki (MA), Ruth Bates (MA), Grace Bello (NY), Teresa Bierce (CT, NY), Sydney Blackwell (MA), Tom Botelho (MA), Wayne Braley (MA), Emily Brunelle (MA), Matt Bua (NY), Rob Buchanan (NY), Rolf Cachat-Schilling (MA, NY, PA), Cathy Carlson (CT), Kurt Carr (PA), Dan Cassedy (NY, PA), Michael Cavanagh (RI), Mark Cedrone (MA), Tommy Charles (GA, SC), David Chase (GA), Craig Cippoli (CT), Anita Cole (MA), David Cole (MA), Robert Conrad (MA), Patrick Cooke (CT, ME, MA, NJ, NY, PA, VT), Mike Coughlin (MA), Thomas Cox (GA), David Cuneo (CT, DE, MA, NJ, NY, PA, RI), Patricia Cridlebaugh (GA), Dennis Curry (MD), Bob Dalbec (MA), Bob DeFosses (CT), Joanna Delaney (MA), Barbara DeLong (CT, ME, MA, NJ, NY, PA, VT), Keith Derting (SC), Terry DeVeau (NB, NS), Charles Devine (CT, RI), Steve DiMarzo (CT, ME, MA, NH, NY, RI), Dennis Donais (CT), Dianna Doucette (MA), Marty Dudek (NH), Don Duffy (MA), Kevin Dunn (MA), Dan Elliott (GA), Dolores Elliott (NJ, NY, PA, VA), Alice Ferguson (MD), Erin Flynn (MA),Tim Fohl (CT, MA, RI, VT), Diana Fox (MA, RI), Mike Futrell (VA), Steve Gabis (MA), James Gage (CT, ME, MA, NH, NY, RI), Mary Gage (MA, RI), Bob Goodby (NH), Dyke Goodin (GA), Mary Green (VA), Chris Groden (MA), Alice Guerrant (DE), Derek Gunn (MA), C. J. Hall (RI), Bruce Hamed (MA), Mike Harmon (NC), Corey Hart (PA), Bob Hasenstab (NY), James Haskins (MA, NY), Lee Hayes (ME), Kenneth Hill (VA), McKayla Hoffman (CT, MA), Nick Holland (MA), Diane Horvath (MA), Alex Houtzager (MA), Matt Howes (MA), Mike Hoye (MA), Jack Hranicky (VA), Gabriel Hrynick (NS), Tommy Hudson (GA), Joanne Hulburt (MA), Nancy Hunt (CT, MA, NH, NJ, RI), Ryan Hurd (PA), H. A. Huscher (GA), Tim Ives (RI), Dan Jesus (MA), Carole Johnson (MA), Brian Jones (CT), Paul Kachinsky (MA), Frank Karkota (MA), Gin Keating (MA), Colin Kennedy (MA), Ken King (ME), Scarlet Kinney (ME), Kathy Klopchin (MA, NY), Kathy Knowles (CT), Sarah Kohler (MA), Brian

Konieczwy (MA), Richard Kramer (MA), Glenn Kreisberg (NY), Greg Lattanzi (NJ), Lucianne Lavin (CT), Ed Lenik (CT, ME, MA, NB, NH, NJ, NY, NS, VT), Ken Leonard (MA), Mike Leonard (MA), Mary Ellen Lepionka (MA), Harvey Lipman (ME, MA), Michael Lombardo (MA), Jon Lothrop (NY), Johannes Loubser (GA, NC, SC), Robert MacDonald (MA), Maryanne MacLeod (MA), Tim MacSweeney (CT, GA, MA, NH, NY, RI, VA), Joe Mahan (GA), Charles Manson (VA), Vic Mastone (MA), Jim Mavor (MA), Bruce McAleer (MA), Gil McCarthy (MA), E. L. McCullough (GA), Linda McElroy (MA), Bill McEntee (MA), Tim McKnight (MD), Gerry McLoughlin (CT, MA, NY), Polly Midgley (CT, NY), Nan Millett (ME), Robert Miner (RI), Bill Moody (MA), Susan Morse (MA), Philip Mulford (VA, WV), Norman Muller (CT, MA, NH, NJ, NY, NC, PA, RI, VT), Larry Mulligan (PA), Rachel Mulroy (MA), Wendi Murray (MA), Susan Myers (NC), Joe Nierman (RI), Henry Norton (MA), Bernard Otto (MA), Tom Paul (CT, NY), Jim Petersen (ME), Vincenzo Petrullo (GA), Chris Pittman (MA), Jim Porter (ME, NH, NY, RI), Dennis and Judy Randall (MA), Ralph Rataul (NY), Sue Reilly (MA), Donald Repsher (CT, NJ, PA, SC), Trudy Lamb Richmond (CT), Fred Robinson (CT), Edward Rose (MA), Jack Rossen (MA), Vicki Rourke (NH, PA), Laurie Rush (NY), Janice Ryalls (NC), Valdimar Samuelson (ME, MA), Gary Sanderson (MA), Alix Saulnier (NB), Judy Savage (MA), Donna Savino (CT, MA, NY), Kristin Scarr (WV), Don Schulz (GA), David Schewe (NY), Doug Schwartz (CT, MA, NY, RI. VT), Rob Sirois (ME), Alan Smith (MA, NH), Jolene Smith (VA), Chris Soccorro (MA), Frank Speck (NY), Dan Stanford (SC), Mark Starr (CT, RI), Robert Stephenson (MD), James Stockbridge (MA), Mary Stowe (VT), Noel Stratton (PA), Ros Strong (ME), Steve Sullwold (MA), Lee Swanson (MA), Anna Szak (NH), Charlotte Taylor (RI), Heather Taylor (PA), Ted Thomas (GA), John Thompson (MA), K. Pat Thorne (CT), Richard Thornton (GA), Ted Timreck (CT, MA, NH, NY), Suzanne Tjoelker (RI), Bob Trotta (MA), G. A. Turner (GA), Teig Tyrson (ME), Walter van Roggen (CT, ME, MA, NH, RI, VT), Peter Waksman (CT, GA, ME, MA, NH, NY, PA, VA), Greg Walwer (CT), M. Weinland (GA), Frederick Werkheiser (CT, NH, PA, SC), Don Wessel (ME), Ernie Wiegand (CT), Mark Williams (GA), Eugene Winter (MA), Ann Wirkkala (CT, ME, MA, NH, NY, PA, QU, RI, VT), Nancy Wisser (NY, PA), D. Wood (GA), Woods Hole Historical Museum (MA), Craig Wright (NY), and Jerry Zerbach (GA).

I also wish to acknowledge the assistance of several individuals who provided me with links to many of the historical documents cited in Chapter 2: Ted Ballard, Rolf Cachat-Schilling, James Gage, Sheila Lynch-Bentinnen, and James Porter. Without their assistance, the sources presented in that chapter would have been considerably less robust. I am also deeply indebted to a number of wise members of indigenous communities who have generously shared their thoughts about these sites with me: Doug Harris and John Brown (Narragansett); Cheryl Andrews-Maltais, Bettina Washington, Kerrie Helme, and Linda Coombs (Aquinnah Wampanoag); and Rolf Cachat-Schilling (Nipmuc/Mohawk).

I also wish to acknowledge the help of two former students, Cory Fournier and Adrienne Edwards, who provided invaluable assistance with converting the data set into GIS format, which permitted several critical types of analysis. Cory undertook a portion of this study as his honors thesis at Bridgewater State University (2013), and continued the work under a grant provided by Bridgewater State's Center for the Advancement of Research and Scholarship, while pursuing his master's degree at Arizona State University. Adrienne Edwards had worked with me during her senior year in 2000–2001 to produce a GIS-based inventory of archaeological sites in the Sudbury–Assabet–Concord watershed in eastern Massachusetts (Hoffman and Edwards 2002), and after earning her master's degree in geoarchaeology at SUNY-Albany, she served as the GIS specialist for the town of Easton, Massachusetts. I engaged her as a consultant to bring the GIS work to completion in 2015–16. I also wish to thank Gordon Bernstein, who generously offered his photographic expertise in taking and preparing some of the images of structures that appear in this volume. Additional photographs were provided by Peter Backes, Steve DiMarzo, Tim Fohl, Bill Moody, Kristopher Radder, and myself.

Finally, I wish to acknowledge the support of the Center for the Advancement of Research and Scholarship at Bridgewater State University, which has provided both generous financial support and course releases that have enabled me to bring this study to fruition. Their special faculty challenge during April 2017 stimulated me to finish the two remaining chapters of the book (Chapters 2 and 11) in less time than it would otherwise have taken. I also wish to thank my colleagues in the Anthropology Department at Bridgewater State, who have shown unfailing interest in and support for this study: Diana Fox, Ellen Ingmanson, Louise Badiane, and Simone Poliandri.

Contents

1

Science, Pseudoscience, and Scientism

Introduction

Scattered throughout the woodlands of the eastern seaboard of the United States and Canada are countless numbers of manmade stone constructions. These have been the subject of speculation and controversy from the time of the very first arrival of European settlers in the early seventeenth century. Up until now, information about these structures, whether from the perspective of professional archaeologists or antiquarian enthusiasts, has been limited in geographical scope and is mostly only anecdotal. The chief purpose of this study is to correct these shortcomings, by providing a robust database upon which a regional framework for understanding these enigmatic structures can be developed, and by providing a set of most probable explanations for their origin. A secondary goal of the study, assuming that the results of the first goal are accepted, is to encourage local, state, and tribal historical preservation planners to engage in dialogue to ensure the long-term preservation of these monuments. No matter who built them, they are definitely part of the human-altered environment, and as such, they deserve the same measure of protection as the National Historic Preservation Act (PL89-665) and its attendant regulations (36CFR800) provide for buried archaeological sites and above-ground standing structures.[1]

While there are many possible approaches that could be taken to study stone structures, for this study I have adopted an "explicitly scientific approach." What I mean by this is that, in addition to providing the historical background for the study in Chapter 2, I will propose four alternative, falsifiable hypotheses as to the identity of the builders, each accompanied by a series of hypothetical test conditions; I will then test them against a far more robust data set than has previously been available. The historical chapter provides an overview of the often-conflicted history of European and Euro-American perceptions of stone structures and their creators throughout the Eastern Seaboard. I will attempt to delineate the differing attitudes towards them, which have ranged from respect to curiosity to zealous hostility, and from benign interest to malign neglect. Following this, Chapter 3 provides a description of the rationale and protocols for the study, and also presents the four alternative research hypotheses to be tested in Chapter 10, along with the test conditions for each of them. Chapter 4 describes the methodology used to obtain the information used in the analysis.

Chapter 5 provides a series of definitions of terms used in the study. Chapters 6–9 present the data set, analyzed according to the terms described in Chapter 5: respectively, general trends, environmental parameters, structure types, and cluster analysis. Readers who do not feel the need to plunge deeply into the weeds of statistical analysis may choose to skip this section and proceed directly to Chapter 10, which provides a quantitative and qualitative evaluation of the results of this testing, to determine which of the four hypotheses best fits the data. This chapter consequently recommends eliminating the disconfirmed hypotheses from further discourse—unless, of course, other researchers can provide contradictory data sets or can show that the data set presented here is somehow significantly biased. Finally, Chapter 11 summarizes the findings and presents some recommendations for site preservation and future research possibilities. A complete bibliography and an index complete the book.

The Challenge

As editor of the *Bulletin of the Massachusetts Archaeological Society* (MAS), I was recently asked by the Society's Board of Trustees to consider some design changes to the format of the *Bulletin*. A questionnaire was included in the Spring 2016 issue of the *Bulletin*, and also posted on the Society's website.[2] While most of the respondents indicated general satisfaction with the *Bulletin* in its current format, there were a few anonymous, unsolicited comments on the content of the journal, one of which caught my attention:

> No pseudo-archaeology &/or speculations based in contemporary religious notions that are neither scientific nor rational nor even empirically and logically demonstrative. And it's not that speculating about such things is bad anthropology: it's that it's *not* anthropology. The inclusion of pseudo-archaeology is the prime reason many institutional libraries and professionals have, sadly for the MAS, dropped their membership, or so they keep telling me. Not only better vetting to keep nonsense articles out of this once highly respected journal, but capable and expert editing with attention to detail and quality are needed.

This was obviously a response to a series of articles that I have allowed to be published in the *Bulletin* since taking over the editorship in 2009 on the subject of stone structures.[3] These articles were indeed carefully edited so as to provide accurate, rational, and detailed descriptions of the structures involved, before moving on to any speculations on the origins, function, or ethnic identity of the producers of the structures. Nor were they the first articles in the *Bulletin* to deal with these structures.[4]

Leaving aside the question of whether the study of religion—which has been embedded in anthropology at least since the days of Edward Tylor—is legitimately part of the discipline, this comment stimulated me to consider the questions of what is, and is not, science, and who gets to decide.[5] In a recent anthology on "fringe archaeology" edited by D. Ryan Grey, the editor defines science in terms of a series of four steps:

> … science is distinguished by its adherence to certain rules, rules that are intended to make its claims universally valid, or at least valid under similar conditions.… To do this, science claims a method typically divided into four steps, consisting of an initial observation, an induction explaining that observation, a deduction of what else follows from that explanation, and then a test of assumptions that follow to corroborate or disprove the original explanation.[6]

As described above, the current study follows this methodology closely. Grey also provides a useful definition of the methodologies used by pseudoscience, thereby positing a bright line between the two:

> Claims relating to these things share many characteristics: an associational approach to evidence rather than a causal or contextual one, a disregard for basic rules of logic in structuring arguments, a tendency to look only for confirmation, an attempt to create mystery rather than resolve it, explanations based on possibility rather than probability, and so on.[7]

Yet that line is not always as bright as Grey's definition represents it to be. The following quote is a response to late nineteenth-century claims of Pleistocene human occupation of North America, by William J. McGee, a reputable geologist of the day:

> Wheresoever workers assemble, there idlers gather to feast on the fruits of honest toil; a part are pitiable paupers, some traffic in unwholesome wares, others swindle the unwary under the cloak of honest dealing and cheat justice by specious pleas, and still others steal and rob.… In like manner the workshops and market-places of science are haunted by harpies; a part are the feeble of mind who always absorb but never produce; some starve and poison hungry minds with the husks of fiction and the lotus of myth, others foist falsehood on the unwary under the guise of science and hide from justice behind shields of skillfully woven words, and still others scoff at reason and rob knowledge of its glory. Thus creative genius is the prey of intellectual parasites, and the progress of knowledge is hindered by the helpless and the perverse.[8]

This kind of *ex cathedra* pronouncement constitutes what we nowadays define as "scientism," which is the dogmatic assertion that what is currently known by scientific experts about any subject is necessarily all that is true, and that any claims to the contrary are not merely false, but downright pernicious. Pseudoscientists, when faced with this kind of criticism of their claims, sometimes resort to conspiracy theories, claiming that for some nefarious reason the professional community must be hiding the evidence that would support their claims from the public. And the reaction of some members of the professional community can be just as biased. For example, at the 2012 Northeastern Anthropological Association's annual meeting, in response to a paper about a stone structure site at which the authors demonstrated the presence of archaeoastronomical elements, the director of a large regional cultural resource management firm warned the students in the audience not to pursue studies of stone structures, lest it jeopardize their career prospects. Thankfully, he was taken to task for his blatant scientism by the director of another large regional cultural resource management firm the following day.

As Bernard Haisch, a prominent astrophysicist, has argued, scientistic claims ought not to be considered to be good science because they violate the "scientific spirit of inquiry" by closing the door on research in certain areas altogether.[9] Similarly, Potawatomi elder and research biologist Robin Wall Kimmerer emphasizes that "science lets us see the dance of the chromosomes, the leaves of moss, and the farthest galaxy. But is it a sacred lens like the *Popol Vuh*? Does science allow us to perceive the sacred in the world, or does it bend light in such a way as to obscure it?"[10] I contend that, if archaeologists are to be considered objective scientists, it should not matter what subject matter is under investigation, so long as the appropriate procedures described by Grey above are followed. In fact, in addition to the existence of Paleo-Indians on this continent to which McGee was objecting, which has long since been accepted by archaeological orthodoxy, there have been numerous other theories that had been labelled by the establishment scientism of their day as pseudoscience (e.g., tectonic plate theory, catastrophic collisions between extra-terrestrial bodies and the Earth, pre-Clovis occupations of North America, and pre-Columbian European explorations of North America, to name a few). All of these are now more or less accepted as mainstream science by the majority of professionals in the field (in the last case, at least we accept that the Vikings were here). While some of these ideas are open to dispute and refinement, as should be the case with all science, they are no longer considered to be in the realm of pseudoscience, even though, in some cases, the ideas had to struggle for decades before sufficient evidence accumulated to convince the majority of researchers in the field—and there remain some who are as yet unconvinced.

Stone Structures: Pseudoscience or Scientism?

With this in mind, I would like to return to the subject of this book, the stone structures that are so often found in the woodlands of eastern North America. Historically, as we shall see in Chapter 2, these structures have mostly been the objects of interest to antiquarian groups and individuals rather than to professional archaeologists. In some portions of the region, the professionals have taken it upon themselves to proclaim the work of these amateurs to be pseudoscience. Below is an example of a rather absolute assertion made in the 2005 issue of the Massachusetts Division of Conservation and Recreation newsletter, *Terra Firma*:

> THE LAST WORD: DEBUNKING THE MYTH OF STONE WALLS, PILES AND CHAMBERS
> Some have suggested a Native American origin for these features. There is no archaeological evidence to support this conclusion. When historians and archaeologists have researched stone walls, piles and chambers, they have <u>invariably</u> demonstrated that these features are associated with the activities of European settlers and have no Native American (or other) origin.… Together, archaeology and ethnohistory provide conclusive evidence that stone walls, piles and chambers are not the work of ancient cultures.[11]

From the perspective of science, of course, there can be no such thing as a "last word" on any subject. Any such assertion may be properly labeled as scientism. What is more disturbing is that nearly identical wording appears as policy on the website of the Massachusetts Historical Commission:

> Piles or continuous walls of fieldstones are common in rural Massachusetts wherever there are rocky soils. When historians and archaeologists have conducted thorough, professional research into such stone piles, they have invariably shown that these features are not associated with the Native American settlement of Massachusetts. When it is possible to determine their origin, stone piles prove to be related to agricultural activities such as clearing of fields for pasture or cultivation, and/or marking property bounds during the eighteenth and nineteenth centuries, pursuits that were once much more common in what may now be residential suburbs. Because stone piles or walls often marked property lines or boundaries between different land uses such as pasture and woodlot, they are often in a linear row or other geometric pattern, some of which may be consistent with cardinal compass points, solstice sunrises or sunsets, or other celestial phenomena.[12]

This policy statement, promulgated without any citations of the professional research to which it refers, has been quoted *verbatim* by cultural resource management professionals and developers to justify the destruction of stone monuments in the state (e.g. SCWA 2016). This is in spite of the fact that the Federally recognized tribes east of the Mississippi have declared these to be their own sacred sites, as the 2003 and 2007 resolutions of the United Southern and Eastern Tribes, Inc. attest (USET 2003, 2007, both reproduced at the end of Chapter 2).

The assertion that these sites are "invariably" non-Native in origin is eminently falsifiable, and as such can be challenged on its own terms, even if only one such site is accepted as authentically Native. Below, in Figure 1, is a listing of some uncalibrated radiocarbon and optically stimulated luminescence (OSL) dates associated with stone structures:

Site	Town	State	Mean		σ	Method	Source
SK155	Richmond	Rhode Island	4340	±	40	radiocarbon	Leveillee & Lance 2008
Flagg Swamp	Marlboro	Massachusetts	4200	±	120	radiocarbon	Huntington 1982
Hall Swamp	Kingston	Massachusetts	3740	±	30	radiocarbon	Flynn & Doucette 2016
Mystery Hill	North Salem	New Hampshire	3475	±	210	radiocarbon	Feldman 1977
Mystery Hill	North Salem	New Hampshire	2995	±	180	radiocarbon	Feldman 1977
Mystery Hill	North Salem	New Hampshire	2120	±	95	radiocarbon	Feldman 1977
Richard's Chamber	Reading	Vermont	1405	±	190	radiocarbon	Whittall 1989
Hall Swamp	Kingston	Massachusetts	1160	±	30	radiocarbon	Flynn & Doucette 2016
Morrill's Point	Salisbury	Massachusetts	965	±	125	radiocarbon	Whittall 1989
Williams Cave	Fort Lewis	Virginia	955	±	75	radiocarbon	Hranicky 2015
Williams Cave	Fort Lewis	Virginia	890	±	70	radiocarbon	Hranicky 2015
Freetown Forest	East Freetown	Massachusetts	875	±	160	radiocarbon	Mavor & Dix 1989
Barrington	Barrington	Rhode Island	860	±	50	radiocarbon	Ballard & Mavor 2010
Cox's Beehive (Pottie Chamber)	Newton	New Hampshire	850	±	140	radiocarbon	Whittall 1989
Barrington	Barrington	Rhode Island	800	±	150	radiocarbon	Ballard & Mavor 2010
Freetown Forest	East Freetown	Massachusetts	790	±	150	radiocarbon	Mavor & Dix 1989
Upton Beehive	Upton	Massachusetts	765	±	115	OSL	Mahan et al. 2015
Rocky Brook	Thompson	Connecticut	705	±	145	radiocarbon	Whittall 1989
Gungywamp	Groton	Connecticut	580	±	240	radiocarbon	Whittall 1989
Upton Beehive	Upton	Massachusetts	515	±	115	OSL	Mahan et al. 2015
Calendar I	Royalton	Vermont	470	±	145	radiocarbon	Mavor & Dix 1989
Calendar I	Royalton	Vermont	435	±	145	radiocarbon	Mavor & Dix 1989

Figure 1: Absolute Dates Associated with Stone Structures (all uncalibrated).

All of these dates are pre-European, some of them by millennia. While any one of these dates and its associations could conceivably be challenged on a case-by-case basis, any reasonable scientist would have to conclude that this evidence, at the very least, calls into question the "invariably" statement—yet it remains embedded in MHC's website and enforced by them as policy.

In the course of my research for this book, I have consulted with state archaeological offices up and down the Eastern Seaboard, and most of them agree that at least some of the structures in their states are of Native origin.[13] However, there are some state offices—Massachusetts included—where the policy is to accept none of these sites as having anything to do with indigenous peoples, pre-Contact or post-Contact. The wording of the Massachusetts Historical Commission's policy quoted above is identical to that found in comment letters sent by the Commission to anyone—professional or avocational—who submits sites of this type for inclusion in their site inventory. The Commission, in fact, categorically refuses to include these sites on its inventory. Listing sites on the state inventory is the only way in which Historical Commissions can legally protect sites by asking for surveys in advance of construction, so the result of this scientistic attitude has been, inevitably, the destruction of the sites. A recent article in the *Journal of Ohio Archaeology* has surveyed state historical commission offices in every state in the U.S. on the issue of stone constructions, and the authors have concluded that the Massachusetts office's categorical refusal to add such sites to their inventory is "the most extreme" in the nation. Staff from the Massachusetts Historical Commission, alone among state historical commissions, would not even return the author's phone calls.[14]

I am well aware that there are also quite a number of pseudoscientific explanations for these structures. These include a recent video by James Vieira, in which he claimed that the structures were built by a race of aliens or giants, whose skulls the Smithsonian Institution has hidden away so as not to allow the public to know about them.[15] That certainly counts as a conspiracy theory! This video was originally presented as a TEDx Talk, but was later withdrawn from their archive due to protests from archaeologists, after which the videographers did their own fact-checking and rejected Vieira's claims as spurious. Also pseudoscientific are the claims by Iceland resident Valdemar Samuelson that all of the stone structures in New England were built by his own Viking ancestors.[16] To bolster his claim, he has provided photographs of stone structures he has documented in Iceland, but in my opinion, they do not greatly resemble the ones found on this side of the Atlantic. Another such pseudoscientific claim has been made about the stone structures on Gilmore Hill in Southborough, Massachusetts, to the effect that, if viewed from 100 feet of altitude, the configuration of stoneworks spells out, in Egyptian hieroglyphics, a message which reads, "when the Sun reaches its furthest point south, celebrate the Winter solstice."[17] A useful message to be sure, but it presumes that the tiny minority of ancient Egyptians who could read hieroglyphics would have been interested in traveling out of their country. The Egyptians generally hired others to do this sort of thing for them, out of concern for the future of their immortal souls if they were not buried in Egyptian soil. It further presumes that they had the technological and mathematical ability to navigate across the Atlantic—under the observation that Egyptian reed boats resemble those in Lake Titicaca in Bolivia, and because such a boat was capable of crossing the Atlantic in the late twentieth century.[18] It also presumes that said ancient explorers had the technology to get themselves 100 feet up in the air to be able to read the message. Last, it presumes that anyone who had the degree of literacy, navigational skills, and airborne capability described above would need to be given this message! A similar claim by Larry Hancock that a cluster of sites in eastern Vermont, if viewed from the air, would form the outline of a winged Phoenician goddess (resulting in his naming of sites with fanciful Phoenician names, such as "The Loins of Bianu") may be dismissed as pseudoscience on the same grounds.

I would also classify some of the more extreme scientistic statements made about stone structures by professional archaeologists in the same category of pseudoscience. For example, Greg Walwer claims that eighteenth-century farmers practiced "aesthetic farm maintenance" by building attractive stone piles in their fields at the Buell Hill site in Killingworth, Connecticut, to keep their children from following Horace Greeley's (probably apocryphal) encouragement to "go West, young man."[19, 20] Another absurd claim was made by Pennsylvania geoarchaeologist Frank Vento to landowners in the Lake Catalpa area, Pennsylvania, to the effect that the stones on their property had rolled downhill and self-organized themselves into piles.[21] It is hard to figure how they would also have organized themselves into the undulating walls, U-shaped structures, enclosures, niches, standing stones, marked stones, and balanced rocks that are found on that property, let alone how some of them contrived to roll uphill to form the piles that are found on the tops of ridges at those sites.

As I stated above, my position, and the theme of this book, is that it is possible to apply scientific methods to the study of these structures. However, I believe that we are only at the very beginning of scientific inquiry about this subject. Until we can get beyond our preconceptions about these structures and begin to replace biased speculations by both avocational pseudoscientists and scientistic archaeologists with explanations built on normative scientific principles, we are likely to continue to observe the antiquarian and professional archaeological communities continuing to talk past each other and not making much headway. But I contend that one difference between pseudoscience and scientism is that pseudoscientists largely address public opinion—as McGee acerbically observed. In terms of site preservation, they are, to borrow a phrase from Douglas Adams, "mostly harmless."[22] On the other hand, professional archaeologists promulgating scientistic views, especially those in State Historic Preservation Offices, influence public policy, which may result (and has resulted) in the irreparable destruction of the sites. This is an out and out loss, no matter who built them. If we adopt a more rational approach, which, at the same time, is respectful of indigenous beliefs about these stone structures, we are likely to learn a great deal more about their position within indigenous cultural systems and we will develop a greater motivation to protect them from destruction. We are also likely to learn that there are ways of differentiating between sites that are genuinely indigenous and those structures that were in fact built by later settlers, as the Massachusetts Historical Commission claims for all such structures. Preserving past traditions of importance to indigenous cultures and engendering intercultural understanding are, after all, among the main goals of anthropology, are they not?

2

Historical Overview

Introduction

The act of arranging stones in ritual configurations has great antiquity. A Neanderthal skull at Monte Circeo in Italy was found carefully placed in the center of a bed of white quartz pebbles.[1] Inside the cave of Drachenloch in Switzerland, also thought to be a Neanderthal site, a stone chamber was built to contain a stack of cave bear skulls.[2] If Neanderthals *c.* 50,000 years ago were physically and cognitively capable of manipulating stones for ritual purposes, we should certainly expect that fully modern *Homo sapiens*, including the earliest inhabitants of North America, were also physically and cognitively capable of such skills. Sites of this sort are found on every other inhabited continent in the world.[3, 4] Thus, it should not come as a surprise to find pre-European stone monuments scattered across the North American continent.

For example, in northern California, the Wintu revere both natural rock formations and intentionally created or altered stones, and these are particularly associated with shamanic practice.[5] A Wintu medicine poem states:

I can't pass a rock
like you
without being mystified
or hypnotized.
I heard stories
of rocks
and have known some
rocks personally
They represent the
world by their presence
wisdom has no
relationship to size
One time, perhaps many times
a man became a rock
thinking that a fine way
to gain immortality.

The Maidu, also residents of northern California, constructed an elaborate solar observatory of stone, with orientations to summer solstice sunset, equinox sunset, and other significant astronomical directions. John Rudolph states of this site:

> To the early people, the sky was a place populated with powerful beings who competed and struggled with each other. The outcome of these struggles could have dire or beneficial consequences for humankind. The native peoples could help stave off disaster and maintain the cosmic balance by performing certain ceremonies at the proper time of the year. It was crucial to them, apparently, to know when the solar year began.[6]

The Hopi, long resident in the Southwest, devote the activities of an entire clan, the Water Clan, to the maintenance of stone structures that provide a calendar for ritual ceremonies:[7]

> Hopi sacred time and space are marked by positions on the horizon where the sun rises and sets at summer and winter solstices. The solstice points in the southeast, where the sun rises at winter solstice (December 21st), and in the northwest, where the sun sets at the summer solstice (June 21st), are known as the sun's houses (Tawaki). The sun chief or priest of the Water (Patki) Clan is responsible for "sun watching" near the solstices. These observations form the basis for the Hopi Calendar within which the sacred ceremonies such as Katsina dances, Social Dances, and planting times occur.[8]

On the high plains are a number of stone structures with features aligned to prominent star positions, known as "medicine wheels." The largest of these, the Bighorn Medicine Wheel in Wyoming, measures 80 feet across and contains both radiating spokes from a central stone pile oriented to first-magnitude star positions and stone circles on the periphery. Radiocarbon dates from this location place its age as early as 10,000 years ago, but it is still in use. Nicole Price comments:

> The Medicine Wheel and Mountain were and are used as a vison quest area by a number of tribes.… The land base for a sacred site is the home or lodge of the spirit life that dwells within, in this case a mountain. The rulers of the universe reside here, not only the rulers of the physical elements but the spiritual elements as well. It is here where the offerings are taken, and the prayers that go with them are accepted or rejected. It is here that the prayers are answered.[9]

Further to the north, on the Montana–Alberta–British Columbia border, and partially within the Blackfoot Indian Reservation, lies Mount Ninaistakis, which the Blackfeet consider to be a sacred mountain. This location is close to the continental divide between rivers that flow eastwards into the Missouri River and those that flow westward into the Columbia River. It is a site that the Piikani band of the Blackfeet still visit for the purpose of undertaking vision quests. As Brian Reeves observes:

> Stone structures were often constructed by vision questers in traditional times and are still constructed today. Old structures continue to be used by later seekers as part of the vision

quest. The dream beds or prayer platforms, as they are called, range from small stone-walled enclosures, large enough for a person to sit or lie in to a platform of flat flagstones or a small cairn of a few rocks. Larger cairns are sometimes present. Archaeological studies of Ninaistakis and the surrounding peaks have found the remains of five ancient structures on Chief Mountain, and over fifty on both the nearby and distant mountain tops.… Structures oriented to Ninaistakis have been found on the mountain tops up to 3,000 metres on the Continental Divide. Some structures are very heavily encrusted with lichens, suggesting they were constructed thousands of years ago. Others, both on Ninaistakis, and on surrounding mountains, continue to be used and built today.[10]

In the far north of the continent, the Inuit are well known for their construction of *inukshuk*, "men/stones"—human effigies made of stacked stones. While these might originally have served as horizon directional markers, since European contact, they have come to symbolize the Inuit themselves, to the point that an *inukshuk* appears on the territorial flag of the autonomous region of Nunavut.[11]

Closer to the area studied in this book, the Jesuit missionary Paul Le Jeune commented in 1636 that the Huron "address themselves to the Earth, to Rivers, to Lakes, to dangerous rocks, but above all, to the Sky; and believe that all these things are animate and that some powerful devil resides there." He also noted that on the way from Huronia to Quebec, particular rocks were often invoked by them, and that "among the Five Nations [Iroquois], the same custom prevailed in regard to the rocks along certain routes."[12]

With so many examples of indigenous stone construction throughout the North American continent, it would be surprising to find them to be absent from the Eastern Seaboard. Nevertheless, as observed in the previous chapter, there is considerable resistance to this idea on the part of both some professional archaeologists and some antiquarians. It will be the purpose of the remainder of this chapter to explore the underlying historical reasons for this resistance, while also providing documentation from historical sources of the indigenous use of stone structures.

Historical Evidence of Indigenous Stone Structures from the Eastern Seaboard

When Europeans first began to establish permanent settlements on the East Coast of North America, they established interactions with indigenous groups wherever they settled. Their motives for settlement were many and diverse: some came seeking religious freedom, some came to profit from the resources of the new land, and many came in hopes of acquiring property. A few of them were learned scholars, who applied their limited understanding of peoples in Europe and the Middle East to the newly discovered indigenous inhabitants. During the first centuries after initial contact, in the course of coming to know about these people, some of the scholars wrote documents in which they recorded their observations of stone monuments built by those inhabitants.

The earliest European expedition into the interior of the Southeast was Hernando de Soto's of 1539–41. Perhaps because de Soto was primarily looking for gold and territorial conquest, his chronicler did not record any examples of stone structures, though he did record some earthen mounds in the towns they visited.[13, 14] The earliest written account I have been able to find of a stone structure in the study area is that of the English explorer John Smith, who reported on his visits to several Powhatan villages in eastern Virginia:

> When any notable accident or encounter had taken place, certain altar stones called by the natives "Pawcorances" were set up, somewhat after Hebrew fashion. Each of these stones had its history, which was recited to any one desiring information. These Pawcorances thus furnished the best records of antiquity to the Virginia Indians, and upon them it was the custom to offer bloud [sic.], deer-suet and Tobacco on any notable occasion, or when the Indians returned victorious from war or successful from the chase. The most remarkable of the Pawcorances was at Uttamassack. It was of solid crystal of great size, and upon it sacrifices were offered at the most solemn festivals.[15]

Smith provided a map of the area on the York River he had explored with his account, sufficiently accurate for me to geolocate the Uttamassack site. Unfortunately, he did not record the locations of any other pawcorances. Robert Beverley, writing of these sites in the early eighteenth century, stated:

> They erect Altars where-ever they have any remarkable occasion, because their principal Devotion consists in Sacrifice, they have a profound respect for these altars. They have one particular Altar, to which, for some mystical reason, many of their Nations pay an extraordinary veneration; of this sort was the Crystal Cube.... The Indians call this by the name of *Pawcoarance*.... When they travel by any of these Altars, they take great care to instruct their Children and Young people in the particular occasion and time of their erection, and recommend the respect which they ought to have for them; so that their careful observance of these Traditions, proves as good a Memorial of such Antiquities, as any Written Records, especially for so long as the same people continue to inhabit in, or near the same place.[16]

When Roger Williams was forced to flee from the Massachusetts Bay Colony in 1634 on account of Puritan opposition to his sympathetic attitude towards the Indians, he established the new colony of Rhode Island and Providence Plantations. Here, he had the opportunity to observe and record many of the customs of the Narragansett people. In his *Key into the Languages of America*, he described one type of stone structure, used as a sweat lodge:

> Pesuponck, a hot house. This Hot house is a kind of little cell or cave, six or eight feet over, round, made on the side of a hill (commonly by some Rivulet or Brook); into this frequently the men enter after they have exceedingly heated it with store of wood, laid upon an heape of stones in the midle. When they have taken out the fire, the stones keepe still a great heat.[17]

On Martha's Vineyard off the southern coast of Massachusetts, Thomas Mayhew, Jr., the first Baptist minister to the island's Native people, was so beloved by his converts that, upon the occasion of his departure to England in 1657 with several young converts, they built a stone pile in his honor:

> Here all the Indian converts met him, about fifteen hundred in number. The chiefs and all their tribes came and formed a semicircle about the place where Mayhew was to stand. Many of these Indians had followed him from Gay Head as he came down towards Edgartown. The service was opened with prayer by Mayhew.… At the close, Hiacoomes came forward and shook the hand of his beloved teacher, and, bursting into tears, placed a white stone at his feet, saying: "I put this stone here in your name and whenever I pass, here I shall place a stone in your memory until you return." Mayhew answered: "Hiacoomes, not in my name, nor in my memory; but in the name and memory of the Great Master of whom I have taught you, Christ." All the chiefs placed a stone where Mayhew stood, and throwing their blankets over their faces and with their heads bowed in grief, followed by their tribes, marched in Indian file over the Plains to their homes.[18]

After Mayhew left for England and his ship was lost at sea, the Native people continued to build the pile in his honor, and Henry Norton himself witnessed its continued use in the late nineteenth century:

> When the writer was a young boy his family had an old Gay Head Indian woman working for them. She was planning to go home, for a short visit and he was to take her as far as West Tisbury where she could get the stage for Gay Head. Just before starting she asked him if he would go by the Indian trail along the South Side. She picked up a white stone, put it in the wagon and they then started on their trip.
>
> At that time the writer knew nothing about "The Place on the Wayside" but as they neared it she told him how, when she was a little girl walking with her grandmother from Gay Head to visit her people on Chappaquiddick, they had stopped and placed a stone in the memory of the Saviour, and the first white man who had taught them to know Him. When they came to the place she got out of the wagon and placed the stone on the pile which must have been between three and four feet high. She said a short prayer and returned to the wagon.
>
> As the writer looks back and sees that old Indian woman, the granddaughter of the last Sachem of Gay Head, and the great grand-daughter of the last Sachem of Chappaquiddick, placing her tribute on that pile of stones, the place becomes Holy Ground. What grander monument could one wish than to have a stone placed to his memory two hundred and forty years after by the Indians because of his work among them![19]

I am informed by local resident William Moody that the stone (shown in Plate 1) is still extant today. Whether this was an isolated act of reverence for a Christian preacher, rather than the continuation of a well-established custom, may be questioned.

The Dutch, in New Amsterdam, recorded several incidents involving stone structures and the displeasure of indigenous people at their attempts to disrupt them:

> "North of Newburgh the rocky peninsula known as Danskammer point is a feature in the landscape as well as in the history of the river. It was at this place that the Indians held their

worship of the devil, on one occasion four or five hundred being seen here engaged in that service. There were two grassy plots on which the dances and other orgies were held, the one called the large Dans-Kammer, and the other the little Dans-Kammer … 'Hans Hansen,'" the story says, "was the son of Jacobus Hansen, one of the first settlers in the vinicity [*sic*.] of Albany, and, except an occasional skirmish with the Indians, had enjoyed undisturbed peace and honor in the small circle that constituted his settlement.… On the evening of the sixth day they reached the Dans-Kammer. The place was known to them, and the company resolved to stop there and partake of some refreshments. Leshee [a squaw guiding the party] remonstrated against visiting the scene of the rites and sacrifices of her tribe … but the evening was beautiful, the place attractive, the Indians at peace, their war-whoop hushed and their sacrificial fires extinguished; hence they resolved to land.… A company of warriors, who had concealed themselves and their canoes above the point, were seen darting forward with appalling velocity. Hans' only hope of escape was his boats…"[20]

Hansen and his bride were captured by the Indians, who were obviously outraged at the desecration of their sacred site, and were burned to death. The other members of the party were released to tell the tale. Unfortunately, we do not know the year in which this incident occurred, but it must have been prior to the 1667 takeover of the New Amsterdam colony by the British and its renaming as New York.

In eastern New York State, as colonists began to lay out their patents to lands, a patent issued by Governor Thomas Dongan to Robert Livingston in 1696 described a Native stone pile:

> … on the north by a Line to be Drawne from a Certain Creek or kill over against the South side of Vastrix Island in Hudsons River Called Wachankasigh to a Place Called by the Natives Wawanaquassick where the Heapes of Stones Lye being near the head of a Certaine kill or Creek Called Nanapenahekan which comes out of Marsh Lyeing near unto said kills of the said Heapes of Stones upon which the Indians throw upon another as they Passe by from an Ancient Custom amongst them…[21]

As we shall see in Chapter 6, "*wawanaquassick*" or "*wawanaqussuck*" is a generic Algonquian name for a cairn honoring a person or event. Note the use of the term "*qussuck*" for stone in Black-Eagle Sun's preface to this book.

When Massachusetts governor Thomas Dudley engaged in peace negotiations with several Abenaki tribal groups in Maine in 1702, he attended a council meeting at Casco village to ratify the agreement. A Native spokesman asserted:

> "That they acknowledged his favour in giving them a visit at such a juncture, with so many of the Council and gentlemen of both Provinces; assuring him, that they aimed at nothing more than peace; and that as high as the sun was above the earth, so far distant should their designs be of making the least breach between each other." And, as a testimony thereof, they presented him with a belt of wampum, and invited him to the two pillars of stones, which at a former treaty were erected, and called by the significant name of the Two Brothers; unto which both parties went and added a greater number of stones.[22]

A cairn was apparently constructed for similar purposes during the period between 1688 and 1703, near the village of Kennebunk:

> [The Abenaki there] whenever they returned, or came in, from their expeditions, they erected near their wigwams a pile of stones, in a conical form, two or three feet high. So long as this pile remained they were at peace with the whites. But when war was to be renewed, the pile was thrown down. They never violated the obligations which were upon them, so long as the monument of stones was undisturbed. It is said by those who lived at this period, that war never continued more than a month or six weeks—and that peace was continued about as long. Whenever they had been out about this length of time, the pile of stones would be again raised, and the Indians soon be at the houses of their old friends with apparently as good feelings as if nothing had happened in the interval.[23]

When James Oglethorpe founded the Georgia colony in 1733, he established good relationships with the local Creek chiefs, especially the Yamaca chief Tamachechi, who helped him in his dealings with the Spanish in Florida and with negotiations with other Native *micos*.

> [When the old chief died in 1739,] Tamachechi was interred in Percival Square (now Wright Square) in a traditional ceremony including the burying with him of certain possessions and offerings to facilitate his journey to the spirit world. Oglethorpe ordered that the ceremony include full military honors accorded by the colonial troops. He ordered also that a pyramid of stone be constructed over the old king's grave. If this were ever done the stones were removed long ago and the exact location of the grave was forgotten. A huge stone boulder was placed in the square and inscribed in his memory a century ago to mark the approximate site of the grave.[24]

Having a European colonial leader construct a stone monument to honor a Native chief certainly turns the tables on the incident with Thomas Mayhew, Jr. on Martha's Vineyard! Joseph Mahan, an ethnographer who studied the Yuchi who had lived in North Georgia before they were removed to Oklahoma, stated that his Yuchi informants had told him that the reason that Oglethorpe was accepted into their lands was that they had learned that he was a Freemason—and so were they! Mahan, who was an ardent diffusionist, documented that Yuchi were in fact among the founders of Georgia's Masonic lodges.[25] But it may be that what they meant by this claim was a reference to the original meaning of the term "mason"—one who works with stone. There are numerous references to Native stonemasons in the colonial literature. The best documented was a seventeenth-century Narragansett known as "Stonewall John", and the tradition was recorded in 1674 by Daniel Gookin, the first Massachusetts Indian Commissioner, as follows:[26]

> But yet let me add this by way of commendation of the Narragansitt [sic.] and Warwick Indians, who inhabit in the jurisdiction, that they are an active, laborious, and ingenious people; which is demonstrated in their labours they do for the English; of whom more are employed, *especially in making stone fences*, and many other hard labours, than of any other Indian people or neighbours.[27]

The tradition of stone-working was apparently widespread among the tribal members for generations:

> Artisans like Russell Spears continued traditions of Narragansett craft. A Narragansett born in Providence, Spears found himself working in Kenyon Dye Mills as a young man but was restless to be working with his hands outdoors. He left the mill and went to work with uncles and other relatives who were masons and learned the craft that tradition says had begun with Stonewall John. Spears built stone walls, patios and fireplaces and worked on buildings in Rhode Island, Connecticut and Cape Cod for nearly seventy years, teaching his sons to shape and carve rock.[28]

In 1753, the Reverend Gideon Hawley, who ministered to the Mashpee on Cape Cod, traveled through eastern New York State with a ministerial companion and a Mohawk guide. At a location along the Schoharie River, while the travelers were resting, he did as follows:

> We perseaved [*sic.*] our Indian looking for a stone, which having found, he caste to a heap, which for ages has been accumulating by passengers like him, who was our guide. We inquired why he observed that rite. He answered that his father practiced it, and enjoyned [*sic.*] it on him. But he did not like to talk on the subject. I have observed in every part of the country, and among every tribe of Indians, and among those where I now am in particular manner, heaps of stones or sticks collected on the like occasion as the above. The largest heap I have ever observed is that large collection of small stones on the mountain between Stockbridge and Great Barrington. We have a Sacrifice rock, as it is termed, between Plymouth and Sandwich, to which stones and sticks are always cast by Indians who pass it. This custom or rite is an acknowledgement of an invisible being. We may style him the unknown God, whom this people worship. This heap is his altar. The stone that is collected is the oblation of the traveler, which, if offered with a good mind, may be as acceptable as a consecrated animal … perhaps these heaps of stones may be erected only to a locally deity, which most probably is the case.[29]

One of the keenest observers of Native stone constructions was the Reverend Ezra Stiles, the president of Yale College, who traveled to the area of Buzzards Bay in 1762. He recounted:

> Mr. Williams told me that on the Road from Sandwich to Plymouth there is a large Stone or Rock in a place free of Stones; and that the Indians immemorially have been used, whenever & as often as they pass this large Stone, to cast a Stone or piece of Wood upon it.… That the Inds. Continue the Custom to this day, tho' they are a little ashamed the English should see them, & accordingly when walking with an Eng. they have made a path round at a quarter Mile's Distance to avoid it. There is also at a little Distance another Stone which they also inject upon, but pass it with less scruple; but are so scrupulous that none was ever known to omit casting Stones or Wood on the other.… The Indians being asked the reason of their Custom & Practice, say they know nothing about it, only that their Fathers and Grandfathers & Great Gr[d]fathers did

so, and charged all their Children to do so; and yᵗ, if they did not cast a Stone or piece of Wood on that Stone as often as they passed by it, they would not prosper, & particularly should not be lucky in hunting Deer. But if they duly observed this Custom, they should have success. The English call them the Sacrificing Rocks, tho' the Indians don't imagine it a Sacrifice—at least they kill & offer no Animals there, & nothing but Wood and Stones.

> N. B. There is such heap of Stones accumulated from such a Custom of passing Indians, between New Haven & Milford about three Miles out of Milford upon the Road. Another Heap at Stockbridge by the Housatunnuck Indians.[30]

Similarly, in the Southeast, Cherokee informants claimed to early settlers that the earthen and stone monuments in their area were not related to their culture; they "denied any knowledge of the purpose the mounds had served, saying only that they were built by another people who had preceded themselves in that area."[31]

Of course, we need not accept the statements made by indigenous informants literally. They would surely have learned by this time that the English, and especially ministers, had little tolerance for their beliefs, and they may have been attempting to conceal the theology behind their ongoing practice of these beliefs by vague circumlocutions (or circumambulations). Stiles observed several worked stones, which he called stone gods or godstones, throughout southern New England.[32] He also reported on the presence of indigenous stonework in the caves where the three judges who had condemned Charles I of England fled to the New World and hid out after the restoration of the monarchy, "a place of Indian worship and powwowing in ancient and forgotten ages."[33]

Negative Associations of Indigenous Stone Structures by Colonial Writers

Despite these observations of stone monuments by colonial writers, the attitude of many of the same writers towards indigenous beliefs was profoundly negative. By his own account, Roger Williams refrained from looking into any types of Narragansett sacred places other than "hot-houses":

> I confesse to have most of these their customes by their owne Relation, for after once being in their Houses and beholding what their Worship was, I durst never bee an eye witnesse, Spectatour, or looker on, least I should have been partaker of Sathans Inventions and Worships, contrary to Ephes. 5. 14.[34]

Robert Geake contends:

> … Williams and other early Puritan ministers were most likely unaware of these sacred sites, that the Native Americans "held back" knowledge of the inscribed rocks, sacred sites and their meanings. Only after a century of near decimation from disease and war, would Ezra Stiles be led to these sites, and by that time there would be few Native Americans remaining to convey their origin and true meaning. In this act of self-exclusion, Williams and other

early interpreters missed an integral thread of Native American language associated with spiritual belief and ritual.[35]

John Eliot, the self-appointed "Apostle to the Indians," after his initial attempts to convert the Nipmuck and Massachuseog in their own villages, complained in 1650:

> [Despite my efforts,] Sathan has taken the advantage to my great grief, whereas of my first preaching at Nashaway sundry did embrace the word, and called upon God and powwowing was wholly silenced among them all, yet now partly being 40 miles off, and principally, by the slow progress of this work, Sathan had so emboldened the powwaws that this winter as I hear to my grief there hath been some powwowing with some of them.[36]

This led directly, in 1654, to his decision, supported by the General Court of Massachusetts, to resettle the Natives into "Praying Villages" situated where the English could keep a closer eye on their activities, and away from their traditional places of worship. This act of removal was supported by three rulings of the General Court in 1646 that forbade blasphemy, forbade Indians the Indians the right to practice their own religion, and made the Colony responsible for converting them to Christianity.[37] The wording of the second ruling was particularly directed towards Native observances:

> It is ordered and decreed by this Court, that no Indian shall at any time powwow, or perform outward worship to their false gods, or to the devil, in any part of our Jurisdiction, whether they be such as shall dwell here, or shall come hither. If any shall transgress this law, the powwawer to pay five pounds, the procurer five pounds, and every assistant countenancing, by his presence or otherwise (being of age of discretion) twenty shillings.[38]

The General Court retained Calvinism as the Massachusetts state religion until 1833, forty-six years after the adoption of the U.S. Constitution and the Bill of Rights, the First Amendment of which prohibits the establishment of a state religion.[39]

In Mi'kmaq territory in eastern Canada, the Jesuit missionary Le Clercq had the opportunity to examine the medicine bundle of a *buoin*, a local shaman, in 1691:

> Le Clercq opened the bag with great curiosity, and found amongst other things the man's *ouahich*, "which was a stone of the size of a nut wrapped in a box, which he called the house of his Devil." Le Clercq recounts how sick Mi'kmaq could be cured by the *buoin*: "the sick person who asks recovery of the juggler, and who implores him to obtain this from his *Ouhaiche*, speaking to him these words, *Emadoui*, as if he were to say, 'Lend me thy Devil'. The juggler answers him, 'If thou wishest that I employ him in thy service…'"[40]

This clearly linked the use of sacred stones with what Le Clercq (and most others of that period) would have termed "devil-worship." The missionaries often demanded that their converts surrender these stones to them, and many of them did, but this was obviously not possible in the case of most constructed stone monuments.[41]

Ezra Stiles, himself, wrote in 1773:

> When the System was intire [*sic.*], it was a direct seeking to Satan; and this the Indians avow
> their Powwows to be to this day (tho' no Powwow now exists in N. England) for they say,
> the good Power will not and never did hurt us—he does nothing but good, he does all the
> good and does it unasked; the Evil Power hurts us, does all the Mischief, and who should
> we seek to prevent or remove Mischief but to him that does it? Some 40 or 50 years ago
> there was a great Drought and the Indians of Narragansett held a great *Powaw* for sundry
> Days. One Babcock or Stanton rebuked them as serving and worshipping the Devil: an old
> Powwow Indian readily owned and justified it—saying all the Corn would die without rain
> and *Chepi* the Evil Power withheld that—now said he, *If I was to beat you, who would you
> pray to? To me or to some Father Ten miles off?* You would pray me to leave off and not beat
> you any more: so we pray to the Devil to leave off affecting us with Evil. Indian Divinity! But
> I suspect this preserves the true principle upon which Satan deceived all the East into the
> complicated system forbid in Deut. 18, 11 and 2 Chron, xxxiii. Whether it might not be well
> to lay this whole Iniquity open, that all the remains of it might be rooted out?[42]

The ministers, of course, were thoroughly conversant with the Biblical text (and Stiles actually could read it in the original Hebrew), so the references to these Biblical passages were quite deliberate. Ephesians 5:11–12 (but not 14) states: "Take no part in the unfruitful works of darkness, but instead expose them. For it is shameful even to speak of the things that they do in secret." Deuteronomy 18:10–12 denounces various pagan practices:

> When thou art come into the land which the Lord thy God giveth thee, thou shalt not learn
> to do after the abominations of those nations. There shall not be found among you any one
> that maketh his son or his daughter to pass through the fire, or that useth divination, or an
> observer of times, or an enchanter, or a witch. Or a charmer, or a consulter with familiar
> spirits, or a wizard, or a necromancer. For all that do these things are an abomination unto
> the Lord: and because of these abominations the Lord thy God doth drive them out from
> before thee.

2 Chronicles 33:15 recounts the repentance of the Judean king, Menasseh, who had previously set up idols (godstones) on the high places for worship: "And he took away the foreign gods and the idol from the house of the Lord, and all the altars that he had built on the mountain of the house of the Lord and in Jerusalem, and he threw them outside of the city." These passages formed the basis both for the later intentional desecration of Native sacred sites and for the persecution of those who continued to worship at them.

Writing about the Salem witch trials of 1696, George Kittredge made a connection between the colonists' fears of witchcraft and indigenous practices:

> There was a very special reason why troubles with the powers of darkness were to be
> expected in New England.… I refer, of course, to the presence of a considerable heathen
> population—the Indians. These were universally supposed to be devil-worshippers—not
> only by the Colonists but by all the rest of the world. Cotton Mather and the Jesuit fathers
> were at one on this point. The religious ceremonies of the Indians were, as we know, in large

part an invocation of spirits and their powwows, or medicine men, supposed themselves to be wizards—were wizards, indeed, so far as sorcery is possible. The Colonial government showed itself singularly moderate in its attitude toward Indian practices of a magical character. Powwowing was, of course, forbidden wherever the jurisdiction of the white men held sway, but it was punishable by fine only, nor was there any idea of inflicting the extreme penalty—although the offence undoubtedly came under Mosaic law, so often quoted on the title-pages of books on witchcraft, "Thou shalt not suffer a witch to live." The existence of all these devil-worshipping neighbors was a constant reminder of the possibility of danger from witchcraft.[43]

As settlers became less dependent on Natives for trade or alliance and the colonists became more concerned with their own internal political issues, interest in the details of Native culture waned, and was replaced by more aggressive policies that sought to deny to indigenous people their rights to the land. Among these was the doctrine of *Terra Nullius*, or "no-man's land": the claim that because most Native groups were transhumant over the course of the seasonal round, they therefore had no land ownership, in the sense of English common law granting private ownership to individuals, with the concomitant right to forbid trespass.[44] This misunderstanding, in turn, led to conflict with indigenous people when they attempted to return to lands over which they considered they had only ceded use-rights, and to their eventual subjugation by Euro-American military force. Part of this subjugation entailed their removal from the land base, for example in the "Trail of Tears" in the Southeast—but also, more pernicious forms of "removal" by means of what would be described today (and prosecuted under international law) as biological warfare. During Pontiac's uprising of 1763, blankets used to wrap smallpox victims were distributed at the advice of Lord Jeffrey Amherst to the Native tribes west of the Appalachians. To justify this, he wrote to Colonel Henry Bouquet, his agent at Fort Pitt (modern Pittsburgh), of the need to "extirpate this execrable race."[45] This practice was repeated many times as settlements moved west. The term we use for this today is erasure: the elimination not only of the people themselves and their relationship to their land base, but even of their cultural history.

In the Southeast, some of the Cherokee bands escaped from the Trail of Tears and made their way back to their homeland, where they re-established their sacred practices. James Mooney recorded many of these, including some relating to the use of stones, in his 1891 ethnography:

> At the creation an *ulunsu'ti* [sacred stone] was given to the white man, and a piece of silver to the Indian. But the white man despised the stone and threw it away, while the Indian did the same with the silver. In going about the white man afterward found the silver piece and put it in his pocket and has prized it ever since. The Indian, in like manner, found the *ulunsu'ti* where the white man had thrown it. He picked it up and has kept it since as his talisman, as money is the talismanic power of the white man.[46]

Mooney also reported that "few inanimate gods are included in the category, the principal being the Stone, to which the shaman prays while endeavoring to find a lost article…"[47] It may perhaps be due to this enduring Native tradition that attitudes among archaeologists in the Southeastern portion of the study area towards stone monuments have been much more accepting of their indigenous origin.

In the Northeast, by contrast, once indigenous people had been marginalized, placed on small reservations, or assimilated into the dominant culture, many farmers who discovered monuments in their fields felt no compunctions about destroying them:

> Near the river, in the Indian field, was a large Indian burying ground; each grave was covered with a small heap of stones. Mr. Stiles, of this place, purchased this field about forty-six years since, of the Indian proprietors, and in ploughing it over, destroyed these relics of antiquity.[48]

> The mound was plowed down by the late William P. Button, superintendent of the Knickerbocker Manor who sowed the field to wheat. He reported unearthing many warriors' bones and weapons of rest in the furrows.[49]

This process of erasure was not restricted to individuals, but in some cases involved local governments. In 1690, the Selectmen of the town of Middleborough, Massachusetts, ordered that a stone structure site in their town be levelled so as to prevent Native people from returning to it to perform ceremonies.[50]

The policy of removal and erasure of indigenous cultures, coupled with the accounts cited above of ministers and traders to the effect that indigenous peoples claimed no knowledge of the stone monuments, resulted in the widespread adoption of a belief in cultural diffusion from the Old World. The diffusionists asserted that the stone and earthen monuments that the Euro-Americans found in the now depopulated Native territories must have been built by some superior, non-Native culture, preferably one related to Europeans themselves or to their cultural predecessors. This "lost race" of Moundbuilders were variously considered to be Celts, Jews, North Africans, or any of a number of other peoples.[51] Despite this obvious bias, some of these diffusionists did record the presence of stone structures. In his *History of the American Indians*, James Adair sought to "prove" that the Native peoples of eastern North America were actually the Ten Lost Tribes of Israel. He commented:

> To perpetuate the memory of any remarkable warriors killed in the woods, I must here observe, that every Indian traveller [*sic.*] as he passes that way throws a stone on the place, according as he likes or dislikes the occasion, or manner of the death of the deceased. In the woods we often see innumerable heaps of small stones in those places, where according to tradition some of their distinguished people were either killed, or buried, till the bones could be gathered: there they add Pelion to Ossa, still increasing each heap, as a lasting monument and honour to them, and an incentive great actions.… Though the Cherakee [*sic.*] do not now collect the bones of their dead, yet they continue to raise and multiply heaps of stones, as monuments for their dead; this the English army remembers well, for in the year 1760, having marched about two miles along a woodland path, beyond a hill where they had seen a couple of these reputed tombs, at the war-woman's creek, they received so sharp a defeat by the Cherakee, that another such must have inevitably ruined the whole

army. Many of those heaps are to be seen, in all parts of the continent of Nort-America [*sic*].… Although the Mohawk Indians may be reasonably expected to have lost their primitive customs, by reason of their great intercourse with foreigners, yet I was told by a gentleman of distinguished character, that they observe the aforesaid sepulchral custom to this day, insomuch, that when they are performing that kindred duty, they cry out, *Mahoom Taguyn Kameneh,* "Grandfather, I cover you."[52]

The Rise of Professional and Avocational Archaeology

The middle half of the twentieth century saw the rise of archaeology as a profession in North America. Numerous avocational societies were also formed during this period. The overwhelming majority of the members of both professional and amateur organizations were (and still are) of European ancestry, and thus, unlike their counterparts in Europe, were biologically and culturally unrelated to the pre-Contact peoples whose cultural material they were excavating. As Sir Mortimer Wheeler famously declared, "archaeology is destruction," and these generations of archaeologists saw nothing wrong in destroying the sites they were excavating, even if they contained human skeletal remains and grave goods.[53] This has given archaeologists a rather negative cachet as grave-robbers among the descendant indigenous populations. This perspective is not altogether unjustified, since archaeologists have seen opportunities in excavating graves that are not as easily available from other contexts. Graves are sealed contexts, referencing only a limited time period; they contain ceremonial objects that are not often found in other contexts, which can give insight into indigenous belief systems; and the skeletal remains themselves can provide a wealth of information about population genetics, demographics, disease, and diet. However, this cavalier attitude toward human remains overlooks strongly held indigenous belief systems, and, with the rise of the Red Power Movement in the 1970s, it led to vociferous protests at excavation sites.[54] It was not until the passage of the Native American Graves Protection and Repatriation Act of 1990 that archaeologists were forced to pay due attention to the sensibilities of indigenous people regarding burials— and, somewhat later, to other locations designated by indigenous peoples as sacred sites.[55]

In any event, as archaeologists became more familiar with the distribution of buried cultural resources in the eastern United States, they soon learned that stone structures were not very productive of artifactual evidence. Unlike the mounds of the Ohio Valley, they rarely covered graves (as had earlier been supposed), and they were also not often located close to the more prolific remains to be found at long-term habitation sites. As ethnographer Frank Speck already noted in 1945:

Brush piles and rock heaps have been well calculated to exalt the poetic fancy of historians and folk-lorists. Archaeologists, however, have so far apparently paid them scant attention. Ethnologists have described them but casually. A systematic search through literature would nevertheless yield abundant references to records of such sites in the old Indian country of the Thirteen Fires. Through New England and southward into the Alleghenian region local historical treatises have mentioned such memorials, the listing of which would prove cumbersome.[56]

His assessment of the relative disinterest in these structures by archaeologists and the greater level of interest in them by speculative researchers remains true, even over seventy years later. Of course, Speck did not have a computer at his disposal to make the listing of such sites less "cumbersome"!

While the exogenous Moundbuilder theory had been thoroughly debunked in professional archaeological circles, by the end of the nineteenth century, it remained (and in some cases still remains) popular among antiquarians.[57] William Goodwin, an Irish American, wrote *The Ruins of Great Ireland in New England* in 1946, in which he sought to "prove" that the monumental stone constructions of New England (especially "Mystery Hill" in North Salem, New Hampshire) had been built by people related to his own Celtic ancestors, who he claimed had crossed the Atlantic fleeing from the Vikings.[58] He liberally reconstructed the site so as to make its stone structures resemble Celtic shaft graves and other monuments, thereby making it very difficult to determine what was originally present at the site.[59]

Goodwin's work inspired several generations of diffusion enthusiasts, who claimed that a variety of peoples from the Old World had crossed the Atlantic before Columbus and established colonies in the New World. By 1964, a group of avocational archaeologists interested in stone structures in the Northeast—especially chambers—had banded together to form the New England Antiquities Research Association (NEARA), whose stated goals are as follows:

> NEARA shall promote disciplined research on the origin and functions of North American lithic structures and related landscape features. Through its publications and meetings, NEARA shall provide an open forum for discussion and debate on the significance of such sites within their cultural context. NEARA shall also engage in advocacy for public awareness of the need to preserve these sites. From our modest beginnings as an outgrowth of the work of William B. Goodwin and his 1946 *The Ruins of Great Ireland in New England*, since 1964 NEARA has grown like a stone in the water spreading like ripples into waves of expanding interests and disciplines. Whether by land or sea we have followed the currents of northern culture from the ice age to the last century.[60]

As their website further states:

> NEARA is not an archeological society, but evolving trends and available academic and scientific research impacts all our studies. We have sponsored research and excavations supervised by accredited archaeologists. Many of our members have participated in projects sponsored by amateur archaeological societies, state and local agencies and historical commissions as well as projects under contract with private owners.[61]

NEARA hosts annual meetings and conferences on the subjects of its interest, publishes a quarterly bulletin, the *NEARA Journal,* as well as a small number of anthologies, and maintains a research library. Its members regularly go on field trips to examine stone structures, and, in some cases, as noted above, to excavate around them to try to establish context.

While NEARA has evolved over the past fifty years to a more nuanced position on the origins of the stone structures, some of its members still hold fast to diffusionist ideas and claims. Of these claims, only one—that of the Vikings—has been supported by indisputable archaeological evidence, on Newfoundland, and on the islands of the Elizabethan Archipelago north of the Canadian mainland.[62, 63, 64] Even in this case, as noted in the previous chapter, some modern Viking enthusiasts (and descendants) claim that all stone structures in the region were built by Vikings, and they have claimed that there are Viking inscriptions along the coast, as far south as Narragansett Bay, not to mention the Kensington Rune Stone in Minnesota.[65] NEARA also remains sympathetic to some outlandish, if not outright pseudoscientific claims of hyperdiffusion, such as those of Barry Fell, whose best-selling books (1976, 1980, 1982) championed the idea of frequent and multiple visits from Old World peoples to the Western Hemisphere.

In response to these largely unsupported claims, and perhaps with a measure of jealousy at the popularity of Fell's publications, as well as his lack of an advanced degree in archaeology (he held a doctorate in invertebrate marine biology), the professional archaeological community has typically reacted vociferously, and sometimes condescendingly, to reject not only the claimants and their claims, but also the sites that they claimed supported their cases. For example, John Cole directed his 1979 archaeological field school students to generate multiple working hypotheses to explain the origins of the "Monks' Caves" and other sites—a total of thirteen sites, mostly chambers—in western Massachusetts. These hypotheses included:

> … habitation, meditation chambers, storage chambers for tools, etc., root cellars, wells, spring houses, chimney supports, tannery structures, astronomical observatories, house foundations, hiding places for escaped slaves or fugitives, forts or defensive outposts, landing sites or constructions of "ancient astronauts," centers of lines of force *à la* "pyramid power," bootlegger or smuggler storage sites, body storage chambers and markers of significant geographical patterns. The cultural sources of the structures proposed included Native Americans, post-Columbian Europeans or Yankees, pre-Columbian Old World visitors such as Celts, Phoenicians, Irish, Egyptians, and/or others, and even extraterrestrial visitors.[66]

Cole's investigation certainly had the appearance of being scientific, but he did not explain his criteria for choosing the sites (other than their proximity to his base at the University of Massachusetts at Amherst), nor the reasons for selecting only these thirteen sites out of more than a hundred, which—as this book will show—are to be found in that part of the state. His principal working hypothesis was that "'Enigmatic stone structures' are evidence of a failed or partially failed experiment [by eighteenth-century farmers—author] in settlement and adaptation to the rocky hill country environment of New England".[67] He concluded that "no evidence was found to suggest that structures preceded historic settlement", without providing any historical documentation for his contention that they therefore must be post-Contact, nor for the existence of such a "failed experiment."[68] Of the thirteen structures investigated, only two contained evidence of post-Contact artifacts.[69] The remainder were artifact-free and were classified by Cole as post-Contact primarily based upon their proximity to logging roads and other historic period structures.

A major turning point for NEARA came in 1989, with the publication of *Manitou: The Sacred Landscape of New England's Native Civilization*, by James Mavor, Jr. and Byron Dix. Mavor and Dix, both engineers (Mavor designed the submersible *Alvin* for Woods Hole Oceanographic Institute, and Dix was an optical systems designer for a geophysical laboratory), engaged in more than a decade of field research at a number of stone structure sites, especially in eastern Vermont, in central Massachusetts, and on Cape Cod. They also delved deeply into many of the same seventeenth- to nineteenth-century historical accounts of stone structure sites that I have cited above. Their work led them to the strongly argued conclusion that these were Native American sacred places. While their accounts of sites were largely anecdotal and qualitative rather than quantitative, they did break new ground by making the claim that the sites were of indigenous origin, and a substantial majority of NEARA members now appear to support this view.

It is at least possible that the change in attitude engendered by the publication of *Manitou,* coupled with concerns about the increasing encroachment of residential development into the uplands of the region, resulted in decisions on the part of descendant indigenous communities to come forward with some information previously kept secret within the tribes about these structures. This has resulted in some productive partnerships, including my own involvement in this issue, which I will describe in detail in the next chapter.

A prevailing view within some quarters of the professional archaeological community has developed—without reference to the published literature, and as far as I can tell solely based upon an aversive reaction to the claims of both non-professionals and tribal groups—to the effect that Native Americans never built stone structures, and that all such structures must be attributed to colonial farmers clearing their fields of rocks, or building staging for stone walls, or—my favorite example of scientism—"aesthetic farm maintenance", the process of beautifying farms so as to entice the younger generation to remain on them with their parents rather than seeking out the richer agricultural lands west of the Appalachians.[70] In some states, these attitudes have resulted in a policy of categorical rejection of all claims that stone structures could have been built by indigenous people. There are even representations that tribal claims to the contrary are simply political posturing on their part, in an attempt to gain influence, and have no basis in indigenous tradition.[71]

Indigenous Perspectives

This attitude is perceived in the indigenous community as being simply one more example of erasure. Having found their voice as a result of the passage of the American Indian Religious Freedom Act of 1978 and the Native American Graves Protection and Repatriation Act of 1990, they do not intend to stand for it any longer. The tribes have brought a number of legal actions to protect their sacred sites and to have them designated by the National Park Service as "Traditional Cultural Properties" (TCPs) or as "Ceremonial Stone Landscapes" (CSLs). These designations now exist in federal regulations, and are increasingly being used in the face of development pressures, sometimes successfully even over the objection of State Historic Preservation Offices.[72]

We can certainly expect that these efforts will continue in the future. Four of the federally recognized southern New England tribes—the Narragansett, the Mashantucket Pequot, the Mohegan, and the Aquinnah Wampanoag—have formed a Sacred Landscapes Coalition to provide a united front in the face of ongoing development and of obtuse responses from state officials, so as to protect these sites intact.[73] They are appealing for support from the general public, as well as from more open-minded members of the archaeological community.

In addition, the federally recognized tribes from Texas to Maine have banded together into a coordinated organization, the United South and Eastern Tribes, Inc. (USET), which meets regularly several times a year. The USET Culture and Heritage Committee has issued two strongly worded resolutions concerning stone structures, the key sections of which are reproduced below (USET 2003, 2007). It is noteworthy that these USET resolutions are addressed to local communities and to the agencies of the federal government, not to State Historic Preservation Offices, for the reason that they have received little support from some of the latter offices, as noted above.

Resolution No. USET 2003:22

SACRED LANDSCAPE WITHIN COMMONWEALTH OF MASSACHUSETTS

WHEREAS,   United South and Eastern Tribes Incorporated (USET) is an intertribal organization comprised of twenty-four (twenty-four) federally recognized tribes; and

WHEREAS,   the actions taken by the USET Board of Directors officially represent the intentions of each member tribe, as the Board of Directors comprises delegates from the members tribe's leadership; and

WHEREAS,   within the Massachusetts towns of Acton, Carlyle, Concord, Lincoln, Littleton, Stowe, Boxborough, and Westford there exists a sacred landscape which is of particular cultural value to certain USET member tribes; and

WHEREAS,   for thousands of years before the immigration of the Europeans, the *pau waus* or medicine people of today's New England region used this sacred landscape to sustain the peoples' reliance on Mother Earth and the spirit energies of balance and harmony; and

WHEREAS,   the properties which comprise this sacred landscape are threatened by the encroachments of imminent development; and

WHEREAS,   the USET Tribes wish to partner with the towns which have stewardship of these properties, in order to create historical preservation plans that will support the permanent protection of the sacred landscape; therefore, be it

RESOLVED   that the USET Board of Directors support the efforts of its member Tribes to partner with the pertinent towns and call upon the towns to join the Tribes in preservation of this unique and irreplaceable Indian resource.

CERTIFICATION

This resolution was duly passed at the USET Annual Board Meeting and EXPO, at which a quorum was present, in Uncasville, CT, Thursday, October 31, 2002.

USET Resolution No. 2007:037

SACRED CEREMONIAL STONE LANDSCAPES FOUND IN THE ANCESTRAL
TERRITORIES OF UNITED SOUTH AND EASTERN TRIBES, INC. MEMBER TRIBES

WHEREAS,   United South and Eastern Tribes Incorporated (USET) is an intertribal organization comprised of twenty-four (twenty-four) federally recognized tribes; and

WHEREAS,   the actions taken by the USET Board of Directors officially represent the intentions of each member tribe, as the Board of Directors comprises delegates from the members tribe's leadership; and

WHEREAS,   within the ancestral territories of the USET Tribes there exists sacred ceremonial stone landscapes and their stone structures which are of particular cultural value to certain USET member Tribes; and

WHEREAS,   for thousands of years before the immigration of the Europeans, the *pau waus* or medicine people of today's New England region used this sacred landscape to sustain the peoples' reliance on Mother Earth and the spirit energies of balance and harmony; and

WHEREAS,   the properties which comprise this sacred landscape are threatened by the encroachments of imminent development; and

WHEREAS,   whether these stone structures are massive or small structures, stacked, stone rows or effigies, these prayers in stone are often mistaken by archaeologists and State Historic Preservation Offices (SHPOs) as the efforts of farmers clearing stones for agricultural or wall building purposes; and

WHEREAS,   archaeologists and SHPOs, categorically thereafter, dismiss these structures as non-Indian and insignificant, permitting them to be the subjects of the sacrilege of archaeological dissection and later destruction during development projects; and

WHEREAS,   Federal laws exist, including, but not limited to, Section 106 of the National Historic Preservation Act (NHPA) as mended with 36 CFR Part 800, the American Indian Religious Freedom Act, Executive Order 13007, and all other related laws, rules, regulations and executive orders that support the rights of Tribal nations, but have yet to proactively influence protection of sacred ceremonial stone landscape sites; and

WHEREAS,   many sacred ceremonial stone landscapes are on lands controlled by or are within projects which are advised, funded, or permitted by government departments and agencies such as the Department of the Interior, Department of the Army, Department of Agriculture, National Park Service, U.S. Forest Service, U.S. Fish & Wildlife Service; Army Corp [sic] of Engineers, Federal Aviation Administration, Federal Communications Commission, National Oceanic & Atmospheric Administration, the Advisory Council on Historic Preservation, and the National Register of Historic Places; and

WHEREAS,   claiming them as products of farm clearing, professional archaeologists and the SHPOs annually pass judgment on the significance and potential protection of these ceremonial stone landscapes and their structures within USET ancestral territories; therefore, be it

RESOLVED	the USET Board of Directors requests that all relevant government departments and agencies actively and formally facilitate consultation with the federally recognized Indian Tribes of the region regarding the sacred ceremonial stone landscapes; and, be it further
RESOLVED	the USET Board of Directors recommends that the Federal departments and agencies facilitate regional workshops between Tribes, State Historic Preservation Offices, archaeologists and Federal Departments and Agencies to facilitate a better comprehension of these concerns and a correction in these dismissive and destructive local policies; and, be it further
RESOLVED	the USET Board of Directors request a draft Federal Government enforcement policy for the protection of the National Historic Preservation Act under Executive Order 13007; and, be it further
RESOLVED	the Federal Government will provide the member Tribes of the United South and Eastern Tribes, Inc. with assistance, when requested, for the protection of historical sites and sacred landscapes within their ancestral territories.

CERTIFICATION

This resolution was duly passed at the USET Impact Week Meeting, at which a quorum was present, in Arlington, VA, on Thursday, February 15, 2007.

This brings the discussion full circle, back to the indigenous communities who are now prepared to claim that their ancestors constructed the monuments, as documented both by tribal traditions and the historical record. It should be noted that the 2007 resolution mentions several different structure types, and it specifically refers to all of them as "prayers in stone." What follows in this volume is an attempt to use quantitative data to test this proposition, and several alternative hypotheses to be presented in the next chapter, against the available facts.

3

Study Goals, Parameters, Protocols, and Hypotheses

As explained in Chapter 1, the goals of this study are to document, inventory, and analyze stone structures throughout the Eastern Seaboard of North America, some or all of which may have been constructed by indigenous peoples; to disseminate information about these structures to state and tribal historic preservation offices (SHPOs and THPOs); and, under the limitations to be described below, to disseminate the information to the general public. Ultimately, the goal is to provide better preservation for these types of cultural resources than is often present currently, and to have them considered on an equal footing with the standing structures of the post-Contact period and the buried archaeological sites of the pre-Contact era by the region's State and Provincial Historic Preservation Offices, which are charged with the responsibility of inventorying and protecting archaeological and historic resources.

The geographic area for this study consists of all areas in the eastern United States and adjacent Canada, which are drained by rivers that flow into the Atlantic Ocean, from the St. John River in Florida to the St. Lawrence River in Quebec and Ontario. The ocean and its embayments constitute the eastern boundary of the study area, while the minor continental divide of the crest of the Appalachian Mountains is the western boundary. In western New York State, where this boundary is not very clear, the Genesee drainage is the westernmost drainage included in the study. Drainages to the west of this river flow into the Niagara River or Lake Erie, and are not included.

This study involves highly sensitive site locational data that was gathered from a variety of sources, in many cases under the explicit oral or written understanding that it be shared only in a limited way, so as to protect sites from the very real possibility of vandalism or desecration. At some state historic preservation offices, I was required to sign contractual documents to this effect. Accordingly, I established the following protocols from the outset:

1. Site locational data for individual sites (such as their Universal Transverse Mercator coordinates) will only be provided to the State Historic Preservation Offices (or the corresponding provincial offices in Canada) and to the Tribal Historic Preservation Offices for the locations in question. These offices, to a certain degree, are exempt from the provisions of the Freedom of Information Act (FOIA) and are not required to share this information outside of their offices, except on a need-to-know basis.

2. In any dissemination of information to the public—whether through public lectures, articles, media interviews, and most importantly in this volume—individual sites will be represented no more accurately than by one-kilometer diameter circles or squares. While in some cases this will result in there being more than one site within the same one-kilometer cell (in some cases, as many as twenty-one), this limitation was considered satisfactory by all of the parties who agreed to share information.

3. Aside from this, the current volume will present the general trends exhibited by the data set, in the form of maps, graphs, tables, and text, without identifying any particular sites by name or number, unless the site is already part of the published record. For example, all of the sites mentioned in the preceding two chapters fall into the latter category.

My Involvement in the Project

While I have been peripherally interested in the problem of stone structures throughout my academic career, the decision to embark on this study was motivated in large part by the involvement of local Native American tribal councils in advocating for the preservation of these structures. The Narragansett Indian Tribe, in particular, has taken the lead in promoting these structures as the "stone prayers" of their people and other tribal groups. I was informed by Doug Harris, the Narragansett Deputy Tribal Historic Preservation Officer (2008), that, starting around 2002, the Narragansett Indian Tribal Council met to discuss their perception that many of these upland sites—which they consider part of their sacred landscape—were rapidly disappearing under the pressure of suburban development. While all present at these meetings acknowledged that these places were the residua of spiritual energy, some thought that the Euro-American developers should be allowed to destroy them and reap the negative consequences of that desecration, while others felt that it might be possible to find towns and individual archaeologists and antiquarians with whom they could partner to preserve them.

The latter opinion prevailed in the council, and the tribal medicine woman, the late Ella Sekatow, and her son-in-law, Doug Harris, arranged a meeting with a group of local antiquarians (Timothy Fohl, Jic Davis, and Peter Waksman) early in 2003 in the town of Carlisle, Massachusetts. I was also invited to this meeting because I was known to the Native community as being sympathetic to their claims. We visited a number of local sites that day, which Ella and Doug declared were definitely sacred places. We agreed to form a working group and to do what we could to encourage local towns to engage in preservation efforts. The Narragansetts, as members of the United South and Eastern Tribes, Inc. (USET), brought the issue before the larger organization, which is comprised of thirty of the federally recognized tribes from Texas to Maine. As noted in the previous chapter, this group's Cultural and Heritage Committee thereafter issued a pair of formal resolutions concerning these sites, categorically identifying them as sacred places (USET 2003, 2007). It is from the second of these resolutions that the title of this book, "*Stone Prayers*," derives.

I subsequently worked with Doug Harris and Tim Fohl to document a stone structure site near Tim's residence in Carlisle.[1] We established a methodology for clearing the structures of surface debris and measuring distances between structures, without actually disturbing the stones. This policy was instituted according to the preferences of the Narragansett tribe. One of the first things that occurred to me to question was whether it is possible, empirically, to discriminate between stone structures associated with colonial farming and Native stone structures. As a pilot study of this, I directed Wendi Field Murray, a gifted undergraduate student then in the Public Archaeology Concentration of Bridgewater State's Anthropology Department, in the writing of an honors thesis on these sites. In this thesis, she documented ten sites in the Carlisle–Acton area that had been identified by Peter Waksman, in terms of the arrangement of the structures, their construction, and their relationship to plowed fields. She found that it was indeed possible to reach empirical conclusions as to the cultural affiliations of most of these structures.[2] Eight of the ten sites were definitively identified as Native, and two as probably Euro-American.

I also assisted Doug, Tim, and a number of other individuals in documenting a large stone structure site in Killingworth, Connecticut, on a property that was slated for development into a housing complex. A surface survey conducted by Walwer Associates had identified eight large, well-constructed cairns on the property, most of which the developer had agreed to avoid disturbing during construction.[3] However, our site visit demonstrated the fact that, in and among these cairns, and scattered throughout the property, were a very large number of smaller stone structures. This site visit and the public meeting which followed it resulted in a determination by then-state archaeologist Nick Bellantoni that Walwer Associates should conduct a thorough inventory of stone structures on the property, assisted by Doug Harris, and that they provide the information to me so that I could perform a statistical analysis of their distribution. I believe that this was the first such quantitative analysis done on a site of this type, at least in the Northeast. A total of 371 structures were identified and mapped before Greg Walwer called a halt to the proceedings so as not to be overwhelmed by the sheer volume of data. In my analysis, I posited five testable hypotheses, each accompanied by corollaries that could be evaluated quantitatively:

a. That the structures were the result of farmers clearing agricultural or pasturage fields;
b. That the structures were staging areas for the construction of stone walls by farmers;
c. That the structures—especially the cairns—were the result of 'aesthetic farm maintenance';
d. That the structures represented archaeoastronomical alignments, either by Native Americans or other pre-Contact peoples;
e. That the structures were the result of repetitive ritual usage by Native Americans.

Each of these hypotheses was tested against a set of seventeen quantifiable environmental and cultural variables. The first three hypotheses satisfied the expectations of at most six of these seventeen variables, while the archaeoastronomical hypothesis satisfied eight and the ritual usage hypothesis satisfied fifteen. The results are shown in Figure 2, below. Observed field conditions that met hypothesis expectations are shown in grey. The only two variables not satisfied by Hypothesis "E" were, in fact, peculiar to the expectations of the archaeoastronomical hypothesis. I therefore concluded that the most likely function of the structures was Native American repetitive ritual use.[4] While this work did not result in the preservation of all of the structures, and while Walwer continues to argue that all the structures are all the work of post-Contact Euro-American settlers, it did provide me with a set of useful methodologies that could be applied to other sites.[5]

Stone Prayers

Hypothesis:	A	B	C	D	E	Actual Conditions
Predictive Statement	Field Clearing	Wall Construction	Beautification	Archaeoastronomy	Repetitive Ritual	
Use of Outcrops	Positive	Some Positive	Positive	Some Positive	Some Positive	Some Positive
External Clustering	Negative	Positive	Positive	Positive	Positive	Positive
Internal Clustering	Negative	Negative	Positive	Positive	Negative	Negative
Elevation	Positive down	Negative	Negative	Positive up	Negative	Positive up
Aspect	Negative	Negative	Negative	Positive	Negative	Positive
Orientation	Negative	Negative	Negative	Positive	Negative	Negative
Slope	Flat	Mixed	Flat	Flat to Moderate	Mixed	Mixed
Distance to Water	Negative	Negative	Negative	Negative	Positive	Positive
Distance to Foundation	Negative	Positive	Positive	Negative	Negative	Negative
Distance to Road	Negative	Some Positive	Positive	Negative	Some Positive	Some Positive
Distance to Wall	Some Positive	Positive	Positive	Negative	Negative	Negative
Similarity to Walls	Negative	Positive	Negative	Negative	Negative	Negative
Types of Piles	Uniform - Unsorted	Uniform - Large	Mixed	Mixed	Mixed	Mixed
Rock Counts	High	High	High	Moderate	Mixed	Mixed
White Rocks	Negative	Negative	Positive	Negative	Some Positive	Some Positive
Evidence of Recent Use	Negative	Negative	Negative	Negative	Positive	Positive
Aesthetics	Negative	Negative	Positive	Negative	Some Positive	Some Positive
Score	4	6	4	8	15	

Figure 2: Testing of Hypotheses at the Buell Hill Site, Killingworth CT.

Research Hypotheses and Test Conditions

The Killingworth study also suggested to me that the same type of quantitative analysis could be applied to the distribution of stone structure sites (not just structures) across the region generally. That was the motivation for the current study. Consequently, I posited a series of four research hypotheses for the study, in part based upon those developed earlier for the Killingworth project. Each of these hypotheses is accompanied by a series of testable quantitative and/or qualitative expectations as to the environmental and cultural positioning of the sites and their configurations, both internally and with respect to other sites. The hypotheses, and their test conditions, are as follows:

A. That the structures are the result of colonial farmers clearing agricultural or pasturage fields or for the construction of stone walls. Test conditions for Hypothesis "A" are as follows:

1. Sites should be located close to or within agricultural fields, either in present or documented historical locations where farming took place;
2. Sites should be in soils which are at least marginally suitable for farming;
3. Sites should be contained within geopolitical boundaries (states, counties, or towns) as established during the period of European settlement;
4. Sites should be widely dispersed throughout the landscape wherever farming took place, and should not be clustered in particular locations;
5. Structures at most sites should reflect only simple piling of stones, or walls, rather than elaborate constructions;
6. Where there are more elaborate constructions, there will be documentation to show that they are the result of "aesthetic farm maintenance";
7. The total number of structure types at sites should be limited;
8. Structures should not be found in such quantities or in such close proximity at a site as to restrict the passage of the types of horse-drawn carts used by farmers to haul away stones;
9. Structures should not be situated at significantly higher elevations than the fields from which they are proposed to have been removed, or on slopes greater than *c.* 15 percent;
10. Walls, if present, should connect at right angles, should generally be straight, and should actually bound parcels;
11. Walls, if present, should not be associated with other types of stone structures;
12. Walls, if present, should be of sufficient height as to serve as boundaries which could keep domestic animals in, and wild animals and trespassers out;
13. Diagnostic artifacts and absolute dates associated with sites should never antedate the earliest European contact in the areas where the sites are located;
14. There should be no preference for sites to be found in the vicinity of watershed boundaries and fault lines;

15. Sites should not be located in areas with topographic place names that indicate deliberate avoidance by colonial farmers, such as names associated with Native Americans or with the Devil;
16. There should be colonial names for the different types of structures, and an absence of indigenous terminology for them;
17. There should be colonial names for individual sites;
18. Any archaeoastronomical alignments should reflect the belief systems of the colonizing English culture, or should be demonstrated to be random orientations.

B. That the structures are natural features of a glaciated landscape, or of downslope erosion. Test conditions for Hypothesis "B" are as follows:

1. Sites should not be found south of the glacial margin;
2. The distribution of sites north of the glacial margin should be essentially random on the small scale, or reflect glacial movement on the large scale;
3. No evidence of human alteration of stones should be present;
4. With the exception of balanced rocks, structures should be found downslope from higher elevations;
5. If balanced rocks are present, they should not be accompanied by other types of structures;
6. If structures are associated with dates, they should be prior to human occupation of the region.

C. That the structures represent the work of pre-Columbian non-Native peoples, either as navigational markers or archaeoastronomical placements. Test conditions for Hypothesis "C" are as follows:

1. Structures should be primarily located along the coast or close to major river transportation corridors, possibly radiating out from these locations to hinterlands;
2. If located close to major river corridors, sites should not be upstream of fall lines which would render the river unnavigable to the type of watercraft used by the incoming culture;
3. Artifactual evidence of specific non-Native cultural materials should be present at the sites which would allow identification of the specific cultures involved—as at L'Anse aux Meadows;
4. Any archaeoastronomical alignments should reflect the belief systems of the non-Native culture;
5. Any representational structures—petroglyphs, pictographs, or effigies—should also be consonant with the belief systems and material culture of the invasive non-Native culture;
6. If the alleged non-Native peoples were literate, sites may contain inscriptions in their languages.

D. That the structures are the result of repetitive ritual usage by Native Americans, either pre- or post-Contact. Test conditions for Hypothesis "D" are as follows:

1. Site locations should reflect patterns of indigenous settlement, though not necessarily be congruent with those patterns;
2. Site locations should not be constrained by post-Contact geopolitical boundaries, unless there is evidence that the site was constructed by post-Contact Native Americans;
3. Sites should have no particular relationship to lands favored by colonial settlers for agricultural activities;
4. Site configurations should be highly clustered, in line with the idea of repetitive usage;
5. The variability of structure types at sites should not be constrained;
6. The total number of structures at sites should also not be constrained;
7. Artifacts and absolute dates associated with sites should include pre-Contact evidence for the particular location of the site, though post-Contact dates and artifacts may also be encountered;
8. Sites should be found throughout the entire study area, without regard for the glacial margin—though they should also be absent from areas lacking in stone materials, such as the coastal plain south of the glacial margin;
9. If walls are present, they should not meet at right angles, or run straight, and may be associated with water features rather than field boundaries;
10. If walls are present, they should not be high enough to bar access or exit;
11. There should be a preference for sites to be found in the vicinity of watershed boundaries and fault lines—and, possibly, head-of-tide locations;
12. Sites may be located in environmental settings unsuitable for agriculture, such as bedrock outcrops, hilltops, steep slopes, and swamps;
13. If structures which may have resulted from glacial action are present (such as balanced rocks), they should be accompanied by structures of other types;
14. Structures should show human alteration, either by the placement of their stones or by evidence of actual alterations to individual stones;
15. The iconography of representational structures—petroglyphs/pictographs, marked stones, and effigies—should be consonant with the belief systems of the Native cultures involved;
16. If archaeoastronomical alignments are present, they should also accord with indigenous belief systems;
17. Inscriptions in non-indigenous scripts should be absent from sites, as should artifacts of non-indigenous origin. If sites are post-Contact, however, they may include some items obtained in trade from Euro-American settlers;
18. Sites may be located in areas with topographic place names that are associated in Euro-American folk traditions with indigenous peoples, or which indicate deliberate avoidance by colonial farmers, such as names associated with the Devil;
19. Sites should be absent, or very infrequent, in areas which are identified as places of deliberate avoidance by indigenous people, based upon their traditions;
20. Indigenous terminology for some specific types of structures should exist.

All of these conditions were tested against the data to determine the most likely hypothesis among the four. It was considered entirely possible that some of the hypotheses might be confirmed for some of the sites, or for certain types of structures, while other hypotheses might more likely be confirmed by other sites or types of structures; and that some hypotheses might be only partially confirmed or disconfirmed.

4

Collection Methodology

My first step in collecting information, starting in the fall of 2012, was to visit the library of the New England Antiquities Research Association (NEARA), at that time housed at New Hampshire Technical College in Concord, New Hampshire. NEARA maintains an extensive set of files on each of the states in which its members have collected data, predominantly the New England states, New York, New Jersey, Pennsylvania, and Nova Scotia. These records cover over fifty years of site reporting. Each site has its own folder, potentially including site forms, photographs, maps, publications, etc. However, I soon found that not all of these sites could be geolocated. In some cases, all that was present in a folder was a single photograph or slide with no clear indication of the location. In others, especially on older forms, members recorded the location of the site in terms of inches from the edges of specific USGS maps. The NEARA library does not contain a very comprehensive set of USGS maps, and the TOPO!© program I used for recording site locations does not always show map boundaries clearly, let alone providing map names or equivalent scales to the original maps. In those cases, where it was impossible to geolocate the sites, the sites were simply not included in the inventory. More recent NEARA report forms have a line for listing the latitudinal and longitudinal coordinates of the sites. As GPS units have become increasingly available to the public, NEARA members have begun reporting sites with increasing precision, sometimes to the extent of "hollow" precision (readings to six decimal places of a degree second, which is a smaller measurement than any of the structures). In addition to the NEARA archives, I was also given access to the extensive site notes of James Mavor, which are housed at the Woods Hole Memorial Library on Cape Cod.

I also consulted with a large number of local antiquarians, especially Peter Waksman for eastern Massachusetts and southern New Hampshire, and Polly Midgley and her group (Gerry McLoughlin, Donna Savino, Teresa Bierce, and Rob Buchanan), who provided me with site locational information for eastern New York state and western Connecticut. In addition, I established a number of additional contacts with antiquarians who provided me with much information about their local areas. Many of these informants were accessed through Peter Waksman's rockpiles blog (2009–2016)—especially Tim MacSweeney for western Connecticut (2009–2016), Kathy Klopchin for the Delaware Valley in New York, Nancy Wisser for eastern Pennsylvania, David Cuneo for Delaware and southern New England, Dennis Donais for northeastern Connecticut, and David Schewe for the Finger Lakes region of New York.

Through my contacts in NEARA, I was able to obtain further information on site locations, especially from James and Mary Gage for northeastern Massachusetts and southeastern New Hampshire (2012); Nancy Hunt for northwestern New Jersey; Tom Paul for south central Connecticut and the Catskills; Larry Mulligan for eastern Pennsylvania; Doug Schwartz for southeastern Connecticut and Vermont; Mark Starr for eastern Connecticut and western Rhode Island; Walter van Roggen for eastern Connecticut, southeastern Massachusetts, and southern New Hampshire; Tim Fohl for the Carlisle area of Massachusetts; Norman Muller for New Jersey, central Massachusetts, and Vermont; Steven DiMarzo for Rhode Island, eastern Connecticut, and southeastern Massachusetts; Peter Anick for central Massachusetts; Ted Ballard and Ken Leonard for southeastern Massachusetts; Terry DeVeau for Nova Scotia; and Ros Strong, Cathy Carlson, and Rob Sirois for Maine. I also obtained information on western Massachusetts sites from Ted Timreck's *The Great Falls* video production.[1]

As it became known that I was undertaking this study, additional Massachusetts antiquarians came forward with information, especially Sarah Kohler and Rolf Cachat-Schilling for western Massachusetts; Richard Kramer for Sharon; Harvey Lipman for Ashland; Paul Kachinsky for Winchendon; Matthew Howes for the Holliston area; Mary Ellen Lepionka for Cape Ann; and Derek Gunn for the Plymouth area.

Each of the sources listed in the above three paragraphs added at least ten sites to the inventory. There were many more who added smaller numbers of sites. A complete list of contributors to the study will be found in the acknowledgments at the beginning of this volume. It must be emphasized that, as with all anecdotal accounts, these reports were potentially colored by the biases of their sources. Some individual antiquarians have tended to specialize in particular structure types, such as chambers, U-shaped structures, and serpent-shaped stone rows, while others have been exclusively focused upon a single area, usually close to where they live. It was obviously impossible for me to visit every site reported to me, though when images of structures were provided to me I used my best judgement as to which to include and which not to include in the inventory. Hopefully, having multiple researchers from the same area will help to cancel out some of these biases. Also, because I have not visited most of the sites, it is impossible to determine how many of them are still extant. I know anecdotally that some of them have been destroyed.

I also obtained site information from the Rhode Island Historic Preservation and Heritage Commission. To expand my sources beyond the Northeast region, in November of 2012, I undertook a road trip southwards, including the state archaeological offices in Georgia, South Carolina, North Carolina, Virginia, Maryland, Delaware, Pennsylvania, and New York. A subsequent trip to South Carolina in January 2013, and an additional trip to Georgia and South Carolina in August 2016, provided considerably more information for the inventory. E-mail contact with the provincial archaeological office in New Brunswick and the West Virginia State Historic Preservation Office provided some additional information. A number of professional archaeologists working in the area were willing to share data with me, particularly Dan Cassedy (2014) for northeastern Pennsylvania and adjacent New York, Alan Smith for central Massachusetts and southern New Hampshire, and Dolores Elliott for the southern tier of New York State and northern Pennsylvania.

The University of Georgia's Natural, Archaeological, and Historic Resources GIS database (www.gnahrgis.com) provided information on a large number of sites recorded by cultural resource management firms and agencies that work within the state. These firms are, in descending order, Southeastern Archaeological Services (184 sites), Pan American Consultants, Inc. (113 sites), the U.S. Forest Service (ninety-five sites), the University of Georgia (sixty-three sites), Brockington and Associates (thirty-five sites), R. S. Webb and Associates, Inc. (twenty-one sites), Carolina Archaeological Consultants (twenty sites), New South Associates (fourteen sites), Garrow and Associates, Inc. (ten sites), the Georgia Department of Natural Resources (eight sites), Apalachee Research (five sites), the Georgia Historic Preservation Division (four sites), the Archaeological Survey Team of Atlanta (three sites), the Georgia Department of Transportation (three sites), Terracon Environmental, Inc. (two sites), the Georgia State Archaeologist's Office (two sites), West Georgia College and State University (two sites), Wynn Consulting (two sites), Kennesaw College (two sites), the Army Corps of Engineers (one site), Braden and Associates (one site), Edward-Pitman Environmental, Inc. (one site), the Georgia Power Company (one site), the Gwinnett Archaeological Research Society (one site), New World Research, Inc. (one site), the U.S. National Park Service (one site), the URS Corporation (one site), Vincenzo Petrullo (one site), Patricia Cridlebaugh (one site), and the Society for Georgia Archaeology (one site).

Publications by Edward Lenik (petroglyphs throughout the Northeast), Philip Mulford (northeastern Virginia), James Mavor and Byron Dix (New England generally), Gerard Fowke (Virginia and North Carolina), Patrick Cooke and Barbara DeLong (general Northeast), Matt Bua (the Catskill region of New York), Frederick Werkheiser and Donald Repsher (Pennsylvania), Russell Gardner, the late Tribal Historian for the Wampanoag tribe (southeastern New England), and Ted Ballard (eastern Massachusetts, the eastern shore of Narragansett Bay) were also consulted, and each contributed multiple site locations.[2] Information on individual sites was obtained from a variety of other published sources.[3] A complete listing of published sources will be found in the bibliography section of this volume. I also participated in a number of field visits with NEARA members and other antiquarians to sites in Maine, Rhode Island, Massachusetts, Pennsylvania, and Connecticut. Wherever sources in this book are unaccompanied by citations, they represent personal communications with the informants.

Finally, I did some prospecting for sites on my own, mostly in eastern Massachusetts. After seeing a considerable number of sites, I developed a kind of intuitive sense of what sorts of landforms are likely to contain sites of this sort. This is, perhaps, what Black-Eagle Sun means by "affective archaeology." However, I believe that any archaeologist who spends sufficient time in the field can develop a similar sense for manmade stone constructions and for the kinds of landforms most likely to contain them. Experience will allow one easily to differentiate manmade constructions from natural formations, such as tree falls and glacial rock dumps, and also to differentiate carefully constructed monuments from farmers' rock disposal piles. These skills are essentially analogous to those archaeologists must develop for discriminating flaked edge tools from natural geofacts. Most archaeologists also utilize this intuitive sense to locate the more ordinary kinds of sites, such as settlements—as do I. I have simply shifted my focus towards a different set of environmental cues than the ones I would use to locate a habitation site. My experience shows me that this is a teachable skill, but one for which book-learning is not a satisfactory substitute for "field truth." I know this, both because I have learned it myself and because I have had success teaching it to others—including Wendi Murray and Cory Fournier, who were involved in the early stages of the study.

Each site was spot-located on USGS 1:25000 topographic maps using the TOPO!© software program, as a flag accompanied by a two-letter state/province code followed by an arbitrarily assigned sequential number within the state, based upon the order in which it was recorded. From these locations, using TOPO!©, I was able to derive the Universal Transverse Mercator (UTM) coordinates, the town and county name (note: town boundaries are not shown on USGS maps of the Southeast, which made town identification more difficult to determine. Towns were assigned to sites on the basis of proximity in these cases), the distance to nearest water, the elevation above sea level, the stream rank, the type of nearest water resource, the main drainage, and the environmental setting of each site. All data was then entered into a pair of Excel spreadsheets, organized alphabetically by state or province and numerically in the order the sites were recorded. One spreadsheet contained the environmental parameters of the site, while the other listed what types of structures were present, where this was known. Data collection continued into mid-September 2016, after which the inventory was closed so that analysis could proceed.

This data was then subjected to a variety of statistical analyses, to be described in subsequent chapters. These included the use of ArcView 10.0 GIS software, for which I relied upon the assistance of two former Bridgewater State University Public Archaeology students, Cory Fournier and Adrienne Edwards. They provided GIS coverages for those environmental parameters which could not easily be calculated from inspection of the maps alone (particularly soil type, slope, distance to fault, distance to watershed boundary, distance to head-of-tide, and distance to nearest neighbor), and also final distribution maps. Cory also assisted in recording Massachusetts sites in the NEARA archive as part of his senior honors thesis. The GIS-based maps which appear in this volume were produced by Adrienne Edwards.

This study was underwritten by three generous grants from Bridgewater State University's Center for the Advancement of Research and Scholarship, awarded during 2012 (Small Grant), 2013 (Travel Grant), and 2016 (Faculty and Librarian Research Grant). In addition to helping to pay for the GIS consultants and for my travel to archaeological offices, these grants provided me with course releases from my teaching responsibilities at Bridgewater State, giving me the time needed to prepare this volume.

5

Definitions of Terms

General Terms

<u>Study Area</u>: The study area for this study includes lands drained by U.S. and Canadian river systems which flow into the Atlantic Ocean, from the St. John River in Florida to the St. Lawrence River in Quebec and Ontario. While the original impetus for the study was centered upon the northeastern states, in the U.S., I soon became aware of parallel efforts in the Southeast and the Ohio Valley, which have produced similar results.[1] After some rumination, I decided to restrict the study area as noted above, extending westwards in New York State to the Genesee drainage, which flows into Lake Ontario, and not to include drainages flowing into the Niagara River, Lake Erie, or the other Great Lakes, though, of course, all of these river systems ultimately empty into the St. Lawrence River. Drainages that flow into the Gulf of Mexico were also excluded. I am aware of the presence of stone structures much further north in Canada, the so-called *Inukshuks*, but I decided to draw the northern boundary at the St. Lawrence River and Lake Ontario.[2] While the southern boundary technically could include east-flowing drainages in Florida, such as the St. John River, the general absence of stone in Florida appears to have entirely precluded the construction of stone structures there, as well as in the Satilla and St. Mary's drainages in southeast Georgia. Of the remaining major river systems north of Florida, from the Altamaha to the St. Lawrence, only the Rappahannock drainage in Virginia and the Miramichi and Restigouche drainages in New Brunswick lacked reported stone structures.

<u>Sites</u>: Sites were defined as any locations at which stone structures that might be attributed to Native Americans were documented. Since it was unfeasible for me to visit each of the 5,550 sites I documented, I had to rely upon the published or oral testimony of many individuals as to both the location and authenticity of the sites as Native American constructions. In some cases (particularly in southeastern Vermont, eastern Massachusetts, western Connecticut, and Rhode Island), informants provided photographs of individual structures, which decreases the probability that these reports are spurious. Nevertheless, some sites may have been misidentified as Native American constructions when in fact some or all of the structures present were of post-Contact colonial origin or even of natural origin. As noted above in the historic overview chapter, there exist considerable biases both in favor of and opposed to accepting stone structures

as Native American. Hopefully, the results of this study will convince most readers that the evidence argues strongly in favor of Native American construction for the majority (but not necessarily all) of the sites included in the inventory.

Individual sites were defined as having their structures separated from any other stone structures by a minimum of 75 meters. In a small number of cases, sites that were located as close together as 50 meters apart, but whose environmental parameters differed, were also inventoried as separate sites. No attempt was made to estimate individual site size, which can vary considerably from a single structure to large areas containing hundreds of structures. Only a single point represents what may in some cases be a much larger site. It is possible that this has resulted in either the separation into different sites of diffuse groupings of structures belonging to the same site, or the conflation of different sites whose structures are located closer to one another. Some of the informants to this study might not agree with this arbitrary parameter for one or both of these reasons. However, at least it is explicit, and it is largely based upon the practical consideration of the placement of separate flags on 1:25000 scale USGS maps in TOPO!©: the separation between sites at distances less than 75 meters would be obscure. In some cases, informants provided highly precise locations for individual structures within sites, using GPS readers; in others, there was only a vague delineation of the site's location. As noted in the previous chapter, some of this precision is surely "hollow," in that measurements of latitude/longitude to six decimal places of a degree second are far smaller than the actual size of any of the individual structures by several orders of magnitude. For management purposes, sites were located by converting latitude/longitude coordinates into Universal Transverse Mercator (UTM) coordinates (using NADB 027) of a single point within the site's perimeter, since this system is more accurate with respect to the Earth's curvature than longitude and latitude are. The calculated northing and easting parameters were rounded up or down, so that the expected accuracy of any site placement is no better than within 5 meters in any case, and is probably considerably less accurate in some cases.

Site names were either provided by the sources consulted, or were attributed by the author on the basis of nearby prominent topographic or geopolitical features. In some states, notably Georgia, South Carolina, Virginia, and West Virginia, the Smithsonian nomenclature was used for site names, consisting of the state number (in alphabetical order), a two-letter county code, and a number representing the sequential order of reporting of the site in the state's inventory of site reports (e.g. 09MO257, for the 257th site reported in Monroe County, Georgia). A different system of simple sequential numeration is used in the New York State Archaeologist's office and at the Rhode Island Historic Preservation and Heritage Commission. Another system employed in a cultural resource management survey in New York and Pennsylvania used a two-letter state code followed by a two-letter county code followed by a sequential number within the study area.[3] Where multiple sites in the same immediate area were reported (or discovered by the author), they were sometimes arbitrarily assigned a topographic site name based on the USGS map, followed by a sequential number. Some of the names in sources reflect traditional nomenclature, while others were assigned based upon supposed attributions by diffusion enthusiasts—sometimes quite fancifully. For example, as noted in Chapter 1, one antiquarian working in Vermont was convinced that the sites he was documenting collectively represented the gigantic figure of a winged ancient Middle Eastern goddess, hence individual site names like "Loins of Bianu" or "Phallus Hill." Since most names of individual sites do not appear in this volume, but only in the information provided to SHPOs and THPOs, all of these designations were retained without comment or correction.

Site Clusters: Site clusters were defined as groups of ten or more sites whose locations (as described in the above paragraphs) were no more distant from their nearest neighbor than ~2.5 kilometers. As with sites, both the number of sites required to form a cluster and the maximum distance between sites in a cluster were chosen arbitrarily. The degree of clustering may be culturally variable, and this is something that will be explored in the discussion of clusters in Chapter 9. The choice of ten sites is arbitrary and could be either too high or too low in some cases. However, there are relatively few close groups of sites consisting of fewer than ten sites throughout the study area. Clusters were named after prominent topographic or geopolitical features and were numbered sequentially within states in the order in which they were defined, preceded by a two-letter code for the state in which they occurred, or (in the case of clusters that overlapped state boundaries) the state in which the majority of their sites occurred.

Environmental Parameters

1. Elevation: The study made extensive use of Topo!©, a series of computer CD-ROM packages which include USGS maps at five scales for the entire eastern seaboard of the U.S.; and of comparable on-line map programs for the Canadian provinces.[4] In addition to providing UTM coordinates, these programs provide the mean elevation (in feet above sea level for U.S. points) for any selected point. Feet were used rather than meters because that is how the contour intervals appear on Topo!©'s USGS maps. This parameter is accurate to the nearest foot, at least as a mean elevation. As with the horizontal UTM coordinates, the single elevation reading for a large site should be considered as a mean, rather than reflecting the range of elevation for that site.

2. Distance to Nearest Water: The Topo!© program is equipped with a "ruler" tool which allows the user to determine the distance between any two points on the map. The units for this tool may be set in either the English or metric systems. Using the metric option, this tool was used to calculate the distance in meters between the site (considered as a point location) and the nearest water source, and it is accurate to within ten meters. It should be noted that even at the 1:25000 scale, USGS maps do not indicate all water sources, such as springs, so it is possible that this parameter is an overestimate in some cases.

3. Major River Drainage: This was obtained by inspection from the USGS maps. Major rivers are those named rivers which flow into the ocean, with or without input from tributary streams.

4. Type of Water Resource: This is a nominal variable, which falls into the following categories:

a. Headwater streams: These are unnamed streams which are at or near the sources of river systems.

b. Named streams, brooks, creeks, runs, etc.: These are flowing water bodies which have given names on the USGS maps. Some of them may be headwater streams, while others, depending on the location, might elsewhere be described as rivers. Obviously, these distinctions are arbitrary and are based upon local usage, which was followed in all cases.

c. Rivers: Similarly, these are flowing water bodies which are so named on the USGS maps, and, as noted above, many small watercourses in New England are named as rivers on the USGS maps which in the Southeast would doubtless be called streams, runs, or creeks. Even major river systems tend to retain their river names all the way to their headwaters. Which branch of the upper reaches of a system was chosen to retain the name appears to be arbitrary, but usually it is the branch most distant from the river's mouth.

d. Lakes: These are generally large bodies of open fresh water, but they also include reservoirs which are the result of post-Contact damming activities and which are more likely to have been stream courses at the time that structures were built along them. As above, local usage, as reflected on the USGS maps, was used in preference to any measurement of water volume or surface area, or with any reference to historic maps drawn prior to the construction of the dams.

e. Ponds: These open water bodies tend to be smaller in size than "lakes," but once again local naming conventions were followed. Along the coast in the intertidal zone, some ponds may contain salt water, at least at high tide, or during flood events.

f. Swamps: These are either fresh or salt water marshy areas, indicated by sedge symbols on the USGS maps. In some cases, these have resulted from drainage alterations or eutrophication during post-Contact times, and they may have been lakes or ponds at the time structures were created near them. However, as above, local naming conventions were followed.

g. The Ocean: This was defined as open salt water, either the Atlantic Ocean itself or any of its bays, coves, straits, etc. Sites on offshore islands were all counted as "ocean" for this parameter, unless the islands had their own internal river systems.

5. Stream Rank: Headwater streams, whether named or unnamed, are considered Rank One streams. Confluences between two Rank One streams form a Rank Two stream; those between two Rank Two streams form a Rank Three stream, and so forth. The highest possible ranking, Eight, is applied only to sites whose closest water body is the ocean, as defined above.

6. Environmental Setting: This parameter describes the general topographic location of the site within the environment, according to the following categories:

a. Hilltops: These are locations which are elevated above the surrounding countryside by at least ten feet, as shown on the USGS contour maps. Sites located within thirty feet of elevation below the top of a hill or mountain were also included in this category.

b. Slopes: These are indicated by bunching of contour lines on USGS contour maps, and they are distinguished from valleys in that their aspects differ from that of the water body which occupies the valley, or in that the sites on them are situated above the valley floor by at least 100 feet of elevation, as determined by using Topo!©'s elevation tool.

   c. Valleys: These are low-lying areas occupied by freshwater bodies (rivers, lakes, streams, or ponds), where the site is at less than 100 feet of elevation above the valley floor and with its aspect oriented towards it, as determined by using Topo!©'s elevation tool.

   d. Plains: These are relatively flat areas, where the contour intervals are at least 100 meters apart in linear distance.

   e. Shores: These are areas within 100 meters of a water body of any of the types described above. Sites which are now underwater as a result of the damming of rivers for flood control or for water supply, or due to sea level rise, were included in this category.

   f. Islands: These are relatively small areas completely surrounded by water, whether in the ocean or its embayments, or in rivers or lakes. Sites which are now on islands due to the damming of rivers for flood control or water supply, or by sea level rise, were included in this category. Large islands, such as Martha's Vineyard in Massachusetts, Block Island in Rhode Island, and Long Island in New York, were not included in this category, but instead were characterized by their environmental setting using the parameters above.

7. Soil Classification: This was retrieved for U.S. sites using a GIS coverage; then the U.S. Department of Agriculture (USDA) web page for each soil type was consulted in order to obtain an evaluation of soil fertility: agriculturally productive, pasturage, low fertility, or naturally infertile. In some cases, no soil type was retrievable, due to the site being on a bedrock outcrop or underwater. In either of these cases, the fertility was evaluated as "naturally infertile." It was not possible to reconcile the Canadian soils data with the U.S. system, so the thirty-two sites in the three Canadian provinces are not included for this parameter.

8. Slope: The Massachusetts Historical Commission, along with several other state historic preservation offices throughout the region, groups slopes into four range variable categories on their site forms: 0–5 percent, 5–15 percent, 15–25 percent, and >25 percent. In most cases, the GIS classification of soil type included the range of slopes for that location, expressed as a percentage of slope. These ranges were sometimes more variable than the MHC ranges above, and many extended well above 25 percent. I calculated the arithmetic mean of each range and used that to fit the site into one of the four categories above.

9. Distance to Fault: The suggestion to investigate this parameter came from antiquarian Doug Schwartz, following an early presentation of my project at a NEARA meeting in 2013. Doug, who lives near the Plainfield Fault in New London County, Connecticut, observed that fault zones sometimes exhibit unusual visual and aural phenomena caused by the friction of tectonic plates. These might have attracted indigenous medicine people, who might also be associated with the construction of stone structures. Accordingly, the GIS specialists were asked to calculate the mean distance between sites and the nearest faults. This was calculated in metric units, using a GIS coverage. GIS returned these distances accurate to the millimeter, but this was considered hollow precision and was rounded up to the nearest hundredth of a kilometer (10 meters). This parameter includes both major and minor fault lines.

10. Distance to Watershed Boundary: This was calculated in metric units, using GIS coverages. GIS provides several scales for measuring this parameter, depending upon the size of the watershed in question. Level Six defines major watershed boundaries, such

as that between the Connecticut and Merrimack River systems. Level Eight defines less major watershed boundaries, such as that between the Concord and Nashoba Rivers, both of which flow into the Merrimack River. Level Ten defines minor watershed boundaries, such as that between the Sudbury and Assabet Rivers, both of which flow into the Concord River. All three levels were examined to see if they would provide meaningful distribution patterns. As with the distance to fault, GIS returned readings accurate to the millimeter. As with that parameter, these were converted into hundredths of kilometers.

11. Distance to Head-of-Tide/Coastline: This parameter was taken into consideration due to a hint provided by Ella Seketau, the late Narragansett Tribal Medicine Woman (2003), to the effect that her people prefer to locate stone structure sites "where water flows in two directions." While she originally referred to sites at or near watershed boundaries, I realized that it could also apply to sites at the edge of the intertidal zone, as indicated by black stippling in the river on the USGS maps. This was measured to the nearest hundredth of a kilometer as a linear distance, either using a GIS coverage or using the UTM coordinates of each site and its distance to the UTM of the head-of-tide of its river system, by means of the Pythagorean Theorem (ΔNorthing^2 + ΔEasting^2 = Distance^2).

12. Nearest Neighbor: This was based on GIS mapping, and is a measure in metric units of the distance between a site and the nearest neighboring site to it. Like the other GIS data, it is returned accurate to ten millimeters. As above, this may be hollow precision, so it was converted into hundredths of a kilometer.

13. Azimuths: These are orientations to various compass points. They were recorded where they were provided, for the most part for U-shaped structures, chambers, stone rows, and effigies. Where possible, they were identified as to degrees away from true north, rather than magnetic north—but this is not always explicitly the case.

Structure Types

Whenever I obtained data about the sites, I made an attempt to determine what types, and in what quantities, were present at them, using the typology described below. Each type was given a spreadsheet column. Separate columns were also included on the spreadsheet for the total number of structures present at a site and the total number of types of structures. The former was not always possible to determine accurately, as descriptions (both written and oral) often were vague, such as "present," "several," "many," etc. In these cases, I have arbitrarily assigned quantities to the sites, such as three for "present," five for "several," and ten for "many." As a cross-check on the accuracy of these estimates, I obtained more specific information about many of the Georgia and Massachusetts sites late in the research process. Specifically, I was granted access to the Georgia online site files maintained at the University of Georgia, and a major antiquarian contributor to the inventory, Peter Waksman, provided me with electronic copies of many of his original site notebooks. While the results of these studies frequently differed somewhat from my estimates at particular sites, the averages for each of the two regions were not far off from the initial estimates.

It should be noted that at the current stage of research there is no universal agreement among researchers as to how to classify stone structures. There are several different systems in use and these differ markedly from one another as to categories, let alone interpretation.[5] More recently, some Native American authors have provided names for many of these structures in the Algonquian languages.[6] What I have used differs somewhat from all of these, and while it may be challenged, at least it is explicit:

1. Cairns: I define these as well-built piles resting on the ground surface. In this, I am following Ives in differentiating them from the category "rock piles."[7] Some of the above researchers object to this classification, on the grounds that "rock piles" are considered by some—by Ives in particular—as all being of post-Contact Euro-American construction, while cairns might not be. I disagree with Ives about this, but I retain the distinction because I think it may be indicative of function.

2. Rock Piles: As above, these are piles which are not so well built as cairns, and/or do not rest on the ground surface but are piled on boulders. They can range from simple "rock-on-rock" piles to elaborate constructions consisting of hundreds of elements.[8] I have not sought to differentiate among these, though some researchers do.

3. Stone Rows: As Allport and Thorson have shown, New England colonial farmers built thousands of miles of stone walls to separate fields, either to control movements of livestock, or as property boundaries.[9] However, these walls are generally made of well-laid stones and are higher than one course of stones, and they also generally run straight in a single direction, meet other walls at right angles, and tend to be continuous for considerable distances, wherever they are not dilapidated or punctured for cart paths. What I am calling "stone rows" lack some or all of these features: they tend to be made of smaller stones which are more haphazardly laid; they may be only one or two courses high, so that they would not be able to function to keep animals in or out; they often curve around, sometimes in sinuous fashion, either horizontally or vertically; they meet other walls at non-right angles; and they often are short segments which begin and end without any clear terminus; or end in bodies of water. Some of the more remarkable rows have what appear to be serpent heads at their ends. These, and the sinuous walls, have been reclassified within the "effigies" category (q.v.).

4. U-shaped Structures: These are deliberate constructions consisting of an arc of stones facing in a particular direction, sometimes with a single isolated stone beyond the opening of the arc and centrally located with respect to it. Some researchers consider these to be "prayer seats," in that it is hypothesized that an individual (rarely are they large enough for more than one) could sit, kneel, lie, or stand within them and sight on a particular direction.[10] Wherever possible, azimuth readings have been supplied— but it is unclear whether the individual using it would have faced out, or in.

5. Chambers/Caves/Subterranean Structures: These are roofed enclosures large enough that at least one person could fit inside them; sometimes they are large enough for several people. They are all dry-lain without any use of mortar. In some cases there is corbelling, in others they have flat lintels.

6. Standing Stones: These are generally elongated stones which are either set up vertically, or have obviously fallen down from a vertical position. Many of them show signs of having been shaped by chipping.

7. Split-filled Boulders: These are most likely naturally-occurring boulders which have been split due to freeze-thaw action, into the splits of which rocks have been deliberately placed. Some researchers have suggested that this is to keep underworld spirits from exiting through the split, but this is highly speculative.[11]

8. Balanced Rocks: These are usually large boulders resting on smaller rocks. While many of them may have been positioned by glacial action, their association with other types of stone structures suggests that some of them were highly regarded by pre-Contact peoples, if not actually moved by them to occupy their present positions.[12, 13] Some of them show alterations by chipping, a human activity. Some of them are finely balanced so that the upper stone can be rocked against the lower, producing a loud sound which may have been used to summon people to ceremonies. Others appear to be fixed in place.

9. Marked Stones: These are generally large natural boulders which have been altered by the deliberate removal of some of the rock, for a variety of possible purposes. They include in-ground mortars, cupules, and shouldered stones of the type referred to as "Manitou stones."[14]

10. Petroglyphs and Pictographs: These are stones into which recognizable designs have been engraved (or, in the case of pictographs, painted).

11. Inscriptions: These are stones into which text has been engraved. Originally petroglyphs and inscriptions were classed in the same category, but it was later decided to separate them, as their environmental parameters turned out to be somewhat different.

12. Stone Circles: These are open or (rarely) filled circles of stones, which may rest on the ground or, less often, on larger boulders.

13. Effigies: These are collections of stones—always more than two—which appear to form the shapes of animals or—more rarely—humans. As noted above, they often include "serpent" walls, as well as turtle effigies. While marked stones, petroglyphs, inscriptions, and effigies are all potentially representational, the former three are subtractive, in that material is removed from the stone to shape it; while effigies are additive, in that they are collections of stones assembled so as to form a shape.

13. Mounds: These are large, circular or oval piles of rocks, sometimes as large as 10 meters in diameter, which tend to have a rounded cross-section, sometimes with a depression at the summit.

14. Platforms: These are similar in size and composition to mounds, except that they have flat cross-sections and tend to be rectilinear in plan.

15. Enclosures: These are open areas bounded by short stone rows, sometimes open on one end, sometimes completely enclosed. Unlike U-shaped structures and stone circles, they tend to lack any coherent form, and they are very variable in size.

16. Niches: These represent gaps in the body of a stone construction that appear to have been intentional rather than being the result of dilapidation or of haphazard rock stacking. In some cases, they penetrate only partway into the structure; in others, they provide a window entirely through the structure.

17. Unique Structures: This is a catch-all category for structure types which have fewer than ten representatives; in many cases they are one-of-a-kind. The utility of this category for statistical analysis is low, but they have been included for completeness.

Sources

As noted in the acknowledgments section, data for this study was gathered from a large number of informants and other sources. These may be grouped into the following categories, which are illustrated in Figure 3 below:

1. Antiquarians: These are individuals who have familiarized themselves with the landscape in their local areas (or occasionally further afield), but who do not possess advanced degrees in archaeology or related fields. All of them are listed in the Acknowledgments. In some cases, they brought me out to sites; in other cases, they simply reported the site locations and their contents to me. As Figure 3 shows, their numbers far outweigh all other sources.
2. Professional Archaeologists: These are either academic or cultural resource management professionals who have reported sites in the course of their fieldwork.
3. State Archives: Several state archaeological offices made their digital site archives available to my research, notably Georgia, South Carolina, Virginia, West Virginia, Maryland, Rhode Island, and Pennsylvania. I was also able to make use of paper records in the North Carolina, Delaware, and New Jersey SHPO offices, and at the New York State Museum.
4. Other Archives: The New England Antiquities Research Association Library, at the time located at New Hampshire Technical Institute in Concord, NH, and the Woods Hole Historic Museum on Cape Cod provided me with access to their paper site records.
5. Published Literature: A limited number of existing articles and monographs which mention stone structures in the region were consulted.
6. Self-Reported: Finally, as noted in the previous chapter, I have acquired some intuitive site recognition skills through my repeated visits to sites, and I have added a number of items to the inventory which I have located myself, chiefly in eastern Massachusetts.

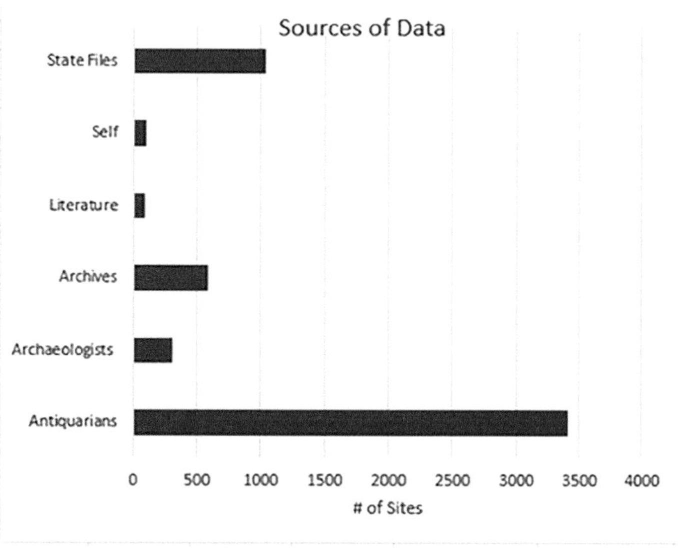

Figure 3: Sources of Site Locational Data.

6

General Results of the Investigation

Introduction

A total of 5,550 sites are included in the inventory, containing an estimated 39,711 individual structures, from all seventeen of the Eastern Seaboard states of the U.S. except Florida, and from three of the adjacent Canadian provinces (New Brunswick, Nova Scotia, and Quebec). No sites were reported from the District of Columbia, despite repeated attempts to contact the City Archaeologist. The total site distribution is shown in Plate 2. While this is a very large and robust database, no representation is made that it is statistically representative or that it constitutes anything like the total number of such sites throughout the region, for reasons discussed below. More sites continue to be reported to me, even from areas that have been intensively investigated in the past. While I have closed the inventory at this point for the purpose of analysis, I maintain records of additional sites as they are reported to me, and I intend to continue to do so. An update on the sites inventoried recently will be found in the concluding chapter of this book.

It must be acknowledged that this collection of sites is undoubtedly only a sample of the total number of stone structure sites present in the environment, and that there are several reasons to question whether it is a representative sample. First, many sites, especially in areas occupied by modern cities, have undoubtedly been destroyed in the process of development, either deliberately by iconoclastic colonists or vandals; by developers, unintentionally, because they were unaware of their significance; or intentionally, because they considered them to be of secondary importance to their own development priorities. In some cases, as noted in Chapter 1, these acts of destruction have been permitted by archaeologists and by historical preservationists who work in state historical commissions, for whom the concept of stone construction by pre-Contact Native peoples was/is not a consideration, for the historical reasons developed in Chapter 2. There are not many sites in the inventory that are within city limits (the total being 492—8.9 percent). As Figure 4 shows, most of these are small to medium-sized cities. Only twelve sites are located in cities with populations above 100,000: Stamford and Waterbury, Connecticut; Athens and Savannah, Georgia; Worcester, Massachusetts; and Philadelphia, Pennsylvania.

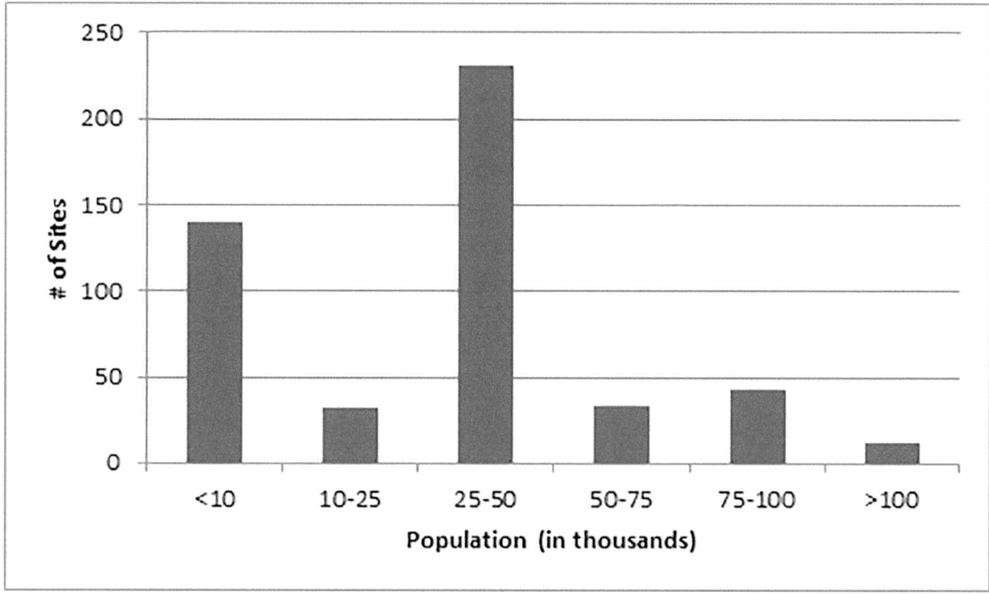

Figure 4: Sites Located Within Cities.

Second, as noted in Chapter 5, to a very large degree, the reporting of sites has been dependent upon local informants, especially in jurisdictions where official archaeological inventories have deliberately excluded sites of this type. Regardless of what ideas these individuals may have expressed about the ethnic identity of the people who produced the structures, their reporting of the sites' geographic locations has been accepted as accurate. In some cases, I have had the opportunity to spot-check this by making field visits, almost always with corroboratory results. While some antiquarian informants have ranged over wide geographic areas in their enthusiastic exploration of these sites, most of them have been primarily cognizant of sites in their local areas. It follows logically that in regions for which there are few informants, there are few reported sites. However, this is also a two-way street: the presence of sites of this type in an area has often been the main stimulus for the antiquarians to become interested in them. Many of my informants reported that this was precisely their motivation to become involved in research regarding these sites. Third, where cultural resource surveys have been performed within the study area, they have often overlooked and failed to report sites of this type, though this is a situation that is in the process of changing. I am pleased to report that the state archaeological inventories in Georgia, South Carolina, North Carolina, Virginia, West Virginia, Maryland, Delaware, Pennsylvania, New York (the State Archaeologist's office, but not the State Historic Preservation Office), Vermont, Rhode Island, New Hampshire, and New Brunswick do include sites of this type.

However, due to these considerations, it is impossible to know how representative this large sample is of the total number of sites that are now present or were once present in the region. Despite this, the large size of the inventory may work to counteract any biases introduced in this manner, at least in part.

Distribution of Sites in the Project Area

The distribution of the inventoried sites is very far from being either random or uniform. Figure 5 shows the distribution by state, both of numbers of sites and estimated numbers of structures, with the area of each state within the study area given in square kilometers and the relative density, given as the number of sites per square kilometer. It should be noted that portions of Georgia, North Carolina, Virginia, West Virginia, Maryland, Pennsylvania, New York, and Quebec lie outside of the boundaries of the study area, and these areas are not included in the area or density calculations below.

State/Province	No. of sites	No. of structures	Area in square kilometers	Density per square kilometer
Connecticut	552	3,921	14,357	0.0387
Delaware	12	34	6,447	0.0019
Georgia	672	3,935	109,905	0.0062
Maine	139	892	91,646	0.0015
Maryland	15	34	32,133	0.0005
Massachusetts	1,778	10,925	27,336	0.0652
New Brunswick	9	105	72,908	0.0001
New Hampshire	223	1,950	24,216	0.0093
New Jersey	81	225	22,588	0.0036
New York	653	3,371	127,890	0.0051
North Carolina	18	63	118,621	0.0002
Nova Scotia	21	145	55,284	0.0004
Pennsylvania	246	2,283	77,366	0.0032
Quebec	2	6	144,900	0.0000
Rhode Island	454	8,517	4,077	0.1136
South Carolina	229	1,632	82,932	0.0028
Vermont	351	1,262	24,901	0.0141
Virginia	67	412	88,320	0.0008
West Virginia	28	88	8,441	0.0033
Total/average	5,550	39,711	1,134,268	0.0049

Figure 5: Distribution of Sites by State.

Most of the states with densities in excess of the average of 0.0049 sites per square kilometer are in the Northeast: in Rhode Island, Massachusetts, Connecticut, Vermont, New Hampshire, Georgia, and New York, in descending order. States or provinces with densities lower than this average were Quebec, New Brunswick, North Carolina, Nova Scotia, Maryland, Virginia, Maine, Delaware, South Carolina, Pennsylvania, West Virginia, and New Jersey, in ascending order. This already suggests that there are two separate concentrations of sites, one in the Northeast and one in Georgia and South Carolina, with a relative gap between them. The Southeast concentration does not extend far northwards into North Carolina, but from what I have seen in the Georgia state site files and what I know of other such sites in the Southeast, it does extend beyond the study area around the southern end of the Appalachians into Alabama and Tennessee.[1] The Northeast concentration does not appear to extend very far south of Pennsylvania, though there is a concentration of sites in the upper Potomac drainage in Maryland, Virginia, and West Virginia, which is known locally as the "Stone Mound Culture" and is identified with the Late Middle Woodland period there.[2] This may be a third, independent center for this activity. The intensity of the Northeast concentration begins to diminish as one moves north and east into Maine, and sites are relatively uncommon in the Maritime provinces of Canada and very uncommon in Quebec. They are also very uncommon north of the Mohawk drainage in New York and in the White Mountains of New Hampshire, though not in the Green Mountains of Vermont.

This bimodal distribution is further confirmed when sites are looked at in terms of their numbers within drainage systems. As noted above, every major drainage system from the Altamaha in Georgia to the St. Lawrence in Quebec contains sites, with the sole exception of the Rappahannock drainage in Virginia and the Miramichi and Restigouche drainages in New Brunswick. But, once again, the distribution is not uniform, as Plate 3 shows. There are large numbers of sites in the Altamaha (431 sites) and Savannah River (385 sites) systems in Georgia and South Carolina, with diminishing numbers in the other two major South Carolina drainages—the Santee (ninety) and the PeeDee (ten)—and in the Ogeechee drainage in Georgia (four), and only one site each in the Cape Fear, Chowan, and York River drainages in North Carolina and Virginia. The distribution begins to pick up again north of the York drainage in Virginia, in the James (nine) and the Potomac (ninety-four) drainages, and with strong numbers in the drainages north and east of that. The Merrimack drainage in New Hampshire and Massachusetts has by far the largest number of sites (1,145), followed by the Connecticut (619), Pawcatuck (377), Hudson (347), Susquehanna (291), Thames (265), Delaware (210), Charles (160), Taunton (141), Housatonic (121), and St. Lawrence (108) drainages. This strong distribution extends as far as the Kennebec River in Maine (thirty-four sites), beyond which the numbers diminish once again. There are few sites in the St. John's (seven), Union (seven), Sheepscot (six), Penobscot (six), St. Croix (five), Mersey (five), Presumpscott (four), St. George's (four), Medway (three), Damariscotta (two), Pemaquid (two), Sackville (two), Clyde (two), Megunticook (one), Nonesuch (one), and Passagassawakeag (one) drainages. South of New York City, sites are absent or nearly absent from counties located in the coastal plain. This, in itself, is not surprising, since the coastal plain south of the glacial margin is generally lacking in rocks with which to construct stone structures. Frank Speck already observed this trend in 1945 with respect to "brush-piles":

The reason for the differentiation in the material of construction of the heaps lies in ecology. On the Coastal Plain from Cape Cod southward along the seaboard, stones being generally absent, the available material is only tree and shrub growths. In the glaciated terrain of New England rounded stones are everywhere within reach and these enter into the mass thrown together to form the marker piles.[3]

I would only disagree with his delineation of the southern limit of the use of stone for structures, as noted above. My informal inspection of site locations by county in the Georgia state archives suggests that stone structures are replaced by earthen mounds (or, in coastal Georgia and Florida, by shell mounds) in areas below the piedmont zone. What is more striking is the general absence of stone structure sites from piedmont North Carolina and Virginia, a terrain in which they are frequent further south. Only in the Shenandoah and upper James valleys in Virginia, west of the Blue Ridge, do sites occur with any frequency, and there are very few sites east of the Blue Ridge in these states.

The pattern of north–south separation is suggested even more strongly when the data are presented county by county, as shown in Plate 4. Sites were found in 255 counties out of a total of 561 within the study area (45.5 percent). The counties with the highest densities of sites are listed in Figure 6, in descending order. These twelve counties, all with densities greater than 0.1 sites per square kilometer, accounted for 43.7 percent of the sites in the inventory, in only 5.5 percent of counties which contained sites. By contrast, 146 counties, 57.3 percent of the total number of counties which contained sites, had site densities less than 0.01 sites per square kilometer. These accounted for 9.0 percent of the sites in the inventory. Of these counties, thirty-nine were in the far northeastern portion of the study area, while twenty-one were in the gap between the southeastern and northeastern cluster. The remaining 34.7 percent of counties (sixty-three) had densities between 0.01 and 0.1 sites per square kilometer. They were scattered throughout the study area, but 30.1 percent of them (nineteen) were located adjacent to the eleven highest density counties.

State	County	Density per sq. km.
Massachusetts	Middlesex	0.33
Rhode Island	Washington	0.32
New York	Putnam	0.30
Rhode Island	Kent	0.20
Georgia	Putnam	0.17
Rhode Island	Newport	0.14
Georgia	Lincoln	0.13
Connecticut	New London	0.12
Massachusetts	Worcester	0.12

Massachusetts	Norfolk	0.11
South Carolina	McCormick	0.11
Georgia	McDuffie	0.11

Figure 6: Highest Site Densities by County.

This uneven distribution is also apparent when considering towns. Sites were reported in 1,248 out of 5,395 towns within the study area (23.1 percent). There are thirteen towns that contain more than fifty-five sites (896 sites total, each $\geq$1.00 percent of the total). These are shown in Figure 7, in descending order. Combined, they account for 16.1 percent of the entire inventory, in only 0.1 percent of the total study area. With the exceptions of Pomfret, Vermont, and Shutesbury, Massachusetts, these towns are all within the eleven highest density counties shown in Figure 6. There were 2,863 sites (51.4 percent of the total) from 192 towns that contained between six and fifty-five sites (0.10 percent to 1.00 percent of the total), and 1,837 sites (33.1 percent of the total) from 1,043 towns which contained fewer than six sites (<0.10 percent of the total).

Town	County	State	No. of Sites	Area (sq. km)	Density per sq. km.
Exeter	Washington	RI	121	151	0.80
Hopkinton	Washington	RI	77	111	0.69
Harvard	Worcester	MA	72	70	1.03
West Greenwich	Washington	RI	71	133	0.53
Voluntown	New London	CT	69	103	0.67
Stanfordville	Putnam	GA	64	62	1.03
Carlisle	Middlesex	MA	62	40	1.55
Pomfret	Windsor	VT	61	102	0.60
Raysville	McDuffie	GA	61	29	2.10
Acton	Middlesex	MA	60	53	1.13
Shutesbury	Franklin	MA	60	70	0.86
Ashland	Middlesex	MA	57	33	1.73
Bolton	Worcester	MA	57	52	1.10
Total			892	1009	0.88

Figure 7: Highest Site Density by Town.

Site Names

Some information about sites can also be gleaned from a study of the site names. As noted in Chapter 5, the choice of names was sometimes arbitrary, but a significant percentage of them are derived from local folk traditions about the sites, rather than having been assigned by modern researchers (the author included). A total of 281 sites in the inventory (5.0 percent) are associated with either Native American place names, or reference "Indians" or specific Contact period Native persons. The most prominent among the latter is King Philip (a.k.a. Pometacom), who is referenced, with historically accurate associations or not in fourteen site names, all but one in Massachusetts (the exception is in Connecticut). Other personages after whom sites are named include Canonchet (six), Weetamoo (three), Agamenticus (two), and one site each is named for Anawan, Awashonks, "Betty," Mantoe, Miantonomo, Sarah Dublet, Tomachechi, Waramaug, and Waskosim.

King Philip's war left an indelible impression upon the English colonists of Massachusetts. The imagery associated with Philip–Pometacom persists to the present day in both Euro-American and indigenous communities, though in the latter communities he is often regarded as a heroic figure. For his colonial adversaries, however, he was sometimes regarded as an agent of the Devil, and sometimes as the scourge of God, dispatched to cleanse the colonists of sin and corruption.[4] Thus, as observed in Chapter 2, it is also not entirely surprising that locations associated with persistent Native religious practices were also associated with the Devil. A total of thirty-five sites (0.6 percent) are named for the Devil, or for persons, places, and activities associated by colonists with him, including seven Devil's Dens, three Purgatories, three Hoccomock/Hobamocks, two Devil's Heads, two Devil's Tombs or Tombstones, two Witch Rocks, and one each of Devil's Dance Chamber, Devil's Foot Rock, Devil's Kitchen, Devil's Potato Patch, Ghost Village, Odzihozo (an Abenaki deity), *Hexenkopf* (Witch's Head), Old Brimstone Road, Satan's Kingdom, Sin and Flesh Brook, Spirit Pond, Spook Rock, Tophet Swamp (Tophet is a Biblical name for Hell), and Witch Brook. All of this suggests that in the minds of the settlers who provided the names for these places, there was an association between the sites and practices considered to be antithetical to normative Christian religious piety. These names are not confined to the areas settled by the New England Puritans, but also include sites as far afield as Quaker Pennsylvania and Dutch Protestant New Amsterdam.

In addition, there were 147 sites (2.6 percent) whose names included the names of indigenous wild animals, which also might indicate a sense that the sites are, or were thought of by those who named them to be, outside of the zone of cultivated land. These include thirty-two references to snakes, twenty references to beavers, nineteen references to bears, eighteen references to wildcats, fourteen references to turtles, ten references to wolves, eight references to turkeys, five references to foxes, four references each to crows, hawks, and eagles, two references each to deer, moose, toads, and whales, and one reference to rabbits.

By contrast, there were only thirty-one sites (0.5 percent) that were named after colonial features (not just the names of the places where the sites were located). These included nine references to cellars, three each to barns, mills, mines, pigpens, and potatoes, and one each to ash-houses, buildings, chimneys, farmer's home places, stills, and town pounds. The overwhelming majority of these sites (twenty-one) are isolated chambers. There were three cases of isolated U-shaped structures and one each of isolated enclosures, mortars, platforms, rock piles, and standing stones associated with colonial names. There were only two sites in this group with multiple structure types: one with a rock pile and a chamber, the other with a stone row and a chamber. These attributions could either have been made after the sites' relationship to indigenous people had been forgotten; or they could be historically accurate.

7

Environmental Preferences

This chapter details the results of analysis for each of the environmental parameters defined in Chapter 5.

Elevation

Elevation above sea level varied between 0 and 3,835 feet (the average being 624.3 feet). On the vertical axis of Figure 8 below:

    1 = 0–249 feet;

    2 = 250–499 feet;

    3 = 500–999 feet;

    4 = 1,000–1,499 feet;

    5 = 1,500–1,999 feet;

    6 = 2,000–2,499 feet; and

    7 = ≥2,500 feet.

As shown in the figure, the largest number of sites (1,996, 36.0 percent) falls between 250 and 500 feet above sea level. By contrast, most Native habitation sites in New England are located between zero and 250 feet above sea level.[1]

Distance to Nearest Water

Distance to nearest water varied between zero and 3,560 meters (the average being 250.8 meters). On the horizontal axis of Figure 9 below:

    1 = 0 meters;

    2 = 1–99 meters;

    3 = 100–249 meters;

    4 = 250–499 meters;

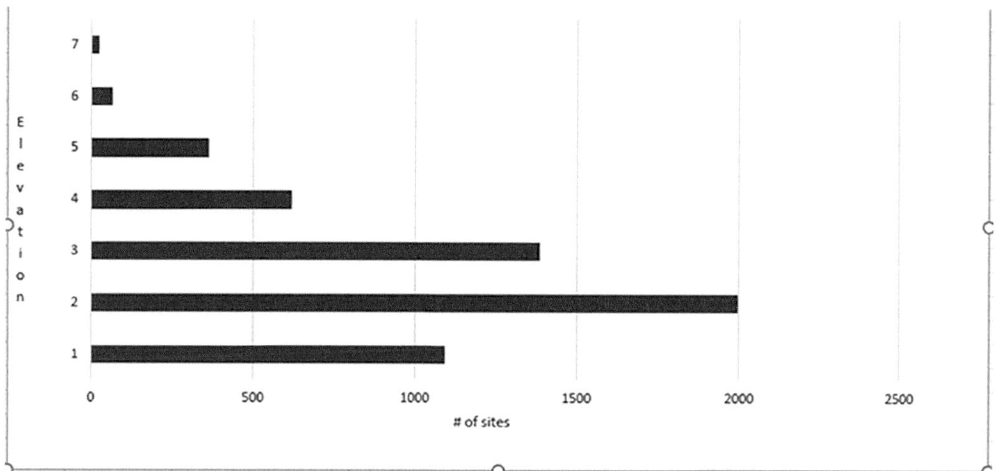

Above: Figure 8: Distribution of Sites by Elevation above Sea Level (in Feet).

Below: Figure 9: Distribution of Sites by Distance to Nearest Water (in Meters).

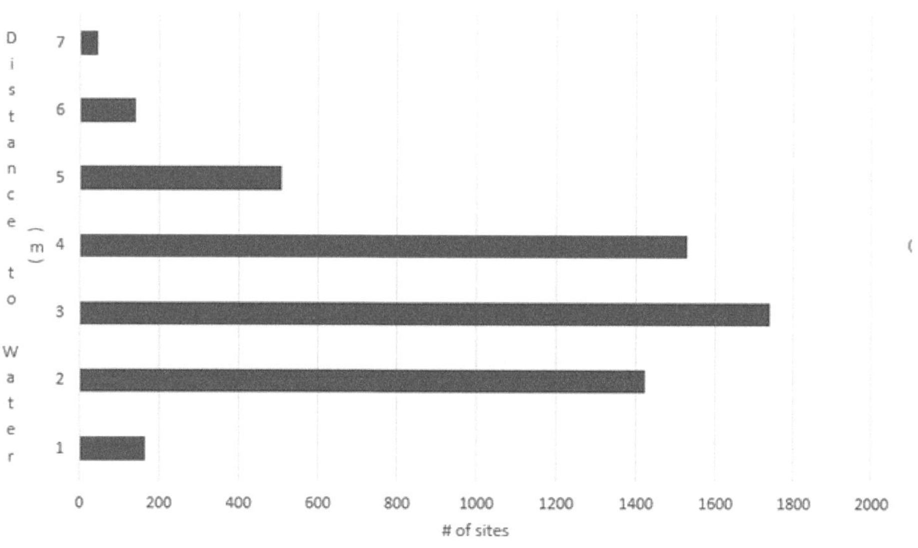

5 = 500–749 meters;
6 = 750–999 meters;
7 = ≥1,000 meters.

The figure shows that the largest number of sites were between 100 and 249 meters (1,740, 31.4 percent), but this was followed closely by sites between 250 and 499 meters (1,530, 27.6 percent), and between 1 and 99 meters (1,422, 25.6 percent). Once again, this is further from water on average than is typical of Native American habitation sites in the regions, which tend to be less than 100 meters from water.[2]

Major River Drainage

Sites were found in a total of 105 river drainages within the study area, which constitute 97.0 percent of the total. The remaining 3.0 percent are along the coast. As noted above, some drainages had very high numbers of sites, while others had as few as a single site. Where estimates of the area of drainages were available (in eighty-nine of the 105 drainages, 84.8 percent), the density of sites within them ranged from 0.48649 per square kilometer (the Pawcatuck drainage in Rhode Island, 378 sites) to 0.00004 per square kilometer (the Cape Fear drainage in North Carolina and Virginia, one site). The average was 0.05604. A total of twenty-nine of the drainages had densities above this average, all of them in New England. There were sixty drainages with densities below the average, scattered throughout the study area.

Type of Water Resource

As shown in Figure 10 below, the largest number of sites (2,320, 41.8 percent) were located adjacent to unnamed headwater streams. Sites adjacent to named streams were next (1,193, 21.5 percent), followed by sites adjacent to swamps (673, 12.1 percent), ponds (529, 9.5 percent), rivers (456, 8.2 percent), lakes (308, 5.5 percent), and the ocean (seventy-one, 1.3 percent). Some sites adjacent to unnamed streams, though included in the category of headwater streams, are actually at higher ranked streams (see next subheading): 253 (10.9 percent) were at Rank Two streams and twenty-six (1.1 percent) were at Rank Three streams.

Type	No. of sites	Percentage
headwater stream	2,320	41.80%
named stream	1,193	21.50%
river	456	8.20%
pond	529	9.50%
swamp	673	12.10%
lake	308	5.50%
ocean	71	1.30%
total	5,550	

Figure 10: Distribution of Sites by Type of Water Resource.

Stream Rank

Stream rank varied from One to Eight (the average being 1.8). As can be seen from Figure 11 below, the overwhelming majority of sites (3,577, 64.5 percent) were associated with Rank One streams, with an additional 17.2 percent (978) at Rank Two streams. Above that, the percentages fall off rapidly. This is once again atypical of Native habitation sites, more of which tend to be at higher ranked streams.[3]

To illustrate this relationship more graphically, in Figure 12 below, the $\log_{10}$ of the number of sites was plotted against the stream rank, with a clear trend line. Only 60.2 percent of sites (2,155) designated as being at Rank One streams were adjacent to unnamed (headwater) streams. There were 617 (17.2 percent) adjacent to swamps, 410 (11.5 percent) adjacent to named streams, 271 (7.6 percent) adjacent to ponds, 100 (2.8 percent) adjacent to lakes, and twenty-four (0.7 percent) adjacent to rivers.

To test whether the above correlation was simply due to there simply being more potential locations at Rank One streams, I examined the distribution of areas at different stream ranks in the largest drainage in the study area for which no sites were reported, the Rappahannock drainage in Virginia. Using USGS maps, the percentage of area at each rank was calculated. As Figure 13 below shows, the results are very comparable to the distribution in Figure 11, with the exception of areas adjacent to Rank Seven streams, which were more than ten times as common in the Rappahannock drainage as were sites at this rank in the inventory. Since this is rank-order data, I compared the two distributions using the Spearman Rank-Order statistic.[4] The result was a Spearman Rho value of 0.62, which is precisely at the critical value at the 0.10 confidence interval with 8 degrees of freedom. While this is a somewhat ambiguous result, it does suggest that the choice of low-ranked streams as site locations may have been at least in part a function of their greater availability rather than of a conscious choice on the part of the builders to construct them in these areas.

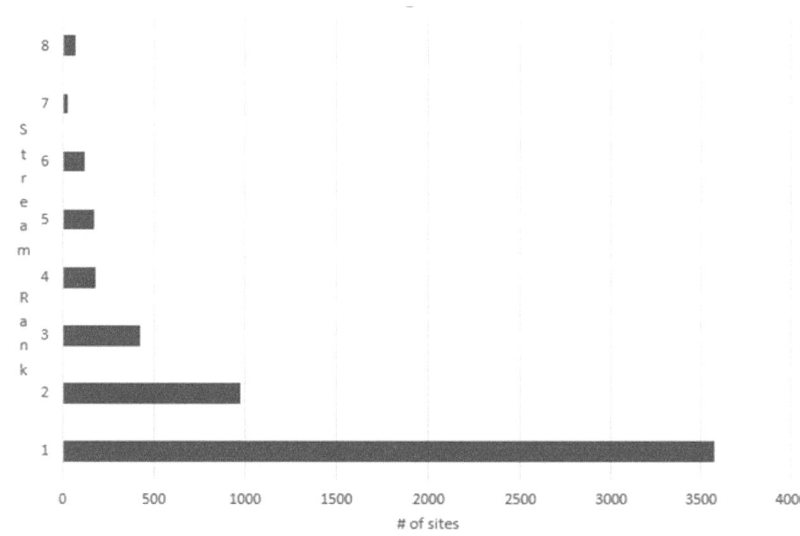

Figure 11: Distribution of Sites by Stream Rank.

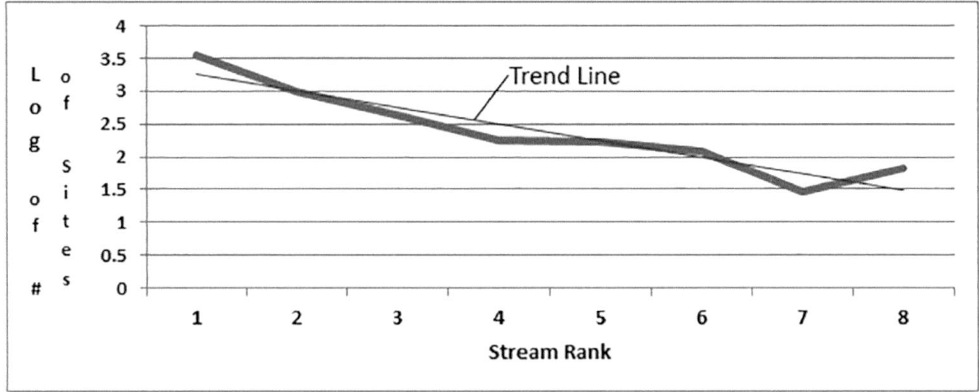

Above: Figure 12: Distribution of $\log_{10}$ of Sites by Stream Rank.

Below: Figure 13: Distribution of Stream Rank Areas in the Rappahannock Watershed.

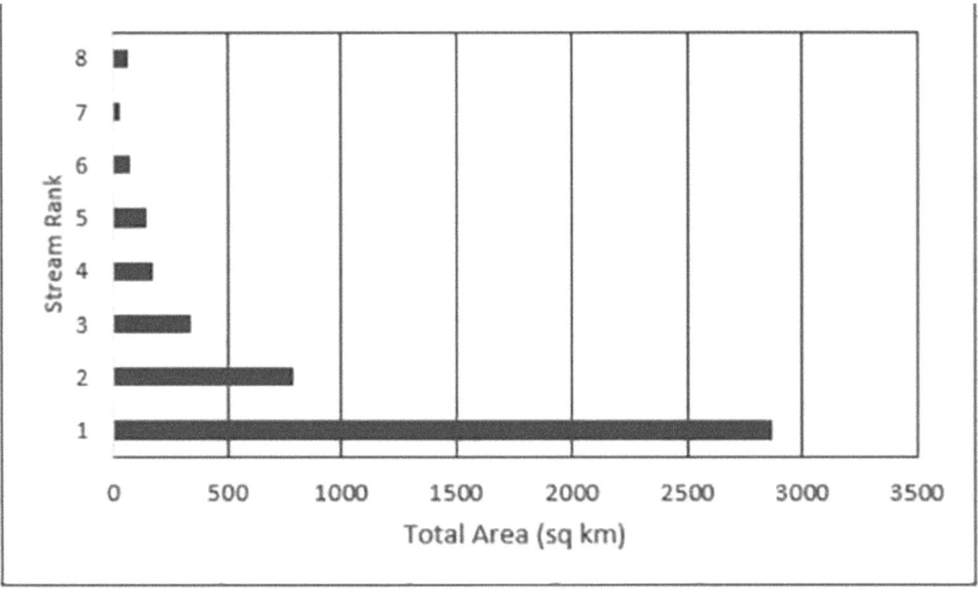

Soil Classification

A total of 5,316 sites (95.8 percent) had soils for which the GIS coverage supplied distinct USDA soil types. A total of 384 different USDA soil types were present at sites in the study area. Most of these types, however, had very few sites in them; only 100 types had percentages above 0.1 percent of the total (> five sites), and only twenty-two had percentages of 1.0 percent or above (≥ fifty-three sites). One soil type—Canton soil—accounted for 10.0 percent (533) of the sites. This was followed by Charlton soils at 7.9 percent (418), Paxton soils at 6.5 percent (343), Hollis soils at 5.9 percent (311), and Chatfield soils at 5.6 percent (300). The remainder had percentages between 0.1 percent and 5.0 percent. The average was 0.3percent. Soil types from twenty-seven of the thirty-two Canadian sites could not be determined, due to the fact that the Canadian system differs from that of the U.S. so much that GIS was unable to reconcile them. There were 192 sites for which there was no description within the USDA system. These included 111 sites in wet or flooded lands, sixty-one sites in disturbed (mostly urban) locations, and twenty sites on bedrock outcrops. All of these are naturally infertile soils. There were eight sites in the U.S. for which no soil type could be found. Thus, the total of sites whose soil fertility could be determined comes to 5,525 (99.5 percent).

The defined soil types belonged to forty-nine trinomial soil classes, but twenty-four of these classes were represented by less than 0.01 percent of the sites ($\leq$ five sites). A total of 3,071 sites (57.3 percent) were in a single class, dystrudepts, followed by kanahapludults at 543 (10.1 percent), haplorthods at 332 (6.2 percent), endoaquepts at 175 (3.3 percent), hapludalfs at 1689 (3.1 percent), quartzipsamments at 2.7 percent, hapludults at 130 (2.4 percent), fragiudepts at 129 (2.4 percent), kandiudults at 106 (2.0 percent), humaquepts at eighty-four (1.6 percent), fragiuquepts at sixty-one (1.1 percent), and udipsamments at sixty-one (1.1 percent). All other types had between 0.1 percent and 1.0 percent of the sites. The average number of sites in any class was 2.0 percent.

These soil classes belonged in turn to eight great groups. As before, one group, the inceptosols, dominated at 67.2 percent (3,608 sites), followed by the ultisols at 15.5 percent (834), the spodosols at 6.5 percent (348), the entisols at 5.5 percent (294), the alfisols at 3.6 percent (195), the histosols at 1.6 percent (eighty-four). There were only four sites in vertisols and one site in mollisols.

The great groups, finally, were reduced to only four categories on the basis of soil fertility, as indicated on the Natural Resources Conservation Services web page entries for each soil type. Figure 14 below provides the results. There was a relatively equal distribution among agriculturally productive soils, soils with low fertility, and naturally infertile soils, with far fewer sites in soils primarily used for pasturage.

Soil Productivity	No.	Percentage
Productively fertile	1,824	33.0%
Pasturage	428	7.7%
Low fertility	1,656	30.0%
Naturally infertile	1,617	29.3%
Total	5,525	

Figure 14: Distribution of Sites by Soil Fertility.

Of the agriculturally productive soils, 40.7 percent were in the unglaciated Southeast. Of the naturally infertile soils, 53.7 percent (868) were on bedrock outcrops and 12.2 percent (197) were in wet environments, either in swamps, or underwater, or in lands subject to flooding. This contradicts Ives' argument (2015) that these soils had once been cultivated by colonial farmers and that their topsoil has since eroded away.

Slope

Where it could be calculated, this parameter varied between 0.0 percent and 75.0 percent (the average being 13.1 percent). As noted in Chapter 5, most soil descriptions (4,756 of them, 85.7 percent of the total) included a range of slopes. The arithmetic mean of the listed range was used to represent the slope in these cases. For some sites (259, or 4.7 percent) where the percentage of slope was not provided, reasonable assumptions were made about it. For example, sites under water were assigned a slope of 0 percent, and sites in muck or peat were assigned ranges of 0–5 percent (the mean being 2.5 percent). Both of these sets of sites fall into the category of slopes from 0–5 percent. Slopes described as "moderately steep" or "sloping" were assigned ranges of 25–40 percent (the mean being 32.5 percent); those described as "steep" or "strongly sloping" were assigned ranges of 40–60 percent (the mean being 50.0 percent); and those described as "very steep" were assigned a range of 60–75 percent (the mean being 67.5 percent). All three of these estimates fall into the category of >25 percent. The remaining 9.6 percent of sites included all thirty-two of the Canadian sites, for which no meaningful soil data was collected, as well as 503 sites whose soil descriptions provided no clear indication of the degree of slope. The distribution of slopes in the four categories is shown below in Figure 15. Once again, this distribution is atypical of Native habitation sites, which tend to be located on shallower slopes. It is also uncharacteristic of farmlands, even marginal farmlands, which tend to be on flat ground.

Percentage of Slope	No. of sites	Percentage
0-5	840	16.75%
5-15	2,748	54.80%
15-25	913	18.21%
>25	514	10.25%
Total	5,015	

Figure 15: Distribution of Sites by Slope.

Environmental Setting

The most common setting was on slopes (45.2 percent), followed by hilltops (21.8 percent) and valleys (20.7 percent). Shorelines, plains, and islands were utilized relatively infrequently (12.3 percent combined). The data are presented in Figure 16:

Setting	No. of sites	Percentage
hilltop	1,212	21.8%
slope	2,510	45.2%
valley	1,148	20.7%
plain	195	3.5%
shore	409	7.4%
island	76	1.4%
total	5,550	

Figure 16: Environmental Settings.

The distribution of most structure types followed these percentages fairly closely, with a few exceptions. These are noted in Chapter 8 in terms of their deviation from expected values, using the chi-square statistic.

When compared with the slope data, the average slope for each of these settings is remarkably similar, varying between 10.0 percent (for shorelines) and 13.1 percent (for valleys). However, the percentage of sites with slopes ≥25 percent is highest for sites on slopes (16.0 percent), followed closely by hilltops (15.0 percent) and valleys (13.8 percent). The average slope percentages for the other three types are lower: 11.1 percent for islands, 11.0 percent for plains, and 9.5 percent for shorelines.

Distance to Fault

Fault line data are available for most jurisdictions within the study area, with the exception of Nova Scotia. The average distance is 4.97 km (range: 0.00–328.72 km). While GIS returns data supposedly accurate to five decimal places of a meter, this was considered to be hollow precision, given that site locations in UTM coordinates

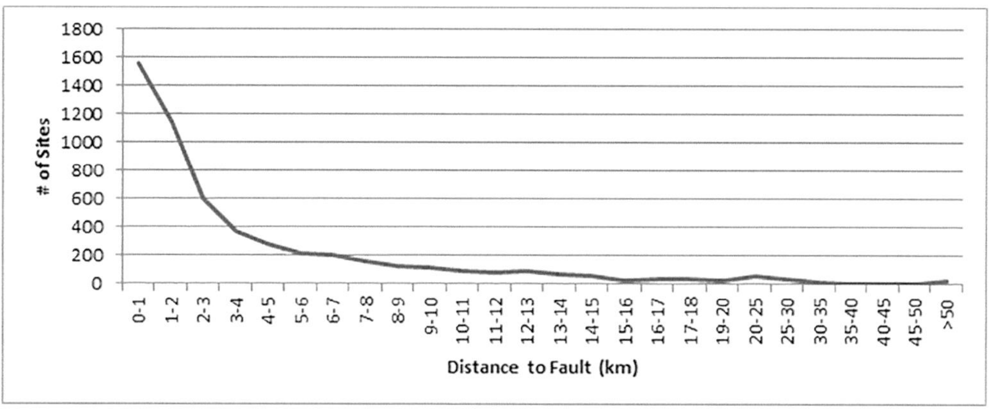

Figure 17: Distribution of Sites by Distance to Nearest Fault (in Kilometers).

themselves are only accurate to 5 meters. Accordingly, distances to faults were rounded up to the nearest kilometer. The distribution is shown in Figure 17 above, and indicates a strong preference for sites to be located close to faults. Sites within 5 km of a fault (the average) constituted 71.7 percent of the total (3,965), with the largest number, 28.1 percent (1,556), within 1 km, and a near-asymptotic decline at greater distances.

Distance to Head-of-Tide/Coastline

This parameter was investigated on the basis of my visit to some sites in Maine, which appeared to be located close to the upper limit of the tidal surge in river systems. Since Native informants had already suggested that preferred locations for stone structures were places "where water flows in two directions," it occurred to me that this condition would be satisfied at head-of-tide locations as well as at watershed boundaries. For river systems, tidal flats are marked on some USGS maps by black stippling in the river, and on others by tan shading, usually adjacent to its banks. The highest point upstream where this stippling or shading was found was taken to be the current head-of-tide line (without making any assumptions about past tidal limits), and its UTM coordinates were compared with those of each site in the drainage, using the Pythagorean theorem to calculate the distance. This method presented a challenge in the case of site locations whose UTM coordinates were in different UTM zones than the head-of-tide location for that drainage. This was resolved, as an approximation, by using Topo!©'s ruler tool to measure the distance to the site. Because of the fact that for some drainages (especially the Altamaha in Georgia) this involved distances in excess of 100 km, it was necessary to use this tool on maps of smaller scale than 1:25000, which decreased the accuracy of the results. At these distances, the curvature of the Earth may also have affected results. For sites that were in coastal locations (e.g. islands, beaches, or near-ocean locations between named river mouths), the distance to the nearest coastline was used instead of head-of-tide, again employing Topo!©'s ruler tool. This applied to 157 sites (2.83 percent of the total): fifty-six in Massachusetts, forty-eight in Rhode Island, twenty-four in Maine, eleven in Connecticut, nine in New York, eight in Nova Scotia, and one in New Hampshire. The average distance is 113.20 km from head-of-tide (range: 0.00–478.62 km). Figure 18 below shows the distribution by 10-km intervals:

There is a strong spike in the distribution from 0–10 km from head-of-tide, and the distribution remains above 300 sites per 10 km of distance up to 100 km, including 65.9 percent of all sites. There are subsidiary spikes at 190–220 km and 250–300 km.

To explore this further, the UTMs were used to examine how this trend was distributed from west to east, with head-of-tide distances averaged at 100-km intervals, adjusted for zone width, starting at the westernmost of the sites, in Georgia. This distribution is shown in Figure 19 below. Sites in the easternmost 800 km of the distribution were on average much closer to head-of-tide than those to the west, all with averages below 100 meters. This includes all of the sites in UTM Zone 19, from about the longitude of the Poquonock River in eastern coastal Connecticut eastwards. These accounted for 38.4 percent of the total, though the greatest number by far are in the first 100 km. If these are subtracted, only 3.0 percent of the total (164) lie to the east of the longitude of Newburyport,

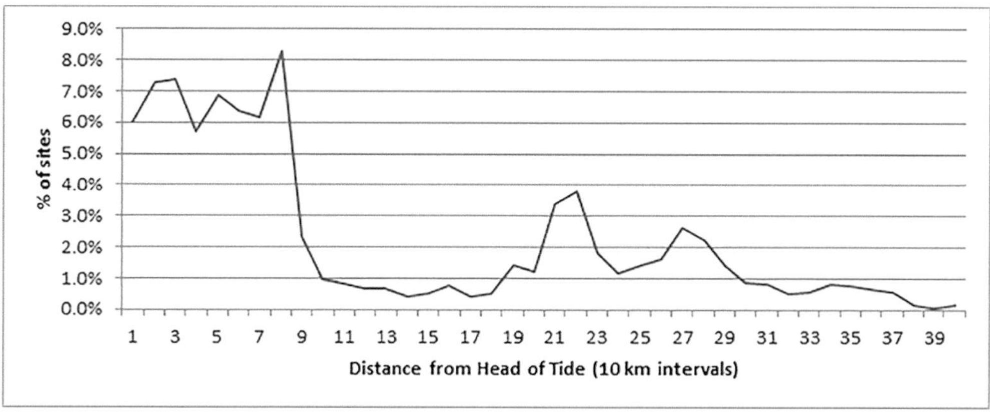

Figure 18: Distribution of Sites (by Percentage) by Distance from Head-of-Tide (in 10-Kilometer Intervals).

Figure 19: Average Distance of Sites to Head-of-Tide by UTM Easting (in 100-Kilometer Intervals).

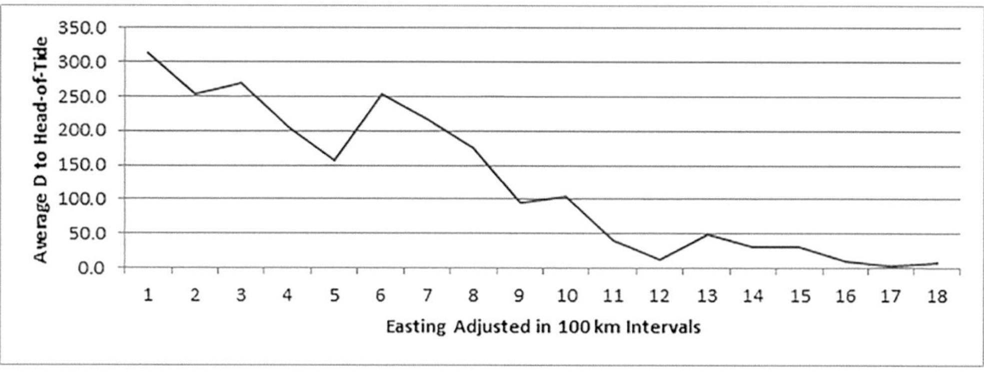

Massachusetts. This indicates that the tendency for sites to cluster close to the head-of-tide is a more easterly, which is also to say a more northerly phenomenon, and may represent a cultural tradition different from that found to the south of New England.

Distance to Watershed Boundary

For major (level six) watersheds, this averaged 14.90 km; for secondary (level eight) watersheds, it averaged 5.51 km; for minor (level ten) watersheds, it averaged 2.26 km. However, there seems to have been an avoidance of sites in the close proximity of major watersheds, measured at 0.5-km intervals. More than half of the sites (2,967, 53.5 percent) were located more than 10 km from a major watershed boundary, and as Figure 20 shows, the distribution of sites closer to the boundary is rather flat, and, with the exception of sites within 0.5 km of a boundary, it does not exceed 150 sites per 0.5-km interval. For secondary watersheds, there is a concentration of sites within 3.5 km of a boundary (2,492, 45.1 percent of the total), but the numbers decline thereafter and there is still a strong concentration of sites more than 10 km away from a watershed

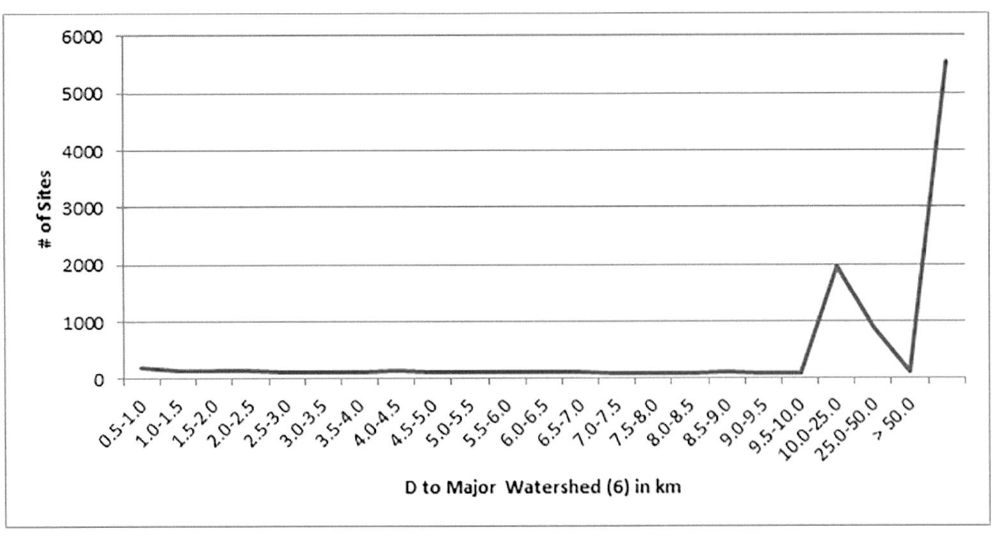

Figure 20: Distribution of Sites by Distance to Level 6 Watershed (in Kilometers).

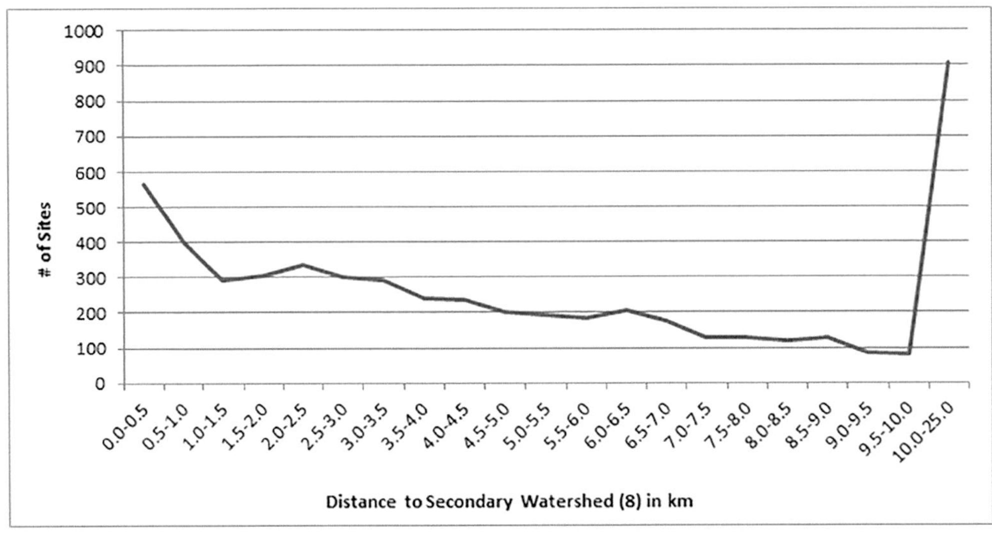

Above: Figure 21: Distribution of Sites by Distance to Level 8 Watershed (in Kilometers).

Below: Figure 22: Distribution of Sites by Distance to Level 10 Watershed (in Kilometers).

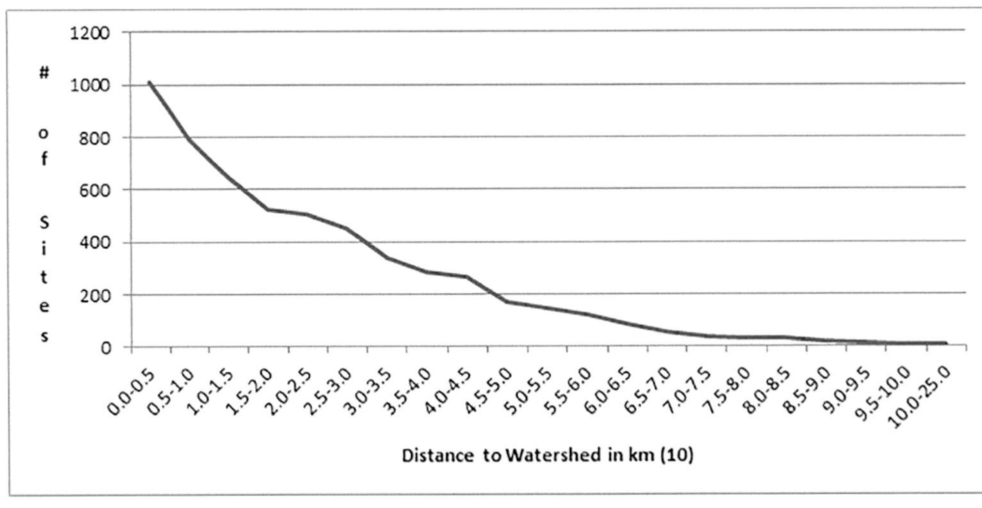

boundary (932 sites, 16.9 percent), as shown in Figure 21. It is only when the minor (level ten) watershed distances are plotted, as shown in Figure 22, that a clear preference for proximity to the boundary emerges: 53.7 percent of sites (2,974) are within 2 km of a level ten watershed boundary, with a smooth asymptotic decline beyond that, and only six sites (0.1 percent) are more than 10 km from a boundary.

Plate 5 presents these three distributions plotted together. This suggests that the distance to minor watershed boundary is a better predictor of site location, and it will be used without reference to the other two levels henceforth.

Site Proximity

This was examined using two methods: variance-mean ratio (VMR) and nearest-neighbor distance (NND).[6] These were particularly employed to test the validity of site clusters (see Chapter 9). The VMR was calculated first by finding the mean number of sites in each cluster per 1-square-kilometer cell, and then comparing that figure with the actual number of sites in each cell (by squaring the difference). The sum of the squared differences for the cluster was divided by the total number of sites to obtain the variance, and this in turn was divided by the mean to calculate the VMR. In cases where VMR ~1.00, the pattern would be defined as random; in cases where it was <1.00, the pattern would be defined as evenly dispersed, while in cases where it was >1.00, it would be defined as clustered. The probability that this ratio was due to random chance or to uniform distribution was further evaluated by multiplying the VMR by the number of 1-square-kilometer cells in the cluster less one, which approximates the chi-square value. The probability for this value in turn was determined from a standard chi-square table.[7] The expectation here was that a probability close to 1.00 would represent a dispersed pattern, while one close to 0.00 would represent a clustered pattern, and a probability intermediate between the two would indicate a random pattern. In all clusters, the VMR was greater than 1.00 and the resulting probability was close to or equal to 0.000, confirming that the pattern was due to clustering. With only one exception, the probability that the sites in clusters were randomly or systematically dispersed was 0.000 at the 0.05 confidence interval. In the one exception (Massachusetts cluster No. 4), the probability was 0.074, still well within the range for clustered patterns.

The NND value for each site was calculated using a GIS coverage, and the mean for each cluster was then calculated. The average NND for the entire sample of 5,550 sites was 2.07 km. The distribution for the entire data set is shown in Figure 23.

As shown in Figures 24 and 25, this is a highly asymptotic curve, with a strong preference for sites being no further than 5 km from their nearest neighbors (5,001 sites, 90.1 percent). Of the forty-two sites further than 25 km from their nearest neighbors, seven are in Virginia, seven in Nova Scotia, six in New York, four each in North Carolina, Georgia, and Pennsylvania, two each in Maine, New Brunswick, and Vermont, and one each in Maryland, Massachusetts, New Hampshire, and West Virginia. None of these sites, obviously, was in a cluster. Sites in clusters were significantly closer to one another on average (0.45 km; range: 0.05–2.82) than were sites outside of clusters (4.06 km; range: 0.05–305.21). Only thirty-two of the 3,058 sites in clusters (1.05 percent) were

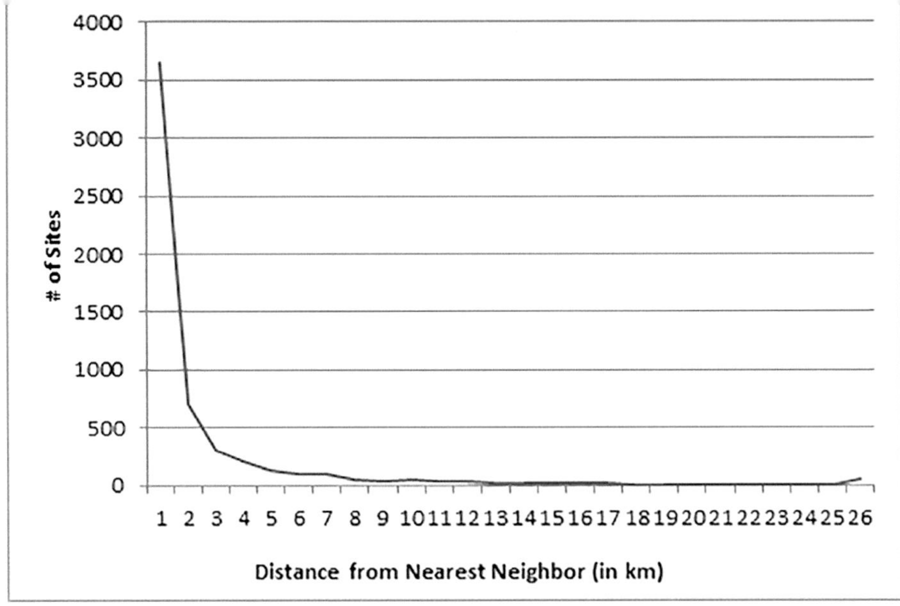

Figurew 23: Distribution of Sites by NND (in Kilometers).

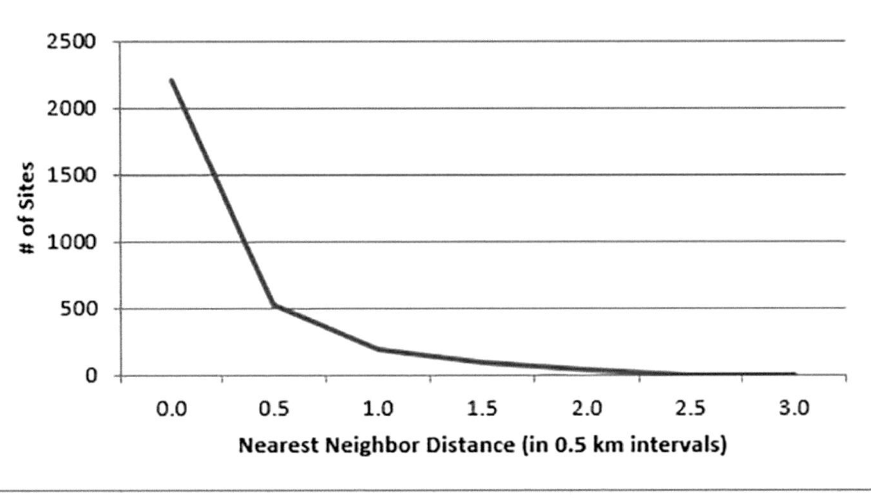

Above: Figure 24: Distribution of Sites in Clusters by NND.

Below: Figure 25: Distribution of Sites outside of Clusters by NND.

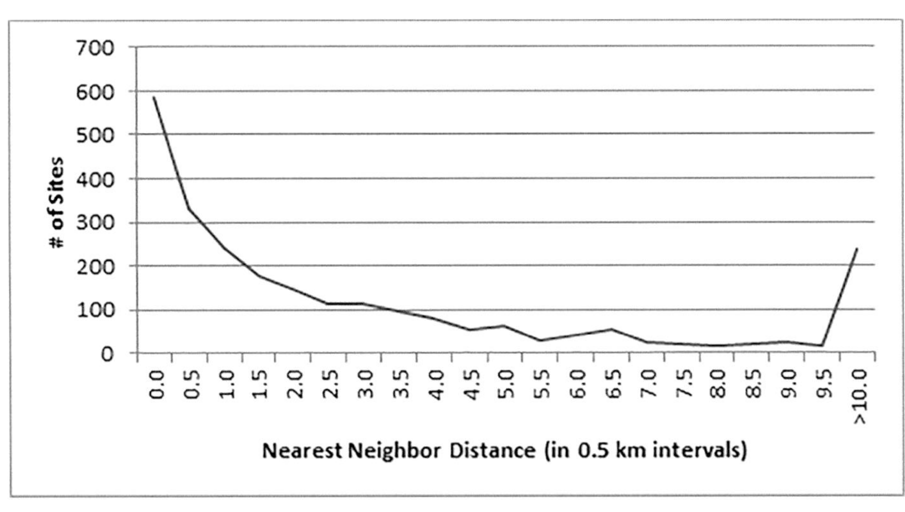

more distant than the sample mean from their nearest neighbor, while only 357 of the 2,492 sites outside of clusters (14.33 percent) were closer than the sample mean to their nearest neighbor, as shown in Figures 24 and 25.

Looking at the total NND across all clusters, it is possible to generate a Z-score that evaluates the likelihood that these distributions are systematic, random, or clustered. Plate 6 shows very clearly that the collective value falls in the left tail of the distribution, which confirms that these sites are, indeed clustered.

Azimuths

Azimuths were recorded for only 412 of the sites in the inventory (7.4 percent). This is not entirely surprising, since structures such as stone piles and cairns can be said to face in all directions and do not have a specific azimuth. However, in some cases, informants noted that there were configurations of stone structures which seemed to be aligned toward particular directions. Sixty of the reported sites had multiple azimuths recorded, for different structures present at the site. There were some serious problems in interpreting the data, since informants often did not always indicate when they gave azimuths in degrees or whether these were degrees from magnetic north or true north. The declination from true north in the Northeast is around 15 degrees east. This may have introduced errors into the figures given. As should be clear from Figure 26, there were strong preferences for key points in the solar year: solstice and equinox sunrises and sunsets, in particular, accounted for 50.9 percent of the sites for which this parameter was recorded. The designations for other directions are derived from Peter Waksman's blog.[8] Associations with secondary aspects such as August 13 sunrise and sunset (associated with the Perseid meteor showers), due north, and lunar standstills were also observed. However, there were also quite a number of orientations that cannot be easily explained on the basis of sky associations. There were also a few notations which were so vague that they could not be resolved to degrees or known aspects.

Degrees	No. of sites	Sky event
0–5	39	axis mundi
5–10	2	
15–20	3	
40–45	2	
55–60	5	
65–70	8	Pleiades rise
70–75	35	summer solstice sunrise
90–95	62	equinox sunrise
110–115	2	
120–125	7	August 13 sunrise
125–130	18	lunar standstill
135–140	75	winter solstice sunrise
155–160	1	

160–165	1	
180–185	40	axis mundi
195–200	1	
200–205	1	
210–215	8	
215–220	3	
220–225	1	
240–245	1	lunar standstill
250–255	62	winter solstice sunset
270–275	51	equinox sunset
295–300	1	
300–305	1	
305–310	8	August 13 sunset
315–320	53	summer solstice sunset
325–330	1	lunar standstill
335–340	2	

Figure 26: Distribution of Sites by Recorded Azimuth (in 5-degree increments).

The distribution of sites with recorded azimuths by state is strongly correlated with the total number of sites from that state; a Spearman Rho test gave a value of 0.92, which for 19 degrees of freedom is significant at the 0.001-confidence interval. Which particular structure was associated with an azimuth was also not often reported, but of the total, 173 sites had only one type of structure present, so only in these cases it is possible to determine this. The largest number of structures in this group were chambers (eighty-two), followed by U-shaped structures (thirty-eight), marked stones (thirteen), standing stones (ten), stone rows (nine), cairns (five), rock piles (five), petroglyphs (two), effigies (two), and unique structures (two).

In addition, there were seventeen sites at which there were multiple azimuths whose numbers were greater than or equal to the number of types present. Adding these to the above gives totals of eighty-three chambers, forty-five U-shaped structures, nineteen marked stones, sixteen stone rows, twelve standing stones, nine rock piles, six cairns, three petroglyphs, three effigies, three unique structures, two split boulders, one balanced rock, one mound, and one niche.

As will be noted in Chapter 9, there are a number of whole clusters most or all of whose sites collectively seem to exhibit consistent azimuths with significant directions. This was most apparent with Connecticut clusters No. 1 and No. 7, which are oriented rather precisely along a winter solstice sunrise–summer solstice sunset line. Local resident Tom Paul has noted that there are a number of additional sites beyond the end of this alignment in both directions that are also aligned with it, terminating in a structure near Montauk Point, Long Island, and continuing westwards at least as far as the Catskills. Beyond this, one would have to factor in the curvature of the earth to determine whether or not the alignment continued to work—something that is beyond the scope of this study. In addition, the southern boundary of Massachusetts cluster No. 14 appears to correspond to a summer solstice sunrise–winter solstice sunset alignment.

8

Structure Types

Individual Structures

The distributions of the eighteen structure types, as defined in Chapter 5, are presented below, in descending order of frequency. Most Algonquian terms were supplied by Rolf Cachat-Schilling, on the basis of his indigenous knowledge and his research into Contact period vocabularies, and some are also found in a recent article by Robinson and Harris.[1, 2] Cachat-Schilling has supplied a general term in Nipmuc for all of these stone sacred places, *Maunumúetash*, "places where we gather."

1. Rock piles (Plates 7, 8): Rock piles, as defined for this study, include a number of forms which are recognized by other researchers as separate types, such as ground piles, rock-on-rock piles, boulder piles, etc.[3] No attempt was made to differentiate between them for this study. A total of 3,035 sites contained rock piles, more than 54 percent of all sites. An equivalent term in the Algonquian languages is *kahtoquwuk*. They were predominantly located in the Northeast (2,123), with fewer in the Southeast (724) and yet fewer in the Middle Atlantic states (190). North Carolina was the only state which lacked rock piles. Of these sites, 18.9 percent (575) had only a single rock pile present. The largest number of rock piles recorded at any one site is approximately 200. At a total of 37.3 percent of the sites (1,133), rock piles were found in combination with other structure types. The most frequent two-way combinations were with stone rows (499) and split boulders (284), both at more than 2σ above the mean. The only site type with which rock piles did not combine above 1σ above the mean was inscriptions, and the only other type with which they did not combine at more than 2σ above the mean was petroglyphs.

    Sites containing rock piles had an average number of 9.1 structures per site (range: 1–644), and an average of 1.8 types of structures per site. The total number of structures could not be determined at 565 of these sites, 18.5 percent of the total. In 266 cases where no information on the type of structures present was provided, the structures were recorded by default as rock piles, which has obviously elevated this percentage. However, I am confident that the rock piles are indeed the most common structure type, on the basis of more precise quantitative descriptions from Rhode Island, Georgia, and South Carolina. They were found at an average elevation of 597.7 feet above sea level (range: 0–3,712 feet) and were on average 253.0 meters from the nearest water resource (range: 0–1,650 meters). Their average stream rank is 1.7 (range: 1–8); their average slope is 12.1 percent (range: 0.5–75.0). They were on average 5.19 km from the nearest fault (range: 0.00–387.27 km); the average distance to the head-of-tide is 125.10 km (range: 0.00–457.98 km); and they were on average 2.23 km from the nearest minor (level ten) watershed boundary (range: 0.00–10.56 km). Their nearest neighbor was on average 1.53 km away (range: 0.51–305.21 km). A total of 1,939 sites, or 63.9 percent, were in clusters. They were predominantly located near headwater streams (1,305), brooks (700), and swamps (396), with smaller numbers at ponds (273), rivers (203), and lakes (145), and very few near the ocean (eleven). Sites in agriculturally productive soils (980) and low fertility soils (927) were about equal in frequency, with slightly fewer in naturally infertile soils (818) and with a smaller number in pasture lands (303). The predominant environmental settings, by far, were slopes (1,505), followed by hilltops (644) and valleys (595). There were relatively fewer on shorelines (163), plains (ninety-seven), and islands (thirty-one).

2. Stone Rows (Plates 9, 10): A total of 896 sites contained stone rows. These may be the equivalent of the Algonquian term *qusukaniyutak*, though this term also appears to apply to enclosures. They were predominantly located in the Northeast (795), with fewer in the Middle Atlantic states (sixty-two) and yet fewer in the Southeast (thirty-nine). Stone rows were absent from Quebec, North Carolina, Virginia, and West Virginia. A total of seventy-seven sites (8.6 percent) had only a single stone row present. The largest number recorded at any one site is thirty-six. A total of 83.4 percent of them (747) were found in combination with other structure types. The most frequent two-way combinations (at more than 2σ above the mean) were with rock piles (499) and chambers (eighty). The only structure type with which stone rows did not occur above 1σ above the mean were inscriptions. Sites containing stone rows had an average number of 14.0 structures per site (range: 1–681), and an average of 3.0 types of structures per site. The total number could not be determined at thirty-seven of these sites, 4.1 percent of the total. They were found at an average elevation of 579.0 feet above sea level (range: 0–2,652 feet), and were on average 261.0 meters from the nearest water resource (range: 0–1,650 meters). Their average stream rank is 1.6 (range: 1–8); their average slope is 13.5 percent (range: 0.0–67.5). They were on average 5.00 km from the nearest fault (range: 0.00–328.65 km); the average distance to the head-of-tide is 78.36 km (range: 0.00–457.48 km); and they were on average 2.15 km from the nearest minor watershed boundary (range: 0.00–100.23 km). Their nearest neighbor was on average 1.38 km away (range: 0.05–63.21 km). A total of 524 sites, or 58.5 percent, were in clusters. They were predominantly located near headwater streams (373), brooks (172), swamps (132), and ponds (100), with smaller numbers at rivers (sixty-six), lakes (forty-six), and the ocean (seven). The largest number (334) were in agriculturally productive soils (323); soils with low fertility (259) and infertile soils (241) were about equal, with a smaller number in pasture lands (sixty-five). The predominant environmental settings are slopes (439), followed by hilltops (195) and valleys (185). There were relatively fewer at shorelines (forty-seven), on plains (twenty-one), and on islands (nine).

3. Cairns (Plates 11, 12): A total of 879 sites contained cairns. These appear to be the equivalent of *wawanaqussuk* (honoring stone) in Algonquian languages. They were predominantly located in the Northeast (685), with fewer in the Middle Atlantic states (124) and yet fewer in the Southeast (seventy). This is the only type which was found in all nineteen states and provinces. Of these sites, 16.6 percent (146) had only a single cairn present. The largest number recorded was "several hundred" (range: 1–*c.* 300). A total of 49.5 percent (435) were found in combination with other structure types. The most frequent two-way combinations were with rock piles (241) (more frequent than 2σ above the mean) and stone rows (185, at more than 1σ above the mean). The only structure type with which cairns did not occur at all were inscriptions. Sites containing cairns had an average number of 17.0 structures per site, and an average of 2.0 types of structures per site. The total number could not be determined at 196 of these sites, 22.4 percent of the total. They were found at an average elevation of 723.0 feet above sea level (range: 0–3,517 feet), and were on average 276.0 meters from the nearest water resource (range: 0–3,560 meters). Their average stream rank is 1.8 (range: 1–8); their average slope is 11.7 percent (range: 0.5–30.0). They were on average 6.52 km from the nearest fault (range: 0.00–93.09 km); the average distance to the head-of-tide is 105.72 km (range: 0.00–410.79 km); and they were on average 2.29 km from the nearest minor watershed boundary (range: 0.00–11.27 km). Their nearest neighbor was on average 2.64 km away (range: 0.06–158.04 km). A total of 447 sites, or 50.9 percent, were in clusters. They were predominantly located near headwater streams (360), brooks (177), and swamps (125), with smaller numbers at ponds (eighty-four), lakes (sixty-five), rivers (fifty-eight), and the ocean (eight). Sites in agriculturally productive soils (288) and naturally infertile soils (279) were about equally frequent, with slightly fewer in low fertility soils (238) and with a smaller number in pasture lands (fifty-nine). The predominant environmental settings are slopes (405), followed by hilltops (214) and valleys (148). There were relatively fewer on shorelines (fifty-six), plains (thirty-one), and islands (five).

4. Chambers (Plates 13, 14) A total of 702 sites contained chambers, caves or other subterranean structures. One possible Algonquian term for them is *hassanegk*, which refers to a cave lined with stones. Roger Williams gives the term *pesuponck* for the type which was used as a sweat lodge.[4] Where most of these were built chambers, they also included three rockshelter sites, a site with two shafts, a burial cave, a crawlway, and a chamber-like bridge over a stream. They were predominantly located in the Northeast (672), with fewer in the Middle Atlantic states (twenty-six) and far fewer in the Southeast (four). Chambers were absent from Delaware, Maryland, New Brunswick, Quebec, South Carolina, Virginia, and West Virginia. Only a single chamber was present at 459 of these sites (65.5 percent). Of these isolated chambers, 51.9 percent (238) were found in just five counties: Putnam, New York (ninety-six), New London, Connecticut (sixty-seven), Windsor, Vermont (twenty-nine), Westchester, New York (twenty-four), and Franklin, Massachusetts (twenty-two). The largest number recorded at any one site is seven (range: 1–7). A total of 30.5 percent (214) were found in combination with other structure types. The most frequent two-way combinations were with stone rows (eighty) and rock

piles (seventy-nine), both more frequent than 1σ above the mean. There were no structure types with which chambers did not co-occur. Sites containing chambers had an average number of 4.5 structures per site (range: 1–305), and an average of 1.7 types of structures per site. The total number could not be determined at twenty of these sites, 2.9 percent of the total. They were found at an average elevation of 646.0 feet above sea level (range: 0–2,852 feet), and were on average 235.4 meters from the nearest water resource (range: 0–1,909 meters). Their average stream rank is 1.6 (range: 1–8); their average slope is 14.8 percent (range: 0.0–67.5). They were on average 4.18 km from the nearest fault (range: 0.00–38.53 km); the average distance to the head-of-tide is 88.50 km (range: 0.00–459.94 km); and they were on average 2.17 km from the nearest minor watershed boundary (range: 0.00–9.32 km). Their nearest neighbor was on average 2.18 km away (range: 0.66–83.68 km). A total of 347 sites, or 49.4 percent, were in clusters. They were predominantly located near headwater streams (283) and brooks (160), with smaller numbers at swamps (eighty-three), ponds (sixty-two), rivers (sixty-one), lakes (forty-six), and the ocean (five). The largest number (241) were in naturally infertile soils; sites with low fertility soils (211) and sites in agriculturally productive soils (205) were about equal in frequency, with a smaller number in pasture lands (forty-two). The predominant environmental settings are slopes (282) and valleys (217), followed by hilltops (109) and shorelines (sixty-four). There were relatively fewer on plains (twenty-seven) and islands (three). It should be noted that this is the only structure type where sites in valleys exceeded those on hilltops by such a wide margin. The chi-square value for valleys (41.1) was significant at the 0.01 confidence interval. However, the majority of chambers which faced valleys (130, 59.9 percent) were isolated and did not have recorded azimuths. This may suggest a different function for this subset of chambers.

5. Balanced Rocks (Plates 15, 16): A total of 487 sites contained balanced rocks. A possible Algonquian term for these is *wanashqueompsk*, which means "on top of the rock(s)." They were predominantly located in the Northeast (451), with fewer in the Middle Atlantic states (thirty-six) and none in the Southeast. Only six were found south of the glacial margin. Balanced rocks were absent from Delaware, Georgia, Maryland, New Brunswick, North Carolina, Nova Scotia, Quebec, South Carolina, Virginia, and West Virginia. In those states where they occurred, 34.9 percent (170) had only a single balanced rock present. These might be solely the result of glacial deposition. The largest number recorded at any one site is thirty-eight. A total of 61.8 percent (301) were found in combination with other structure types. The most frequent two-way combinations were with rock piles (215) (more frequent than 2σ above the mean); and with split-filled boulders (113) and stone rows (110) (both more frequent than 1σ above the mean). The only structure types with which balanced rocks did not co-occur were inscriptions. Sites containing balanced rocks had an average number of 14.5 structures per site (range: 1–217), and an average of 2.9 types of structures per site. The total number could not be determined at 9 of these sites, 1.9 percent of the total. They were found at an average elevation of 548.8 feet above sea level (range: 0–3,835 feet), and were on average 295.9 meters from the nearest water resource (range: 0–1,060 meters). Their average stream rank is

1.5 (range: 1–8); their average slope is 14.1 percent (range: 0.5–67.5). They were on average 4.35 km from the nearest fault (range: 0.02–34.88 km); the average distance to the head-of-tide is 52.13 km (range: 0.01–478.62 km); and they were on average 1.89 km from the nearest minor watershed boundary (range: 0.25–8.94 km). Their nearest neighbor was on average 1.59 km away (range: 0.05–35.01 km). A total of 284 sites, or 58.3 percent, were in clusters. They were predominantly located near headwater streams (163), brooks (115), and swamps (100), with smaller numbers at ponds (forty-eight), rivers (thirty-six), lakes (twenty), and the ocean (five). Most sites were in naturally infertile soils (242), with similar frequencies for sites in low fertility soils (214) and agriculturally productive soils (205), and fewer (forty-two) in pasturage. The predominant environmental settings are slopes (238) and hilltops (135), followed by valleys (eighty). There were relatively few on shorelines (eighteen), plains (fourteen), and islands (two).

6. Marked Stones (Plates 17, 18, 19): A total of 415 sites contained marked stones. Where defined (in 184 cases, 44.3 percent), these included eighty-two stones described as *manitous*, fifty-one mortars, twenty-two cupules, six altered boulders, four holes, three bowls, two depressions, two serpents, two stone faces, and one each of swirls, triangles, arrows, butterflies, cup and saucer, feline profiles, grindstones, pyramid stones, scallops, and smoothing stones.[5] The Algonquian term for mortars is *toqhumoq*. A possible term for cupules is *axsinalaxaqat*, which designates a stone with a hole in it. Eleven sites contained more than one type of marked stone. They were predominantly located in the Northeast (305), with fewer in the Middle Atlantic states (sixty-three) and in the Southeast (forty-seven). Marked stones were absent from Delaware, Maryland, New Brunswick, Nova Scotia, Quebec, and West Virginia. A total of 108 of these sites (26.0 percent) had only a single marked stone present. The largest number recorded at any one site is 200. A total of 63.4 percent (263) were found in combination with other structure types. The most frequent two-way combinations were with rock piles (157) (at more than 2σ above the mean); and with stone rows (110) (more frequent than 1σ above the mean). There were no structure types with which marked stones did not co-occur. Sites containing marked stones had an average number of 14.6 structures per site (range: 1–681), and an average of 2.9 types of structures per site. The total number could not be determined at fifty-six of these sites, 13.5 percent of the total. They were found at an average elevation of 530.6 feet above sea level (range: 0–2,680 feet), and were on average 231.2 meters from the nearest water resource (range: 0–1,030 meters). Their average stream rank is 2.0 (range: 1–8); their average slope is 13.4 percent (range: 0.0–67.5). They were on average 4.08 km from the nearest fault (range: 0.02–33.47 km); the average distance to the head-of-tide is 68.30 km (range: 0.00–371.40 km); and they were on average 2.48 km from the nearest minor watershed boundary (range: 0.00–9.91 km). Their nearest neighbor was on average 2.36 km away (range: 0.07–35.41 km). A total of 216 sites, or 52.0 percent, were in clusters. They were predominantly located near headwater streams (139), brooks (ninety-four), and swamps (sixty-seven), with smaller numbers at ponds (forty-four), rivers (forty-four), lakes (fourteen), and the ocean (thirteen). Sites in agriculturally productive soils (148) and in soils with low

fertility (136) were about equal, with a slightly smaller number of sites in naturally infertile soils (100) and much fewer in pasture lands (thirty-one). The predominant environmental settings are slopes (157), followed by hilltops (ninety-seven) and valleys (ninety-three). There were relatively fewer sites on shorelines (forty-one), plains (nineteen), and islands (nine).

7. Split-filled Boulders (Plates 20, 21): A total of 386 sites contained split-filled boulders. A possible Algonquian term for this type is *pindaxsenakan*—literally, "a living being enters into something," on the idea that these were considered spirit portals to the underworld. They were predominantly located in the Northeast (371), with fewer in the Middle Atlantic states (fifteen) and none in the Southeast. Only two were south of the glacial margin. Split-filled boulders were absent from Georgia, Maryland, New Brunswick, North Carolina, Nova Scotia, North Carolina, South Carolina, and West Virginia. Of these sites, 6.7 percent (twenty-six) had only a single split-filled boulder present. The largest number recorded at any one site is thirty-one (range: 1–31). A total of 90.2 percent (348) were found in combination with other structure types. The most frequent two-way combinations were with rock piles (284) (more than 2σ above the mean); and balanced rocks (113) (more than 1σ above the mean). There were no structure types with which split boulders did not co-occur. Sites containing split-filled boulders had an average number of 21.8 structures per site (range: 1–681), and an average of 3.8 types of structures per site. The total number could not be determined at twenty-four of these sites, 6.2 percent of the total. They were found at an average elevation of 446.2 feet above sea level (range: 0–2,574 feet), and were on average 250.1 meters from the nearest water resource (range: 0–1,280 meters). Their average stream rank is 1.6 (range: 1–8); their average slope is 12.5 percent (range: 0.5–67.5). They were on average 4.13 km from the nearest fault (range: 0.00–31.14 km); the average distance to the head-of-tide is 53.64 km (range: 0.00–299.08 km); and they were on average 1.99 km from the nearest minor watershed boundary (range: 0.00–8.96 km). Their nearest neighbor was on average 0.93 km away (range: 0.05–30.30 km). A total of 299 sites, or 77.5 percent, were in clusters. They were predominantly located near headwater streams (137), brooks (eighty-seven), and swamps (eighty-six), with smaller numbers at ponds (forty-four), rivers (twenty-one), the ocean (eight), and lakes (four). Sites in agriculturally productive soils (132) and in soils with low fertility (131) were about equal, with a smaller number of sites in naturally infertile soils (seventy-six) and pasture lands (forty-seven). The predominant environmental settings are, by far, slopes (209), followed by valleys (seventy-three) and hilltops (sixty-seven). There were relatively fewer on shorelines (twenty-two), plains (ten), and islands (five).

8. Effigies (Plates 22, 23, 24): A total of 379 sites contained effigies. Where defined (in 317 cases, 83.4 percent), and as interpreted by informants, 144 (38.0 percent) of these appear to represent turtles and 131 (34.6 percent) appear to represent snakes or serpents. The Algonquian term for turtle effigies is *toonuppusoq*. It is my understanding that the Algonguian term *qusukaniyutak*, which applies to stone rows and enclosures, also may be used to define serpentine walls. The Algonquian term for snake, *skug*, does not appear to be applied to these structures.[6] In addition, there

were six birds, four eagles, four human female figures, three other human figures, three panthers, three whales, two faces, two footprints, two fish, two heads, and one each of effigies described as boat-shaped, commas, elephants (?), eyebrows, frogs, alligators (?), hands, hawks, bears, and wolves. A total of twenty-two sites had more than one type of effigy present. They were predominantly located in the Northeast (341), with fewer in the Middle Atlantic states (thirty) and yet fewer in the Southeast (eight). Effigies were absent from Delaware, Maryland, New Brunswick, North Carolina, Quebec, Virginia, and West Virginia. Of these sites, 18.5 percent (seventy) had only a single effigy present. The largest number recorded at any one site is seven (range: 1–7). A total of 77.0 percent (292) were found in combination with other structure types. The most frequent two-way combinations were with rock piles (196, more frequent than 2σ above the mean), stone rows (145), and petroglyphs (twenty-three), all more frequent than 1σ above the mean). There were no structure types with which effigies did not co-occur. Sites containing effigies had an average number of 17.6 structures per site (range: 1–681), and an average of 3.2 types of structures per site. The total number could not be determined at sixty of these sites, 15.9 percent of the total. They were found at an average elevation of 621.2 feet above sea level (range: 0–3,517 feet), and were on average 256.3 meters from the nearest water resource (range: 0–1,650 meters). Their average stream rank is 1.6 (range: 1–8); their average slope is 14.0 percent (range: 0.0–67.5). They were on average 3.91 km from the nearest fault (range: 0.02–25.22 km); the average distance to the head-of-tide was 62.56 km (range: 0.00–367.88 km); and they were on average 2.35 km from the nearest minor watershed boundary (range: 0.00–9.92 km). Their nearest neighbor was on average 1.38 km away (range: 0.06–31.32 km). A total of 240 sites, or 63.3 percent, were in clusters. They were predominantly located near headwater streams (136), brooks (seventy-three), and swamps (sixty-eight), with smaller numbers at ponds (fifty-one), rivers (thirty-two), lakes (thirteen), and the ocean (five). The largest number (142) were in agriculturally productive soils, while naturally infertile soils (109) and soils with low fertility (ninety-eight) were about equal, with a smaller number in pasture lands (twenty-six). The predominant environmental settings are slopes (175), followed by hilltops (ninety-one) and valleys (seventy-seven). There were relatively few on shorelines (thirteen), plains (nine), and islands (four).

9. Standing Stones (Plates 25, 26): A total of 343 sites contained standing stones. These structures are termed *sunsh nipamu* in Algonquian languages. While most of them are flat slabs (either standing upright or fallen in place), at one site they were described as "obelisks." They were predominantly located in the Northeast (321), with fewer in the Middle Atlantic states (eighteen) and yet fewer in the Southeast (four). Standing stones are absent from Delaware, Maryland, New Brunswick, Quebec, Virginia, and West Virginia. A total of sixty-seven of these sites (19.6 percent) had only a single standing stone present. The largest number recorded at any one site is twenty-eight. A total of 74.1 percent (254) were found in combination with other structure types. The most frequent two-way combination which exceeded 2σ above the mean was with rock piles (141). The most frequent combinations which exceeded 1σ above the mean were with stone rows (117) and petroglyphs (twenty-nine). The only structure

type with which standing stones did not co-occur were inscriptions. Sites containing standing stones had an average number of 16.2 structures per site (range: 1–681), and an average of 3.3 types of structures per site. The total number could not be determined at thirty-one of these sites, 9.0 percent of the total. They were found at an average elevation of 742.3 feet above sea level (range: 0–3,476 feet), and were on average 300.8 meters from the nearest water resource (range: 0–1,909 meters). Their average stream rank is 1.5 (range: 1–8); their average slope is 15.5 percent (range: 0.0–52.5). They were on average 5.77 km from the nearest fault (range: 0.00–35.23 km); the average distance to the head-of-tide is 97.29 km (range: 0.14–354.67 km); and they were on average 2.16 km from the nearest minor watershed boundary (range: 0.00–8.91 km). Their nearest neighbor was on average 1.60 km away (range: 0.05–57.22 km). A total of 209 sites, or 60.9 percent, were in clusters. They were predominantly located near headwater streams (150) and brooks (seventy-two), with smaller numbers at swamps (forty-three), ponds (thirty-nine), rivers (twenty-eight), lakes (seven), and the ocean (three). Sites in soils with low fertility (112), sites in agriculturally productive soils (106) and infertile soils (101) were about equal in frequency, with a smaller number in pasture lands (twenty-two). The predominant environmental settings are slopes (166), followed by hilltops (ninety-one) and valleys (fifty-eight). There were relatively few on shorelines (nineteen), plains (six), and islands (three).

10. U-shaped structures (Plates 27, 28): A total of 305 sites contained U-shaped structures, or prayer seats. The Algonquian term for these is *shwihwakuwi.* They were predominantly located in the Northeast (286), with fewer in the Middle Atlantic states (fourteen) and yet fewer in the Southeast (five). U-shaped structures are absent from Delaware, Maryland, New Brunswick, North Carolina, Nova Scotia, Quebec, South Carolina, Virginia, and West Virginia. Of these sites, 30.5 percent (ninety-three) had only a single structure present. A total of 64.6 percent (197) were found in combination with other structure types. The largest number recorded at any one site is eight (range: 1–8). The most frequent two-way combination was with rock piles (118), at more than 2σ above the mean; and with stone rows (eighty-one) and cairns (seventy-nine), both at more than 1σ above the mean. The only structure type with which U-shaped structures did not co-occur were inscriptions. Sites containing U-shaped structures had an average number of 17.0 structures per site (range: 1–681), and an average of 3.0 types of structures per site. The total number could not be determined at nine of these sites, 3.0 percent of the total. They were found at an average elevation of 489.2 feet above sea level (range: 2–1,935 feet), and were on average 251.0 meters from the nearest water resource (range: 0–1,360 meters). Their average stream rank is 1.5 (range: 1–7); their average slope is 11.5 percent (range: 0.0–67.5). They were on average 4.40 km from the nearest fault (range: 0.02–43.58 km); the average distance to the head-of-tide is 59.95 km (range: 0.40–352.25 km); and they were on average 2.10 km from the nearest minor watershed boundary (range: 0.00–9.75 km). Their nearest neighbor was on average 1.04 km away (range: 0.07–35.01 km). A total of 347 sites, or 72.1 percent, were in clusters. They were predominantly located near headwater streams (115), brooks (sixty), and swamps

(sixty), with smaller numbers at ponds (thirty-eight), rivers (nineteen), lakes (twelve), and the ocean (one). Sites in agriculturally productive soils (ninety-seven), in soils with low fertility (ninety-five), and in naturally infertile soils (eighty-nine) were about equal, with a smaller number in pasture lands (twelve). The predominant environmental settings are slopes (145), followed by hilltops (eighty-two) and valleys (forty-nine). There were relatively fewer on shorelines (twenty), plains (seven), and islands (two).

11. Petroglyphs and Pictographs (Plates 29, 30): A total of 230 sites contained petroglyphs, and eight contained pictographs. Where they were defined and interpreted by informants (fifty cases, or 21.7 percent), these included seven hands, six circles, six ferns, four birds, three Xs, three eyes, three human figures, two turtles, two footprints, two parallel lines, and one each of arrows, atl-atls, butterflies, dots, crosses, phalli, faces, serpents, fish, ships, horned heads, spirals, and a map. There are no known Algonquian terms equivalent to these images. Six sites contained more than one type of petroglyph. They were predominantly located in the Northeast (157), with fewer in the Southeast (forty-seven) and yet fewer in the Middle Atlantic states (twenty-six). Petroglyphs are absent from Delaware and Quebec. Of these sites, 42.6 percent (ninety-eight) had only a single petroglyph present. The largest number recorded at any one site is six. A total of 39.6 percent (ninety-one) were found in combination with other structure types. The most frequent two-way combinations were with stone rows (thirty), standing stones (twenty-nine), rock piles (twenty-five), and inscriptions (two), all more frequent than 1σ above the mean. There were no structure types with which petroglyphs did not co-occur. Sites containing petroglyphs had an average number of 5.2 structures per site (range: 1–217), and an average of 1.9 types of structures per site. The total number could not be determined at fifty-one of these sites, 22.2 percent of the total. They were found at an average elevation of 827.2 feet above sea level (range: 0–3,770 feet), and were on average 242.3 meters from the nearest water resource (range: 0–985 meters). Their average stream rank is 2.4 (range: 1–8); their average slope is 18.6 percent (range: 0.0–75.0). They were on average 8.39 km from the nearest fault (range: 0.01–77.21 km); the average distance to the head-of-tide is 154.43 km (range: 0.00–399.30 km); and they were on average 4.36 km from the nearest minor watershed boundary (range: 0.00–10.14 km). Their nearest neighbor was on average 4.52 km away (range: 0.09–66.44 km). A total of seventy-four sites, or 32.2 percent, were in clusters. They were predominantly located near headwater streams (ninety-three), rivers (forty-eight) and brooks (forty-six), with smaller numbers at swamps (thirteen), the ocean (thirteen), ponds (ten), and lakes (eight). Sites in agriculturally productive soils (seventy-six), naturally infertile soils (seventy), and soils with low fertility (sixty-six) were about equal in frequency, with a smaller number in pasture lands (sixteen). The predominant environmental settings are slopes (ninety), followed by valleys (fifty-four), hilltops (thirty-nine), and shores (twenty-six). There were relatively few on islands (twelve) and plains (nine). This was the only structure type for which the percentage for sites on islands was larger than that for sites on plains. The chi-square value for islands (40.2) was significant at the 0.01 confidence interval.

12. Enclosures (Plates 31, 32): A total of 173 sites contained enclosures. Where these were defined, four of them were described as terraces, two as amphitheaters, and one each as boulder outlines, cist graves, cistern-like, curved structures, earthwork forts, foundations, keystone-shaped, and L-shaped. These may be the equivalent of the Algonquian term *qusukaniyutak*, though this term also appears to apply to stone rows. They were predominantly located in the Northeast (166), with far fewer in the Middle Atlantic states (five) and in the Southeast (two). Enclosures are absent from Delaware, Maryland, New Brunswick, North Carolina, Nova Scotia, Quebec, South Carolina, and Virginia. Of these sites, 8.1 percent (fourteen) had only a single enclosure present. The largest number recorded at any one site is ten (range: 1–10). A total of 87.9 percent (152) were found in combination with other structure types. The most frequent two-way combinations were with rock piles (116, more than 2σ above the mean) and stone rows (eighty-two, more than 1σ above the mean). The only structure type with which enclosures did not co-occur were inscriptions. Sites containing enclosures had an average number of 20.4 structures per site (range: 1–681), and an average of 3.1 types of structures per site. The total number could not be determined at nine of these sites, 5.2 percent of the total. They were found at an average elevation of 482.9 feet above sea level (range: 1–2,224 feet), and were on average 218.4 meters from the nearest water resource (range: 0–880 meters). Their average stream rank is 1.4 (range: 1–8); their average slope is 11.6 percent (range: 0.5–37.5). They were on average 2.94 km from the nearest fault (range: 0.07–43.45 km); the average distance to the head-of-tide is 54.86 km (range: 0.13–457.98 km); and they were on average 2.58 km from the nearest minor watershed boundary (range: 0.00–9.88 km). Their nearest neighbor was on average 0.87 km away (range: 0.08–13.38 km). A total of 132 sites, or 76.3 percent, were in clusters. They were predominantly located near headwater streams (fifty-three), swamps (forty-four), and brooks (thirty-eight), with smaller numbers at ponds (twenty-four), rivers (nine), lakes (four), and the ocean (one). The largest number (sixty-two) were in agriculturally productive soils, while soils with low fertility (fifty) and naturally infertile soils (forty) were about equal in frequency, with a smaller number in pasture lands (eighteen). The predominant environmental settings by far were slopes (102), followed by hilltops (thirty-two) and valleys (twenty-nine). There were much fewer sites on shorelines (seven) and plains (three), and none on islands.

13. Stone Circles (Plates 33, 34): A total of 161 sites contained stone circles. The Algonquian term for these is *wagaagapoak*. They were predominantly located in the Northeast (141), with far fewer in the Middle Atlantic states (eleven) and in the Southeast (nine). Stone circles are absent from Delaware, New Brunswick, North Carolina, and Nova Scotia. Of these sites, 2.3 percent (twenty) had only a single stone circle present. The largest number recorded at any one site is twelve. A total of 83.3 percent (135) were found in combination with other structure types. The most frequent two-way combinations were with rock piles (ninety-five), more than 2σ above the mean; and stone rows (fifty-six), more frequent than 1σ above the mean. The only structure types with which stone circles did not co-occur were inscriptions. Sites containing

stone circles had an average number of 24.6 structures per site (range: 1–681), and an average of 3.8 types of structures per site. The total number could not be determined at nine of these sites, 5.6 percent of the total. They were found at an average elevation of 555.2 feet above sea level (range: 2–1,820 feet), and were on average 282.1 meters from the nearest water resource (range: 0–1,110 meters). Their average stream rank is 1.5 (range: 1–7); their average slope is 12.4 percent (range: 0.5–67.5). They were on average 4.43 km from the nearest fault (range: 0.05–27.93 km); the average distance to the head-of-tide is 68.57 km (range: 0.47–361.34 km); and they were on average 2.12 km from the nearest minor watershed boundary (range: 0.00–8.91 km). Their nearest neighbor was on average 1.72 km away (range: 0.05–34.94 km). A total of 108 sites, or 67.1 percent, were in clusters. They were predominantly located near headwater streams (fifty-six) and brooks (thirty-eight), with smaller numbers at swamps (twenty-nine), ponds (twenty-four), rivers (ten), and lakes (four); none were found near the ocean. The largest number (seventy-one) were in soils with low fertility; sites in naturally infertile soils (forty-six) and agriculturally productive soils (thirty-nine) were about equal, with a smaller number in pasture lands (four). The predominant environmental settings are slopes (eighty), followed by hilltops (thirty-nine) and valleys (thirty-two). There were relatively few on shorelines (eight) and only one each on plains and islands.

14. Niches (Plates 35, 36): A total of 149 sites contained niches. The Algonquian term for these is *wallkasuu*. They were predominantly located in the Northeast (143), with far fewer in the Middle Atlantic states (six) and none in the Southeast. Niches are absent from Delaware, Georgia, Maryland, New Brunswick, North Carolina, Nova Scotia, Quebec, South Carolina, Virginia, and West Virginia. Only three (2.0 percent) were recorded as being solitary. The largest number recorded at any one site is twenty (range: 1–20). A total of 98.0 percent (146) were found in combination with other structure types—because a niche is essentially a gap in another structure. The most frequent two-way combinations were with rock piles (127, which exceeded 2σ above the mean) and stone rows (seventy, which exceeded 1σ above the mean). The only structure types with which niches did not co-occur were inscriptions. Sites containing niches had an average number of 32.2 structures per site (range: 1–681), and an average of 5.0 types of structures per site. The total number could not be determined at four of these sites, 2.7 percent of the total. They were found at an average elevation of 514.8 feet above sea level (range: 12–2,011 feet), and were on average 275.9 meters from the nearest water resource (range: 0–1,070 meters). Their average stream rank is 1.4 (range: 1–4); their average slope is 13.1 percent (range: 0.5–67.5). They were on average 3.66 km from the nearest fault (range: 0.03–43.58 km); the average distance to the head-of-tide is 39.78 km (range: 1.91–227.14 km); and they were on average 1.70 km from the nearest minor watershed boundary (range: 0.00–8.79 km). Their nearest neighbor was on average 0.68 km away (range: 0.07–13.20 km). A total of 107 sites, or 71.8 percent, were in clusters. They were predominantly located near headwater streams (fifty-four), swamps (thirty-nine), and brooks (thirty), with smaller numbers at ponds (thirteen), rivers (eight), and lakes (four); none were found near the ocean. The largest number (seventy) were

in soils with low fertility; sites in naturally infertile soils (forty) and agriculturally productive soils (thirty-two) were about equal, with a smaller number in pasture lands (six). The predominant environmental settings are slopes (eighty-nine), followed by valleys (twenty-seven) and hilltops (twenty-three). There were relatively few on shorelines (five), plains (four), and islands (one).

15. Mounds (Plates 37, 38): A total of 126 sites contained mounds. Nine of them were noted as having depressions at their summits. *Winohketash* is an Algonquian term equivalent to this type. They were predominantly located in the Northeast (101), with far fewer in the Southeast (thirteen) and the Middle Atlantic states (twelve). Mounds are absent from Delaware, Maryland, New Brunswick, North Carolina, Nova Scotia, South Carolina, Vermont, Virginia, and West Virginia. Of these sites, 12.0 percent (fifteen) had only a single mound present. The largest number recorded at any one site is fourteen. A total of 82.5 percent (104) were found in combination with other structure types. The most frequent two-way combinations were with rock piles (eighty-seven, more than 2σ above the mean) and stone rows (forty-three, more than 1σ above the mean). The only structure type with which mounds did not co-occur were inscriptions. Sites containing mounds had an average number of 12.9 structures per site (range: 1–107), and an average of 3.2 types of structures per site. The total number could not be determined at six of these sites, 4.8 percent of the total. They were found at an average elevation of 637.6 feet above sea level (range: 52–1,911 feet), and were on average 273.3 meters from the nearest water resource (range: 0–1,290 meters). Their average stream rank is 1.5 (range: 1–6); their average slope is 13.8 percent (range: 0.5–67.5). They were on average 4.29 km from the nearest fault (range: 0.00–15.58 km); the average distance to the head-of-tide is 91.60 km (range: 0.25–372.42 km); and they were on average 2.06 km from the nearest minor watershed boundary (range: 0.00–6.04 km). Their nearest neighbor was on average 1.31 km away (range: 0.05–31.32 km). A total of seventy-six sites, or 60.3 percent, were in clusters. They were predominantly located near headwater streams (forty-nine), brooks (twenty-eight), and swamps (twenty-five), with smaller numbers at rivers (nine), ponds (seven), and lakes (seven); none were found near the ocean. Sites in agriculturally productive soils (thirty-eight), naturally infertile soils (thirty-eight), and soils with low fertility (thirty-four) were about equal in frequency, with a smaller number in pasture lands (fifteen). The predominant environmental settings by far were slopes (seventy-three), followed by hilltops (twenty-five) and valleys (eighteen). There were relatively few sites on shorelines (eight), and only one each on plains and islands.

16. Unique Structures (Plates 39, 40): A total of sixty-nine sites contained unique structures. Where defined (in forty-four cases, 64.7 percent), these included five altars, four slabs, three bridges, three dams, two crescents, two pits, two aqueducts, two benches, two triangles, two lintels, two steps, and one each of embankments, sun daggers, berms, dolmens, forked walls, gateways, offering holes, pavements, pools, pyramids, shrines, spillways, depressions, tetrahedral structures, V-shaped structures, and walk-throughs. There are no known Algonquian terms equivalent to any of these. They were predominantly located in the Northeast (fifty-seven),

with far fewer in the Middle Atlantic states (seven) and in the Southeast (five). Unique structures were absent from Delaware, Maryland, New Brunswick, New Hampshire, North Carolina, Nova Scotia, Quebec, Virginia, and West Virginia. Of these sites, 17.4 percent (twelve) had only a single unique structure present. The largest number recorded at any one site is eight (range: 1–8). A total of 78.3 percent (fifty-four) were found in combination with other structure types. The most frequent two-way combinations were with rock piles (twenty-nine, which exceeded 2σ above the mean) and stone rows (seventeen, which exceeded 1σ above the mean). The only structure types with which unique structures did not co-occur were platforms and inscriptions. Sites containing unique structures had an average number of 15.2 structures per site (range: 1–305), and an average of 3.2 types of structures per site. The total number could not be determined at 4 of these sites, 4.5 percent of the total. They were found at an average elevation of 595.5 feet above sea level (range: 52–3,093 feet), and were on average 218.8 meters from the nearest water resource (range: 0–880 meters). Their average stream rank is 1.5 (range: 1–6); their average slope is 14.4 percent (range: 0.5–67.5). They were on average 3.23 km from the nearest fault (range: 0.06–20.32 km); the average distance to the head-of- tide was 86.99 km (range: 0.90–361.95 km); and they were on average 2.30 km from the nearest minor watershed boundary (range: 0.03–8.79 km). Their nearest neighbor was on average 2.40 km away (range: 0.08–16.58 km). A total of 30 sites, or 43.5 percent, were in clusters. They were predominantly located near headwater streams (thirty-one), with smaller numbers at brooks (twelve), swamps (eleven), ponds (nine), and rivers (six); none were found near lakes or the ocean. Sites in agriculturally productive soils (twenty-five), naturally infertile soils (twenty-four), and soils with low fertility (nineteen) were about equal, with only one in pasture lands. The predominant environmental settings are slopes (twenty-nine), followed by plains (twenty), valleys (twenty), and hilltops (thirteen). There were relatively few on shorelines (five), and none on islands. This is the only type where sites on plains had such a high frequency. The chi-square value for plains (107.8) was highly significant at the 0.01 confidence interval.

17. Platforms (Plates 41, 42): A total of fifty-six sites contained platforms. Five of these were recorded as "pavements," and one was recorded as having a depression at the summit. There is no known Algonquian term equivalent to this. They were predominantly located in the Northeast (fifty), with far fewer in the Southeast (five) and the Middle Atlantic states (one). Platforms were only present in Connecticut, Georgia, Massachusetts, New Hampshire, New York, Pennsylvania, and Rhode Island. Of these sites, 16.1 percent (nine) had only a single platform present. The largest number recorded at any one site is six. A total of 83.9 percent (forty-seven) were found in combination with other structure types. The most frequent two-way combination was with rock piles (thirty-nine, at more than 2σ above the mean). The only structure type with which platforms did not co-occur were unique structures. Sites containing cairns had an average number of 20.4 structures per site (range: 1–681), and an average of 3.1 types of structures per site. The total number could not

be determined at three of these sites, 5.5 percent of the total. They were found at an average elevation of 482.9 feet above sea level (range: 72–1,434 feet), and were on average 218.4 meters from the nearest water resource (range: 0–830 meters). Their average stream rank is 1.4 (range: 1–4); their average slope is 11.0 percent (range: 0.5–37.5). They were on average 2.94 km from the nearest fault (range: 0.03–18.12); the average distance to the head-of-tide is 46.85 km (range: 10.06–374.21 km); and they were on average 2.58 km from the nearest minor watershed boundary (range: 0.04–6.66). Their nearest neighbor was on average 0.87 km away (range: 0.07–9.12). A total of forty-three sites, or 76.8 percent, were in clusters. They were predominantly located near brooks (eighteen) and headwater streams (sixteen), with smaller numbers at swamps (ten), ponds (nine), rivers (two), and lakes (two); none were found near the ocean. Sites in naturally infertile soils (twenty), soils with low fertility (nineteen), and agriculturally productive soils (sixteen) were about equal, with none in pasture lands. The predominant environmental settings are slopes (thirteen), followed by valleys (eleven) and hilltops (ten). There were very few on shorelines and plains (two each) and none on islands.

18. Inscriptions (Plates 43, 44): A total of eighteen sites contained inscriptions. There is no known Algonquian term equivalent to this. They were predominantly located in the Northeast (seventeen), with only one in the Middle Atlantic states and none in the Southeast. Inscriptions were only present in Connecticut, Massachusetts, New York, Nova Scotia, Pennsylvania, Rhode Island, and Vermont. Of these sites, 55.6 percent (ten) had only a single inscription present. The largest number recorded at any one site is three. A total of 38.9 percent (seven) were found in combination with other structure types. The most frequent two-way combinations were with marked stones (three, at more than 2σ above the mean), platforms (two), chambers (two), and petroglyphs (two) (all at more than 1σ above the mean). The structure types with which inscriptions did not co-occur were cairns, U-shaped structures, standing stones, split boulders, balanced rocks, effigies, mounds, enclosures, niches, and unique structures. Sites containing inscriptions had an average number of 3.3 structures per site (range: 1–25), and an average of 1.6 types of structures per site. They were found at an average elevation of 252.4 feet above sea level (range: 0–1,530 feet), and were on average 148.3 meters from the nearest water resource (range: 0–820 meters). Their average stream rank is 3.6 (range: 1–8); their average slope is 9.0 percent (range: 0.0–47.5). They were on average 11.69 km from the nearest fault (range: 0.18–89.86 km); the average distance to the head-of-tide is 37.70 km (range: 0.00–198.93 km); and they were on average 9.70 km from the nearest minor watershed boundary (range: 0.06–7.90 km). Their nearest neighbor was on average 12.57 km away (range: 0.32–68.30 km). A total of four sites, or 22.2 percent, were in clusters—the lowest percentage of any structure type. They were predominantly located near the ocean (six), with smaller numbers near ponds (three), swamps (three), headwater streams (two), brooks (two), and rivers (two); none were found near lakes. The largest number (eleven) were in naturally infertile soils, with smaller numbers in agriculturally productive soils (four) and soils with low fertility (one), and none in pasture lands. The predominant environmental settings are shorelines

(six) and slopes (five), with few in valleys (three), plains, (two), hilltops and islands (one each). This distribution is very different from what is found for all other structure types, and the chi-square value of 22.3 for shorelines is significant at the 0.01 confidence interval.

Discussion

For the seven quantifiable environmental variables (elevation, distance to water, slope, distance to fault, distance to head-of-tide, distance to level ten watershed boundary, and distance to nearest neighbor), the averages for each of the eighteen types presented above were tabulated and the standard deviations were calculated to see whether there were any statistically significant deviations from the mean for particular structure types. The results are given in Figure 27 below. Values which deviated from the mean by >2σ are shown in grey or black.

As should be apparent, inscriptions deviate significantly from the mean for all seven parameters, being more than 2σ further from faults, watershed boundaries, and nearest neighbors; at more than 2σ lower elevations and slopes; and at more than 1σ closer to nearest water and head-of-tide. Petroglyphs, by contrast, are located at more than 2σ higher elevations, slopes, and distances from head-of-tide, and more than 1σ more distant from faults. Standing stones are more than 1σ higher elevations, distances from water, and slopes than average. Cairns are more than 1σ higher elevations and distances to head-of-tide than average. Platforms are at more than 1σ lower slopes and distances to faults. Rock piles are at more than 1σ distances to head-of-tide. Enclosures are at more than 1σ closer to faults. Niches are at more than 1σ closer to head-of-tide. Unique structures are at more than 2σ closer to water. All other frequencies are within 1σ of the average.

Type	Elevation (ft.)	Distance to Water	Slope	Distance to Fault	Distance to Head-of-Tide	Distance to 10 Watershed	Distance to Nearest Neighbor
Cairn	723.0	276.0	11.7	6.5	105.7	2.3	2.6
Rock Pile	597.7	253.0	12.1	5.2	125.1	2.2	1.5
Stone Row	579.0	261.0	13.5	5.0	78.4	2.2	1.4
Prayer Seat/U-Shaped	489.2	251.0	11.5	4.4	60.0	2.1	1.0
Subterranean/ Chamber/Cave	646.0	235.4	14.8	4.2	88.5	2.2	2.2
Standing Stone	748.8	301.4	15.6	6.1	97.3	2.2	1.7
Split Boulder	446.2	250.1	12.5	4.1	53.6	2.0	0.9
Balanced Rock	548.8	295.9	14.1	4.4	52.1	1.9	1.6
Marked Stone	530.6	231.2	13.4	4.1	68.3	2.5	2.4
Petroglyph	827.2	242.3	18.6	8.4	154.4	4.4	4.5
Inscription	252.4	148.3	9.0	11.7	37.7	9.7	12.6
Stone Circle	555.2	282.1	12.4	4.4	68.6	2.1	1.7
Effigy	621.2	256.3	14.0	3.9	62.6	2.4	1.4
Mound	637.6	273.3	13.8	4.3	91.6	2.1	1.3
Platform	482.9	218.4	11.0	2.9	46.9	2.6	0.9
Enclosure	482.9	218.4	11.6	2.9	54.9	2.6	0.9
Niche	514.8	275.9	13.1	3.7	39.8	1.7	0.7
Unique Structure	563.4	144.0	14.6	5.5	49.5	2.3	2.5
Average	569.3	245.2	13.2	5.1	74.2	2.7	2.3
Standard Deviation	124.4	41.9	2.0	2.0	30.4	1.8	2.6

Figure 27: Comparison of Average Values for Quantitative Environmental Variables (≥+2σ in grey; ≥-2σ in black).

Combinations of Structure Types

Fully 30.2 percent of sites (1,682) contained more than one type of structure. The distribution is shown in Figure 28 below. This percentage is very likely an underestimate. Many sites are reported only to have stone structures "present," as noted in Chapter 5, and these were arbitrarily attributed to the category "rock piles." When the author had the opportunity to review the digital notebooks for the Metro–West Massachusetts area provided by Peter Waksman, it was possible to add more specific quantitative information about over 100 of these, including numerous sites with more than one structure type. Unfortunately, the first fifteen of his notebooks are no longer extant. If this level of information were available for all sites, it is probable that the percentage of sites with multiple structure types would increase. While there is a general decrease in the number of sites as the number of types increases, there are ten sites that contained ten or more of the eighteen types delineated for this study. The highest number of types recorded at any one site was thirteen.

No. of types	Total	Percentage
1	3,858	69.5%
2	937	16.9%
3	390	7.0%
4	168	3.0%
5	92	1.7%
6	47	0.8%
7	19	0.3%
8	23	0.4%
9	6	0.1%
10	4	0.1%
11	3	0.1%
12	1	0.0%
13	2	0.0%
	5,550	30.3%

Figure 28: Number of Types per Site.

There is also a fairly strong correlation between the number of structures at a site and the number of types present, as Figure 29 below demonstrates. This is a log-linear plot, with the y-axis representing the number of structures expressed as the $\log_{10}$ of the actual number.

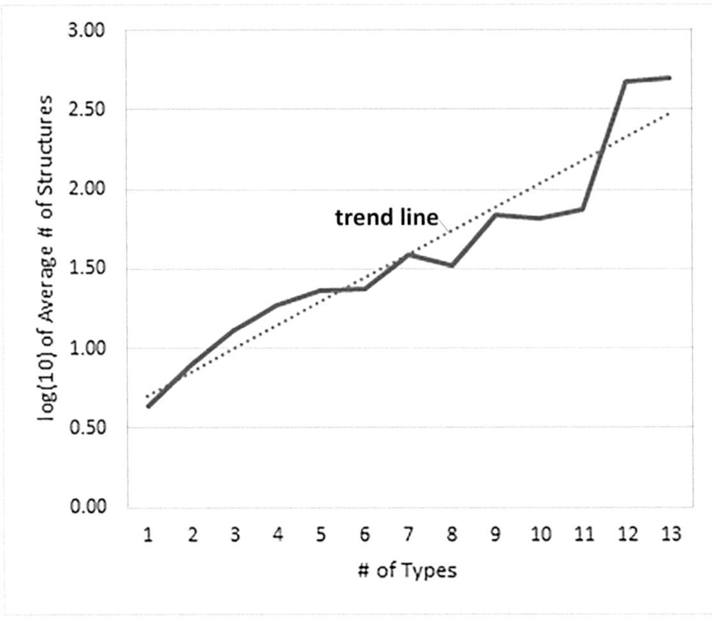

Figure 29: Log$_{10}$ of Number of Structures by Number of Types.

Structures	Total	Percentage	No. combined	Percentage	Solitary	Percentage
stone pile	3,035	54.7%	1,133	37.3%	575	18.9%
stone row	897	16.2%	748	83.4%	75	8.4%
cairn	879	15.8%	435	49.5%	146	16.6%
chamber	701	12.6%	214	30.5%	459	65.5%
balanced rock	487	8.8%	301	61.8%	170	34.9%
marked stone	415	7.5%	263	63.4%	108	26.0%
split boulder	386	7.0%	348	90.2%	26	6.7%
effigy	379	6.8%	292	77.0%	70	18.5%
standing stone	343	6.2%	254	74.1%	67	19.5%
U-shaped	305	5.5%	197	64.6%	93	30.5%
petroglyph	230	4.1%	91	39.6%	98	42.6%
enclosure	173	3.1%	152	87.9%	14	8.1%
stone circle	161	2.9%	135	83.9%	20	12.4%
niche	149	2.7%	146	98.0%	3	2.0%
mound	126	2.3%	104	82.5%	15	11.9%
unique structure	69	1.2%	54	78.3%	12	17.4%
platform	56	1.0%	47	83.9%	9	16.1%
inscription	18	0.3%	7	38.9%	10	55.6%
	8,809		4,921	55.9%	1,970	22.4%

Figure 30: Associated and Non-Associated Structure Types.

However, certain types were more likely to be combined with other types. Figure 30 above shows this, as well as showing at how many sites each type was found in isolation—

that is, only one example of that type of structure was present. It should be immediately apparent from this figure that chambers, rock piles, inscriptions, and petroglyphs were the least likely to be combined with other structure types proportional to their numbers, all with 40 percent or fewer of their occurrences combined.

Niches were by far the most likely to be combined (for the reason—as noted above—that a niche is necessarily part of another structure), followed by split boulders, enclosures, stone circles, stone rows, mounds, and platforms, all of which were combined in more than 80 percent of their occurrences. Chambers and inscriptions were most likely to be found as solitary items, with more than 50 percent of them being solitary; while niches, split boulders, enclosures, and stone rows were least likely to be solitary items, with less than 10 percent of them being solitary.

It is further possible to evaluate the frequency with which types co-occurred. This was done for two-way comparisons, by dividing the sum of all combinations of any one of the eighteen types with the other types by seventeen to find the mean, and then calculating the standard deviation (σ) from the mean by summing the squared differences between the actual count for each combination and the mean, dividing the sum by seventeen, and taking the square root of this number. Then the amount to which the count deviated from the mean could be calculated in terms of the number of standard deviations above or below the mean. The two-way combinations are shown on Plate 45. These are color-coded, as follows:

> Values $\geq 2\sigma$ above the mean are shown in red;
> Values $\geq 1\sigma$ but $<2\sigma$ above the mean are shown in orange;
> Values between 1σ above the mean and 1σ below the mean are shown in yellow;
> Values $>1\sigma$ below the mean but $<2\sigma$ below the mean are shown in green;
> Values $\geq 2\sigma$ below the mean are shown in blue.

Rock piles obviously have the highest likelihood of being combined with other types, only falling less than 1σ above the mean for inscriptions, and only falling below 2σ above the mean for petroglyphs. This is partly due to their being present at by far the largest number of sites; but it should also be kept in mind that sites with these types of structures were also among the most likely to be found without combination with other types. The next highest type in combinations are stone rows, which are found combined with rock piles and chambers at higher than 2σ above the mean σ at higher than 1σ above the mean for all other types except for platforms and inscriptions; and at more than 1σ below the mean only for inscriptions and platforms. By far the most frequent combination is between stone rows and rock piles, at 499 sites (9.0 percent of all sites). Only one other combination, between inscriptions and marked stones, occurs more than 2σ above the mean, and there are only eight other combinations which occur more than 1σ above the mean: cairns and U-shaped structures, chambers and inscriptions, standing stones and petroglyphs, split boulders and rock piles, split boulders and balanced rocks, petroglyphs and inscriptions, effigies and petroglyphs, and platforms and inscriptions. Inscriptions are most often combined at more than 2σ below the mean, rising to $<1\sigma$ below the mean only for stone rows, split boulders, mounds, and platforms. Mounds and unique structures also never rise above 1σ below the mean, but mounds are only more than 2σ below the mean in combination with petroglyphs; and unique structures are only more than 2σ below the mean in combination with U-shaped structures and stone circles.

The same procedure was followed for three-way comparisons for all pairs in Plate 45 whose value exceeded 1σ above the mean, dividing by sixteen rather than seventeen. The results are given in Plate 46. For three-way combinations of structure types, once again rock piles and stone rows are predominant, with almost all combinations with sufficient numbers to be significant at least 1σ above the mean. The only exception, for rock piles, is with chambers and inscriptions (three); for stone rows, it is with chambers and effigies (six). The highest number of combinations was between rock piles, stone rows, and split boulders (116). For rock piles, the only combinations between 1σ and 2σ above the mean are with chambers and standing stones (nine), petroglyphs and effigies (nine), and petroglyphs and stone rows (nine). For stone rows, the only combinations between 1σ and 2σ above the mean are with split boulders and balanced rocks (fifty-two), rock piles and stone circles (forty), cairns and U-shaped structures (thirty-seven), rock piles and petroglyphs (nine), inscriptions and effigies (seven), and chambers and inscriptions (five). All other combinations exceed 2σ above the mean. For cairns, combinations with rock piles and stone rows (ninety), and stone rows and chambers (twenty-five), exceed 2σ above the mean, while combinations with rock piles and effigies (fifty-nine), stone rows and effigies (forty-seven), stone rows and standing stones (forty-six), stone rows and marked stones (thirty-nine), rock piles and U-shaped structures (thirty-eight), stone rows and stone circles (twenty-three), rock piles and mounds (twenty-two), stone rows and unique structures (eight), rock piles and platforms (seven), and rock piles and petroglyphs (seven) exceed 1σ above the mean. For split boulders, combinations with rock piles and stone rows (116), and rock piles and balanced rocks (ninety-five) exceed 2σ above the mean, while combinations with rock piles and effigies (fifty-seven), rock piles and niches (fifty-three), rock piles and enclosures (fifty-three), stone rows and balanced rocks (fifty-two), rock piles and marked stones (fifty), rock piles and U-shaped structures (forty-three), rock piles and standing stones (forty-one), rock piles and stone circles (thirty-seven), and rock piles and platforms (seven) are between 1σ and 2σ above the mean. For balanced rocks, combinations with rock piles and chambers (twenty-six) exceed 2σ above the mean, while combinations with rock piles and split boulders (ninety-five), rock piles and niches (forty-six), rock piles and marked stones (forty-five), rock piles and U-shaped structures (forty-one), rock piles and standing stones (forty), rock piles and stone circles (thirty-four), stone rows and stone circles (twenty-two), rock piles and petroglyphs (seven), chambers and standing stones (seven), rock piles and unique structures (three), and stone rows and unique structures (three) exceed 1σ above the mean. The only other combinations that exceed 1σ above the mean are between stone rows, effigies, and petroglyphs (ten), standing stones, stone rows, and petroglyphs (ten), rock piles, petroglyphs, and effigies (nine), standing stones, petroglyphs, and effigies (seven), stone rows, effigies, and unique structures (seven), standing stones, rock piles, and petroglyphs (seven), rock piles, effigies, and platforms (six), rock piles, platforms, and enclosures (six), chambers, inscriptions, and effigies (five), standing stones, inscriptions, and effigies (five), chambers, inscriptions, and effigies (five), standing stones, rock piles, and unique structures (three), and rock piles, enclosures, and unique structures (three). On the lower end of the distribution, as before most combinations with inscriptions are more than 2σ below the mean, with the exception of those with chambers and effigies (five) and chambers and standing stones (four), which are above than 1σ below the mean; and stone rows and petroglyphs (one) and rock piles and platforms (one), both of which are more than 1σ below the mean. Two other structure types are combined no more often than 1σ below the mean: platforms and unique structures. Sixteen combinations with platforms are more than 2σ below the mean (cairns and rock piles, cairns and stone rows, cairns and U-shaped structures, chambers and effigies, chambers and standing stones, petroglyphs and effigies, rock piles and balanced rocks, rock piles and chambers, rock piles and niches, rock piles and standing stones, rock piles and stone circles, rock piles and stone rows, rock piles and petroglyphs, split boulders and balanced rocks, stone rows and stone circles, and stone rows and unique structures), while seven combinations with unique structures are more than 2σ below the mean (cairns and rock piles, chambers and effigies, rock piles and platforms, rock piles and split boulders, rock piles and stone circles, rock piles and stone rows, and split boulders and balanced rocks). Two additional structure types, petroglyphs and mounds, had only one combination each within 1σ of the mean: for petroglyphs, with chambers and standing stones (five); for mounds, with rock piles and platforms (five). For petroglyphs, there were eleven combinations lower than 2σ below the mean (with cairns and rock piles, cairns and stone rows, cairns and U-shaped structures, rock piles and enclosures, rock piles and niches, rock piles and platforms, rock piles and split boulders, rock piles and stone rows, rock piles and U-shaped structures, stone rows and enclosures, and stone rows and niches). For mounds, there were three combinations lower than 2σ below the mean (with chambers and effigies, petroglyphs and effigies, and split boulders and balanced rocks). No other combinations with any other structures were lower than 2σ below the mean.

For four-way combinations, as shown in Plate 47, the same procedure was followed for all groups of three whose values exceeded 2σ above the mean, dividing by fifteen rather than seventeen. There were no four-way combinations that included inscriptions, so they were eliminated from the table. The choice of 1σ was made due to the large number of groups of three which exceeded 1σ, many of which had very small numbers of examples. The highest number of occurrences was forty-seven, for the combination of rock piles, stone rows, split boulders, and balanced rocks. The totals, obviously, are far lower than for three-way combinations, with only five in excess of 2σ above the mean. For cairns, these are combinations with rock piles, stone rows, and chambers (fourteen); and rock piles, stone rows, and platforms (six). For rock piles, these are combinations with stone rows, petroglyphs, and effigies (seven). For stone rows, these are combinations with rock piles, split boulders, and balanced rocks (forty-seven); and rock piles, chambers, and effigies (ten). There are many combinations which are between 1σ and 2σ above the mean σ especially for split boulders (twelve), cairns (eight), balanced rocks (nine), and effigies (eight). Enclosures (four), marked stones (three), niches (three), and standing stones (two) all had combinations are between 1σ and 2σ above the mean. On the lower end of the distribution, all combinations with platforms are more than 2σ below the mean. All combinations with petroglyphs and unique structures are more than 1σ below the mean, with only two each between 1σ and 2σ below the mean (for petroglyphs, with rock piles, chambers, and balanced rocks; and with rock piles, chambers, and effigies; for unique structures, with cairns, stone rows, and chambers; and with stone rows, petroglyphs, and effigies). All combinations with mounds are also more than 1σ below the mean, but eleven are between 1σ and 2σ below the mean. For chambers, there is only one combination less than 1σ below the mean, with stone rows, petroglyphs, and effigies; and eight combinations more than 2σ below the mean. No other combinations with any other structures were lower than 2σ below the mean.

It would be conceivably possible to continue to chart five-way combinations and above, but this would result in diminishing returns, which might not be statistically significant. For example, the highest number of five-way combinations is of cairns, rock piles, stone rows, chambers, and marked stones, but there are only seventeen of them. It should be kept in mind that for many of the sites the number of structures is not quantitatively defined—either the number is given as a range (and is thus indefinite), or no number is specified and instead there is a qualitative entry in the inventory, such as "many," "several," "some," etc. (and is thus unspecified). This may also mean that there are actually more combinations than are documented above. Figure 31 below documents the number of sites with indefinite and unspecified numbers of structures of each type, and also the percentage of these two combined of the total number of sites containing each type of structure. The highest percentage of these was for petroglyphs, followed by cairns, rock piles, unique structures, effigies, stone rows, and marked stones, all of which had higher percentages than the average of 13.7 percent. Thus, Plates 45–47 should be considered to provide underestimates of the actual number of combinations present.

Structures	Total	Indefinite	Unspecified	Percentage
balanced rock	487	1	7	1.6%
cairn	877	49	145	22.1%
chamber	700	1	9	1.4%
effigy	378	2	61	16.7%
enclosure	173	0	7	4.0%
inscription	18	0	2	11.1%
marked stone	415	0	65	15.7%
mound	125	0	6	4.8%
niche	148	0	4	2.7%
petroglyph	230	0	54	23.5%
platform	55	0	3	5.5%
rock pile	3,060	33	543	18.8%

split boulder	387	1	23	6.2%
standing stone	342	3	18	6.1%
stone circle	162	1	8	5.6%
stone row	897	0	143	15.9%
unique structure	68	0	11	16.2%
U-shaped	305	2	6	2.6%
Total	8,827	93	1,115	13.7%

Figure 31: Indefinite and Unspecified Numbers of Structures.

Figure 32 below shows the distribution of all eighteen types across the nineteen states and provinces in the study area. These are arranged from left to right roughly from north to south and from east to west. While nearly all of the categories are obviously overrepresented in Massachusetts, the table does show strong concentrations in some other states: cairns and chambers in New York; petroglyphs and standing stones in Vermont; niches, balanced rocks, cairns, enclosures, inscriptions, and stone circles in Rhode Island; cairns, chambers, and effigies in Connecticut; marked stones in North Carolina; and rock piles in Georgia. More importantly, the absence of many structure types in both the extreme northeastern and southwestern ends of the continuum is striking. This data will be reconsidered in Chapter 10.

State	Cairn	Rock Pile	Stone Row	Seat/U-shaped
CT	141	192	124	36
DE	6	2	3	0
GA	13	602	30	5
ME	30	51	24	9
MD	6	3	1	0
MA	170	1,173	351	133
NB	4	3	1	0
NH	61	82	37	14
NJ	5	11	8	3
NY	122	254	75	23
NC	8	0	0	0
NS	8	3	2	0
PA	83	114	50	11
QU	1	1	0	0
RI	97	277	125	56
SC	48	121	9	0
VT	49	86	57	15
VA	11	47	0	0
WV	14	13	0	0
Total	877	3,035	897	305

State	Petroglyph	Inscription	Stone Circle	Effigy
CT	8	1	11	72
DE	0	0	0	0
GA	23	0	5	5
ME	13	0	8	7
MD	5	0	1	0
MA	28	8	54	144
NB	1	0	0	0
NH	11	0	1	5
NJ	6	0	2	3
NY	12	1	12	38
NC	2	0	0	0
NS	7	2	0	1
PA	5	1	5	27
QU	0	0	0	0
RI	12	6	49	52
SC	22	0	4	2
VT	65	1	7	23
VA	9	0	2	0
WV	1	0	1	0
Total	230	20	162	379

Figure 32: Distribution of Types by State/Province.

Subterranean/ Chamber/Cove	Standing Stone	Split Boulder	Balanced Rock	Marked Stone
144	42	26	48	66
0	0	1	0	0
2	2	0	0	4
22	9	5	19	5
0	0	0	0	0
113	108	178	151	138
0	0	0	0	0
44	14	10	20	8
8	4	5	21	16
204	32	14	37	16
1	1	0	0	6
1	1	0	0	0
16	14	8	15	42
0	0	0	0	0
45	38	125	153	56
0	1	0	0	37
99	77	14	23	16
3	0	1	0	5
0	0	0	0	0
702	343	387	487	415

Mound	Platform	Enclosure	Niche	Unique Structure
3	5	15	17	7
0	0	0	0	0
13	4	2	0	3
8	0	6	2	6
0	0	0	0	0
74	35	52	50	26
0	0	0	0	0
5	2	3	5	0
1	0	1	1	1
7	1	12	8	6
0	0	0	0	0
0	0	0	0	0
11	1	3	5	5
0	0	0	0	0
3	5	74	59	9
0	0	0	0	2
0	0	3	1	3
0	0	0	0	0
0	0	1	0	0
125	54	172	148	68

Site Clusters

As explained in Chapter 5, site clusters were defined as groups of ten or more sites whose locations (to be described below) were no more distant from their nearest neighbor than ~2.5 kilometers. A total of sixty-four site clusters fit this definition, comprising 59.82 percent of all sites in the inventory (3,057) and 56.37 percent of all structures (*c.* 22,387), though occupying only 0.51 percent of the total study area. So as to conform to the study's protocol of not disclosing precise site locations, clusters were plotted on Excel spreadsheets as schematic grids, using the first three digits of their eastings as columns and the first four digits of their northings as rows, as derived from the UTM coordinates. The UTM zone(s) appears in the upper left cell. This produced cells that were 1 square kilometer in area. Total cluster area was determined by adding to the number of 1-square-kilometer cells in the cluster that contained sites the number of cells containing no sites, both between the cells containing sites and in a single perimeter of 1-square-kilometer cells surrounding the cells containing sites. For example, a cluster whose sites were located in only four adjacent 1-square-kilometer cells arranged in a square (e.g. Virginia Cluster No. 1—see Figure 96) was considered to have a total area of 16 square kilometers. This means that the area calculations are slightly conservative overestimates. The clusters ranged in area from 15 to 888 square kilometers (the average being 89.89), and contained between ten and 613 sites (the average being 47.84). The locations of clusters are shown in Plate 48. Because the clusters in southeastern New England are so close together, Plate 49 shows these at a larger scale. In the schematics that follow, the UTM coordinates have been removed so as to satisfy concerns of the THPOs about revealing site locations. Cells containing no known sites are shown in grey.

While most clusters were contained within individual states, there were five clusters that overlapped state lines (between New Hampshire and Massachusetts, Rhode Island and Connecticut, Connecticut and New York, New York and Pennsylvania, and South Carolina and Georgia), twenty-two additional clusters which overlapped county lines (two in Connecticut, five in Georgia, seven in Massachusetts, three in New York, two in Pennsylvania, one in Rhode Island, and one in Vermont), and thirty additional clusters that overlapped town boundaries (four in Connecticut, eight in Georgia, ten in Massachusetts, two each in New Hampshire, Rhode Island, South Carolina, and

Vermont, and one each in New York and Rhode Island). Only seven clusters were confined within the boundaries of one town (four in Rhode Island and one each in Georgia, Massachusetts, and Virginia). Clusters were absent from North Carolina, Maryland, Delaware, New Jersey, and Maine, and were also absent from the Canadian provinces of New Brunswick, Nova Scotia, and Quebec.

Cluster Descriptions

The following are descriptions of each of the clusters (those which overlap state boundaries and some others are shown both as schematic grids and as GIS maps).

Connecticut Cluster No. 1: Hammonassett—West (Figure 33, Plate 50)

This is a cluster of fifty-seven sites containing *c.* 861 structures in south central Connecticut, within an area of 87 square kilometers (density: 0.66 sites per square kilometer). It is unlike any of the other clusters in that most of the sites in it are oriented along a single linear alignment, the "Hammonassett line," which further corresponds to winter solstice sunrise–summer solstice sunset. This line shows up very clearly on Plate 50, a GIS map of this cluster combined with Connecticut Cluster No. 7 (q.v.). Most of the sites were reported by NEARA member Tom Paul, who actually lives within the cluster. It overlaps the boundary between Middlesex and New Haven Counties. Two were identified by Tim MacSweeney and one is from the NEARA archives.[1] While the majority of sites (thirty-nine) are in the Hammonassett River drainage, the cluster extends both eastwards and westwards from this watershed into the drainages of the East and West Rivers, the Housatonic River, and the Farm and Indian Rivers. The cluster has a VMR of 3.93 and a chi-square value of 338.39, which means that there is a 0.00 chance of its sites being randomly or uniformly distributed. The average NND is 0.39 km (range: 0.07–1.62 km). The average number of structures per site is well above the average of 5.5, 14.7 (range: 1–263), with an average of 2.3 types of structures per site. Cairns (thirty-seven sites), marked stones (twenty-six), stone rows (fifteen), U-shaped structures (twelve), and standing stones (eleven) are most common, while petroglyphs, inscriptions, mounds, and enclosures are absent. The average stream rank is 1.3 (range: 1–3); the average slope is 12.4 percent (range: 0.0–30.0). The average elevation is 379.8 feet (range: 266–721 feet); the average distance to nearest water is 145.8 meters (range: 0–430 meters). The average distance to nearest fault is 2.41 km (range: 0.11–14.97 km); the average distance to the head-of-tide is 13.52 km (range: 8.43–18.16 km); the average distance to minor watershed boundary is 3.94 km (range: 0.00–6.91 km). Sites are found equally on headwater streams (thirteen sites), lakes (thirteen), swamps (thirteen), and ponds (eleven); no sites were adjacent to rivers or the ocean. Soil fertility is strongly skewed towards low fertility (twenty-three sites) and naturally infertile (twenty) soils, with smaller numbers in agriculturally productive soils (fourteen); no sites were in pasture lands. The predominant environmental settings are slopes (twenty-five) and hilltops (nineteen); there are fewer in valleys (eight) and at shores (five), and none on islands or plains.

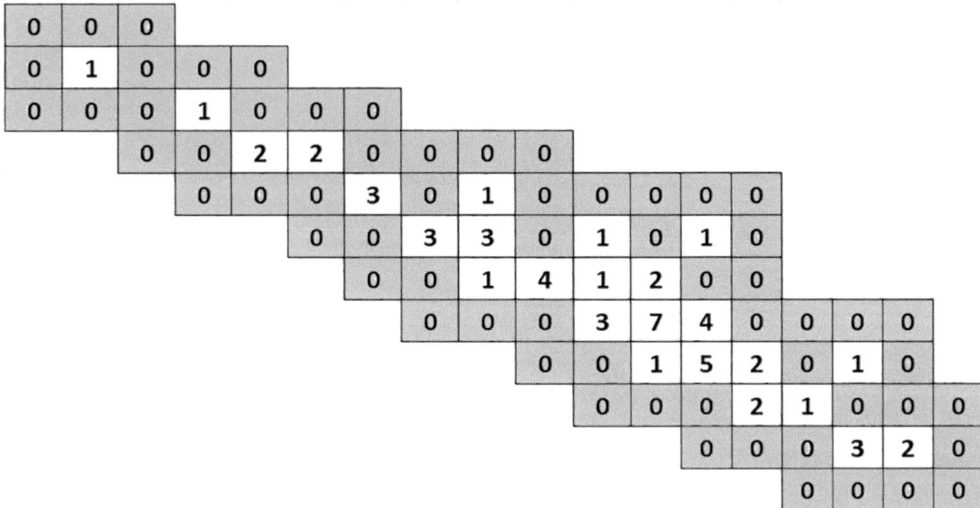

Figure 33: Schematic of Connecticut Cluster No. 1.

Connecticut Cluster No. 2: Woodbridge (Figure 34)

This is a roughly oval cluster of twelve sites containing *c.* 138 structures in west central Connecticut, within an area of 24 square kilometers (density: 0.50 per square kilometer). Its orientation is approximately southwest to northeast. Most of the sites were reported by NEARA member Tim MacSweeney, with one identified by Peter Waksman.[2] It is located in New Haven County, entirely within the town of Woodbridge. Most of the sites (twelve) are in the Housatonic drainage, with three in the adjacent West River drainage. The cluster has a VMR of 6.33 and a chi-square value of 145.67, which means that there is a 0.00 chance of its sites being randomly or uniformly distributed. The average NND is 0.39 km (range: 0.15–0.95 km). The average number of structures per site is well above the average of 5.5, 11.5 (range: 1–48), with an average of 3.1 types of structures per site. Rock piles (nine) and stone rows (six) predominate, while U-shaped structures, chambers, petroglyphs, inscriptions, stone circles, mounds, platforms, and unique structures are absent. The average stream rank is 1.4 (range: 1–3); the average slope is 17.8 percent (range: 0.0–30.0). The average elevation is 479.6 feet (range: 354–579 feet); the average distance to nearest water is 232.1 meters (range: 0–530 meters). The average distance to nearest fault is 2.24 km (range: 0.08–8.40 km); the average distance to the head-of-tide is 9.04 km (range: 7.64–10.73 km); the average distance to minor watershed boundary is 2.19 km (range: 0.00–5.09 km). Sites were preferentially located near headwater streams (five) and rivers (four); and lakes, the ocean, and ponds were not utilized. Soil fertility is strongly skewed towards agriculturally productive soils (twelve); no sites are in low fertility soils, naturally infertile soils, or pasture lands. The predominant environmental settings are hilltops (five), slopes (four), and valleys (three); no other settings occur.

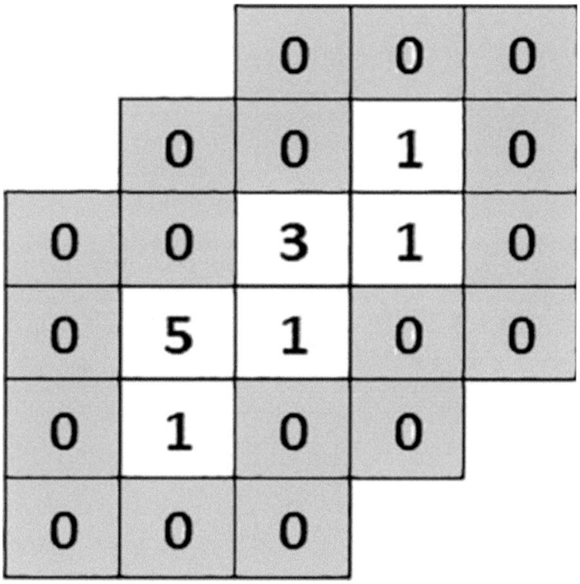

Figure 34: Schematic of Connecticut Cluster No. 2.

Connecticut Cluster No. 3: Nonewaug (Figure 35)

This is a somewhat dispersed cluster of thirty-two sites containing *c.* 119 structures in west central Connecticut, within an area of 79 square kilometers (density: 0.41 per square kilometer). All of the sites were reported by NEARA member Tim MacSweeney, who lives within the cluster.[3] It is located in Litchfield County, and all of the sites are in the Housatonic drainage. The cluster has a VMR of 6.51 and a chi-square value of 507.65, which means that there is a 0.00 chance of its sites being randomly or uniformly distributed. The average NND is 0.56 km (range: 0.06–2.01 km). The average number of structures per site is below the average of 5.5, 3.7 (range: 1–9), with an average of 1.8 types of structures per site. Stone rows (eighteen), rock piles (fourteen), and effigies (thirteen) predominate, while inscriptions, stone circles, mounds, platforms, enclosures, niches, and unique structures are absent. The average stream rank is 2.0 (range: 1–3); the average slope is 12.9 percent (range: 5.0–30.0). The average elevation is 576.1 feet (range: 333–845 feet); the average distance to nearest water is 241.4 meters (range: 25–720 meters). The average distance to nearest fault is 1.44 km (range: 0.01–3.88 km); the average distance to the head-of-tide is 31.41 km (range: 23.09–35.47 km); the average distance to minor watershed boundary is 2.51 km (range: 0.02–4.62 km). Most sites are located adjacent to headwater streams (twelve), rivers (nine), and brooks (seven); and the ocean was not utilized. Soil fertility is slightly skewed against agriculturally productive sites (seven), with relatively equal numbers in low fertility (twelve) and infertile (thirteen) soils; only one site is in pasture lands. The predominant environmental settings are slopes (thirteen) and valleys (twelve), with smaller numbers on hilltops (five) and shorelines (two); there are none on plains or islands.

0	0	0			0	0	0	
0	1	0	0	0	0	1	0	
0	0	0	0	3	1	0	0	
	0	0	2	7	1	0	0	0
0	0	1	0	0	0	0	2	0
0	3	1	0	0	0	0	0	0
0	0	2	1	0	1	0		
	0	1	0	0	0	0		
	0	1	1	0	1	0		
	0	0	0	0	0	0		
	0	1	0					
	0	0	0					

Figure 35: Schematic of Connecticut Cluster No. 3.

Connecticut Cluster No. 4: Pequot (Figure 36)

This is a rather dispersed cluster of forty-one sites containing *c.* 271 structures in southeastern Connecticut, within an area of 126 square kilometers (density: 0.33 per square kilometer). Most of the sites were reported by NEARA member Doug Schwartz, who lives within the cluster. It is located in New London County. Some were reported by Connecticut State Archaeologist Brian Jones, Peter Waksman, and Walter van Roggen, and some were in the NEARA Archive.[4] Most of the sites (thirty-six) are within the Thames drainage, with smaller numbers in the adjacent Mystic, Pawcatuck, and Poquonock drainages. The cluster has a VMR of 5.15 and a chi-square value of 644.24, which means that there is a 0.00 chance of its sites being randomly or uniformly distributed. The average NND is 0.84 km (range: 0.01–2.27 km). The average number of structures per site is well below the average of 5.5, 1.7 (range: 1–77), with an average of 1.0 types of structures per site. Chambers (twenty-six) occur well above average; the only other structure types present were rock piles (fourteen), stone rows (fourteen), cairns (two), and standing stones (one). The average stream rank is 1.2 (range: 1–3); the average slope is 11.0 percent (range: 0.0–30.0). The average elevation is 225.0 feet (range: 85–531 feet); the average distance to nearest water is 184.0 meters (range: 0–590 meters). The average distance to nearest fault is 1.42 km (range: 0.03–6.88 km); the average distance to the head-of-tide is 12.24 km (range: 0.82–13.17 km); the average distance to minor watershed boundary is 1.79 km (range: 0.05–5.49 km). There is a marked preference for sites adjacent to swamps (sixteen), headwater streams (fourteen), and brooks (ten). Lakes, the ocean, and rivers were not utilized. Soil fertility is strongly skewed against agriculturally productive sites

				0	0	0							
0	0	0	0	0	1	0							
0	1	0	1	0	0	0							
0	1	0	0	1	0	0	0	0	0				
0	0	0	0	5	1	3	0	1	0				
0	1	0	0	0	1	0	0	0	0				
0	0	0	1	2	0	0	2	0					
0	1	0	0	0	0	1	1	0					
0	1	0	0	0	0	0	0	0					
0	0	0	0	2	0	0	1	0	0	0	0	0	0
		0	0	2	0	0	1	0	0	1	0	1	0
		0	4	0	0	0	0	0	0	0	1	1	0
		0	0	0		0	0	1	0	0	0	0	0
							0	0	0				

Figure 36: Schematic of Connecticut Cluster No. 4.

(four), with high numbers in low fertility (twenty-two) and infertile (fourteen) soils; no sites are in pasture lands. The predominant environmental settings are slopes (eighteen) and valleys (twelve), with fewer on hilltops (seven), at shores (three), or on plains (one); there are none on islands.

Connecticut Cluster No. 5: Hatchet Pond (Figure 37, Plate 51)

This is a tightly packed oval cluster of forty-seven sites containing *c.* 253 structures in northeastern Connecticut, within an area of 23 square kilometers (density: 2.04 per square kilometer). Its orientation is roughly north-south. All of the sites were reported by Dennis Donais, who lives near the cluster in adjacent Worcester County, Massachusetts. All but one of the sites are located in Windham County, within the town of Woodstock (the exception is just over the county line in adjacent Tolland County), and all sites are within the Thames drainage. It is associated with the eighteenth-century Wabaquassett Native reservation, which was established at one of John Eliot's 1674 group of Praying Towns and was officially recognized shortly after the Revolutionary War, not long before the final border between Connecticut and Massachusetts was drawn in 1804.[5] The sites go up to the border but do not cross it. The cluster has a VMR of 3.74 and a rather low chi-square value of 82.28, but even so there is a 0.00 chance of its sites being randomly or uniformly distributed. The average NND is 0.15 km (range: 0.06–0.48 km). The average number of structures per site is below the average of 5.5, 3.2 (range: 1–10), with an average of 1.6 types of structures per site. Rock piles (twenty-four), cairns (twenty-two), marked stones (ten), and stone rows (nine) predominate, while chambers, inscriptions, stone circles, mounds, platforms, enclosures, and unique structures are absent. All sites are at Rank One streams; the average slope is 13.2 percent (range: 0.0–30.0). The average elevation is 856.2 feet (range: 786–1,000 feet); the average distance to nearest water is 292.2 meters (range: 0–660 meters). The average distance to nearest fault is 1.23 km (range: 0.43–1.77 km); the average distance to the head-of-tide is 57.82 km (range: 56.56–59.15 km); the average distance to minor watershed boundary is 1.70 km (range: 0.70–2.74 km). There is a marked preference for sites adjacent to headwater streams (thirty-five) and ponds (fourteen). Lakes, the ocean, swamps, and rivers were not utilized. Soil fertility is strongly skewed towards low fertility sites (twenty-two), with equal numbers in agriculturally productive (fourteen) and naturally infertile (fourteen) soils; only one site is in pasture lands. The predominant environmental settings are slopes (forty-seven), with smaller numbers in valleys (twelve), hilltops (eight), plains (two), and shorelines (one); there are none on islands.

Connecticut Cluster No. 6: Montville (Figure 38)

This is an elongated oval cluster of seventeen sites containing *c.* 217 structures in southeastern Connecticut, within an area of 60 square kilometers (density: 0.28 per square kilometer). Its orientation is roughly east-southeast to west-northwest—similar to Clusters 1 and 7, so it is possibly also along a solstice alignment. Most of the sites were reported by NEARA member Doug Schwartz, who lives near the cluster. Some were reported by Mohegan Tribal Historic Preservation Officer Elaine Thomas (2015), by James Gage, Norman Muller, and in the NEARA Archive. It is located in New London County. All but one of the sites is in the Thames drainage; the exception is in the drainage of the Connecticut River. The cluster has a VMR of 4.33 and a chi-square value of 255.29, which means that there is a 0.00 chance of its sites being randomly or uniformly distributed. The average NND is 0.94 km (range: 0.38–1.84 km). The average number of structures per site is well above the average of 5.5, 12.8 (range: 1–115), with an average of 1.5 types of structures per site. Chambers (fifteen) predominate, and the only other structures present are cairns (four), stone rows (two), U-shaped structures (two), rock piles (one), and balanced rocks (one). The average stream rank is 1.8 (range: 1–3); the average slope is 14.9 percent (range: 5.5–30.0). The average elevation is 300.9 feet (range: 141–460 feet); the average distance to nearest water is 134.4 meters (range: 0–360 meters). The average distance to nearest fault is 7.40 km (range: 3.73–10.17 km); the average distance to the head-of-tide is 13.30 km (range: 8.15–48.20 km); the average distance to minor watershed boundary is 1.10 km (range: 0.17–3.03 km). There is a marked preference for sites with regard to headwater streams (nine); and the ocean, rivers, and swamps were not utilized. Soil fertility is strongly skewed against agriculturally productive sites (one), with high numbers of sites in low fertility soils (ten) and lower numbers in naturally infertile (six) soils; no sites were in pasture lands. The environmental settings are about evenly divided among slopes (six), valleys (five), and hilltops (four), with fewer on shores (two); there are none on islands or plains.

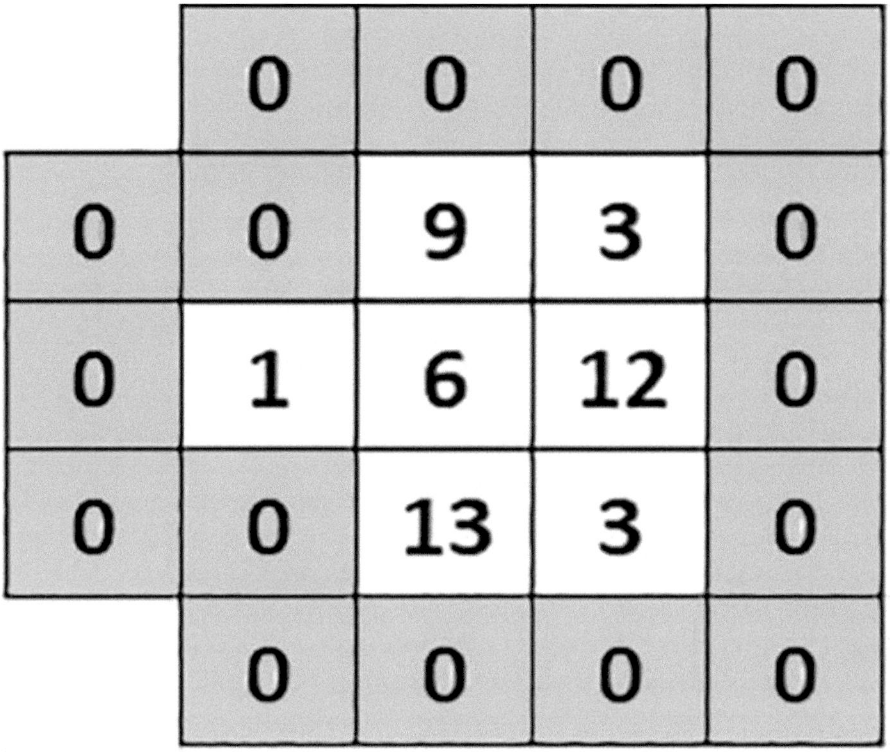

0	0	0	0

0	0	9	3	0

0	1	6	12	0

0	0	13	3	0

0	0	0	0

Above: Figure 37: Schematic of Connecticut Cluster No. 5.

Below: Figure 38: Schematic of Connecticut Cluster No. 6.

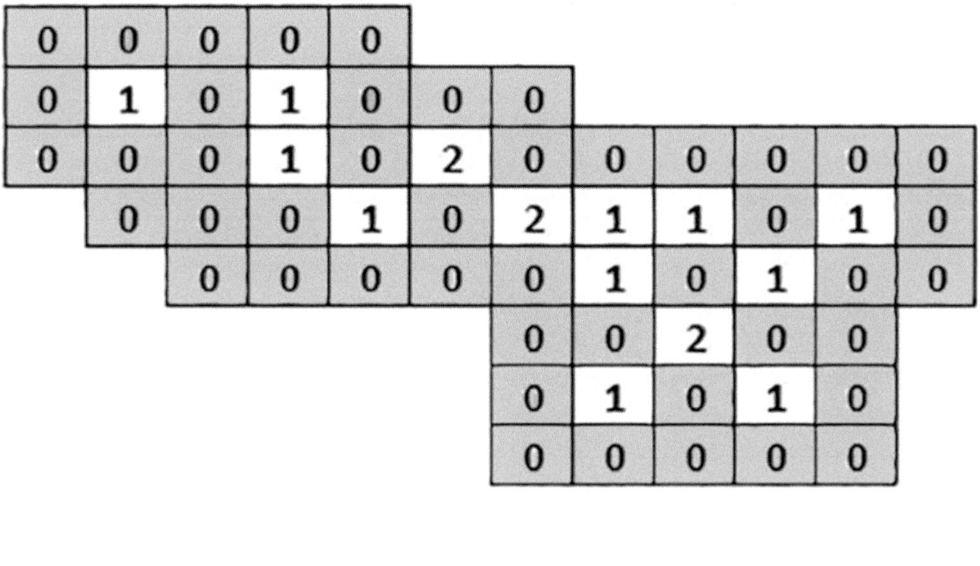

0	0	0	0	0
0	1	0	1	0	0	0
0	0	0	1	0	2	0	0	0	0	0	0
			0	0	0	1	0	2	1	1	0	1	0
				0	0	0	0	0	1	0	1	0	0
							0	0	2	0	0
							0	1	0	1	0
							0	0	0	0	0

Connecticut Cluster No. 7: Hammonassett—East (Figure 39, Plate 50)

This is a linear cluster of eleven sites containing *c.* eighty-three structures in southern Connecticut, within an area of 47 square kilometers (density: 0.23 per square kilometer). It is located in Middlesex County, in small coastal drainages including the Menunkeetesuck and the Patchogue. Most of the sites were reported by NEARA member Tom Paul, and it is a direct continuation of his Hammonassett Line (see Plate 50), but the westernmost site in the cluster is about 5 km from the easternmost site in Connecticut Cluster 1, so it was counted as a separate cluster. One site was reported by Tim MacSweeney.[6] The cluster has a VMR of 4.05 and a chi-square value of 186.28, which means that there is a 0.00 chance of its sites being randomly or uniformly distributed. The average NND is 1.00 km (range: 0.46–2.04 km). The average number of structures per site is only slightly above the average of 5.5, 7.5 (range: 2–17), with an average of 2.3 types of structures per site. Marked stones, stone circles, mounds, platforms, enclosures, niches, and unique structures are absent. The average stream rank is 2.3 (range: 1–8); the average slope is 12.1 percent (range: 5.5–30.0). The average elevation is 113.4 feet (range: 16–179 feet); the average distance to nearest water is 181.8 meters (range: 20–360 meters). The average distance to nearest fault is 10.30 km (range: 9.43–12.72 km); the average distance to the head-of-tide is 3.59 km (range: 0.00–7.09 km); the average distance to minor watershed boundary is 1.70 km (range: 0.01–2.95 km). There is a preference for sites adjacent to ponds (five). Lakes and rivers were not utilized. Soil fertility is slightly skewed towards low fertility soils (five), with equal numbers in agriculturally productive (three) and naturally infertile soils (three); no sites are in pasture lands. The predominant environmental settings are hilltops (six), with fewer on slopes (two) or on plains, shores, or in valleys (one each); there are none on islands.

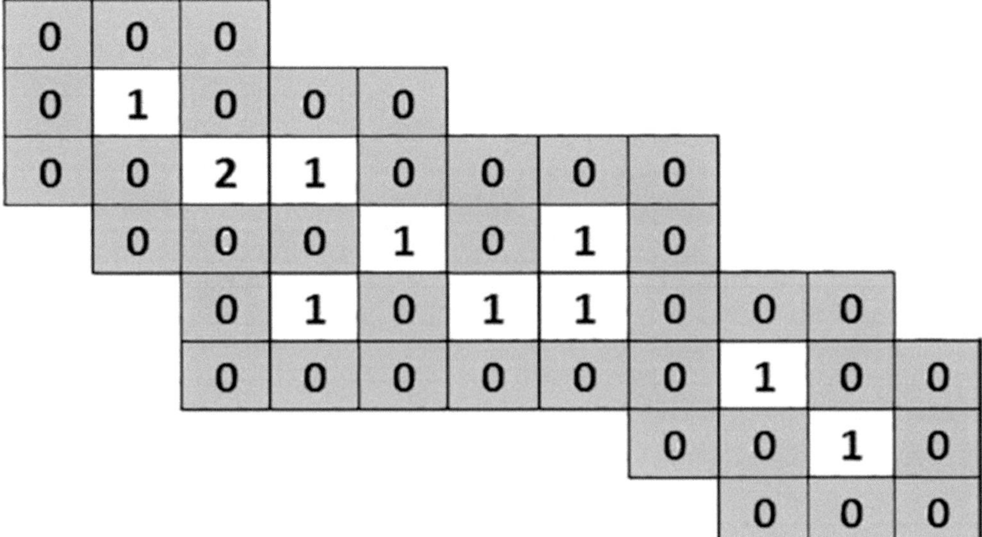

Figure 39: Schematic of Connecticut Cluster No. 7.

In Connecticut, 40.5 percent of sites are outside of clusters (223; density: 0.02 per square kilometer). Most of the sites were provided by Doug Schwartz, Tim MacSweeney, and the NEARA archive, with smaller numbers contributed by Bob de Fosses, Cathy Carlson, Charles Devine, Craig Cippoli, Connecticut Parks and Recreation, David Cuneo, Patrick Cooke and Barbara De Long, Dennis Donais, Ed Lenik, Ernie Wiegand, Fred Robinson, Gerry McLoughlin and Donna Savino, Greg Walwer, James and Mary Gage, Kathy Knowles, Lucianne Lavin, McKayla Hoffman, Nancy Hunt, Peter Waksman, Peter Anick, Polly Midgley, Steve DiMarzo, Ted Timreck, Teresa Bierce, Tim Fohl, Tom Paul, Trudy Lamb Richmond, Walter Van Roggen, Frederick Werkheiser and Donald Repsher, and the author. The writings of Ezra Stiles also contributed one site. These sites have an average number of 4.7 structures per site (range: 1–51), and an average of 1.7 types per site. All site types are found outside of clusters in Connecticut, but the predominant types are chambers (seventy-seven), rock piles (seventy-three), stone rows (fifty-nine), effigies (thirty-seven), and cairns (thirty-four). Their average elevation is 487.1 feet (range: 0–1,491 feet); their average distance to water is 210.1 meters (range: 0–1,030 meters). Their average stream rank is 2.1 (range: 1–8); their average slope is 13.9 percent (range: 0.0–52.5). Their average distance to fault was 3.56 km (range: 0.01–43.44 km); the average distance to the head-of-tide is 33.37 km (range: 0.00–478.62 km); their average distance to minor watershed is 1.73 km (range: 0.00–6.82 km). Their average NND is 2.67 km (range= 0.10–22.83 km). All water resources are utilized, but sites are most often found near headwater streams (seventy-eight), with smaller numbers at named brooks (forty-seven), rivers (twenty-nine), ponds (twenty-four), and swamps (twenty-two). Agriculturally productive soils predominate (130), with smaller numbers of sites in low fertility soils (fifty-five) and naturally infertile soils (thirty-six), and only one site in pasture lands. The predominant environmental settings are slopes (seventy-nine), hilltops (sixty), and valleys (fifty-two), with fewer on shorelines (twenty-three) and far fewer on plains (six) and islands (three).

Georgia Cluster No. 1: Greene County West (Figure 40)
This is a relatively circular cluster of thirty-seven sites containing 267 structures eastern Georgia, within an area of 51 square kilometers (density: 0.73 per square kilometer). All of the sites are in Greene County, in the Altamaha drainage. All of the sites were on file at the University of Georgia Archaeology Laboratory, and were reported by Brockington & Associates, Southeastern Archaeological Services, and the University of Georgia. The cluster has a VMR of 5.72 and a chi-square value of 285.91, which means that there is a 0.00 chance of its sites being randomly or uniformly distributed. The average NND is 0.29 km (range: 0.09–1.13 km). The average number of structures per site is slightly above the average of 5.5, 6.1 (range: 1–23), with an average of 1.0 types of structures per site. This is due to the fact that the only type of structure at all of these sites is rock piles. The average stream rank is 1.8 (range: 1–6); the average slope is 11.5 percent (range: 4.0–22.5). The average elevation is 505.7 feet (range: 436–574 feet); the average distance to nearest water is 238.2 meters (range: 0–854 meters). The average distance to nearest fault is 10.43 km (range: 7.33–12.90 km); the average distance to the head-of-tide is 277.80 km (range: 275.36–281.72 km); the average distance to minor

Stone Prayers

		0	0	0	
		0	2	0	0
	0	0	0	1	0
0	0	2	0	0	0
0	3	0	0	0	0
0	1	0	9	3	0
0	0	0	8	3	0
	0	0	1	0	0
	0	1	2	1	0
	0	0	0	0	0

Figure 40: Schematic of Georgia Cluster No. 1.

watershed boundary is 0.72 km (range: 0.04–8.11 km). There is a marked preference for sites at headwater streams (thirty-one); and brooks, lakes, the ocean, and swamps were not utilized. Soil fertility is strongly skewed in favor of sites in agriculturally productive soils (thirty-four), with only three in low fertility soils and no sites in infertile soils or in pasture lands. The predominant environmental settings are slopes (twenty-five); there are fewer in valleys (six), on hilltops (three), at shores (two), or on plains (one); there are none on islands.

Georgia Cluster No. 2: Southwestern Putnam County (Figure 41)

This is a roughly oval cluster of ninety-two sites containing 548 structures in central Georgia, within an area of 126 square kilometers (density: 0.73 per square kilometer). All of the sites were on file at the University of Georgia Archaeology Laboratory, and were reported by Brockington & Associates, Carolina Archaeological Consultants, R. S. Webb & Associates, Southeastern Archaeological Services, the U.S. Forest Service, and the University of Georgia. Most of the sites are within Putnam County, but the cluster overlaps into the northern part of Jones County. All but one of the sites is in the Altamaha drainage; the exception is in the Savannah drainage. The cluster has a VMR of 2.83 and a chi-square value of 353.76, which means that there is a 0.00 chance of its sites being randomly or uniformly distributed. The average NND is 0.42 km (range: 0.05–2.09 km). The average number of structures per site is slightly above the average of 5.5, 6.0 (range: 1–60), with an average of 1.1 types of structures per site. The overwhelming majority of structures at these sites (ninety) are rock piles, with a few stone rows (three) and mounds

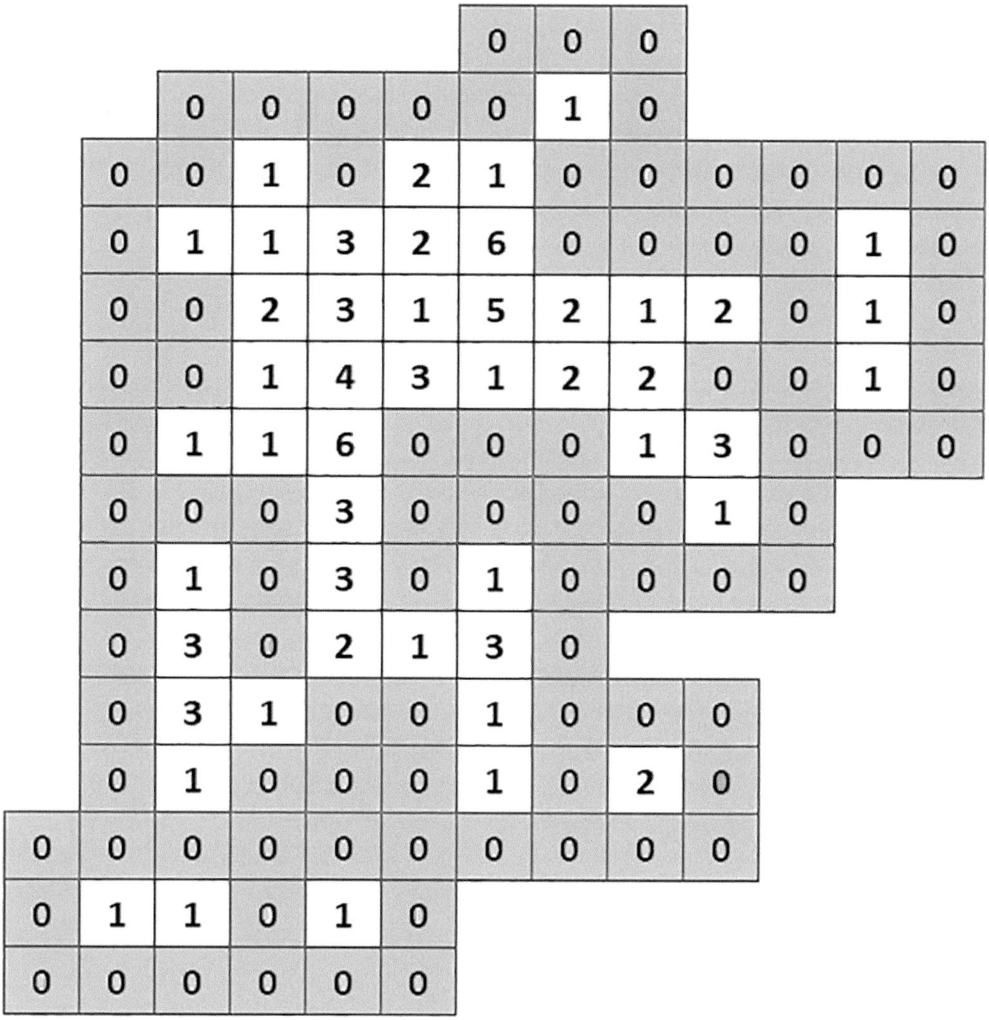

						0	0	0				
		0	0	0	0	0	1	0				
	0	0	1	0	2	1	0	0	0	0	0	0
	0	1	1	3	2	6	0	0	0	0	1	0
	0	0	2	3	1	5	2	1	2	0	1	0
	0	0	1	4	3	1	2	2	0	0	1	0
	0	1	1	6	0	0	0	1	3	0	0	0
	0	0	0	3	0	0	0	0	1	0		
	0	1	0	3	0	1	0	0	0	0		
	0	3	0	2	1	3	0					
	0	3	1	0	0	1	0	0	0			
	0	1	0	0	0	1	0	2	0			
0	0	0	0	0	0	0	0	0	0			
0	1	1	0	1	0							
0	0	0	0	0	0							

Figure 41: Schematic of Georgia Cluster No. 2.

(two), and one stone circle and one effigy are present. The average stream rank is 1.3 (range: 1–4); the average slope is 9.7 percent (range: 0.0–17.5). The average elevation is 527.2 feet (range: 400–637 feet); the average distance to nearest water is 330.8 meters (range: 0–989 meters). The average distance to nearest fault is 1.73 km (range: 0.04–5.56 km); the average distance to the head-of-tide is 278.63 km (range: 267.39–283.03 km); the average distance to minor watershed boundary is 2.10 km (range: 0.01–7.53 km). There is a marked preference for sites at headwater streams (seventy-nine); and lakes, the ocean, and swamps were not utilized. Soil fertility is strongly skewed in favor of sites in agriculturally productive soils (ninety-one), with only one site in naturally infertile soils and no sites in low fertility soils or in pasture lands. The predominant environmental settings are slopes (sixty-one), with fewer on hilltops (eighteen), in valleys (twelve), or on plains (one); there are none on islands or shores.

Georgia Cluster No. 3: Ocmulgee (Figure 42)

This is a relatively linear cluster of fourteen sites containing 196 structures in central Georgia, within an area of 39 square kilometers (density: 0.36 per square kilometer). The orientation is roughly east-southeast to west-northwest. All of the sites are in Monroe County, in the Altamaha drainage. All of the sites were on file at the University of Georgia Archaeology Laboratory, and were reported by Garrow & Associates, Southeastern Archaeological Services, and the University of Georgia. The cluster has a VMR of 3.78 and a chi-square value of 143.47, which means that there is a 0.00 chance of its sites being randomly or uniformly distributed. The average NND is 0.54 km (range: 0.23–1.25 km). The average number of structures per site is well above the average of 5.5, 14.0 (range: 1–93), with an average of 1.2 types of structures per site. The overwhelming majority of structures at these sites (fourteen) are rock piles, with only two cairns, two mounds, and one enclosure present. The average stream rank is 1.4 (range: 1–2); the average slope is 9.0 percent (range: 0.0–20.0). The average elevation is 450.9 feet (range: 331–512 feet); the average distance to nearest water is 237.5 meters (range: 106–468 meters). The average distance to nearest fault is 7.31 km (range: 4.80–10.35 km); the average distance to the head-of-tide is 289.05 km (range: 286.51–292.17 km); the average distance to minor watershed boundary is 2.48 km (range: 0.01–6.62 km). There is a preference for sites with respect to headwater streams (nine) and brooks (five); and lakes, the ocean, rivers, and swamps were not utilized. Soil fertility is skewed in favor of sites in agriculturally productive soils (ten), with only three sites in naturally infertile soils and one site in low fertility soils. No sites are located in pasture lands. The predominant environmental settings are slopes (nine) and hilltops (five); no other environmental settings were used.

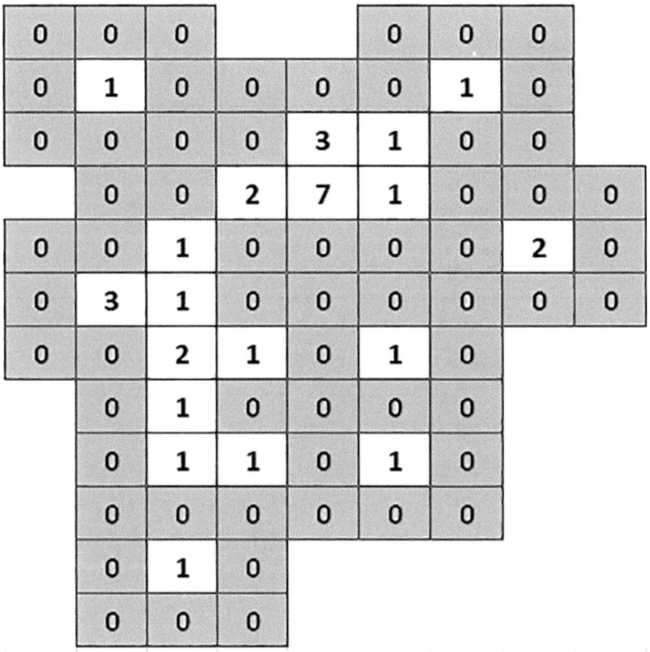

<table>
<tr><td>0</td><td>0</td><td>0</td><td></td><td></td><td>0</td><td>0</td><td>0</td><td></td></tr>
<tr><td>0</td><td>1</td><td>0</td><td>0</td><td>0</td><td>0</td><td>1</td><td>0</td><td></td></tr>
<tr><td>0</td><td>0</td><td>0</td><td>0</td><td>3</td><td>1</td><td>0</td><td>0</td><td></td></tr>
<tr><td></td><td>0</td><td>0</td><td>2</td><td>7</td><td>1</td><td>0</td><td>0</td><td>0</td></tr>
<tr><td>0</td><td>0</td><td>1</td><td>0</td><td>0</td><td>0</td><td>0</td><td>2</td><td>0</td></tr>
<tr><td>0</td><td>3</td><td>1</td><td>0</td><td>0</td><td>0</td><td>0</td><td>0</td><td>0</td></tr>
<tr><td>0</td><td>0</td><td>2</td><td>1</td><td>0</td><td>1</td><td>0</td><td></td><td></td></tr>
<tr><td></td><td>0</td><td>1</td><td>0</td><td>0</td><td>0</td><td>0</td><td></td><td></td></tr>
<tr><td></td><td>0</td><td>1</td><td>1</td><td>0</td><td>1</td><td>0</td><td></td><td></td></tr>
<tr><td></td><td>0</td><td>0</td><td>0</td><td>0</td><td>0</td><td>0</td><td></td><td></td></tr>
<tr><td></td><td>0</td><td>1</td><td>0</td><td></td><td></td><td></td><td></td><td></td></tr>
<tr><td></td><td>0</td><td>0</td><td>0</td><td></td><td></td><td></td><td></td><td></td></tr>
</table>

Figure 42: Schematic of Georgia Cluster No. 3.

Georgia Cluster No. 4: Western Putnam County (Figure 43)

This is a roughly linear cluster of nineteen sites containing 161 structures in central Georgia, within an area of 47 square kilometers (density: 0.40 per square kilometer). It is located entirely within Putnam County, within the Altamaha drainage. Its orientation is relatively east-southeast to west-northwest. All of the sites were on file at the University of Georgia Archaeology Laboratory, and were reported by New South Associates, Pan American Consultants, R. S. Webb & Associates, Southeastern Archaeological Services, the U.S. Forest Service, and the University of Georgia. The cluster has a VMR of 3.54 and a chi-square value of 162.23, and there is a 0.00 chance of its sites being randomly or uniformly distributed. The average NND is 0.72 km (range: 0.17–2.74 km). The average number of structures per site is slightly above the average of 5.5, 7.9 (range: 1–42), with an average of 1.1 types of structures per site. The overwhelming majority of structures at these sites (seventeen) are rock piles, with only one stone row and one mound present. The average stream rank is rather high, 2.8 (range: 1–5); the average slope is 11.4 percent (range: 8.0–17.5). The average elevation is 485.4 feet (range: 406–558 feet); the average distance to nearest water is 253.1 meters (range: 65–539 meters). The average distance to nearest fault is 9.56 km (range: 6.30–11.74 km); the average distance to the head-of-tide is 287.48 km (range =284.35–290.33 km); the average distance to minor watershed boundary is 1.83 km (range: 0.28–3.96 km). There is a marked preference for sites with respect to rivers (eight) and headwater streams (eight); and lakes, the ocean, and swamps were not utilized. Soil fertility is very strongly skewed in favor of sites in agriculturally productive soils (nineteen), with no sites in infertile soils, low fertility soils, or pasture lands. The predominant environmental settings are slopes (thirteen), with far fewer in valleys (four), on hilltops or plains (one each); there are none on islands or shores.

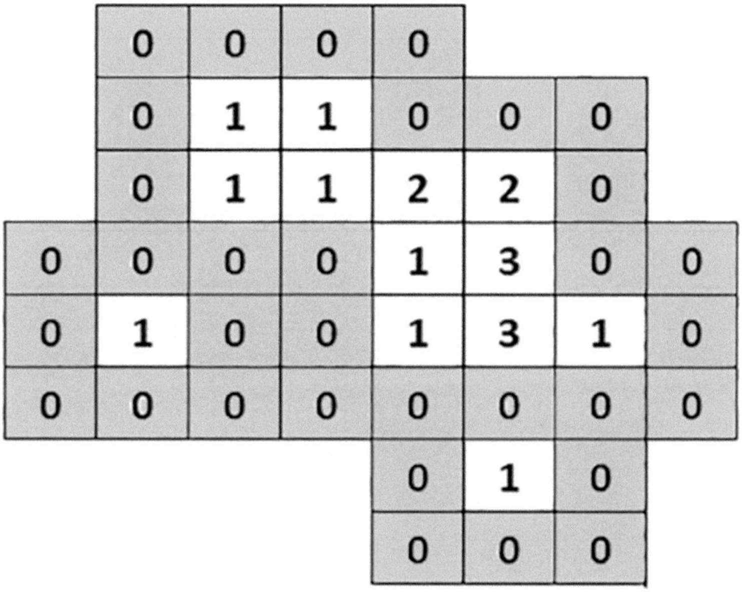

Figure 43: Schematic of Georgia Cluster No. 4.

Georgia Cluster No. 5: McDuffie County (Figure 44)

This is a roughly oval cluster of seventy-six sites containing 567 structures in eastern Georgia, within an area of 98 square kilometers (density: 0.78 per square kilometer). It is located mostly within McDuffie County, with a few sites in adjacent Lincoln and Wilkes Counties. All of the sites are within the Savannah drainage. Its orientation is relatively east-west. All of the sites were on file at the University of Georgia Archaeology Laboratory, and were reported by the Army Corps of Engineers, Carolina Archaeological Consultants, New South Associates, Pan American Consultants, and Southeastern Archaeological Services. The cluster has a VMR of 2.59 and a chi-square value of 251.59, so there is a 0.00 chance of its sites being randomly or uniformly distributed. The average NND is 0.38 km (range: 0.06–1.83 km). The average number of structures per site is slightly above the average of 5.5, 7.5 (range: 1–59), with an average of 1.0 types of structures per site. The overwhelming majority of structures at these sites (seventy-six) are rock piles, with three stone rows present; no other structure types are present. The average stream rank is rather high, 3.6 (range: 1–5); the average slope is 10.3 percent (range: 0.0–50.0). The average elevation is 371.8 feet (range: 331–462 feet); the average distance to nearest water is 180.4 meters (range: 0–665 meters). The average distance to nearest fault is 4.85 km (range: 0.67–10.33 km); the average distance to the head-of-tide is 221.88 km (range: 217.20–226.96 km); the average distance to minor watershed boundary is 1.47 km (range: 0.03–6.84 km). There is a marked preference for sites with respect to brooks (thirty) and rivers (twenty-five), with fewer at headwater streams (sixteen); and the ocean, ponds, and swamps were not utilized. Soil fertility is very strongly skewed in favor of sites in agriculturally productive soils (sixty-five), with few sites in low fertility soils (nine) or infertile soils (two) and

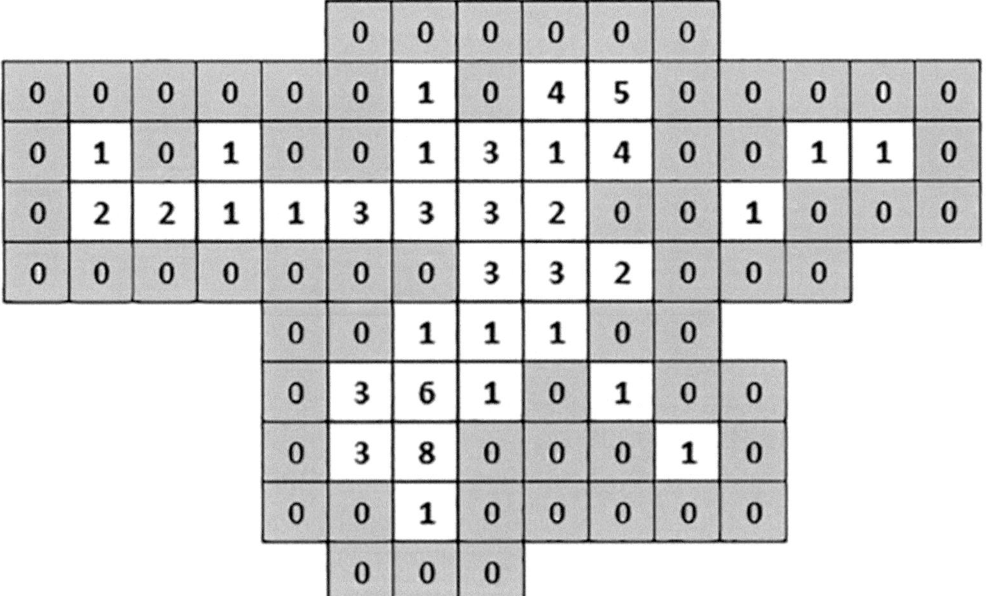

Figure 44: Schematic of Georgia Cluster No. 5.

none in pasture lands. The predominant environmental settings are slopes (fifty-eight); there were far fewer on shores (eight), hilltops (six), islands and valleys (two each); and none on plains.

Georgia Cluster No. 6: Lincoln County No. 1 (Figure 45)

This is a roughly circular cluster of thirty-four sites containing 147 structures in eastern Georgia, within an area of 42 square kilometers (density: 0.81 per square kilometer). It is located entirely within Lincoln County, within the Savannah drainage. All of the sites were on file at the University of Georgia Archaeology Laboratory, and were reported by New South Associates, Pan American Consultants, and the University of Georgia. The cluster has a VMR of 4.89 and a chi-square value of 200.32, so there is a 0.00 chance of its sites being randomly or uniformly distributed. The average NND is 0.27 km (range: 0.05–1.70 km). The average number of structures per site is somewhat above the average of 5.5, 8.4 (range: 1–28), with an average of 1.4 types of structures per site. The overwhelming majority of structures at these sites (thirty-four) are rock piles, with only one stone row and one stone circle present. The average stream rank is rather high, 3.5 (range: 1–5); the average slope is 8.1 percent (range: 0.0–17.5). The average elevation is 417.3 feet (range: 331–368 feet); the average distance to nearest water is 116.9 meters (range: 20–240 meters). The average distance to nearest fault is 3.01 km (range: 0.58–5.37 km); the average distance to the head-of-tide is 219.98 km (range: 218.15–222.40 km); the average distance to minor watershed boundary is 4.58 km (range: 0.14–8.76 km). There is a marked preference for sites with respect to lakes (thirty-seven), due to its proximity to the flooded basin of the Savannah River, with fewer at brooks (nine); and the ocean, ponds, rivers, and swamps were not utilized. Soil fertility is very strongly skewed in

0	0	0	0	0	0
0	1	5	2	1	0
0	0	2	1	0	0
0	0	0	2	3	0
0	1	3	10	0	0
0	1	1	0	0	
0	1	0	0		
0	0	0			

Figure 45: Schematic of Georgia Cluster No. 6.

favor of sites in agriculturally productive soils (forty-seven), with few sites in naturally infertile soils (two), and none in lower fertility soils or in pasture lands. The predominant environmental settings are about equally divided between slopes (fifteen) and shores (fourteen), with fewer on hilltops or islands (two each), and plains (one); there are none in valleys.

Georgia Cluster No. 7: Lincoln County No. 2 (Figure 46)

This is a roughly linear cluster of eighteen sites containing fifty-seven structures in eastern Georgia, within an area of 54 square kilometers (density: 0.33 per square kilometer). It is located entirely within Lincoln County, within the Savannah drainage. Its orientation is relatively east-northeast to west-southwest. All of the sites were on file at the University of Georgia Archaeology Laboratory, and were reported by Patricia Cridlebaugh, New South Associates, Pan American Consultants, and the University of Georgia. The cluster has a VMR of 5.43 and a chi-square value of 282.4, so there is a 0.00 chance of its sites being randomly or uniformly distributed. The average NND is 0.72 km (range: 0.09–1.38 km). The average number of structures per site is somewhat below the average of 5.5, 3.2 (range: 1–8), with an average of 1.0 types of structures per site. This is due to the fact that the only type of structure at all of these sites was rock piles (seventeen). The average stream rank is quite high, 4.5 (range: 1–6); the average slope is 13.4 percent (range: 3.0–75.0). The average elevation is 357.2 feet (range: 331–407 feet); the average distance to nearest water is 139.4 meters (range: 0–430 meters). The average distance to nearest fault is 4.15 km (range: 0.57–11.77 km); the average distance to the head-of-tide is 224.76 km (range: 213.44–348.85 km); the average distance to minor watershed boundary is 6.38 km (range: 0.42–8.76 km). There is a preference for sites with respect to lakes (nine),

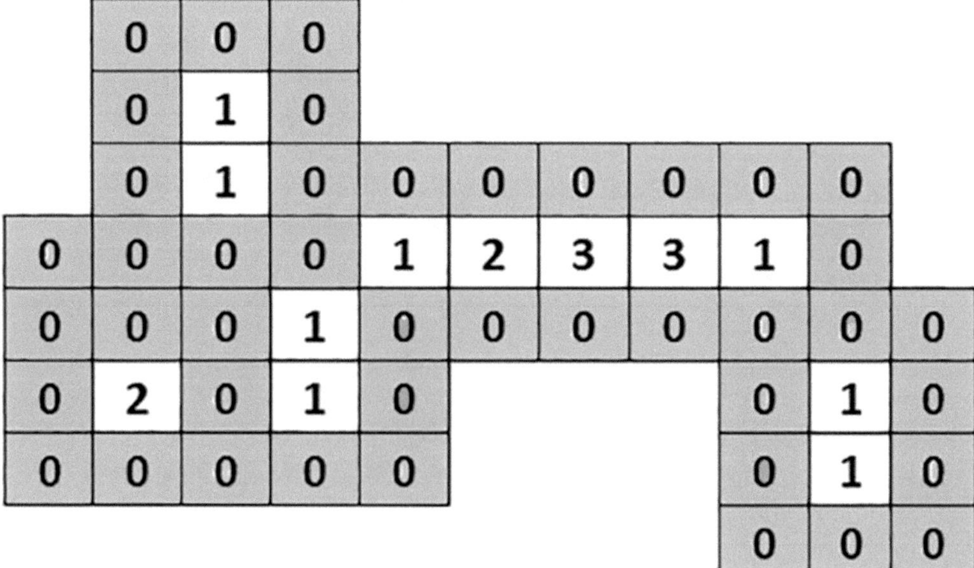

Figure 46: Schematic of Georgia Cluster No. 7.

rivers (five), and headwater streams (four); and the ocean, ponds, and swamps were not utilized. Soil fertility is skewed in favor of sites in agriculturally productive soils (seven) and low fertility soils (six), with only two sites in low fertility soils, and three in pasture lands. The predominant environmental settings are evenly divided between hilltops and slopes (five each), with fewer on shores (four), islands (two), plains and valleys (one each).

Georgia Cluster No. 8: Gladesville (Figure 47)

This is a roughly linear cluster of twelve sites containing 144 structures in central Georgia, within an area of 38 square kilometers (density: 0.32 per square kilometer). It is located entirely within the town of Gladesville in Jasper County, within the Altamaha drainage. Its orientation is relatively east-northeast to west-southwest. All of the sites were on file at the University of Georgia Archaeology Laboratory, and were reported by the Georgia Department of Transportation, R. S. Webb & Associates, Southeastern Archaeological Services, and the U.S. Forest Service. The cluster has a VMR of 4.28 and a chi-square value of 158.29, so there is a 0.00 chance of its sites being randomly or uniformly distributed. The average NND is 0.61 km (range: 0.33–2.25 km). The average number of structures per site is well above the average of 5.5, 12.0 (range: 1–36), with an average of 1.0 types of structures per site. This is due to the fact that the only type of structure at all of these sites was rock piles. The average stream rank is 1.6 (range: 1–2); the average slope is 9.0 percent (range: 3.0–17.5). The average elevation is 547.1 feet (range: 476–631 feet); the average distance to nearest water is 249.8 meters (range: 103–624 meters). The average distance to nearest fault is 8.73 km (range: 4.47–11.45 km); the average distance

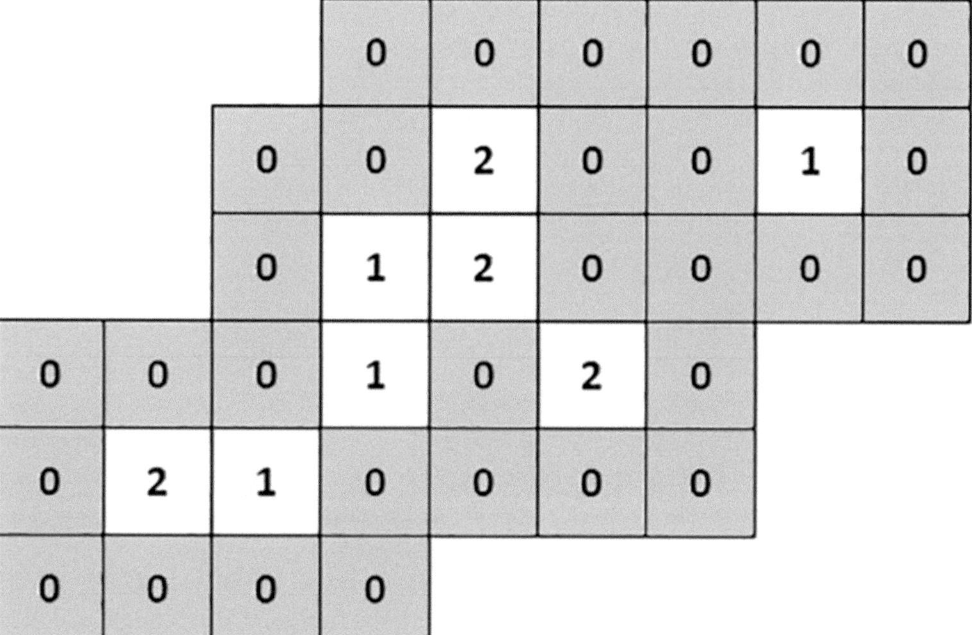

Figure 47: Schematic of Georgia Cluster No. 8.

to the head-of-tide is 294.51 km (range: 293.06–295.42 km); the average distance to minor watershed boundary is 1.81 km (range: 0.12–4.20 km). There is a slight preference for sites with respect to brooks (eight); and lakes, the ocean, ponds, rivers, and swamps were not utilized. Soil fertility is very strongly skewed in favor of sites in agriculturally productive soils (eleven), with only one site in low fertility soils, and none in naturally infertile soils or in pasture lands. The predominant environmental settings are on slopes (seven), with fewer on hilltops (three), on plains or in valleys (one each); there are none on islands or shores.

Georgia Cluster No. 9: Stephens County (Figure 48)

This is a diffuse cluster of eleven sites containing twenty-five structures in north central Georgia, within an area of 54 square kilometers (density: 0.20 per square kilometer). Most sites are located in Stephens County, with a few in adjacent Habersham County. All of the sites are within the Savannah drainage. All of the sites were on file at the University of Georgia Archaeology Laboratory, and were reported by Southeastern Archaeological Services and the U.S. Forest Service. The cluster has a VMR of 3.55 and a chi-square value of 206.01, so there is a 0.00 chance of its sites being randomly or uniformly distributed. The average NND is 1.21 km (range: 0.33–2.03 km). The average number of structures per site is well below the average of 5.5, 2.3 (range: 1–9), with an average of 1.0 types of structures per site. However, in contrast to the other Georgia clusters, there is a diversity of structure types present at these sites—rock piles (five), U-shaped structures (two), stone rows (one), standing stones (one), marked stones (one), and platforms (one)— though there is only one type per site. No other structure types are present. The average stream rank is 1.7 (range: 1–3); the average slope is 16.6 percent (range: 4.0–42.5). The average elevation is 1,041.5 feet (range: 781–1,456 feet); the average distance to nearest water is 153.1 meters (range: 20–393 meters). The average distance to nearest fault is 8.46 km (range: 1.79–12.32 km); the average distance to the head-of-tide is 350.55 km (range: 346.47–354.67 km); the average distance to minor watershed boundary is 1.97 km (range: 0.25–2.61 km). There is a strong preference for sites with respect to headwater streams (eight); and lakes, the ocean, ponds, and swamps were not utilized. Soil fertility is skewed in favor of sites in low fertility soils (five) and naturally infertile soils (four), with only two sites in agriculturally productive soils, and none in pasture lands. The predominant environmental settings are valleys (six) and slopes (five), with none on shores, hilltops, islands, or plains.

Georgia Cluster No. 10: Lawrence Shoals (Figure 49)

This is a tightly packed oval cluster of twenty-six sites containing 318 structures in central Georgia, within an area of 39 square kilometers (density: 0.67 per square kilometer). It is located entirely within the town of Rockville in Putnam County, within the Altamaha drainage. Its orientation is relatively east-southeast to west-northwest. Most of the sites were the result of a cultural resource management survey (Gresham 1990), with the remainder on file at the University of Georgia Archaeology Laboratory, and were reported by Brockington & Associates, Garrow and Associates, Inc., Southeastern Archaeological Services, and the University of Georgia. The cluster has a VMR of 5.92

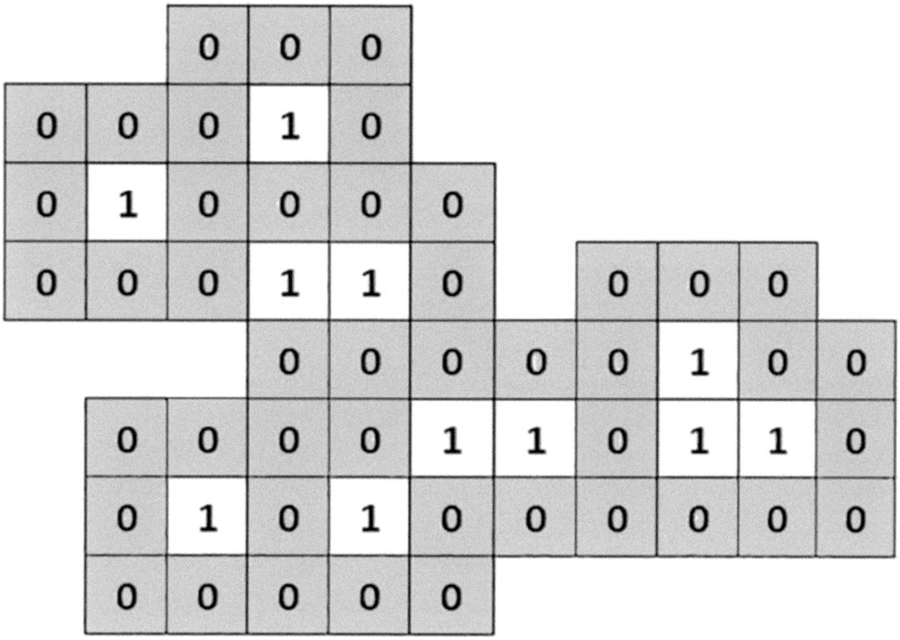

Above: Figure 48: Schematic of Georgia Cluster No. 9.

Below: Figure 49: Schematic of Georgia Cluster No. 10.

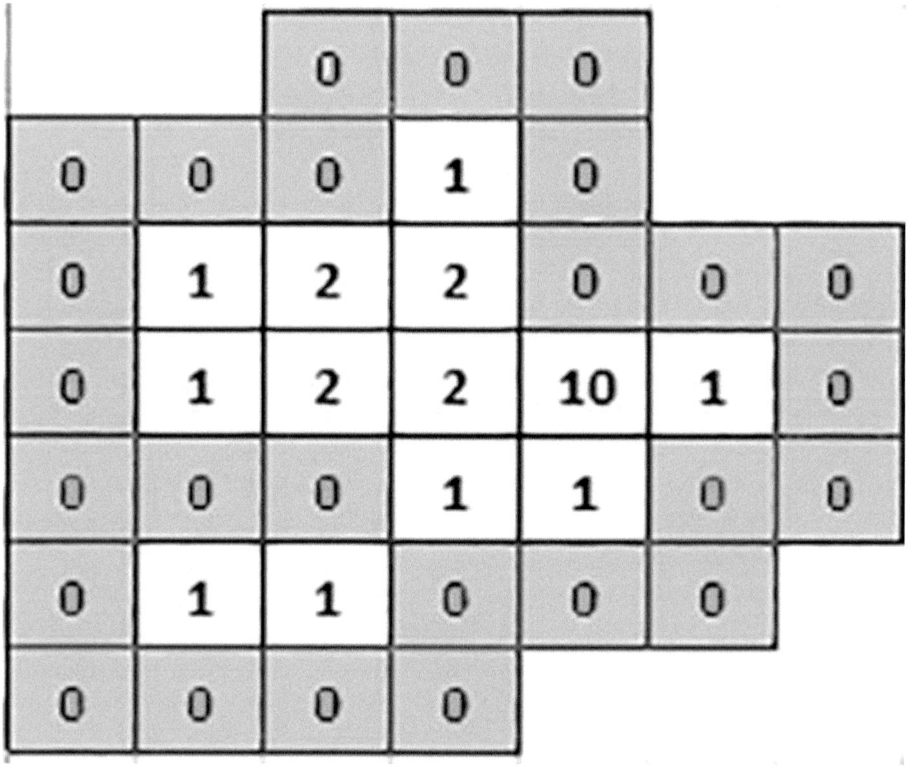

and a chi-square value of 225.08, so there is a 0.00 chance of its sites being randomly or uniformly distributed. The average NND is 0.33 km (range: 0.12–1.34 km). The average number of structures per site is well above the average of 5.5, 12.2 (range: 1–153), with an average of 1.0 types of structures per site. The overwhelming majority of structures at these sites (twenty-four) are rock piles, with one cairn and two effigies present. The average stream rank is 1.6 (range: 1–6); the average slope is 14.6 percent (range: 0.0–50.0). The average elevation is 514.8 feet (range: 415–646 feet); the average distance to nearest water is 219.2 meters (range: 40–438 meters). The average distance to nearest fault is 5.91 km (range: 4.7–6.91 km); the average distance to the head-of-tide is 269.71 km (range: 268.76–271.57 km); the average distance to minor watershed boundary is 1.59 km (range: 0.30–2.45 km). There is a strong preference for sites with respect to headwater streams (twenty-three); and lakes, the ocean, ponds, brooks, and swamps were not utilized. Soil fertility is very strongly skewed in favor of sites in agriculturally productive soils (twenty-two), with only one site in low fertility soils and two in naturally infertile soils. None were in pasture lands. The predominant environmental settings are slopes (seventeen), with fewer on hilltops (six), shores (two), and valleys (one); there are none on islands or plains.

Georgia Cluster No. 11: Richland Creek (Figure 50)

This is a roughly oval cluster of eleven sites containing eighteen structures in east central Georgia, within an area of 28 square kilometers (density: 0.39 per square kilometer). It is located entirely within Greene County, in the Altamaha drainage. Its orientation is relatively northeast to southwest. All of the sites were on file at the University of Georgia Archaeology Laboratory, and were reported by Braden & Associates, Brockington & Associates, and Southeastern Archaeological Services. The cluster has a VMR of 5.25 and a chi-square value of 141.69, so there is a 0.00 chance of its sites being randomly or uniformly distributed. The average NND is 0.44 km (range: 0.12–1.15 km). The average number of structures per site is far below the average of 5.5, 1.6 (range: 1–7), with an average of 1.0 types of structures per site. This is due to the fact that the only type of structure at all of these sites was rock piles. The average stream rank is 1.5 (range: 1–3); the average slope is 11.5 percent (range: 0.0–22.5). The average elevation is 496.3 feet (range: 457–524 feet); the average distance to nearest water is 270.5 meters (range: 65–556 meters). The average distance to nearest fault is 8.51 km (range: 7.56–10.23 km); the average distance to the head-of-tide is 285.47 km (range: 283.74–286.44 km); the average distance to minor watershed boundary is 0.98 km (range: 0.19–1.58 km). There is a strong preference for sites with respect to headwater streams (eight); and lakes, the ocean, ponds, rivers, and swamps were not utilized. Soil fertility is very strongly skewed in favor of sites in agriculturally productive soils (nine), with only one site each in low fertility soils and naturally infertile soils, and none in pasture lands. The predominant environmental settings are slopes (eight), with fewer in valleys (three); no other environmental settings are used.

Site Clusters 133

		0	0	0	
	0	0	1	0	
0	0	2	0	0	0
0	4	1	0	1	0
0	0	0	2	0	0
		0	0	0	

Figure 50: Schematic of Georgia Cluster No. 11.

Georgia Cluster No. 12: McElheny's Crossroads (Figure 51)

This is a small, concentrated oval cluster of thirteen sites containing 115 structures in central Georgia, within an area of 19 square kilometers (density: 0.68 per square kilometer). It is located entirely within Jasper County, within the Altamaha drainage. Its orientation is relatively northeast to southwest. All of the sites were on file at the University of Georgia Archaeology Laboratory, and were reported by R. S. Webb & Associates, the U.S. Forest Service, and the University of Georgia. The cluster has VMR of 6.25 and a chi-square value of 106.25, and there is a 0.00 chance of its sites being randomly or uniformly distributed. The average NND is 0.61 km (range: 0.33–2.25 km). The average number of structures per site is well above the average of 5.5, 12.0 (range: 1–36), with an average of 1.0 types of structures per site, since all of the structures at these sites are rock piles. The average stream rank is 1.6 (range: 1–2); the average slope is 9.0 percent (range: 3.0–10.5). The average elevation is 547.1 feet (range: 509–718 feet); the average distance to nearest water is 249.8 meters (range: 134–624 meters). The average distance to nearest fault is 8.73 km (range: 4.47–10.43 km); the average distance to the head-of-tide is 294.52 km (range: 293.06–295.15 km); the average distance to minor watershed boundary is 2.24 km (range: 0.48–6.09 km). There is a strong preference for sites with respect to brooks (eight) and headwater streams (five); and lakes, the ocean, ponds, and swamps were not utilized. Soil fertility is very strongly skewed in favor of sites in naturally infertile soils (six), with fewer sites in low fertility soils (three), agriculturally productive soils (three), and in pasture lands (one). The predominant environmental settings are slopes (seven), with fewer on hilltops (three), in valleys (two) and on plains (one); there are none on islands or shores.

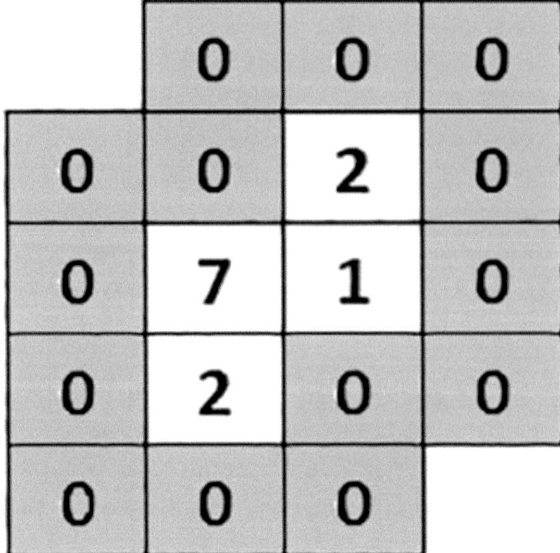

Figure 51: Schematic of Georgia Cluster No. 12.

Georgia Cluster No. 13: Elbert County (Figure 52)

This is a rather diffuse cluster of twelve sites containing thirty-four structures in the Savannah River drainage of eastern Georgia, within an area of 51 square kilometers (density: 0.24 per square kilometer). It is mostly located on the southeastern edge of Elbert County, with one site across the Little River in Lincoln County. All of the sites were on file at the University of Georgia Archaeology Laboratory, and were reported by Pan American Consultants, Southeastern Archaeological Services, and West Georgia College and State University. The cluster has VMR of 8.39 and a chi-square value of 409.33, and there is a 0.00 chance of its sites being randomly or uniformly distributed. The average NND is 0.70 km (range: 0.16–2.12 km). The average number of structures per site is below the average of 5.5, 2.0 (range: 1–11), with an average of 1.0 types of structures per site. The overwhelming majority of structures at these sites (ten) are rock piles, with one stone row and one U-shaped structure present. The average stream rank is 4.3 (range: 1–6); the average slope is 11.8 percent (range: 4.0–20.0). The average elevation is 406.5 feet (range: 335–451 feet); the average distance to nearest water is 238.1 meters (range: 0–460 meters). The average distance to nearest fault is 178.3 km (range: 0.7–328.7 km); the average distance to the head-of-tide is 258.6 km (range: 254.8–261.9 km); the average distance to minor watershed boundary is 1.46 km (range: 0.23–5.38 km). There is a strong preference for sites with respect to rivers (eight); and the ocean, ponds, and swamps were not utilized. Soil fertility is very strongly skewed in favor of sites in agriculturally productive soils (nine), with two sites in low fertility soils, one in naturally infertile soils, and none in pasture lands. The predominant environmental settings are slopes (seven), with fewer on hilltops (three) and shores (two); there are none on islands, plains, or in valleys.

In Georgia, 42.6 percent of sites are outside of clusters (286; density: 0.00 per square kilometer). Most of these sites were found on file at the University of Georgia Archaeology Laboratory, where they were reported by Apalachee Research, the Archaeological Survey

0	0	0							
0	1	0			0	0	0		
0	0	0	0	0	0	1	0	0	
0	2	0	4	0	0	0	0	0	0
0	1	0	0	1	0		0	2	0
0	0	0	0	0	0		0	1	0
							0	0	0

Figure 52: Schematic of Georgia Cluster No. 13.

Team of Atlanta, Brockington & Associates, D. Wood, Dan Elliott, David W. Chase, Don Schultz, Dyke Goodin, E. L. McCullough, Edward-Pitman Environmental, G. A. Turner, Garrow and Associates, Inc., the Georgia Department of Natural Resources, the Georgia Department of Transportation, the Georgia Historic Preservation Commission, the Georgia Power Company, the Georgia State Archaeologist, Gwinnett Archaeological Research Society, H.A. Huscher, Jerry Zerbach, Kennesaw College, M. Weinland, New South Associates, New World Research, Inc., Pan American Consultants, Vincenzo Petrullo, R. S. Webb & Associates, the Society for Georgia Archaeology, Southeastern Archaeological Services, Ted Thomas, Terracon Environmental, Inc., the U.S. Forest Service, the National Park Service, the University of Georgia, the URS Corporation, and West Georgia College and State University. Small numbers of sites were also contributed by Joseph Mahan, Tim MacSweeney, Richard Thornton, Tommy Hudson, and Tommy Charles. These sites have an average number of 4.7 structures per site (range: 1–84), and an average of 1.1 types per site. Most structure types are found outside of clusters in Georgia, with the exception of split boulders, balanced rocks, inscriptions, and niches. Rock piles overwhelmingly predominate (237), with smaller numbers of petroglyphs (twenty-three), stone rows (seventeen), and cairns (ten). Their average elevation is 707.7 feet (range: 43–2,435 feet); their average distance to water is 217.5 meters (range: 0–1,000 meters). Their average stream rank is 1.9 (range: 1–6); their average slope is 10.9 percent (range: 0.0–75.0). Their average distance to fault is 9.88 km (range: 0.05–133.63 km); the average distance to the head-of-tide is 311.61 km (range: 9.35–411.17 km); their average distance to minor watershed is 2.38 km (range: 0.00–8.03 km). Their average NND is 3.31 km (range: 0.05–63.21 km). Sites are predominantly located near headwater streams (165), followed by named streams (eighty-two). Swamps and the ocean were not utilized. Relatively equal numbers of sites are found in naturally infertile soils (105) and agriculturally productive soils (103), with fewer in low fertility soils (seventy-two) and pasture lands (fourteen). The predominant environmental settings are on slopes (123), followed by valleys (eighty-one) and hilltops (forty-nine), with far fewer on plains (sixteen), shores (thirteen), or islands (four).

Massachusetts Cluster No. 1: College Rock (Figure 53, Plate 52)

This is a large oval cluster of ninety-four sites containing *c.* 900 structures in east central Massachusetts, within an area of 90 square kilometers (density: 1.04 per square kilometer). It is located at the junction of Middlesex, Worcester, and Norfolk Counties, and is mostly in the Charles drainage and partly in the Merrimack and Blackstone drainages. Its orientation is relatively east to west. A number of researchers have reported sites in this cluster, including Matt Howes, Peter Waksman, Bruce McAleer, Walter van Roggen, Joanne Hulburt, Peter Anick, Norman Muller, and the author.[7] The cluster has a VMR of 6.48 and a chi-square value of 576.38, and there is a 0.00 chance of its sites being randomly or uniformly distributed. The average NND is 0.34 km (range: 0.13–2.36 km). The average number of structures per site is somewhat above the average of 5.5, 9.6 (range: 1–110), with an average of 2.8 types of structures per site. There is a high diversity of structure types present, with rock piles (seventy-one), stone rows (thirty-two), split boulders (twenty-five), balanced rocks (twenty-four), marked stones (fourteen), effigies (eleven), stone circles (nine), enclosures (eight), mounds (six), and unique structures (five) occurring well above average. The only structure types which are absent are petroglyphs, inscriptions, and platforms. The average stream rank is 1.4 (range: 1–3); the average slope is 12.2 percent (range: 0.5–50.0). The average elevation is 338.6 feet (range: 247–563 feet); the average distance to nearest water is 195.1 meters (range: 0–700 meters). The average distance to nearest fault is 1.35 km (range: 0.00–4.00 km); the average distance to the head-of-tide is 41.99 km (range: 36.57–86.83 km); the average distance to minor watershed boundary is 2.31 km (range: 0.01–6.40 km). There is a strong preference for sites with respect to headwater streams (thirty-nine), swamps (twenty-three), and brooks (fifteen); and the ocean was not utilized. Soil fertility is very strongly skewed in favor of sites in naturally infertile soils (forty) and low fertility soils (twenty-five), with smaller numbers in agriculturally productive soils (fifteen) and in pasture lands (fourteen). The predominant environmental settings are slopes (forty-one), hilltops (twenty-eight), and valleys (sixteen), with fewer on shores (six) or plains (three); and none on islands.

Massachusetts Cluster No. 2: Hopkinton State Park (Figure 54)

This is a roughly circular cluster of thirty sites containing *c.* 188 structures in east central Massachusetts, just to the north of Cluster No. 1, within an area of 63 square kilometers (density: 0.48 per square kilometer). It is entirely located within Middlesex County, and all but one site is in the Merrimack drainage; the exception is within the Charles drainage. A number of researchers reported sites in this cluster, including Matt Howes, Peter Waksman, Walter van Roggen, Nick Holland, David Cuneo, and the

					0	0	0		0	0	0	
			0	0	0	1	0	0	0	1	0	
0	0	0	0	1	0	3	2	2	1	1	0	0
0	4	0	0	0	3	10	3	7	1	0	1	0
0	2	0	1	0	3	2	6	1	0	0	1	0
0	0	0	1	2	10	3	1	1	1	0	0	0
	0	0	0	1	6	1	3	5	0	1	0	
		0	0	0	1	0	0	0	0	0		
				0	0	0						

Figure 53: Schematic of Massachusetts Cluster No. 1.

0	0	0							
0	1	0	0	0	0	0			
0	0	0	1	1	2	0	0		
	0	3	0	3	0	3	0		
	0	2	0	0	0	0	0	0	0	0
	0	0	1	5	1	0	0	0	1	0
		0	0	0	0	2	0	0	0	0
				0	0	0	4	0	0
					0	0	0		

Figure 54: Schematic of Massachusetts Cluster No. 2.

author.[8] The cluster has a VMR of 6.04 and a chi-square value of 374.73, and there is a 0.00 chance of its sites being randomly or uniformly distributed. The average NND is 0.35 km (range: 0.11–1.69 km). The average number of structures per site is slightly above the average of 5.5, 6.1 (range: 1–29), with an average of 1.8 types of structures per site. There is a high diversity of structure types present, with rock piles (twenty-five), stone rows (nine), split boulders (four), and balanced rocks (three) occurring well above average. The only structure types which are absent are U-shaped structures, petroglyphs, inscriptions, mounds, and platforms. The average stream rank is 1.7 (range: 1–4); the average slope is 12.0 percent (range: 1.5–42.5). The average elevation is 338.7 feet (range: 95–518 feet); the average distance to nearest water is 255.3 meters (range: 0–630 meters). The average distance to nearest fault is 2.32 km (range: 0.01–1.62 km); the average distance to the head-of-tide is 80.67 km (range: 37.33–83.66 km); the average distance to minor watershed boundary is 1.93 km (range: 0.11–5.04 km). There is a strong preference for sites with respect to headwater streams (fourteen); and brooks and the ocean were not utilized. Soil fertility is somewhat skewed in favor of sites in agriculturally productive soils (twelve), with smaller numbers in naturally infertile soils (eight) and low fertility soils (seven) and fewer in pasture lands (three). The predominant environmental settings are slopes (twelve) and hilltops (eleven), with fewer on plains or in valleys (three each) and shores (one); there are none on islands.

Massachusetts Cluster No. 3: Ashland Town Forest (Figure 55)

This is a large oval cluster of forty-five sites containing *c.* 437 structures in east central Massachusetts, to the east-northeast of Cluster No. 2, within an area of 42 square kilometers (density: 1.10 per square kilometer). It is almost entirely located in Middlesex County, with one site in Worcester County; and it is entirely within the Merrimack drainage. Its orientation is relatively east to west. Most sites were located by Harvey Lipman and by the author, both of whom are local residents, with number of other researchers reporting sites in this cluster, including Matt Howes, Peter Anick, Robert Austin, Peter Waksman, Walter van Roggen, Alan Smith, and David Cuneo.[9] The cluster has a VMR of 5.63 and a chi-square value of 197.09, and there is a 0.00 chance of its sites being randomly or uniformly distributed. The average NND is 0.22 km (range: 0.05–0.64 km). The average number of structures per site is somewhat above the average of 5.5, 8.6 (range: 1–75), with an average of 2.6 types of structures per site. There is a high diversity of structure types present, with rock piles (thirty-one), split boulders (sixteen), stone rows (thirteen), effigies (eleven), marked stones (nine), balanced rocks (six), niches (six), stone circles (five), and mounds (five) occurring well above average. The only structure types that are absent are chambers, petroglyphs, inscriptions, and platforms. The average stream rank is 1.1 (range: 1–4); the average slope is 9.4 percent (range: 0.5–20.0). The average elevation is 325.9 feet (range: 202–420 feet); the average distance to nearest water is 195.8 meters (range: 0–440 meters). The average distance to nearest fault is 0.97 km (range: 0.02–1.51 km); the average distance to the head-of-tide is 77.31 km (range: 75.90–78.23 km); the average distance to minor watershed boundary is 3.60 km (range: 0.03–5.76 km). There is a strong preference for sites with respect to headwater

0	0	0	0	0	0	0
0	1	2	0	1	1	0
0	0	4	17	7	0	0
	0	1	5	3	3	0
	0	0	0	1	0	
			0	0	0	

Figure 55: Schematic of Massachusetts Cluster No. 3.

streams (twenty-seven); and lakes and the ocean were not utilized. Soil fertility is equally skewed in favor of sites in in low fertility soils (twenty-one) and naturally infertile soils (seventeen) and with smaller numbers in agriculturally productive soils (five) and two in pasture lands. The predominant environmental settings are slopes (twenty-six), with fewer on hilltops (ten) and in valleys (nine); there are none on islands, plains, or shores.

Massachusetts Cluster No. 4: Fall River (Figure 56)

This is a somewhat linear cluster of fifteen sites containing forty-eight structures in southeastern Massachusetts, within an area of 42 square kilometers (density: 0.36 per square kilometer). It is located in Bristol County, and is mostly in the Taunton drainage, with two sites in the adjacent Westport drainage. Its orientation is relatively north-northwest to south-southeast. A number of researchers reported sites in this cluster, including Ted Ballard, Steve DiMarzo, Walter van Roggen, Carole Johnson, Edward Rose, and Alex Houtzager.[10] The cluster has a VMR of 3.30 and a chi-square value of 54.75. This is the only cluster in the study in which the chance of its sites being randomly distributed is greater than zero, at 0.074. The average NND is 0.61 km (range: 0.13–2.30 km). The average number of structures per site is well below the average of 5.5, 2.9 (range: 1–9), with an average of 1.4 types of structures per site. While more than half of the sites contain rock piles (nine), this is not significantly above the average for this structure type. Sites with marked stones (three) are well above the average. Cairns, standing stones, inscriptions, effigies, platforms, niches, and unique structures do not occur in this cluster. The average stream rank is 1.7 (range: 1–5); the average slope is 10.7 percent (range: 0.5–25.0). The average elevation is 126.7 feet (range: 3–236 feet); the average distance to nearest water is 308.5 meters (range: 0–690 meters). The average distance to nearest fault is 2.62 km (range: 0.67–4.52 km); the average distance to the head-of-tide is 8.04 km (range: 0.52–23.94 km); the average distance to minor watershed boundary is 2.14 km (range: 0.94–6.19 km). There was a relatively equal preference for sites with respect to brooks (four), rivers (four), and headwater streams (four); lakes and the ocean were not utilized. Soil fertility skewed in favor of sites in agriculturally productive soils (eight), with lower numbers in low fertility soils (five), in naturally infertile soils (two), and in pasture lands (one). The predominant environmental settings are slopes (eight), with fewer on shores (three), and hilltops and valleys (two each); there are none on islands or plains.

Massachusetts Cluster No. 5: Lakeville Ponds (Figure 57)

This is a small, somewhat diffuse cluster of ten sites containing *c.* sixty-seven structures in southeastern Massachusetts, within an area of 39 square kilometers (density: 0.26 per square kilometer). It is located on the border of Plymouth and Bristol Counties, and is mostly in the Taunton drainage, with a few sites in the adjacent Acushnet and Slocums River drainages. Most of the sites in this cluster were reported by Ken Leonard (2010), who resides there, and by James Mavor and Byron Dix.[11] Other sites were reported by Sue Reilly and Walter van Roggen. The cluster has a VMR of 6.02 and a chi-square value of 228.76, and there is a 0.00 chance of its sites being randomly or uniformly distributed. The average NND is 0.68 km (range: 0.12–2.46 km). The average number of structures per site is slightly above the average of 5.5, 6.7 (range: 1–35), with an average of 1.8 types of structures per site. The distribution of types strongly favors stone rows (four), marked stones (four), and rock piles (three). Split boulders, petroglyphs, inscriptions, stone circles, effigies, mounds, platforms, enclosures, niches, and unique structures do not occur in the cluster. All sites are at Rank One streams; the average slope is 7.1 percent (range: 5.5–11.5). The average elevation is 120.2 feet (range: 77–165 feet); the average distance to nearest water is 215.0 meters (range: 90–370 meters). The average distance to nearest fault is 1.14 km (range: 0.62–1.68 km); the average distance to the head-of-tide is 11.27 km (range: 8.36–13.42 km); the average distance to minor watershed boundary is 0.70 km (range: 0.30–1.57 km). There was a light preference for sites with respect to swamps (four); and brooks, lakes, and the ocean were not utilized. Soil fertility is somewhat skewed in favor of sites in naturally infertile soils (five), with smaller numbers in agriculturally productive soils (three), in low fertility soils (two), and in pasture lands (one). The predominant environmental settings are hilltops (seven), with fewer on slopes (three); no other environmental settings are used.

Massachusetts Cluster No. 6: Nobscot Hill (Figure 58)

This is a small, roughly oval cluster of twenty-one sites containing *c.* ninety structures in east central Massachusetts, within an area of 43 square kilometers (density: 0.49 per square kilometer). It is entirely located in Middlesex County, entirely within the Merrimack drainage. Its orientation is roughly east-northeast to west-southwest. Some of the sites in this cluster were reported by Lee Swanson, who resides there, and others by Peter Waksman and Peter Anick, who live in adjacent towns.[12] The cluster has a VMR of 3.98 and a chi-square value of 166.95, and there is a 0.00 chance of its sites being

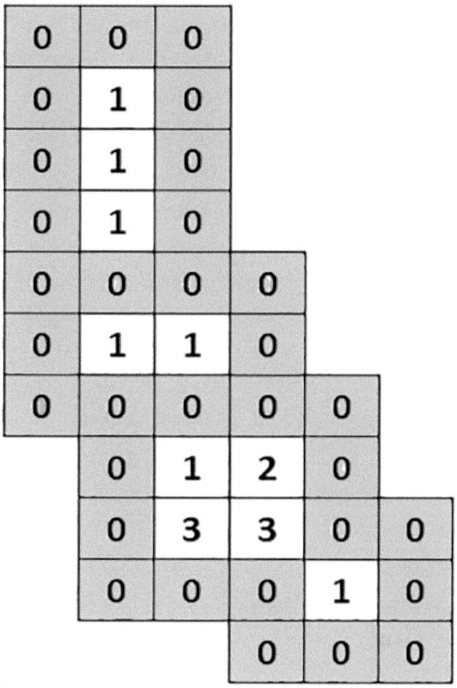

Right: Figure 56: Schematic of Massachusetts Cluster No. 4.

Below: Figure 57: Schematic of Massachusetts Cluster No. 5.

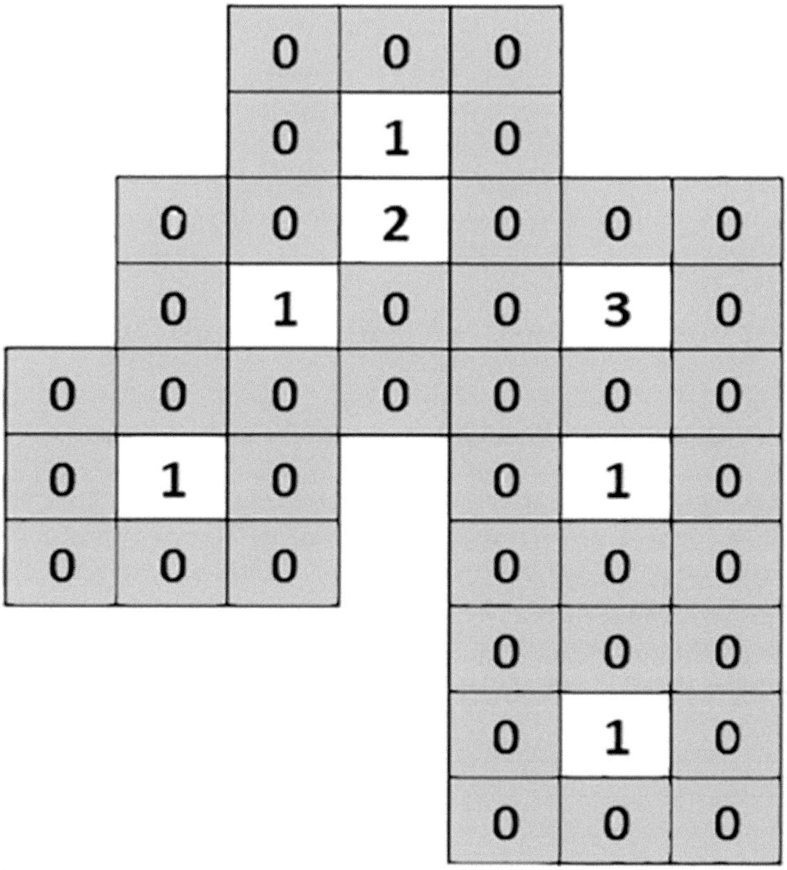

randomly or uniformly distributed. The average NND is 0.49 km (range: 0.13–1.36 km). The average number of structures per site is slightly below the average of 5.5, 4.3 (range: 1–13), with an average of 1.4 types of structures per site. The distribution of types strongly favors cairns (twenty-three), rock piles (fifteen), stone rows (six), and marked stones (three). Chambers, standing stones, petroglyphs, inscriptions, stone circles, effigies, mounds, platforms, enclosures, niches, and unique structures do not occur in the cluster. The average stream rank is 1.0 (range: 1–2); the average slope is 13.0 percent (range: 1.5–25.0). The average elevation is 333.1 feet (range: 194–501 feet); the average distance to nearest water is 250.7 meters (range: 25–630 meters). The average distance to nearest fault is 0.60 km (range: 0.12–1.44 km); the average distance to the head-of-tide is 71.42 km (range: 68.48–73.46 km); the average distance to minor watershed boundary is 3.89 km (range: 0.44–5.54 km). There was a very strong preference for sites with respect to headwater streams (fifteen); and brooks, lakes, rivers, and the ocean were not utilized. Soil fertility is skewed in favor of sites in naturally infertile soils (ten) and agriculturally productive soils (eight), with smaller numbers in low fertility soils (three), and none in pasture lands. The predominant environmental settings are slopes (eleven), with smaller numbers in valleys (five), on hilltops (four), or on shores (one); there are none on islands or plains.

Massachusetts Cluster No. 7 Cape Ann (Figure 59)

This is a rather diffuse cluster of thirteen sites containing *c*. thirty-six structures in northeastern Massachusetts, within an area of 56 square kilometers (density: 0.23 per square kilometer). It is located within Essex County, and is mostly in the Annisquam drainage, a tidal drainage which separates Gloucester and Rockport from the mainland, with some sites along the coast. Some of the sites in this cluster were reported by Mary Ellen Lepionka, who resides there, and by Mary and James Gage, Walter van Roggen, and the author.[13] The cluster has a VMR of 5.98 and a chi-square value of 328.70, and there is a 0.00 chance of its sites being randomly or uniformly distributed. The average NND is 0.37 km (range: 0.14–0.88 km). The average number of structures per site is well below the average of 5.5, 2.8 (range: 1–8), with an average of 1.6 types of structures per site. Rock piles (seven), split boulders (four), and balanced rocks (three) predominate. Chambers, standing stones, petroglyphs, inscriptions, stone circles, mounds, platforms, enclosures, niches, and unique structures do not occur in the cluster. The average stream rank is 3.2 (range: 1–8); the average slope is 10.3 percent (range: 0.5–30.0). The average elevation is 79.5 feet (range: 0–173 feet); the average distance to nearest water is 187.3 meters (range: 0–500 meters). The average distance to nearest fault is 0.70 km (range: 0.13–1.43 km); the average distance to the head-of-tide is 2.75 km (range: 0.00–5.95 km); the average distance to minor watershed boundary is 0.80 km (range: 0.00–2.79 km). There is an equal preference for sites with respect to the ocean (three), rivers (three), and brooks (three); and ponds were not utilized. Soil fertility is skewed in favor of sites in low fertility soils (seven) and agriculturally productive soils (four), with smaller numbers in naturally infertile soils (two) and none in pasture lands. The predominant environmental settings are hilltops (six), slopes (four), and shores (three); no other environmental settings are used.

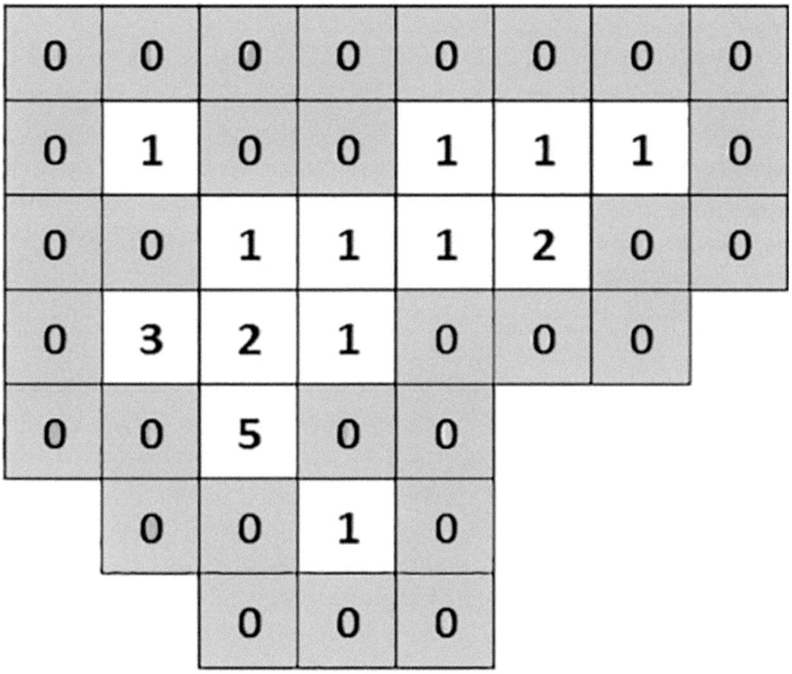

Above: Figure 58: Schematic of Massachusetts Cluster No. 6.

Below: Figure 59: Schematic of Massachusetts Cluster No. 7.

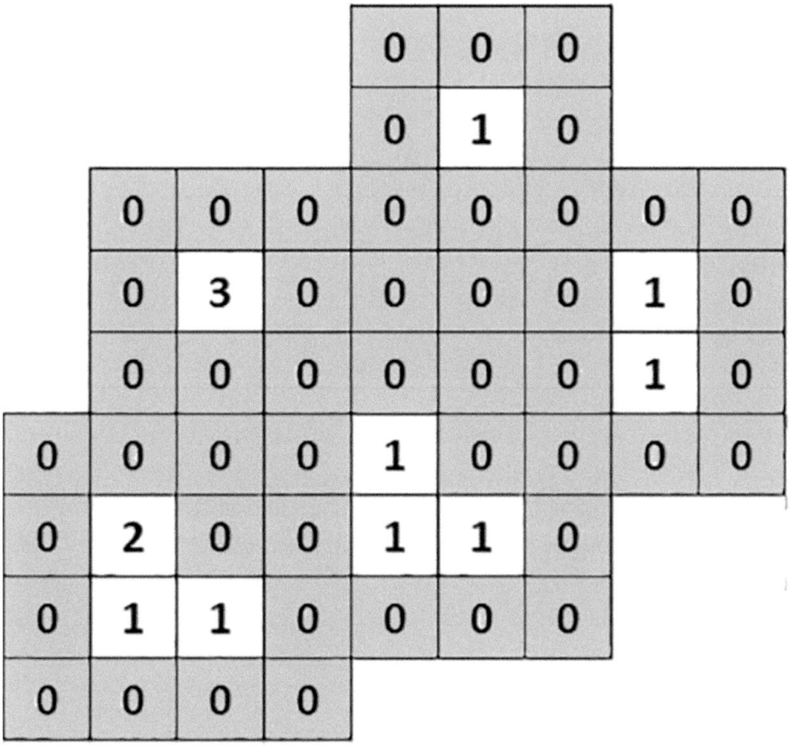

Massachusetts Cluster No. 8 Falmouth (Figure 60)

This is a small, somewhat diffuse, L-shaped cluster of thirteen sites containing *c.* 122 structures in western Cape Cod, Massachusetts, within an area of 24 square kilometers (density: 0.54 per square kilometer). It is located entirely within the town of Falmouth in Barnstable County, and the majority of the sites relate to Buzzards Bay, an arm of the Atlantic Ocean. The remainder are in the small coastal Wild Harbor drainage. All of the sites in this cluster were reported by James Mavor, whose records are housed at the Woods Hole Historical Museum.[14] The cluster has a VMR of 7.10 and a chi-square value of 163.36, and there is a 0.00 chance of its sites being randomly or uniformly distributed. The average NND is 0.47 km (range: 0.19–1.78 km). The average number of structures per site is well above the average of 5.5, 9.4 (range: 1–27), with an average of 1.2 types of structures per site. The distribution of types strongly favors rock piles (thirteen); other than this only chambers (two) occur. All sites are at Rank One streams; the average slope is 12.4 percent (range: 0.5–25.0). The average elevation is 93.2 feet (range: 49–146 feet); the average distance to nearest water is 759.2 meters (range: 350–1,320 meters). The average distance to nearest fault is 17.22 km (range: 16.51–19.00 km); the average distance to the head-of-tide is 2.77 km (range: 1.19–9.06 km); the average distance to minor watershed boundary is 2.35 km (range: 0.84–5.53 km). There is a strong preference for sites with respect to ponds (nine); and brooks, lakes, rivers, and the ocean were not utilized. Soil fertility is skewed in favor of sites in naturally infertile soils (seven) and agriculturally productive soils (four), with smaller numbers in low fertility soils (two); none were in pasture lands. The predominant environmental settings are hilltops (thirteen); no other environmental settings are used.

Massachusetts Cluster No. 9 Dighton-Rehoboth (Figure 61)

This is a somewhat diffuse oval cluster of twenty-nine sites containing *c.* fifty structures in southeastern Massachusetts, within an area of 81 square kilometers (density: 0.36 per square kilometer). It is located entirely within Bristol County, and is mostly in the Taunton drainage (sixteen), with nine sites in the adjacent Warren River drainage. The orientation is roughly east-northeast to west-southwest. Most of the sites in this cluster were reported by Ted Ballard, who resides there, with a few deriving from the NEARA archives and one from Edward Lenik.[15] The cluster has a VMR of 5.98 and a chi-square value of 478.62, and there is a 0.00 chance of its sites being randomly or uniformly distributed. The average NND is 0.50 km (range: 0.07–1.74 km). The average number of structures per site is well below the average of 5.5, 1.7 (range: 1–8), with an average of 1.2 types of structures per site. The distribution of types strongly favors U-shaped structures (fifteen); with fewer balanced rocks (five), marked stones (four), and chambers (three); split boulders, petroglyphs, inscriptions, stone circles, effigies, mounds, enclosures, niches, and unique structures were not present. Average stream rank is 1.41 (range: 1–3); the average slope is 9.4 percent (range: 0.5–35.0). The average elevation is 131.7 feet (range: 56–213 feet); the average distance to nearest water is 162.4 meters (range: 0–390 meters). The average distance to nearest fault is 10.81 km (range: 8.67–13.83 km); the average distance to the head-of-tide is 9.80 km (range: 4.75–13.84 km); the average distance to minor watershed boundary is 1.81 km (range: 0.13–5.99 km). There is a strong

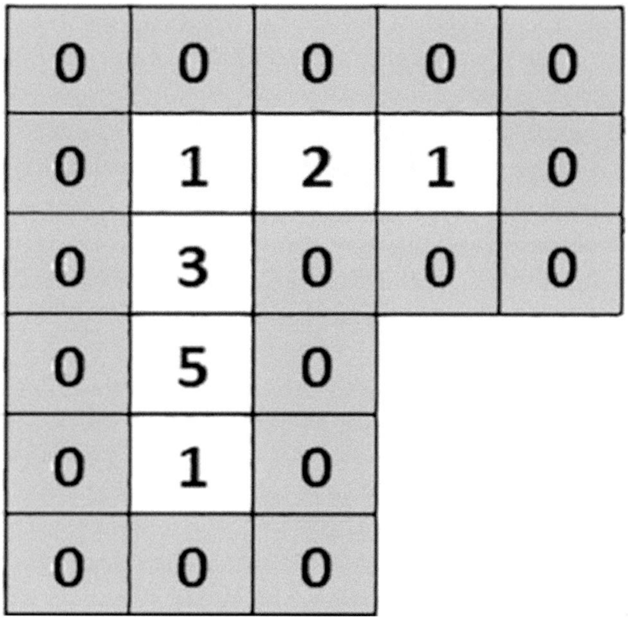

Figure 60: Schematic of Massachusetts Cluster No. 8.

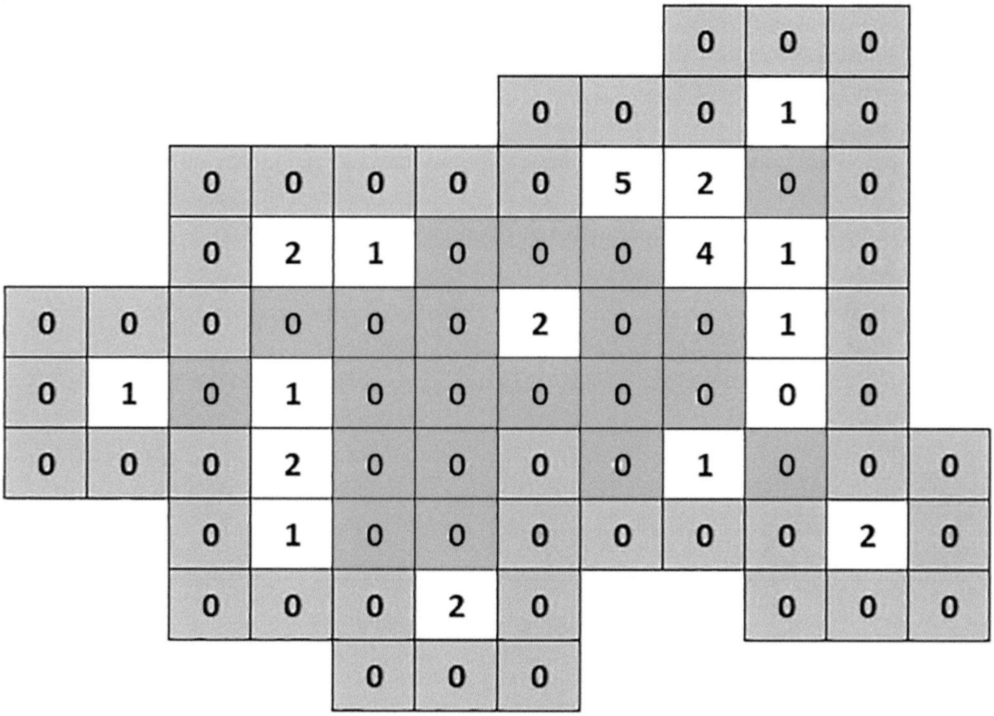

Figure 61: Schematic of Massachusetts Cluster No. 9.

preference for sites with respect to headwater streams (seventeen); and lakes, ponds, and the ocean were not utilized. Soil fertility is skewed in favor of sites in naturally infertile soils (fourteen) and agriculturally productive soils (twelve), with smaller numbers in low fertility soils (two); and one was in pasture lands. The predominant environmental settings are slopes (twelve); islands were not used.

Massachusetts Cluster No. 10 Noon Hill (Figure 62)

This is a small, oval cluster of twelve sites containing fifty-seven structures in eastern Massachusetts, within an area of 26 square kilometers (density: 0.46 per square kilometer). It is located entirely within Norfolk County, within the Charles drainage. Most of the sites in this cluster were reported by Peter Waksman.[16] Other sites were reported by John Thompson and by Tim MacSweeney.[17] The cluster has a VMR of 5.75 and a chi-square value of 143.64, and there is a 0.00 chance of its sites being randomly or uniformly distributed. The average NND is 0.53 km (range: 0.19–1.72 km). The average number of structures per site is slightly below the average of 5.5, 4.8 (range: 1–12), with an average of 1.6 types of structures per site. The distribution of types strongly favors rock piles (eleven) and stone rows (three). The only other types which occur in the cluster are mounds (two), and balanced rocks, marked stones, and enclosures, with one example of each. The average stream rank is 1.4 (range: 1–3); the average slope is 12.8 percent (range: 1.0–32.5). The average elevation is 199.3 feet (range: 133–285 feet); the average distance to nearest water is 138.8 meters (range: 20–280 meters). The average distance to nearest fault is 0.45 km (range: 0.01–1.04 km); the average distance to the head-of-tide is 30.58 km (range: 28.70–31.11 km); the average distance to minor watershed boundary is 2.27 km (range: 0.99–6.04 km). There is a preference for sites with respect to headwater streams (five); and lakes and the ocean were not utilized. Soil fertility is skewed in favor of sites in low fertility soils (five), with smaller numbers in agriculturally productive soils (three),

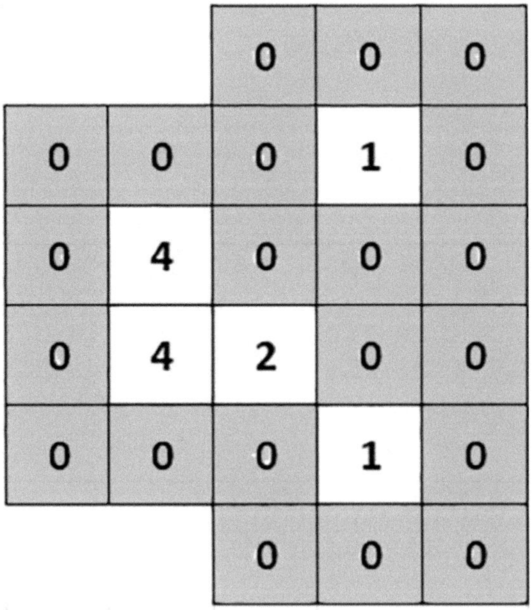

Figure 62: Schematic of Massachusetts Cluster No. 10.

naturally infertile soils (two), and pasture lands (two). The predominant environmental settings are slopes (six), with fewer in valleys (three), on shores (two), or on hilltops (one); there are none on islands or plains.

Massachusetts Cluster No. 11 King Philip's Rock (Figure 63)

This is a roughly linear cluster of twenty sites containing *c.* 113 structures in eastern Massachusetts, within an area of 35 square kilometers (density: 0.57 per square kilometer). It is located on the border of Norfolk and Bristol Counties, with all but one of the sites in Norfolk County, and is entirely in the Taunton drainage. The orientation is approximately east-southeast to west-northwest. Most of the sites in this cluster were reported by Richard Kramer, who resides there, and by Ted Ballard.[18] One site was reported by Bill McEntee. The cluster has a VMR of 5.83 and a chi-square value of 198.15, and there is a 0.00 chance of its sites being randomly or uniformly distributed. The average NND is 0.40 km (range: 0.09–2.18 km). The average number of structures per site is well below the average of 5.5, 2.8 (range: 1–12), with an average of 1.6 types of structures per site. The distribution of types strongly favors U-shaped structures (thirteen), stone rows (five) rock piles (four), standing stones (two), and marked stones (two). Cairns, split boulders, petroglyphs, inscriptions, effigies, mounds, platforms, enclosures, and unique structures do not occur in the cluster, and rock piles are well below average (four). The average stream rank is 1.6 (range: 1–3); the average slope is 9.9 percent (range: 0.0–30.0). The average elevation is 267.2 feet (range: 194–331 feet); the average distance to nearest water is 113.5 meters (range: 0–240 meters). The average distance to nearest fault is 0.65 km (range: 0.32–1.35 km); the average distance to the head-of-tide is 28.29 km (range: 23.30–29.45 km); the average distance to minor watershed boundary is 1.01 (range: 0.05–4.58 km). There is a strong preference for sites with respect to swamps (eight), ponds (six), and headwater streams (five); and brooks,

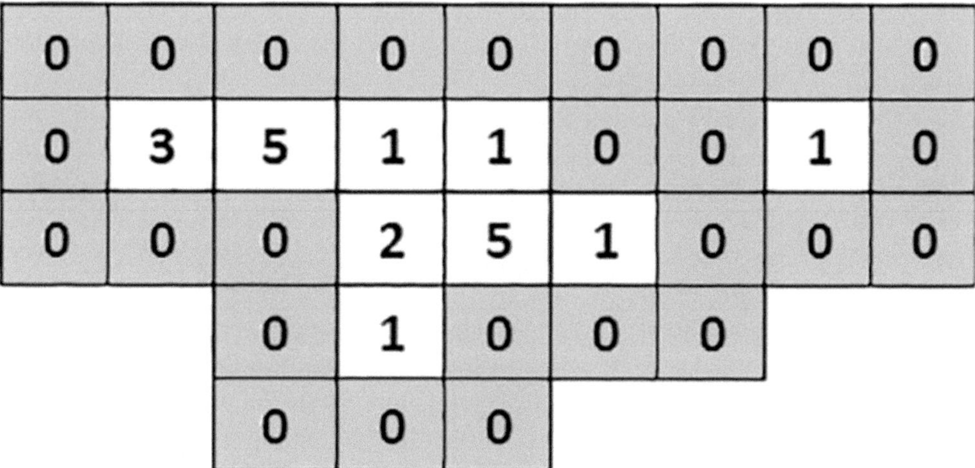

Figure 63: Schematic of Massachusetts Cluster No. 11.

lakes, and the ocean were not utilized. Soil fertility is skewed in favor of sites in naturally infertile soils (nine) and agriculturally productive soils (seven), with smaller numbers in low fertility soils (three) and in pasture lands (one). The predominant environmental settings are slopes (nine) and hilltops (seven), with fewer in valleys (three) or on shores (one); there are none on islands or plains.

Massachusetts Cluster No. 12 Leverett-New Salem (Figure 64)

This is a large, oval cluster of 129 sites containing *c.* 1,546 structures in central western Massachusetts, within an area of 234 square kilometers (density: 0.55 per square kilometer). It is located entirely within Franklin County and within the Connecticut drainage. Its orientation is roughly northeast to southwest. Most of the sites in this cluster were reported by Sarah Kohler and Rolf Cachat-Schilling, who reside there, and by Ted Timreck in his film *The Great Falls*.[19] Other sites were reported by Patrick Cooke and Barbara De Long on their website, and by Peter Waksman, Ken Leonard, Matt Howes, and in the NEARA archive.[20] The cluster has a VMR of 7.20 and a very high chi-square value of 1,679.10, and there is a 0.00 chance of its sites being randomly or uniformly distributed. The average NND is 0.49 km (range: 0.01–2.19 km). The average number of structures per site is well above the average of 5.5, 10.6 (range: 1–92), with an average of 2.1 types of structures per site. The distribution of types strongly favors rock piles (sixty-eight), cairns (thirty-three), standing stones (twenty), stone rows (nineteen), effigies (nineteen), mounds (nineteen), chambers (eighteen), marked stones (fourteen), stone circles (thirteen), U-shaped structures (eleven), and petroglyphs (eleven). The only types which do not occur in the cluster are inscriptions. The average stream rank is 1.3 (range: 1–3); the average slope is 12.1 percent (range: 0.0–42.5). The average elevation is 962.0 feet (range: 427–1,296 feet); the average distance to nearest water is 322.2 meters (range: 20–1,030 meters). The average distance to nearest fault is 2.06 km (range: 0.04–5.59 km); the average distance to the head-of-tide is 84.60 km (range: 75.84–93.01 km); the average distance to minor watershed boundary is 1.79 km (range: 0.02–6.08 km). There is a strong preference for sites with respect to headwater streams (sixty-six), brooks (twenty-two), and swamps (twenty); the ocean was not utilized. Soil fertility is about equally distributed among sites in low fertility soils (sixty-four) and naturally infertile soils (fifty-two), with smaller numbers in agriculturally productive soils (eight) and pasture lands (five). The predominant environmental settings are slopes (sixty-two), followed by valleys (thirty-two), hilltops (twenty-one), and shores (ten); there are only four on plains and none on islands.

Massachusetts Cluster No. 13 Wrentham (Figure 65)

This is a relatively oval cluster of forty-two sites containing 157 structures with a small westward extension in eastern Massachusetts, within an area of 53 square kilometers (density: 0.79 per square kilometer). It is located entirely within Norfolk County, and is mostly in the Taunton drainage, but it overlaps into the adjacent Charles, Neponset, and Seekonk drainages. Several of the sites in this cluster were reported by Ted Ballard and by the author.[21] Other sites were reported by Norman Muller, Peter Waksman, Ted

Above: Figure 64: Schematic of Massachusetts Cluster No. 12.[22]

Below: Figure 65: Schematic of Massachusetts Cluster No. 13.

Timreck, and Walter van Roggen.[23] The cluster has a VMR of 6.83 and a chi-square value of 389.05, and there is a 0.00 chance of its sites being randomly or uniformly distributed. The average NND is 0.31 km (range: 0.07–2.40 km). The average number of structures per site is somewhat below the average of 5.5, 3.7 (range: 1–42), with an average of 1.8 types of structures per site. The distribution of types strongly favors rock piles (twenty-one), balanced rocks (seventeen), stone rows (twelve), and U-shaped structures (nine). Petroglyphs, inscriptions, effigies, mounds, platforms, and unique structures do not occur in the cluster. The average stream rank is 1.3 (range: 1–2); the average slope is 10.8 perfect (range: 0.0–25.0). The average elevation is 336.9 feet (range: 207–424 feet); the average distance to nearest water is 351.0 meters (range: 40–760 meters). The average distance to nearest fault is 1.34 km (range: 0.05–2.91 km); the average distance to the head-of-tide is 31.13 km (range: 27.07–42.24 km); the average distance to minor watershed boundary is 1.07 km (range: 0.01–3.24 km). There is a strong preference for sites with respect to headwater streams (sixteen), brooks (fourteen), and swamps (eight); rivers and the ocean were not utilized. Soil fertility is strongly skewed in favor of sites in naturally infertile soils (thirty-one), with smaller numbers in agriculturally productive soils (five) and low fertility soils (four), and no sites in pasture lands. The predominant environmental settings are hilltops (twenty-one) and slopes (seventeen), with far fewer in valleys (three) or on plains (one); there are none on islands or on shores.

Massachusetts Cluster No. 14 Metro-West (Figure 66, Plate 53)

This is the largest cluster in the study, both in numbers of sites and of area, with a total of 613 sites containing *c.* 3,680 structures in eastern and central Massachusetts, within an area of 868 square kilometers (density: 0.71 per square kilometer). It is roughly triangular in shape, with its southern edge being roughly west-southwest to east-northeast, and its northern edge being southwest to northeast. The vertex of the triangle is south of the Wachusett Reservoir in Boylston, and its eastern edge corresponds roughly to Route 3, from Bedford to Tyngsborough. It is located within Middlesex and Worcester Counties, and is entirely within the Merrimack drainage. Most of the sites in this cluster were reported by Peter Waksman, who resides there, and by Tim Fohl, Walter van Roggen, Peter Anick, Lee Swanson, and Robert MacDonald, all of whom also live within the cluster.[24] Other sites were reported by Ted Ballard, Robert Conrad, Sidney Blackwell, Frank Karkota, Colin Kennedy, Alan Smith, the Massachusetts Division of Conservation and Recreation, Fredrick Huntington, Eugene Winter, James Mavor and Byron Dix, and in the NEARA archive.[25] The cluster has a VMR of 3.80 and a very high chi-square value of 3,296.82, and there is a 0.00 chance of its sites being randomly or uniformly distributed. The average NND is 0.45 km (range: 0.07–2.34 km). The average number of structures site is close to the average of 5.5, 6.0 (range: 1–101), with an average of 1.5 types of structures per site. The distribution of types strongly favors rock piles (390), stone rows (ninety-five), split boulders (sixty-four), effigies (fifty-seven), cairns (fifty-five), platforms (twenty-two), and standing stones (nineteen). All eighteen structure types occur in the cluster. The average stream rank is 1.4 (range: 1–6); the average slope is 10.3 percent (range: 0.0–30.0). The average elevation is 293.6 feet (range: 109–669 feet); the average distance to nearest water is 222.6 meters (range: 0–1,040 meters). The

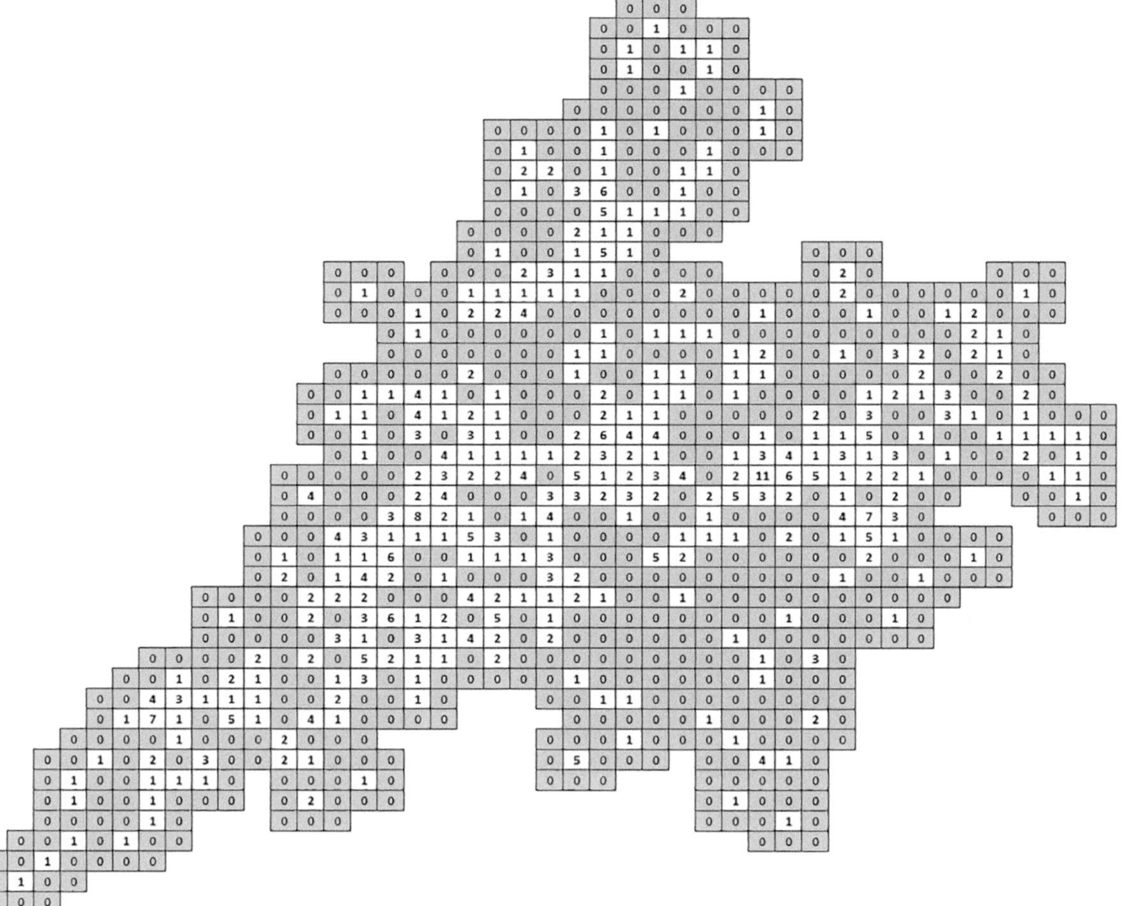

Figure 66: Schematic of Massachusetts Cluster No. 14.

average distance to nearest fault is 1.20 km (range: 0.01–5.37 km); the average distance to the head-of-tide is 60.62 km (range: 41.02–86.26 km); the average distance to minor watershed boundary is 2.49 km (range: 0.01–7.00 km). There is a strong preference for sites with respect to headwater streams (241), brooks (146), swamps (115), and ponds (ninety-six); the ocean was not utilized. Soil fertility is somewhat skewed in favor of sites in naturally infertile soils (248) and agriculturally productive soils (211), with smaller numbers in low fertility soils (137) and in pasture lands valleys (136). There are fewer on shores (thirty-three), plains (twenty-one), and islands (three).

                    Stone Prayers

Massachusetts Cluster No. 15 Fitchburg-Wachusett (Figure 67, Plate 54)

This is a large, somewhat diffuse cluster of 177 sites containing *c.* 827 structures in north central Massachusetts, overlapping into southern New Hampshire, within an area of 384 square kilometers (density: 0.41 per square kilometer). Its primary axis is roughly north-northwest to south-southeast. It is mostly located in Worcester County, with a small number of sites in adjacent Middlesex County and in Hillsborough County, New Hampshire, and it is almost entirely in the Merrimack drainage, with two sites in the adjacent Connecticut drainage. Most of the sites in this cluster were reported by Peter Waksman.[26] Other sites were reported by James and Mary Gage, Patrick Cooke and Barbara DeLong on their website, Steve Gabis, Tim MacSweeney, in the NEARA archive, and by James Mavor and Byron Dix.[27] The cluster has a VMR of 3.67 and a very high chi-square value of 1,341.94, and there is a 0.00 chance of its sites being randomly or uniformly distributed. The average NND is 0.49 km (range: 0.07–2.16 km). The average number of structures per site is slightly below the average of 5.5, 4.5 (range: 1–30), with an average of 1.6 types of structures per site. The distribution of types strongly favors rock piles (106), stone rows (thirty-eight), mounds (eleven), and enclosures (eleven). Petroglyphs and inscriptions are the only types which do not occur in the cluster. The average stream rank is 1.3 (range: 1–4); the average slope is 11.1 percent (range: 0.05–50.0). The average elevation is 949.7 feet (range: 486–1,574 feet); the average distance to nearest water is 267.0 meters (range: 0–970 meters). The average distance to nearest fault is 1.83 km (range: 0.19–5.82 km); the average distance to the head-of-tide is 81.06 km (range: 10.47–91.43 km); the average distance to minor watershed boundary is 1.77 km (range: 0.02–5.69 km). There is a strong preference for sites with respect to headwater streams (seventy-four), with fewer at brooks (thirty-three) and ponds (thirty-three); and the ocean was not utilized. Soil fertility is skewed in favor of sites in low fertility soils (seventy-five) and naturally infertile soils (fifty), with smaller numbers in agriculturally productive soils (thirty-six) and in pasture lands (sixteen). The predominant environmental settings are slopes (ninety-one), with equal numbers (thirty-nine) on hilltops and in valleys, and far fewer on shores (seven) and plains (one); there are none on islands.

Massachusetts Cluster No. 16 Upton (Figure 68)

This is a relatively oval cluster of thirty-eight sites containing *c.* 266 structures in south central Massachusetts, within an area of 90 square kilometers (density: 0.41 per square kilometer). Its primary axis is east-northeast to west-southwest. It is located on the border of Worcester and Middlesex Counties, and overlaps the watershed between the Merrimack and Blackstone drainages. Most of the sites in this cluster were reported by Peter Waksman, with smaller numbers by James Haskins, David Cuneo, the author, and in the NEARA archive.[28] The cluster has a VMR of 2.35 and a chi-square value of 209.07, and there is a 0.00 chance of its sites being randomly or uniformly distributed. The average NND is 0.59 km (range: 0.10–1.83 km). The average number of structures per site is slightly above the average of 5.5, 6.0 (range: 1–32), with an average of 2.0 types of structures per site. The distribution of types strongly favors rock piles (thirty-three), stone rows (thirteen), mounds (five), niches (five), split boulders (four), and effigies (four). Petroglyphs, inscriptions, and unique structures do not occur in the cluster. The

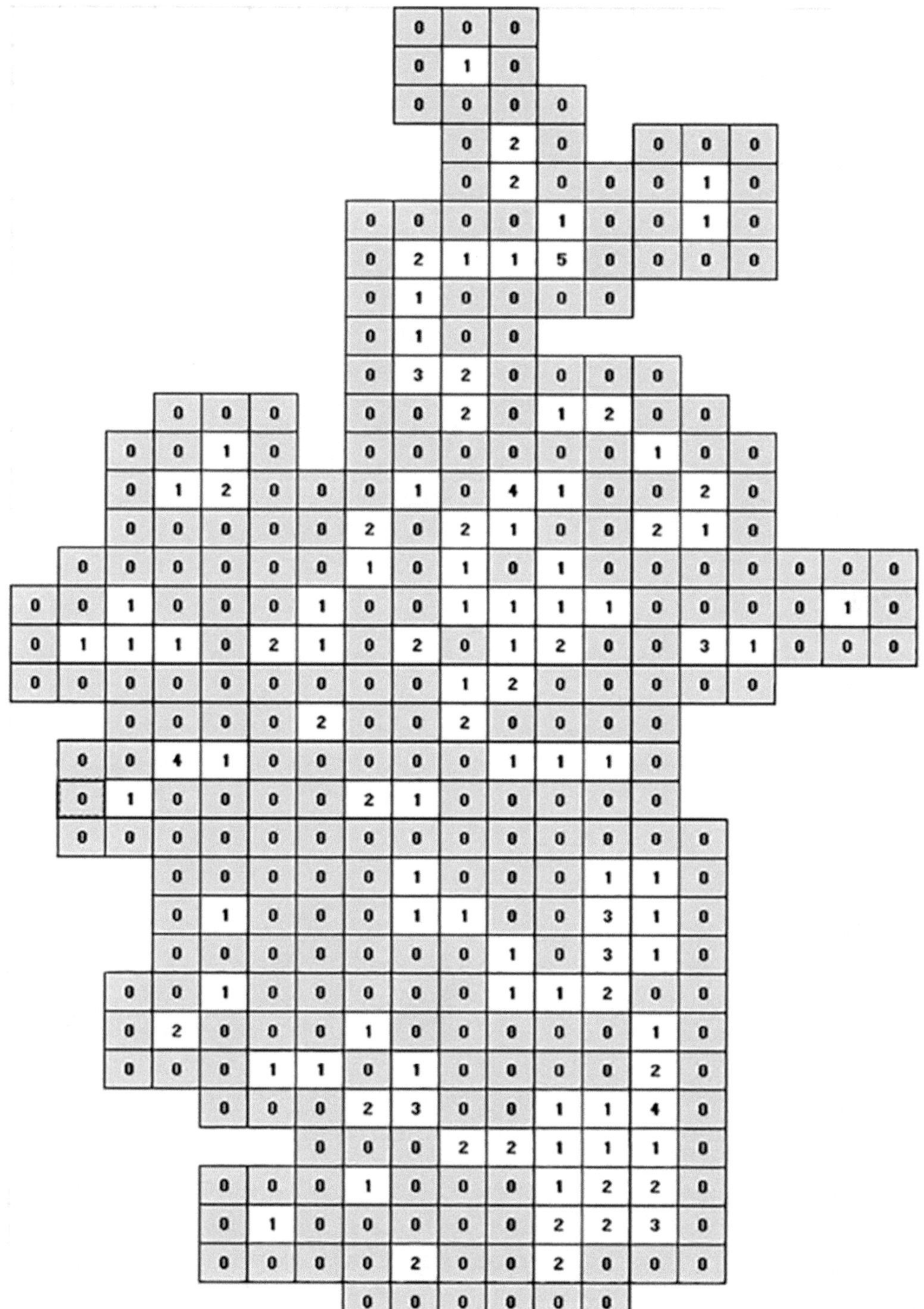

Figure 67: Schematic of Massachusetts Cluster No. 15.

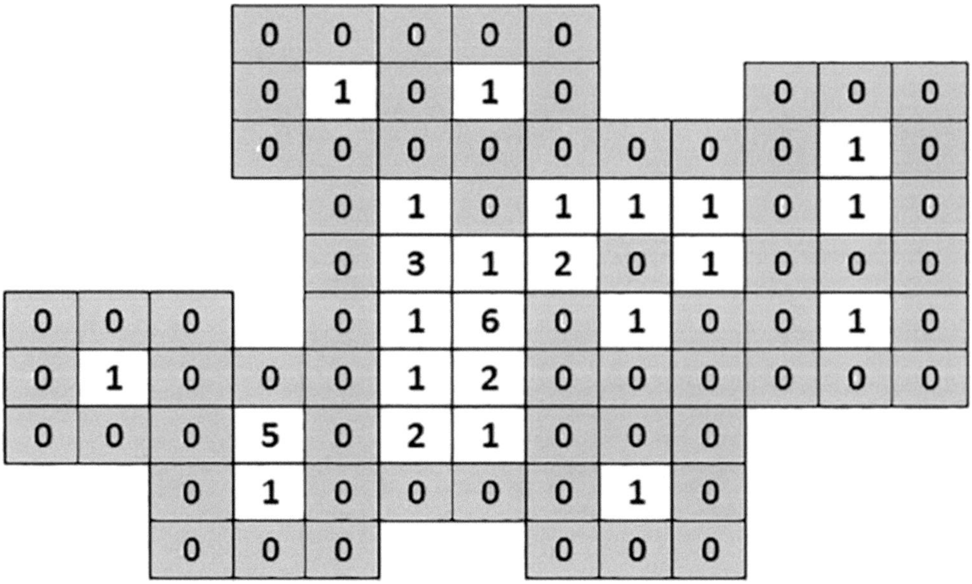

<table>
<tr><td></td><td></td><td></td><td>0</td><td>0</td><td>0</td><td>0</td><td>0</td><td></td><td></td><td></td><td></td><td></td></tr>
<tr><td></td><td></td><td></td><td>0</td><td>1</td><td>0</td><td>1</td><td>0</td><td></td><td></td><td>0</td><td>0</td><td>0</td></tr>
<tr><td></td><td></td><td></td><td></td><td>0</td><td>0</td><td>0</td><td>0</td><td>0</td><td>0</td><td>0</td><td>1</td><td>0</td></tr>
<tr><td></td><td></td><td></td><td></td><td>0</td><td>1</td><td>0</td><td>1</td><td>1</td><td>1</td><td>0</td><td>1</td><td>0</td></tr>
<tr><td></td><td></td><td></td><td></td><td>0</td><td>3</td><td>1</td><td>2</td><td>0</td><td>1</td><td>0</td><td>0</td><td>0</td></tr>
<tr><td>0</td><td>0</td><td>0</td><td></td><td>0</td><td>1</td><td>6</td><td>0</td><td>1</td><td>0</td><td>0</td><td>1</td><td>0</td></tr>
<tr><td>0</td><td>1</td><td>0</td><td></td><td>0</td><td>1</td><td>2</td><td>0</td><td>0</td><td>0</td><td>0</td><td>0</td><td>0</td></tr>
<tr><td>0</td><td>0</td><td>0</td><td></td><td>5</td><td>0</td><td>2</td><td>1</td><td>0</td><td>0</td><td>0</td><td></td><td></td></tr>
<tr><td></td><td></td><td></td><td>0</td><td>1</td><td>0</td><td>0</td><td>0</td><td>0</td><td>1</td><td>0</td><td></td><td></td></tr>
<tr><td></td><td></td><td></td><td>0</td><td>0</td><td>0</td><td></td><td></td><td>0</td><td>0</td><td>0</td><td></td><td></td></tr>
</table>

Figure 68: Schematic of Massachusetts Cluster No. 16.

average stream rank is 1.5 (range: 1–3); the average slope is 11.9 perfect (range: 0.5–30.0). The average elevation is 446.6 feet (range: 305–698 feet); the average distance to nearest water is 189.9 meters (range: 0–660 meters). The average distance to nearest fault is 0.48 km (range: 0.03–1.58 km); the average distance to the head-of-tide is 52.78 km (range: 38.89–89.14 km); the average distance to minor watershed boundary is 1.55 km (range: 0.07–3.39 km). There is a strong preference for sites with respect to headwater streams (twenty-six); and the ocean and rivers were not utilized. Soil fertility is skewed in favor of sites in agriculturally productive soils (eighteen) and naturally infertile soils (fourteen), with smaller numbers in low fertility soils (three) and in pasture lands (four). The predominant environmental settings are on slopes (eighteen), in valleys (eleven), and on hilltops (eight), with fewer on shores (two); there are none on islands or plains.

Massachusetts Cluster No. 17 Andover (Figure 69)

This is a small, roughly linear cluster of eighteen sites containing *c.* seventy-eight structures in northeastern Massachusetts, within an area of 56 square kilometers (density: 0.32 per square kilometer). It is located on the border of Essex and Middlesex Counties, and is entirely in the Merrimack drainage. Its axis of orientation is east-northeast to west-southwest. All but two of the sites in this cluster were reported by Peter Waksman, the exceptions being from Ted Timreck, and from the NEARA archive.[29] The cluster has a VMR of 5.67 and a chi-square value of 311.59, and there is a 0.00 chance of its sites being randomly or uniformly distributed. The average NND is 0.72 km (range: 0.25–2.47 km). The average number of structures per site is slightly below the average of 5.5, 4.3 (range: 1–12), with an average of 1.4 types of structures per site. The distribution of types

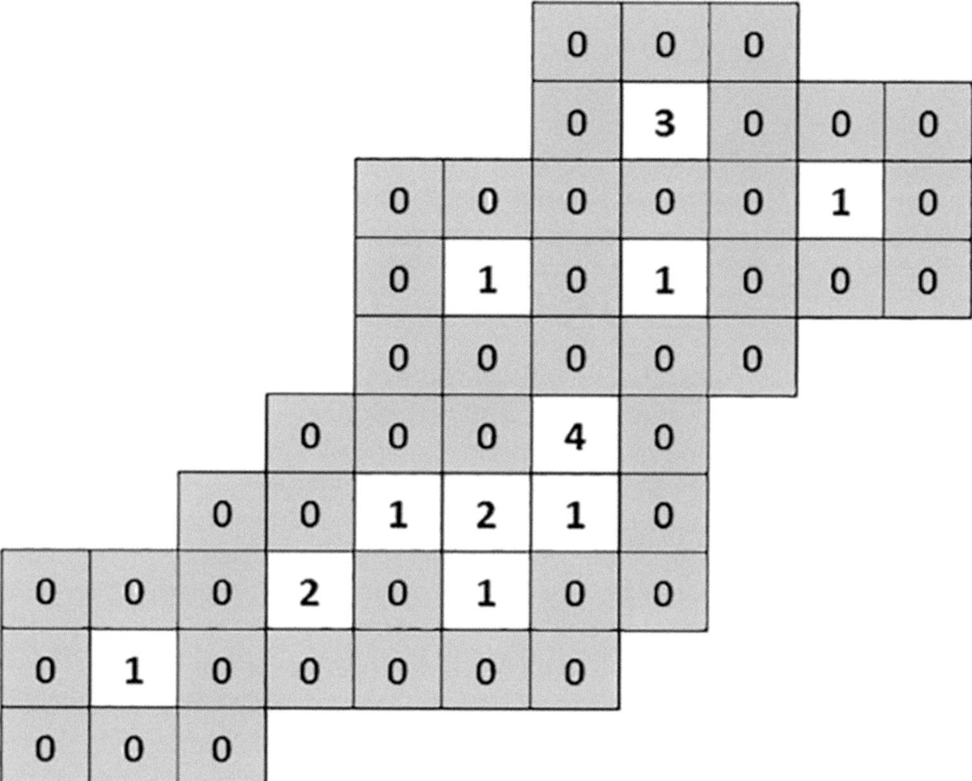

Figure 69: Schematic of Massachusetts Cluster No. 17.

strongly favors rock piles (fifteen). Cairns, U-shaped structures, chambers, marked stones, petroglyphs, inscriptions, stone circles, mounds, platforms, enclosures, niches, and unique structures do not occur in the cluster. The average stream rank is 1.3 (range: 1–2); the average slope is 9.1 percent (range: 0.5–20.0). The average elevation is 167.9 feet (range: 71–287 feet); the average distance to nearest water is 212.2 meters (range: 40–460 meters). The average distance to nearest fault is 1.52 km (range: 0.05–2.98 km); the average distance to the head-of-tide is 32.23 km (range: 28.19–37.83 km); the average distance to minor watershed boundary is 1.09 km (range: 0.32–2.14 km). There is a strong preference for sites with respect to headwater streams (nine); and lakes, rivers, and the ocean were not utilized. Soil fertility is skewed in favor of sites in naturally infertile soils (seven) and agriculturally productive soils (seven), with smaller numbers in low fertility soils (four) and none in pasture lands. The predominant environmental settings are on slopes (nine) or in valleys (seven), with fewer on plains or shores (one each); there are none on hilltops or islands.

Massachusetts Cluster No. 18 Lincoln (Figure 70)

This is a small, somewhat diffuse cluster of twenty-five sites containing *c.* ninety-five structures in eastern Massachusetts, within an area of 81 square kilometers (density: 0.31 per square kilometer). It is located within Middlesex County, and is on the watershed between the Merrimack and Charles drainages. All but one of the sites in this cluster were reported by Peter Waksman, the exception being from the NEARA archive.[30] The cluster has a VMR of 4.19 and a chi-square value of 335.19, and there is a 0.00 chance of its sites being randomly or uniformly distributed. The average NND is 0.61 km (range: 0.08–1.78 km). The average number of structures per site is somewhat below the average of 5.5, 3.8 (range: 1–20), with an average of 1.3 types of structures per site. The distribution of types strongly favors rock piles (twenty-one) and stone rows (twenty-one). Chambers, standing stones, marked stones, petroglyphs, inscriptions, stone circles, mounds, enclosures, niches, and unique structures do not occur in the cluster. The average stream rank is 1.4 (range: 1–3); the average slope is 10.3 percent (range: 0.5–20.0). The average elevation is 226.6 feet (range: 143–217 feet); the average distance to nearest water is 253.2 meters (range: 90–830 meters). The average distance to nearest fault is 0.78 km (range: 0.02–2.00 km); the average distance to the head-of-tide is 26.22 km (range: 5.50–61.19 km); the average distance to minor watershed boundary is 1.79 km (range: 0.00–5.20 km). There is a strong preference for sites with respect to brooks (fifteen); and lakes, rivers, and the ocean were not utilized. Soil fertility is skewed in favor of sites in naturally infertile soils (twelve), agriculturally productive soils (seven), and low fertility soils (six); and none in pasture lands. The predominant environmental settings are on hilltops (ten), slopes (eight), and in valleys (six), with fewer on plains (one); there are none on islands or shores.

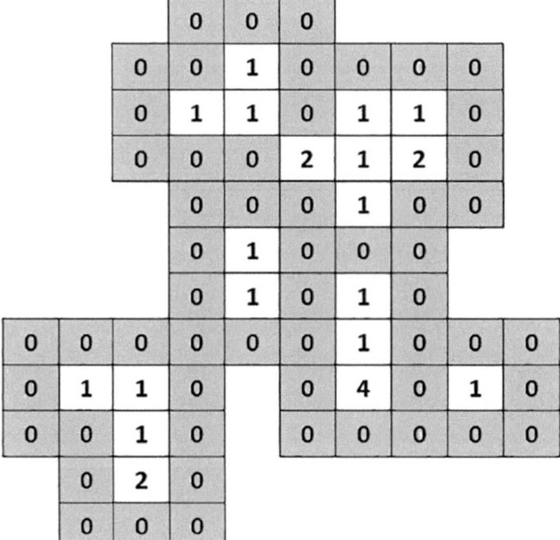

Figure 70: Schematic of Massachusetts Cluster No. 18.

Massachusetts Cluster No. 19 Weston (Figure 71)

This is a small, roughly oval cluster of eleven sites containing *c.* fifty structures in eastern Massachusetts, within an area of 40 square kilometers (density: 0.28 per square kilometer). Its main axis is east-northeast to west-southwest. It is entirely located within Middlesex County, and is on the watershed between the Merrimack and Charles drainages. The sites in this cluster were reported by Peter Waksman and Tim Fohl, both of whom live nearby.[31] The cluster has a VMR of 3.81 and a chi-square value of 148.54, and there is a 0.00 chance of its sites being randomly or uniformly distributed. The average NND is 0.87 km (range: 0.26–1.71 km). The average number of structures per site is slightly below the average of 5.5, 4.5 (range: 1–11), with an average of 1.7 types of structures per site. The distribution of types strongly favors rock piles (eight) and stone rows (four). Cairns, chambers, split boulders, petroglyphs, inscriptions, effigies, platforms, enclosures, niches, and unique structures do not occur in the cluster. The average stream rank is 1.4 (range: 1–2); the average slope is 8.4 percent (range: 0.5–25.0). The average elevation is 236.2 feet (range: 186–331 feet); the average distance to nearest water is 169.1 meters (range: 40–420 meters). The average distance to nearest fault is 0.66 km (range: 0.08–1.38 km); the average distance to the head-of-tide is 40.91 km (range: 16.75–67.48 km); the average distance to minor watershed boundary is 1.92 km (range: 0.15–4.36 km). There was a slight preference for sites with respect to headwater streams (five); and rivers and the ocean were not utilized. Soil fertility is skewed in favor of naturally infertile soils (nine), with small numbers in agriculturally productive soils (one) and in pasture lands (one), and none in low fertility soils. The predominant environmental settings are on hilltops and slopes (four each), with fewer in valleys (two) and shores (one); there are none on islands or plains.

In Massachusetts, 24.1 percent of sites are outside of clusters (428; density: 0.02 per square kilometer). Most of these sites were contributed by Peter Waksman, James Mavor and Byron Dix, Ted Timreck, in the NEARA Archive, and at the Woods Hole

				0	0	0			
				0	2	0	0	0	0
	0	0	0	0	0	0	1	1	0
0	0	1	2	1	0	0	0	0	0
0	1	1	0	1	0				
0	0	0	0	0	0				

Figure 71: Schematic of Massachusetts Cluster No. 19.

Historical Museum, with smaller numbers contributed by Alan Smith, Anita Cole, Ted Ballard, Bernard Otto, Bill Moody, Bob Dalbec, Brian Konieczny, Bruce Harned, Bruce Mcaleer, Chris Groden, Chris Soccorro, John Coles, Dan Jesus, David Cuneo, Patrick Cooke and Barbara De Long, Dennis and Judy Randall, Derek Gunn, Diana Fox, Diane Horvath, Dianna Doucette, Doug Schwartz, Emily Brunelle, Erin Flynn and Dianna Doucette, Frederick Pohl, Gary Sanderson, Gerry McLoughlin and Donna Savino, Gil McCarthy, Henry Norton, Jack Rossen, Mary and James Gage, James Stockbridge, Jeffrey Cedrone, Judy Savage, Karen Bartnicki, Ken Leonard, Ed Lenik, Mary Ellen Lepionka, Matt Howes, Maurice Robbins McKayla Hoffman, Michael Lombardo, Mike Hoye, Mike Leonard, Nancy Hunt, Nancy Klopchin, Nick Holland, Norman Muller, Paul Kachinsky, Peter Anick, Richard Kramer, Robert Trotta, Ruth Bates, Sarah Kohler, Steve DiMarzo, Steve Gabis, Steve Sullwold, Susan Morse, Tim Fohl, Tim MacSweeney, Tom Botelho, Valdemar Samuelson, Vic Mastone, Walter Van Roggen, Wayne Braley, and the author. These sites have an average number of 5.8 structures per site (range: 1–309), and an average of 1.6 types per site. All structure types are found in sites outside of clusters in Massachusetts, but the predominant types are rock piles (183), stone rows (eighty-nine), chambers (fifty-three), marked stones (fifty-two), balanced rocks (forty-five), cairns (thirty-seven), split boulders (thirty-three), effigies (thirty-three), and standing stones (thirty). Their average elevation is 415.6 feet (range: 0–2,423 feet); their average distance to water is 254.0 meters (range: 0–1,090 meters). Their average stream rank is 1.7 (range: 1–8); their average slope is 10.9 perfect (range: 0.0–50.0). Their average distance to fault is 3.90 km (range: 0.00–77.22 km); the average distance to the head-of-tide is 40.59 km (range: 0.00–133.11 km); their average distance to minor watershed is 1.97 km (range: 0.00–8.79 km). Their average NND is 2.25 km (range: 0.08–43.34 km). All water types were utilized, but there is a predominance of sites near headwater streams (130), followed by swamps (ninety-seven), ponds (seventy-four), and named streams (sixty-seven). Sites in low fertility soils predominate (192), followed by naturally infertile soils (107), agriculturally productive soils (ninety-seven), and pasture lands (thirty-one). The predominant environmental settings are hilltops (125) and slopes (122), followed by valleys (eighty-seven), shores (fifty-nine), plains (twenty-three), and islands (twelve).

New Hampshire Cluster No. 1 New Hampshire Border No. 1 (Figure 72)

This is a small, roughly circular cluster of twenty-six sites containing *c.* 488 structures in southeastern New Hampshire, within an area of 89 square kilometers (density: 0.29 per square kilometer). It is entirely located within Rockingham County, and all but two of the sites are within the Merrimack drainage; the exceptions are in the adjacent Piscataqua drainage. Most sites in this cluster were reported by James and Mary Gage, who live nearby, or are from the NEARA archive.[32] It includes the famous Mystery Hill site.[33] The cluster has a VMR of 5.75 and a chi-square value of 506.31, and there is a 0.00 chance of its sites being randomly or uniformly distributed. The average NND is 0.75 km (range: 0.20–1.78 km). The average number of structures per site is far above the average of 5.5, 18.8 (range: 1–206), with an average of 1.5 types of structures per site. The distribution of types strongly favors cairns (nineteen) and split boulders (five). Marked stones, inscriptions, stone circles, effigies, platforms, enclosures, niches, and

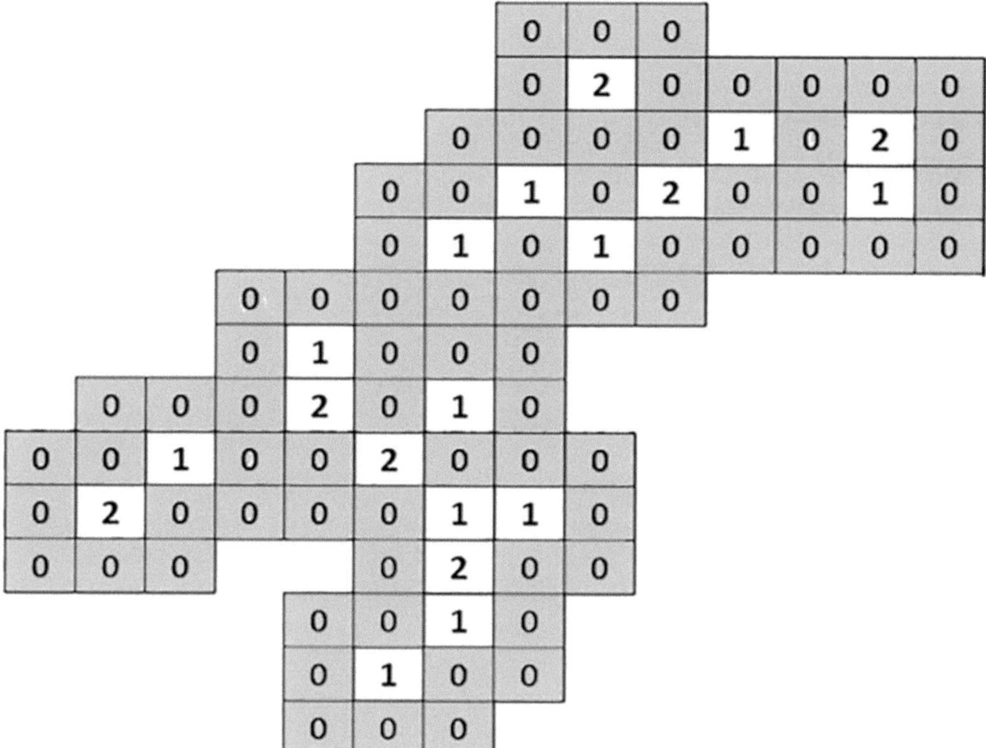

Figure 72: Schematic of New Hampshire Cluster No. 1.

unique structures do not occur in the cluster. The average stream rank is 1.8 (range: 1–3); the average slope is 14.4 percent (range: 0.5–47.5). The average elevation is 257.0 feet (range: 60–364 feet); the average distance to nearest water is 257.5 meters (range: 50–450 meters). The average distance to nearest fault is 2.34 km (range: 0.06–5.99 km); the average distance to the head-of-tide is 25.51 km (range: 20.58–38.46 km); the average distance to minor watershed boundary is 1.61 km (range: 0.03–4.39 km). There is a strong preference for sites with respect to headwater streams (thirteen), with lower numbers of ponds (seven); and lakes, swamps, rivers, and the ocean were not utilized. Soil fertility is skewed in favor of sites in low fertility soils (eleven) and naturally infertile soils (eight), with smaller numbers in agriculturally productive soils (three) and in pasture lands (four). The predominant environmental settings are on slopes (ten) and hilltops (nine), with smaller numbers in valleys (three), on islands (two), plains and shores (one each).

New Hampshire Cluster No. 2 New Hampshire Border No. 2 (Figure 73)

This is a small, diffuse cluster of eleven sites containing *c.* forty-two structures in southeastern New Hampshire, within an area of 29 square kilometers (density: 0.38 per square kilometer). All but one of the sites are located in Hillsborough County, with the exception being in Rockingham County, and it is entirely within the Merrimack drainage. The sites in this cluster were all reported by Peter Waksman.[34] The cluster

		0	0	0	
		0	3	0	
0	0	1	0	0	
0	2	0	1	0	0
0	3	0	0	1	0
0	0	0	0	0	0

Figure 73: Schematic of New Hampshire Cluster No. 2.

has a VMR of 4.99 and a chi-square value of 139.77, and there is a 0.00 chance of its sites being randomly or uniformly distributed. The average NND is 0.58 km (range: 0.30–2.05 km). The average number of structures per site is somewhat below the average of 5.5, 3.8 (range: 1–11), with an average of 1.7 types of structures per site. The distribution of types strongly favors rock piles (eleven) and stone rows (three). Cairns, chambers, standing stones, balanced rocks, marked stones, petroglyphs, inscriptions, mounds, platforms, niches, and unique structures do not occur in the cluster. All sites were at Rank One streams; the average slope is 13.6 percent (range: 4.0–25.0). The average elevation is 304.9 feet (range: 213–435 feet); the average distance to nearest water is 192.3 meters (range: 20–550 meters). The average distance to nearest fault is 1.19 km (range: 0.08–3.43 km); the average distance to the head-of-tide is 40.78 km (range: 39.37–41.64 km); the average distance to minor watershed boundary is 5.22 km (range: 3.88–7.42 km). There is a strong preference for sites with respect to headwater streams (seven), with slightly lower numbers for brooks (three); and rivers, lakes, ponds, and the ocean were not utilized. Soil fertility is skewed in favor of sites in naturally infertile soils (seven), with smaller numbers in low fertility soils (three) and pasture lands (one); none were in agriculturally productive soils. The predominant environmental settings are on slopes (six), with fewer on hilltops and in valleys (two each), and on shores (one); there are none on islands or plains.

New Hampshire Cluster No. 3 New Hampshire Border No. 3 (Figure 74)

This is a small, roughly oval cluster of eleven sites containing *c.* 136 structures in southeastern New Hampshire, within an area of 25 square kilometers (density: 0.44 per square kilometer). Its main axis is east-southeast to west-northwest. It is entirely located within Rockingham County, and all but one of the sites are within the Merrimack drainage; the exception is in the adjacent Piscataqua drainage. The sites in this cluster were reported by James and Mary Gage, or are in the NEARA archive.[35] The cluster has a VMR of 5.82 and a chi-square value of 139.64, and there is a 0.00 chance of its sites being randomly or uniformly distributed. The average NND is 0.55 km (range: 0.15–2.17 km). The average number of structures per site is rather high,

12.4 (range: 1–44), with an average of 1.2 types of structures per site. The distribution of types strongly favors cairns (nine). The only other types which occur in the cluster are chambers (two), standing stones (one), and balanced rocks (one). The average stream rank is 1.2 (range: 1–2); the average slope is 15.6 percent (range: 0.0–37.5). The average elevation is 166.6 feet (range: 108–257 feet); the average distance to nearest water is 204.5 meters (range: 0–490 meters). The average distance to nearest fault is 4.91 km (range: 2.25–6.17 km); the average distance to the head-of-tide is 14.90 km (range: 8.96–38.29 km); the average distance to minor watershed boundary is 4.03 km (range: 3.36–4.74 km). There is a strong preference for sites with respect to headwater streams (seven); and brooks, lakes, rivers and the ocean were not utilized. Soil fertility is skewed in favor of sites in low fertility soils (seven), with smaller numbers in agriculturally productive soils (two), naturally infertile soils (one) and in pasture lands (one). The predominant environmental settings are on hilltops (seven), with smaller numbers on shores or in valleys (two each); no other environmental settings are used.

In New Hampshire, 75.8 percent of sites are outside of clusters (169; density: 0.01 per square kilometer). Most of these sites are derived from the NEARA Archive, and from Peter Waksman and Walter Van Roggen, with smaller numbers contributed by Alan Smith, Anna Szak, Ted Ballard, Robert Goodby *et al.*, Patrick Cooke and Barbara De Long, Ed Lenik, James and Mary Gage, Jim Porter, Nancy Hunt, Norman Muller, Peter Anick, Steve DiMarzo, Ted Timreck, Tim MacSweeney, Victoria Rourke, and the author. These sites have an average number of 7.5 structures per site (range: 1–130), and an average of 1.4 types per site. Almost all structure types are found outside of clusters in New Hampshire, except for inscriptions and unique structures. The predominant types are rock piles (sixty-six), chambers (thirty-nine), cairns (thirty-three), and stone rows (thirty-one). Their average elevation is 561.9 feet (range: 6–3,835 feet); their average distance to water is 257.0 meters (range: 0–1,110 meters). Their average stream rank is 1.7 (range: 1–8); their average slope is 14.1 percent (range: 0.0–42.5). Their average distance to fault is 2.77 km (range: 0.02–15.40 km); the average distance to the head-of-tide is

0	0	0	0	0	0	0
0	1	0	1	1	1	0
0	0	0	0	5	2	0
			0	0	0	0

Figure 74: Schematic of New Hampshire Cluster No. 3.

77.34 km (range: 0.00–401.07 km); their average distance to minor watershed is 2.45 km (range: 0.01–9.32 km). Their average NND is 3.69 km (range: 0.06–40.47 km). All water types are utilized, but there is a predominance of sites near headwater streams (seventy-seven), followed by named streams (thirty-five) and lakes (twenty-two). Sites in agriculturally productive soils predominate (eighty-two), followed by low fertility soils (fifty-three), naturally infertile soils (thirty), and pasture lands (four). The predominant environmental settings are slopes (seventy-two), followed by valleys (thirty-five), hilltops (thirty), plains and shores (twelve each), and islands (eight).

New York Cluster No. 1 Putnam County (Figure 75, Plate 55)

This is a very large, roughly oval cluster of 216 sites containing *c.* 518 structures in southeastern New York and western Connecticut, within an area of 550 square kilometers (density: 0.39 per square kilometer). Its main axis is east to west. It is mostly located within Putnam County, but it overlaps into Westchester County to the south, Dutchess County to the north, and Litchfield County in Connecticut to the east. Nearly all of the sites are within the Hudson drainage, with one exception each in the Housatonic, Rippowam, and Saugatuck drainages. Most of the sites in this cluster were reported by a team of NEARA-affiliated local researchers: Polly Midgley, Teresa Bierce, Donna Savino, Rob Buchanan, and Gerry McLaughlin, as well as in the NEARA archive. Additional sites were reported by David Cuneo, Patrick Cooke and Barbara DeLong, Doug Schwartz, Peter Waksman, and Tim MacSweeney.[36] The cluster has a VMR of 4.09 and a very high chi-square value of 3,629.47, and there is a 0.00 chance of its sites being randomly or uniformly distributed. The average NND is 0.61 km (range: 0.09–2.57 km). The average number of structures per site is well below the average of 5.5, 2.4 (range: 1–31), with an average of 1.2 types of structures per site. The distribution of types overwhelmingly favors chambers (157), with smaller numbers of stone rows (twenty-eight) and cairns (fourteen). All other types except for inscriptions and unique structures are found in this cluster. The average stream rank is 1.5 (range: 1–4); the average slope is 16.4 percent (range: 0.0–67.5). The average elevation is 686.2 feet (range: 238–1,081 feet); the average distance to nearest water is 174.0 meters (range: 0–650 meters). The average distance to nearest fault is 1.17 km (range: 0.03–4.88 km); the average distance to the head-of-tide is 86.05 km (range: 36.50–99.41 km); the average distance to minor watershed boundary is 2.41 km (range: 0.00–9.25 km). There is a very strong preference for sites with respect to headwater streams (seventy-five), with somewhat lower numbers for swamps (forty-one), lakes (thirty-five), ponds (thirty-three), and brooks (twenty-three); the ocean was not utilized. One reason for the elevated number of sites at lakes is the existence of several artificial reservoirs in the area's river basins created by damming. Prior to dam construction in the nineteenth and early twentieth century, presumably these sites would have been closest to rivers and streams. Soil fertility is skewed in favor of sites in low fertility soils (111), with smaller numbers in naturally infertile soils (fifty-four), agriculturally productive soils (forty-three), and in pasture lands (twelve). The predominant environmental settings are valleys (eighty-two) and slopes (seventy-six), followed by shores (thirty-six), hilltops (twenty-one), and plains (five); there are none on islands. This is the only cluster in which valleys predominated over all other environmental settings.

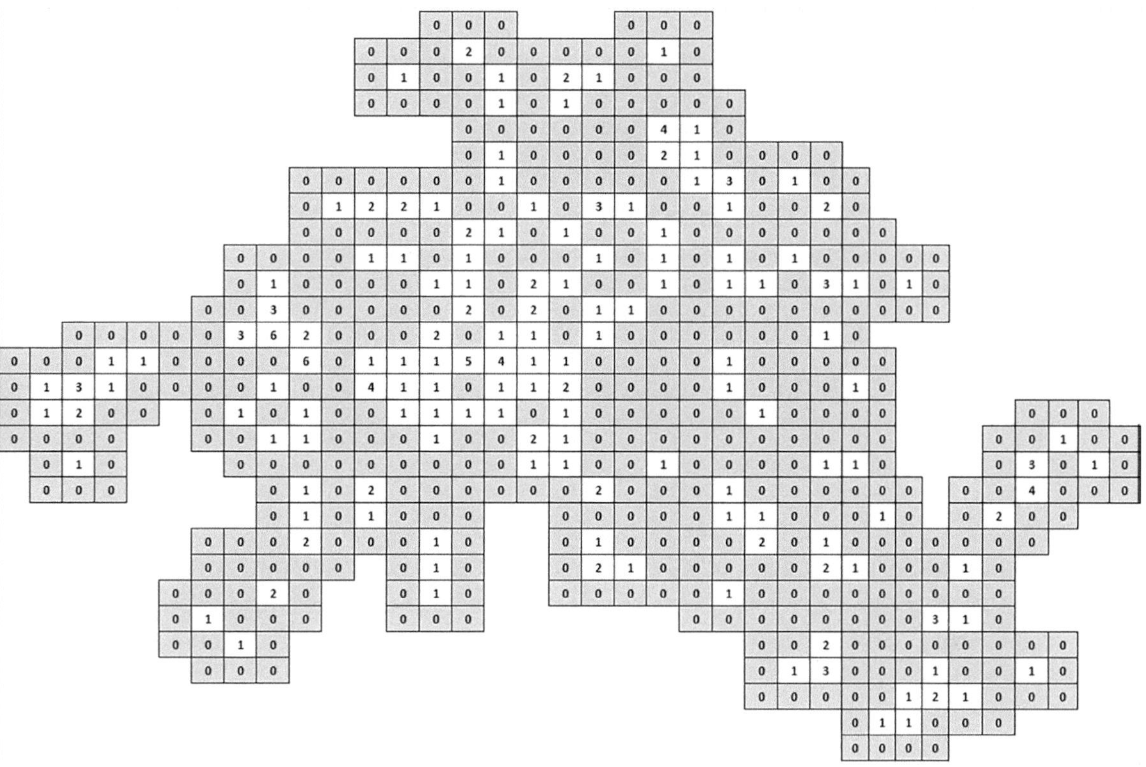

Figure 75: Schematic of New York Cluster No. 1.

New York Cluster No. 2 Kensico (Figure 76)

This is a small, roughly circular cluster of ten sites containing *c.* fifty-one structures in southeastern New York, just to the south of New York Cluster No. 1, within an area of 19 square kilometers (density: 0.53 per square kilometer). It is entirely located within Westchester County, and is on the watershed between the Hudson and Mamaroneck drainages, with one site in the Bronx River drainage. Most sites in this cluster were reported by Doug Schwartz and in the NEARA archive; the remainder were reported by Polly Midgley and by Grace Bello, who is a local resident. The cluster has a VMR of 5.13 and a chi-square value of 92.34, and there is a 0.00 chance of its sites being randomly or uniformly distributed. The average NND is 0.37 km (range: 0.13–1.05 km). The average number of structures per site is close to the average of 5.5, 5.1 (range: 1–26), with an average of 1.4 types of structures per site. The distribution of types strongly favors chambers (ten). The only other types which occur in the cluster, with one example each, are cairns, stone rows, and standing stones. All sites are at Rank One streams; the average slope could not be determined since only one of the sites had a slope indicated (32.5 percent). The average elevation is 374.4 feet (range: 305–435 feet); the average distance to nearest water is 120.5 meters (range: 25–290 meters). The average distance to nearest fault

0	**0**	**0**	
0	**1**	**0**	**0**
0	**0**	**2**	**0**
0	**2**	**5**	**0**
0	**0**	**0**	**0**

Figure 76: Schematic Map of New York Cluster No. 2.

is 0.65 km (range: 0.14–1.49 km); the average distance to the head-of-tide is 28.39 km (range: 11.64–49.07 km); the average distance to minor watershed boundary is 0.59 km (range: 0.05–1.17 km). There was a slight preference for sites with respect to headwater streams (five); and brooks, lakes, rivers and the ocean were not utilized. Soil fertility is slightly skewed in favor of sites in naturally infertile soils (five), with smaller numbers in low fertility soils (three) and in pasture lands (two), and none in agriculturally productive soils. The predominant environmental settings are hilltops (five), followed by slopes and shores (two each) and valleys (one); there are none on plains or islands.

New York Cluster No. 3 Upper Susquehanna No. 1 (Figure 77)

This is a large, diffuse, roughly U-shaped cluster of thirteen sites containing twenty-five structures in south central New York, within an area of 61 square kilometers (density: 0.21 per square kilometer). Its main axis is north to south. It is mostly located within Chenango County, with a few sites in adjacent Broome and Delaware counties. Most sites are within the Susquehanna drainage, with one site in the adjacent Delaware drainage. Most of the sites in this cluster were reported by Polly Midgley, Dan Cassedy, and Kathy Klopchin.[37] Additional sites were reported by Tom Paul and Dolores Elliott. The cluster has a VMR of 4.87 and a chi-square value of 282.02, and there is a 0.00 chance of its sites being randomly or uniformly distributed. The average NND is 0.84 km (range: 0.16–1.86 km). The average number of structures per site is well below the average of 5.5, 1.9 (range: 1–7), with an average of 1.1 types of structures per site. The distribution of types strongly favors rock piles (nine) and cairns (four). The only other type which occurs in the cluster is a single example of a balanced rock. The average stream rank is 1.2 (range: 1–2); the average slope is 13.6 percent (range: 0.0–67.5). The average elevation is 1,502.1 feet (range: 985–2,009 feet); the average distance to nearest water is 475.4 meters (range: 0–800 meters). The average distance to nearest fault is 1.06 km (range: 0.08–2.08 km); the average distance to the head-of-tide is 289.72 km (range: 226.67–298.29 km); the average distance to minor watershed boundary is 2.01 km (range: 0.04–4.03 km). There is a strong preference for sites with respect to headwater streams (nine); otherwise, only brooks are utilized. Soil fertility is about equally distributed between pasture lands (five)

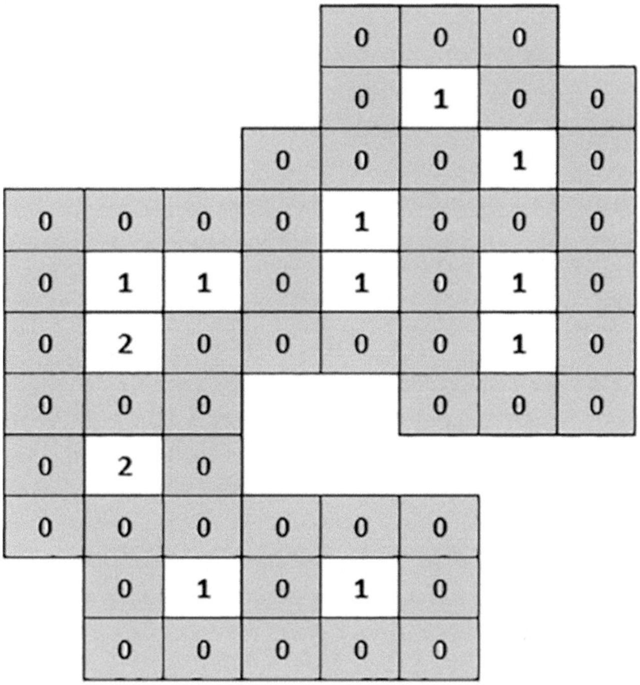

				0	0	0	
				0	1	0	0
			0	0	0	1	0
0	0	0	0	1	0	0	0
0	1	1	0	1	0	1	0
0	2	0	0	0	0	1	0
0	0	0			0	0	0
0	2	0					
0	0	0	0	0	0		
	0	1	0	1	0		
	0	0	0	0	0		

Figure 77: Schematic Map of New York Cluster No. 3.

and low fertility soils (four) and with smaller numbers in naturally infertile soils (three) and agriculturally productive soils (one). The predominant environmental settings are slopes (ten), with smaller numbers in valleys (two) and on hilltops (one); no other environmental settings are used.

New York Cluster No. 4 Hi-Tor (Figure 78)

This is a medium-sized, roughly oval cluster of fifty-three sites containing *c.* 225 structures in western New York, within an area of 103 square kilometers (density: 0.51 per square kilometer). Its main axis is northeast to southwest. All but three of the sites are located within Yates County, with the remainder in Ontario County, and it is entirely in the Oswego drainage, which flows into Lake Ontario, which in turn flows into the St. Lawrence River. All of the sites in this cluster were reported by local resident David Schewe. The cluster has a VMR of 3.76 and a chi-square value of 383.36, and there is a 0.00 chance of its sites being randomly or uniformly distributed. The average NND is 0.46 km (range: 0.18–2.38 km). The average number of structures per site is slightly below the average of 5.5, 4.2 (range: 1–19), with an average of 1.1 types of structures per site. The distribution of types strongly favors rock piles (fifty-one); the only other types which occur in the cluster are cairns (three), U-shaped structures (one), stone circles (one), and mounds (one). The average stream rank is 1.1 (range: 1–3); the average slope is 11.5 percent (range: 0.5–47.5). The average elevation is 1,590.2 feet (range: 750–1,974 feet); the average distance to nearest water is 461.9 meters (range: 0–1,360 meters). The average distance to nearest fault is 1.21 km (range: 0.03–2.85 km); the average distance to the head-of-tide is 70.08 km (range: 67.90–70.99 km); the average distance to minor watershed boundary is 1.77 km (range: 0.01–4.40 km). There is a strong preference for sites with respect to headwater streams (forty-one) and brooks (eleven); no other water resources were utilized. Soil fertility is skewed in favor of sites in pasture lands (thirty-two), with smaller numbers in agriculturally productive soils (eight) and in low fertility soils (ten), and few in naturally infertile soils (three). The predominant environmental settings are on slopes (forty-three), with smaller numbers in valleys (nine) and hilltops (one); no other environmental settings were used.

New York Cluster No. 5 Upper Susquehanna No. 2 (Figure 79, Plate 56)

This is a rather diffuse cluster of fifteen sites containing *c.* 115 structures in an area of 64 square kilometers (density: 0.23 per square kilometer) which overlaps the New York–Pennsylvania border in Broome County New York and Susquehanna County, Pennsylvania. Most of the sites were reported as the result of a cultural resource management survey by Dan Cassedy, with some sites reported by Dolores Elliott.[38] It has a VMR of 4.14, and a chi-square value of 260.59, so there is a 0.00 chance that the distribution is random. The average NND is 0.83 km (range: 0.13–2.82 km). The average number of structures per site is somewhat above the average of 5.5, 7.7 (range: 1–26), and the average number of types of structures per site is 1.1 (range: 1–2). The average stream rank is 1.1 (range: 1–2); the average slope is 19.3 percent (range: 5.5–52.5). The distribution of types strongly favors rock piles (fourteen), and the only other type present is cairns (two). The average elevation is 1,512.0 feet (range: 170–1,789 feet); the average distance to water is 479.7 meters (range: 70–1,070 meters). The average distance to nearest fault is 3.80 km (range: 1.12–6.09 km); the average distance to the head-of-tide is 259.27 km (range: 209.71–275.88 km); the average distance to minor watershed boundary is 1.34 km (range: 0.02–3.67 km). There a strong preference for sites with respect to brooks (eleven), and otherwise only headwater streams were utilized. Soil fertility was skewed towards sites in pasture lands (eight) and low fertility soils (six), with only one in agriculturally productive soils and none in naturally infertile soils. The predominant environmental settings are slopes (eight) and hilltops (five), with smaller numbers on plains and in valleys (one each); islands and shores and the ocean were not used.

In New York, 55.0 percent of sites are outside of clusters (359; density: 0.00 per square kilometer). Most of these sites were obtained from Dan Cassedy, Dolores Elliott, David Schewe, Kathy Klopchin, Polly Midgley, Tom Paul, in the NEARA Archive, and from the New York State Museum. Smaller numbers were contributed by Robert Hasenstab, Craig Wright, Doug Schwartz, Ed Lenik, Gerry McLoughlin, Glenn Kreisberg, James and Mary Gage, James Haskins, Laurie Rush, Matt Bua, Nancy Hunt, Nancy Wisser, Norman Muller, Peter Anick, Peter Backes, Peter Waksman, Rob Buchanan, Steve DiMarzo, Ted Timreck, Teresa Bierce, Tim MacSweeney, the New York State Historic Preservation Office, and the author. These sites have an average number of 6.2 structures per site (range: 1–103), and an average of 1.4 types per site. With the exception of platforms, all structure types are found outside of clusters in New York. The predominant types are rock piles (180), cairns (ninety-nine), stone rows (forty-seven), and chambers (forty-six). Their average elevation is 1,290.8 feet (range: 0–3,517 feet); their average distance to water

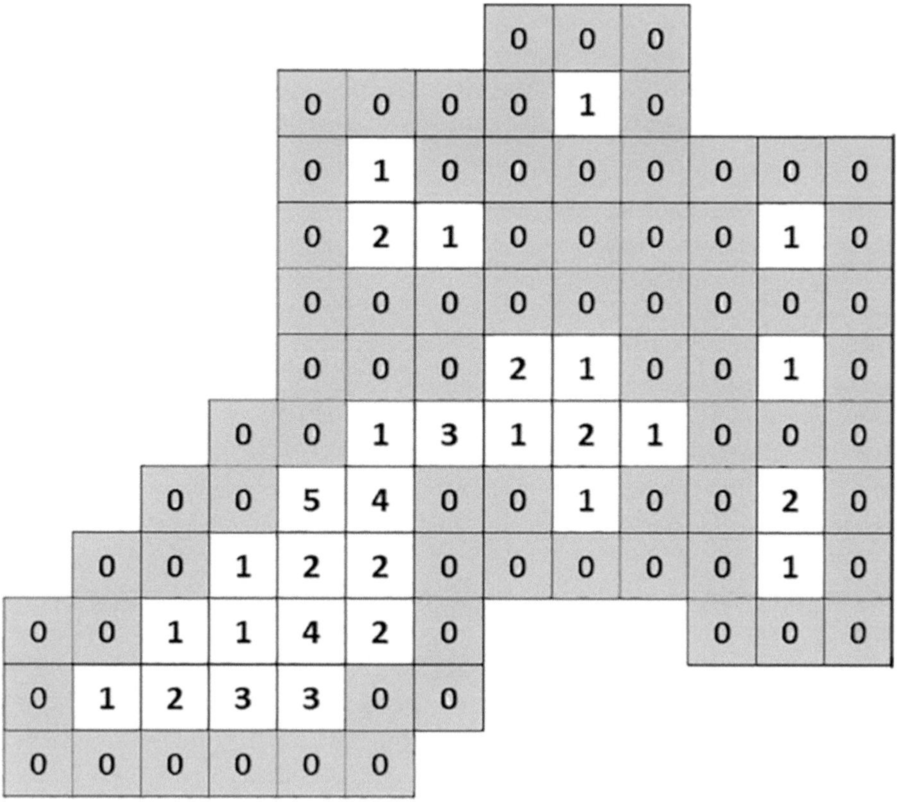

Above: Figure 78: Schematic Map of New York Cluster No. 4.

Right: Figure 79: Schematic Map of New York Cluster No. 5.

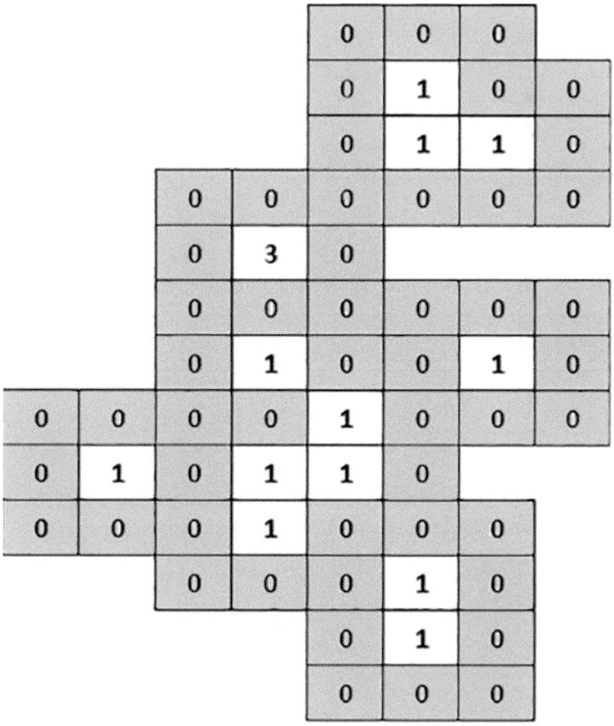

is 356.0 meters (range: 0–3,650 meters). Their average stream rank is 1.8 (range: 1–8); their average slope is 17.9 percent (range: 0.0–67.5). Their average distance to fault is 2.54 km (range: 0.00–35.23 km); the average distance to the head-of-tide is 194.01 km (range: 0.00–370.37 km); their average distance to minor watershed is 2.59 km (range: 0.00–11.20 km). Their average NND is 4.39 km (range: 0.10–49.18). All water types are utilized, but there is a predominance of sites near headwater streams (191), followed by named streams (eighty-three) and rivers (forty). Sites in naturally infertile soils predominate (148), followed by agriculturally productive soils (102), low fertility soils (seventy-eight), and pasture lands (thirty-one). The predominant environmental settings are slopes (142), hilltops (ninety-three), and valleys (eighty-two), with fewer on shores (twenty-four) and plains (eighteen); there are none on islands or the ocean.

Pennsylvania Cluster No. 1 Lake Catalpa (Figure 80)

This is a tightly packed, roughly circular cluster of forty-seven sites containing *c.* 585 structures in eastern Pennsylvania, within an area of 43 square kilometers (density: 1.09 per square kilometer). It is located on the border of Luzerne and Wyoming Counties, and is entirely within the Susquehanna drainage. The sites in this cluster were all reported by Heather Taylor, who serves as caretaker for the large single property on which they are located. The cluster has a VMR of 2.25 and a chi-square value of 94.53, and there is a 0.00 chance of its sites being randomly or uniformly distributed. The average NND is 0.32 km (range: 0.13–0.74 km). The average number of structures per site is significantly above the average of 5.5, 12.4 (range: 1–67), with an average of 2.6 types of structures per site. The distribution of types strongly favors rock piles (thirty-four), stone rows (twenty), cairns (eighteen), effigies (eleven), niches (five), standing stones (five), and marked stones (five). The only types which do not occur are inscriptions and stone circles. The average stream rank is 1.1 (range: 1–2); the average slope is 14.4 percent (range: 4.0–50.0). The average elevation is 1,366.3 feet (range:

	0	0	0	0	0
0	0	7	2	3	0
0	3	2	2	5	0
0	3	2	2	0	0
0	1	3	3	0	0
0	0	1	4	3	0
	0	1	0	0	0
	0	0	0		

Figure 80: Schematic of Pennsylvania Cluster No. 1.

1,162–1,675 feet); the average distance to nearest water is 302.1 meters (range: 0–880 meters). The average distance to nearest fault is 11.263 km (range: 8.73–13.11 km); the average distance to the head-of-tide is 200.89 km (range: 198.02–202.85 km); the average distance to minor watershed boundary is 866.2 km (range: 0.00–2.47 km). There is a strong preference for sites with respect to headwater streams (twenty-nine) and swamps (thirteen); and brooks, ponds, rivers and the ocean were not utilized. Soil fertility is skewed in favor of sites in low fertility soils (twenty-six) and pasture lands (twenty), with only one in agriculturally productive soils and none in naturally infertile soils. The predominant environmental settings are on slopes (twenty-nine), with smaller numbers in valleys (eight), on hilltops (seven), on shores (two), and on plains (one); islands are not used.

Pennsylvania Cluster No. 2 Unami-Hacking (Figure 81)
This is a small, oval cluster of eighteen sites containing *c*. 385 structures in eastern Pennsylvania, within an area of 43 square kilometers (density: 0.42 per square kilometer). Its main axis is northeast to southwest. All but one of its sites are located within Montgomery County, the exception being in adjacent Bucks County, and the cluster is entirely within the Delaware drainage. The sites in this cluster were all recorded in the archives of the Pennsylvania Historical and Museum Commission. The cluster has a VMR of 2.92 and a chi-square value of 122.63, and there is a 0.00 chance of its sites being randomly or uniformly distributed. The average NND is 0.74 km (range: 0.32–1.36 km). The average number of structures per site is very high, 21.4 (range= 1–288), with an average of 2.1 types of structures per site. The distribution of types strongly favors marked stones (thirteen), rock piles (six), and stone rows (six). U-shaped structures, chambers, balanced rocks, petroglyphs, inscriptions, mounds, platforms, enclosures, niches, and unique structures do not occur in the cluster. The average stream rank is 1.7 (range: 1–3); the average slope is 17.4 percent (range: 4.0–50.0). The average elevation is 379.8 feet (range: 253–585 feet); the average distance to nearest water is 234.7 meters (range: 65–720 meters). The average distance to nearest fault is 4.64 km (range: 2.38–7.54 km); the average distance to the head-of-tide is 58.55 km (range: 57.07–59.84 km); the average distance to minor watershed boundary is 7.29 km (range: 3.83–9.92 km). There is a strong preference for sites at brooks (twelve) and headwater streams (six); no other water resources are utilized. Soil fertility is skewed in favor of sites in agriculturally productive soils (thirteen), with smaller numbers in low fertility soils (three), naturally infertile soils (one), and in pasture lands (one). The predominant environmental settings are slopes (seven), hilltops and valleys (five each); there are fewer on shores (one); none are located on islands or plains.

In Pennsylvania, 70.7 percent of sites are outside of clusters (174; density: 0.00 per square kilometer). Most of these sites were obtained from Dan Cassedy, Dolores Elliott, Nancy Wisser, in the NEARA Archive, and at the Pennsylvania Historical and Museum Commission. Smaller numbers were contributed by Corey Hart, David Cuneo, Patrick Cooke and Barbara DeLong, Larry Mulligan, Norman Muller, Peter Waksman, Richard Adverbly, Rolf Cachat-Schilling, Ryan Hurd, Victoria Rourke, Frederick Werkheiser and Donald Repsher, and the author. These sites have an average number of 7.4 structures

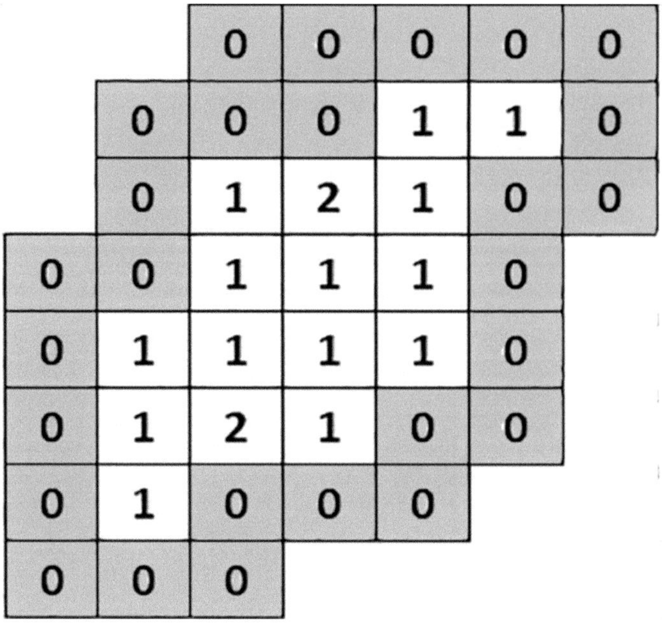

Figure 81: Schematic of Pennsylvania Cluster No. 2.

per site (range: 1–72), and an average of 1.4 types per site. Most structure types are found outside of clusters in Pennsylvania, with the exception of platforms, enclosures, and niches. The predominant types are rock piles (sixty-eight), cairns (963), stone rows (twenty-four), and marked stones (twenty-four). Their average elevation is 1,086.2 feet (range: 95–2,328 feet); their average distance to water is 364.5 meters (range: 0–1,610 meters). Their average stream rank is 2.4 (range: 1–7); their average slope is 15.5 percent (range: 0.0–67.5). Their average distance to fault is 8.01 km (range: 0.03–33.17 km); the average distance to the head-of-tide is 173.58 km (range: 36.94–279.82 km); their average distance to minor watershed is 2.73 km (range: 0.01–11.27 km). Their average NND is 4.42 km (range: 0.10–38.72 km). Sites near headwater streams (sixty-five) and named streams (fifty-eight) are nearly equally predominant, followed by rivers (thirty-one); no sites are adjacent to the ocean, on which Pennsylvania has no frontage. Sites are predominantly in low fertility soils (seventy-three) and naturally infertile soils (fifty-eight), with smaller numbers in agriculturally productive soils (twenty-seven) and pasture lands (fifteen). The predominant environmental settings are slopes (sixty-eight) and hilltops (sixty-five), with fewer in valleys (twenty-three), on islands and plains (seven each), and on shores (four).

Rhode Island Cluster No. 1 Pachaug-Beach Pond (Figure 82, Plate 57)

This is a very large, irregularly shaped cluster of 252 sites containing *c.* 1,938 structures, overlapping the border between New London County in eastern Connecticut and Washington County in western Rhode Island, within an area of 228 square kilometers (density: 1.11 per square kilometer). Its main axis is east-northeast to west-southwest. It is located on the watershed between the Pawcatuck and Thames drainages. Most of the sites in this cluster were reported by Steve DiMarzo, James and Mary Gage, Walter van

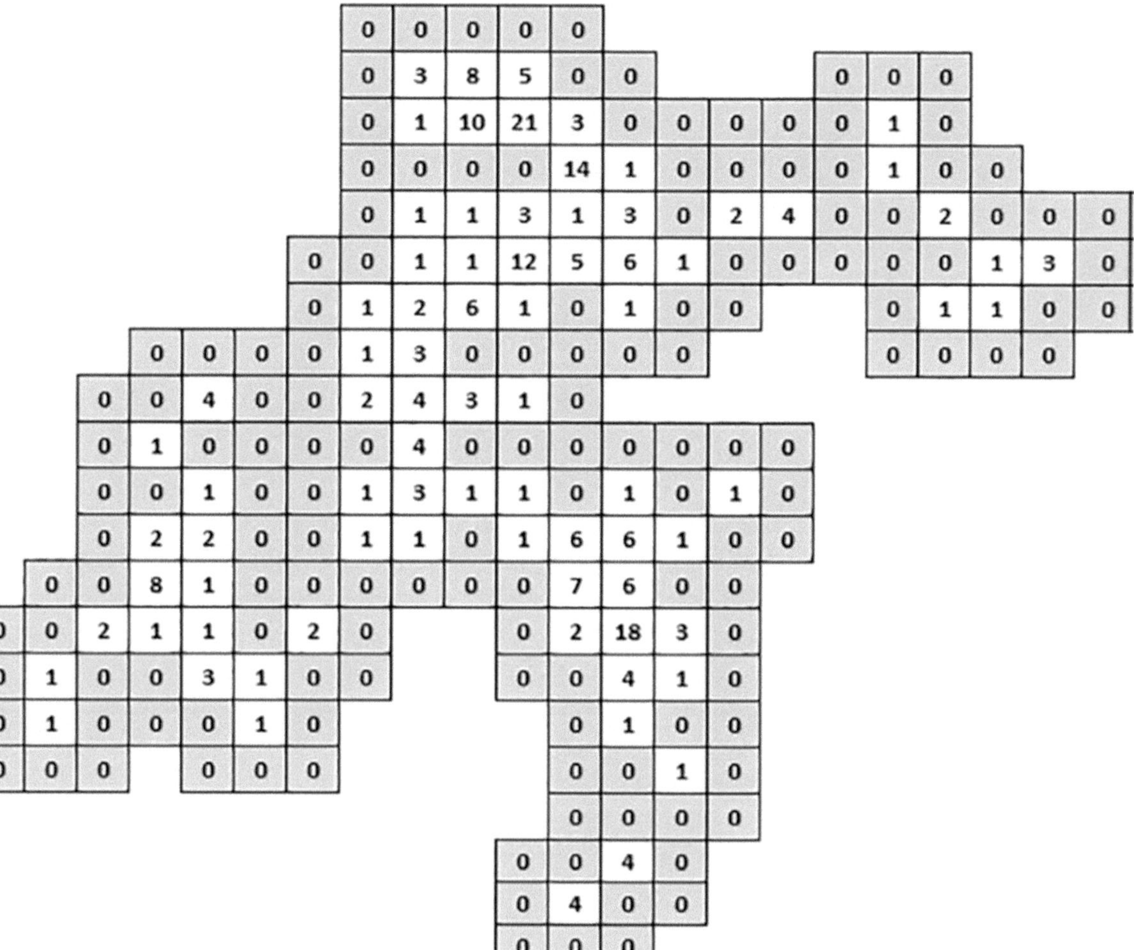

Figure 82: Schematic of Rhode Island Cluster No. 1.

Roggen, and Mark Starr, with others reported by Norman Muller, Doug Schwartz, Peter Anick, a web denizen of Peter Waksman's rockpiles blog whose handle is "badbadpotato," and the NEARA Archive.[39] The cluster has a VMR of 3.75 and a chi-square value of 847.40, and there is a 0.00 chance of its sites being randomly or uniformly distributed. The average NND is 0.24 km (range: 0.07–2.02 km). The average number of structures per site is very high, 21.5 (range: 1–681), with an average of 2.4 types of structures per site. The distribution of types strongly favors rock piles (136), cairns (eighty-nine) and stone rows (sixty), with lesser but still significant numbers of balanced rocks (fifty-six), split boulders (forty), U-shaped structures (thirty-nine), effigies (thirty-two), enclosures (thirty-two), niches (thirty), and chambers (twenty-nine). All other structure types occur in the cluster. The average stream rank is 1.2 (range: 1–3); the average slope is 10.9 percent (range: 0.0–52.5). The average elevation is 359.3 feet (range: 103–501 feet); the average distance to nearest water is 260.1 meters (range: 0–900 meters). The average distance to nearest fault is 3.22 km (range: 0.09–8.79 km); the average distance to the head-of-tide is 18.50 km (range: 1.84–33.04 km); the average distance to minor watershed boundary is 0.92 km (range: 0.00–3.78 km). There is a strong preference for sites with respect to swamps (102), brooks (sixty-four), ponds (forty-three), and headwater streams (forty); and lakes and the ocean were not utilized. Soil fertility is strongly skewed in favor of sites in low fertility soils (157) and naturally infertile soils (seventy-three), with smaller numbers in agriculturally productive soils (twenty) and in pasture lands (five). The predominant environmental settings are slopes (145), with lesser numbers in valleys (forty-four) and on hilltops (forty-three), and much fewer on shores (fourteen), plains (five), and islands (one).

Rhode Island Cluster No. 2 Carr's Pond (Figure 83)

This is a small, roughly linear cluster of twenty-one sites containing 330 structures in western Rhode Island, within an area of twenty-eight square kilometers (density: 0.75 per square kilometer). Its main axis is northeast to southwest. It is entirely within the town of West Greenwich in Kent County, and is entirely within the Pawtuxet drainage. Most of the sites in this cluster were reported by Steve DiMarzo and James and Mary Gage, with others reported by Tom Paul and the Rhode Island Historic Preservation and Heritage Commission.[40] The cluster has a VMR of 4.52 and a chi-square value of 122.14, and there is a 0.00 chance of its sites being randomly or uniformly distributed. The average NND is 0.22 km (range: 0.10–0.46 km). The average number of structures per site is fairly high, 15.7 (range: 1–58), with an average of 2.3 types of structures per site. The distribution of types strongly favors rock piles (eleven), split boulders (ten), enclosures (six), and balanced rocks (five). Petroglyphs, inscriptions, stone circles, mounds, platforms, and unique structures do not occur in the cluster. The average stream rank is 1.2 (range: 1–2); the average slope is 12.3 percent (range: 1.0–25.0). The average elevation is 356.0 feet (range: 293–423 feet); the average distance to nearest

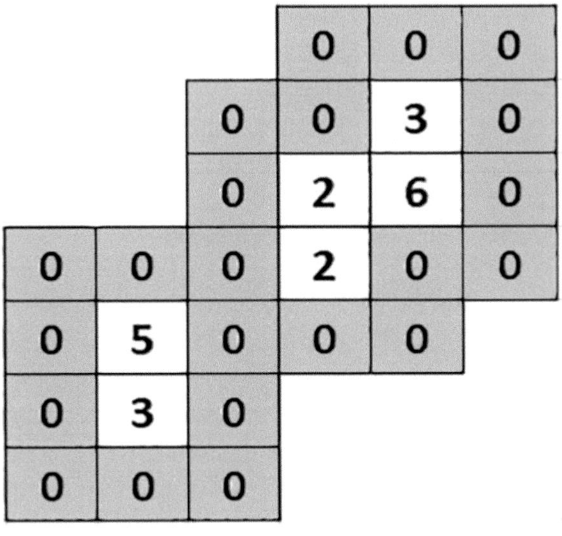

Figure 83: Schematic of Rhode Island Cluster No. 2.

water is 188.3 meters (range: 0–620 meters). The average distance to nearest fault is 4.51 km (range: 1.26–7.59 km); the average distance to the head-of-tide is 38.39 km (range: 18.87–45.17 km); the average distance to minor watershed boundary is 0.53 km (range: 0.03–1.93 km). There is a strong preference for sites with respect to Carr's Pond itself (eleven); and lakes and the ocean were not utilized. Soil fertility is about equal among sites in low fertility soils (seven) and naturally infertile soils (eight), and agriculturally productive soils (six); and none in pasture lands. The predominant environmental settings are on slopes (sixteen), with smaller numbers in valleys (four) and on hilltops (one); there are none on islands, plains, or shores.

Rhode Island Cluster No. 3 Wickaboxet (Figure 84)

This is a small, roughly oval cluster of forty-one sites containing *c.* 814 structures in western Rhode Island, within an area of 41 square kilometers (density: 1.00 per square kilometer). Its main axis is east-southeast to west-northwest. It is entirely within the town of West Greenwich in Kent County, and is entirely within the Pawcatuck drainage. All but one of the sites in this cluster were reported by Steve DiMarzo; the exception was on file at the Rhode Island Historic and Heritage Preservation Commission. The cluster has a VMR of 2.46 and a chi-square value of 98.54, and there is a 0.00 chance of its sites being randomly or uniformly distributed. The average NND is 0.21 km (range: 0.08–0.97 km). The average number of structures per site is rather high, 19.9 (range: 1–109), with an average number of types of 3.4. There was a predominance of rock piles (thirty-five), split boulders (twenty-four), and balanced rocks (twenty-two). Petroglyphs, inscriptions, mounds, and platforms do not occur in the cluster. The average stream rank is 1.3 (range: 1–2); the average slope is 10.3 percent (range: 4.0–25.0). The average elevation is 430.1 feet (range: 286–560 feet); the average distance to nearest water is 215.1 meters (range: 0–800 meters). The average distance to nearest fault is 5.59 km (range: 0.06–14.42 km); the average distance to the head-of-tide is 37.36 km (range: 35.51–39.58 km); the average distance to minor watershed boundary is 1.63 km (range:

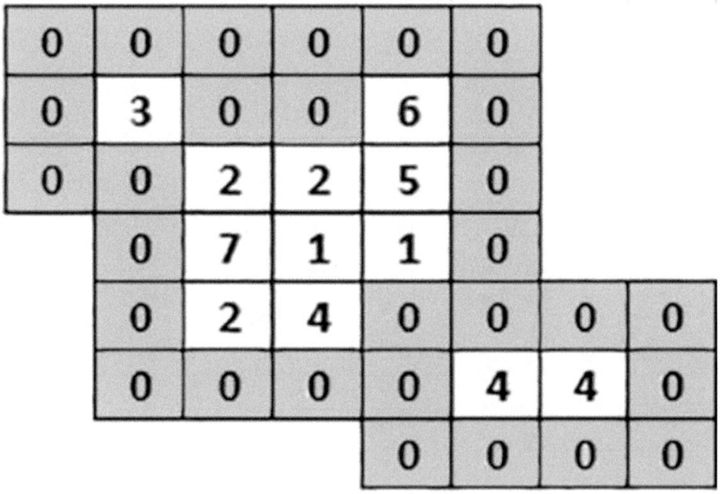

0	0	0	0	0	0	
0	3	0	0	6	0	
0	0	2	2	5	0	
	0	7	1	1	0	
0	2	4	0	0	0	0
0	0	0	0	4	4	0
			0	0	0	0

Figure 84: Schematic of Rhode Island Cluster No. 3.

0.11–4.41 km). There is a strong preference for sites with respect to brooks (twenty-one) and swamps (twelve); and rivers, lakes, and the ocean were not utilized. Soil fertility is skewed in favor of sites in low fertility soils (twenty-five) and naturally infertile soils (twelve), with smaller numbers in agriculturally productive soils (four) and none in pasture lands. The predominant environmental settings are on slopes (twenty-five) and in valleys (fourteen), with fewer on hilltops (two); there are none on islands, plains, or shores.

Rhode Island Cluster No. 4 Barber Road (Figure 85)

This is a small, tightly packed circular cluster of seventeen sites containing 272 structures in western Rhode Island, within an area of 15 square kilometers (density: 1.13 per square kilometer). It is entirely located within Washington County, and is entirely within the Pawcatuck drainage. The sites in this cluster were all reported by Steve DiMarzo. The cluster has a VMR of 5.59 and a chi-square value of 78.30, and there is a 0.00 chance of its sites being randomly or uniformly distributed. The average NND is 0.17 km (range: 0.07–0.82 km). The average number of structures per site is fairly high, 16.0 (range: 1–56), with an average of 3.7 types of structures per site. The distribution of types strongly favors rock piles (fifteen) and balanced rocks (ten). Chambers, petroglyphs, inscriptions, and platforms do not occur in the cluster. The average stream rank is 1.9 (range: 1–3); the average slope is 7.4 percent (range: 4.0–20.0). The average elevation is 308.5 feet (range: 254–373 feet); the average distance to nearest water is 380.0 meters (range: 20–640 meters). The average distance to nearest fault is 2.79 km (range: 1.38–4.40 km); the average distance to the head-of-tide is 31.97 km (range: 31.48–32.97 km); the average distance to minor watershed boundary is 2.47 km (range: 1.45–2.83 km). There is a strong preference for sites with respect to swamps (nine) and rivers (eight); no other locations were utilized. Soil fertility is skewed in favor of sites in low fertility soils (nine) and agriculturally productive soils (six), with smaller numbers in naturally infertile soils (two) and none in pasture lands. The predominant environmental settings are on slopes (sixteen), with only one in a valley; no other environmental settings are used.

0	0	0	
0	3	0	0
0	10	4	0
0	0	0	0

Figure 85: Schematic of Rhode Island Cluster No. 4.

Rhode Island Cluster No. 5 Coventry (Figure 86)

This is a small, roughly oval cluster of thirty-one sites containing 600 structures in central Rhode Island, within an area of 31 square kilometers (density: 1.00 per square kilometer). Its main axis is east-southeast to west-northwest. It is located on the boundary between Providence and Kent Counties, and is also on the watershed between the Pawcatuck and Pawtuxet drainages. Most of the sites in this cluster were reported by Steve DiMarzo, with four in the NEARA archive and one reported by Norman Muller. The cluster has a VMR of 5.07 and a chi-square value of 152.15, and there is a 0.00 chance of its sites being randomly or uniformly distributed. The average NND is 0.45 km (range: 0.09–0.64 km). The average number of structures per site is fairly high, 19.4 (range: 1–130), with an average of 2.6 types of structures per site. The distribution of types strongly favors rock piles (twenty-four) and balanced rocks (thirteen). Petroglyphs, inscriptions, mounds, and unique structures do not occur in the cluster. The average stream rank is 1.7 (range: 1–2); the average slope is 9.0 percent (range: 4.0–20.0). The average elevation is 481.8 feet (range: 396–605 feet); the average distance to nearest water is 258.7 meters (range: 40–800 meters). The average distance to nearest fault is 5.86 km (range: 0.34–14.43 km); the average distance to the head-of-tide is 39.44 km (range: 24.58–48.53 km); the average distance to minor watershed boundary is 2.10 km (range: 0.35–4.33 km). There was a very strong preference for sites with respect to brooks (twenty-two) and headwater streams (six); the only other type of water resources utilized was swamps (three). Soil fertility is skewed in favor of sites in low fertility soils (twenty), with smaller numbers in agriculturally productive soils (eight) and naturally infertile soils (three) and none in pasture lands. The predominant environmental settings are slopes (twenty), with fewer in valleys (eight), hilltops (two), and shores (one); none are on islands or plains or the ocean.

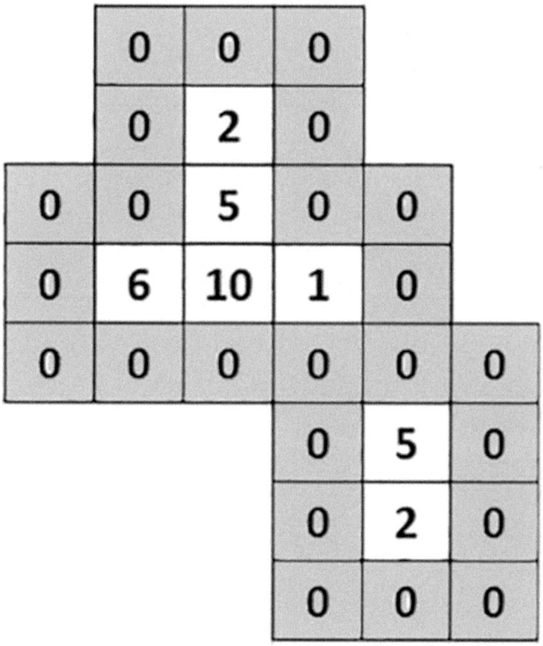

Figure 86: Schematic of Rhode Island Cluster No. 5.

Rhode Island Cluster No. 6 Nelson Pond (Figure 87)

This is a small, roughly oval cluster of fifteen sites containing thirty-four structures in southeastern Rhode Island, within an area of 23 square kilometers (density: 0.65 per square kilometer). Its main axis is southeast to northwest. It is entirely within the town of Middletown in Newport County, and is in the coastal zone. The sites in this cluster were all reported by Steve DiMarzo. The cluster has a VMR of 6.85 and a chi-square value of 150.61, and there is a 0.00 chance of its sites being randomly or uniformly distributed. The average NND is 0.37 km (range: 0.08–1.58 km). The average number of structures per site is well below the average of 5.5, 2.3 (range: 1–6), with an average of 1.3 types of structures per site. The distribution of types strongly favors enclosures (seven) and rock piles (five). Chambers, split boulders, balanced rocks, inscriptions, stone circles, effigies, mounds, platforms, niches, and unique structures do not occur in the cluster. The average stream rank is 1.9 (range: 1–8); the average slope is 1.7 perfect (range: 0.0–5.5). The average elevation is 32.9 feet (range: 0–66 feet); the average distance to nearest water is 83.3 meters (range: 0–260 meters). The average distance to nearest fault is 0.87 km (range: 0.16–1.43 km); the average distance to the head-of-tide is 0.48 km (range: 0.00–0.88 km); the average distance to minor watershed boundary is 0.61 km (range: 0.02–0.97 km). There is a strong preference for sites with respect to Nelson Pond (eleven); and brooks, lakes, and swamps were not utilized. Soil fertility is skewed in favor of sites in naturally infertile soils (thirteen), with smaller numbers in agriculturally productive soils (one) and in low fertility soils (one), and none in pasture lands. The predominant environmental settings are on shores (six), with smaller numbers on hilltops (four), in valleys (three), and on slopes and the ocean (one each); there are none on islands or plains.

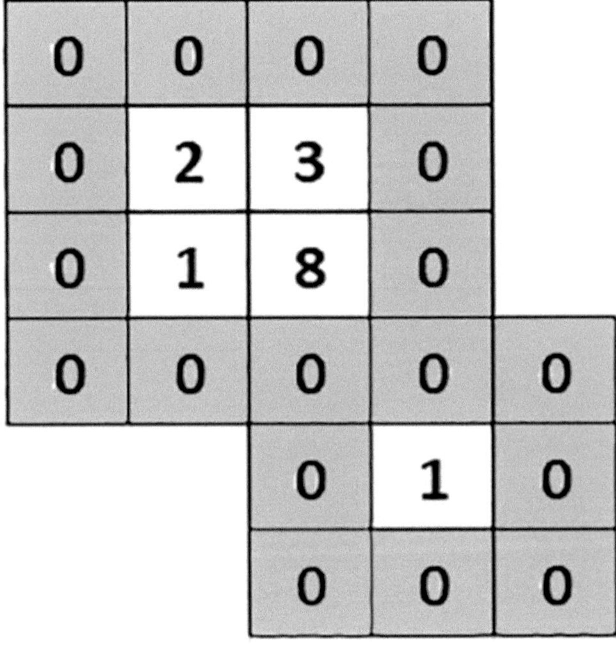

Figure 87: Schematic of Rhode Island Cluster No. 6.

Rhode Island Cluster No. 7 Tefft Hill (Figure 88)

This is a small, roughly oval cluster of twenty-eight sites containing 557 structures in western Rhode Island, within an area of 34 square kilometers (density: 0.82 per square kilometer). Its main axis is east-southeast to west-northwest. It is entirely located within Washington County, and is entirely within the Pawcatuck drainage. The sites in this cluster were all reported by Steve DiMarzo. The cluster has a VMR of 4.39 and a chi-square value of 149.20, and there is a 0.00 chance of its sites being randomly or uniformly distributed. The average NND is 0.14 km (range: 0.08–0.31 km). The average number of structures per site is rather high, 19.9 (range: 1–62), with an average of 3.4 types of structures per site. The distribution of types strongly favors rock piles (twenty-seven), standing stones (fourteen), and split boulders (fourteen). Inscriptions, mounds, and platforms do not occur in the cluster. The average stream rank is 1.1 (range: 1–2); the average slope is 8.7 percent (range: 0.0–20.0). The average elevation is 351.1 feet (range: 232–479 feet) the average distance to nearest water is 347.9 meters (range: 20–1,000 meters). The average distance to nearest fault is 3.23 km (range: 1.91–5.04 km); the average distance to the head-of-tide is 31.53 km (range: 30.15–33.09 km); the average distance to minor watershed boundary is 1.63 km (range: 0.23–3.57 km). There was a very strong preference for sites with respect to swamps (nineteen); and lakes and the ocean were not utilized. Soil fertility is skewed in favor of sites in low fertility soils (twenty) and agriculturally productive soils (eight), and there were none in naturally infertile soils or pasture lands. The predominant environmental settings are on slopes (twenty-four), with smaller numbers in valleys (three) and on plains (one); there are none on hilltops, islands, or shores.

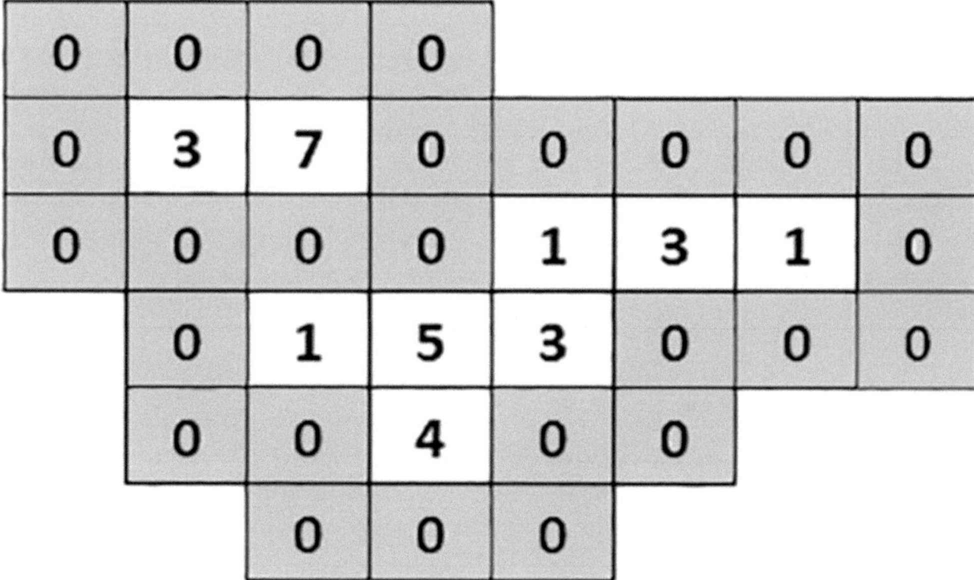

Figure 88: Schematic of Rhode Island Cluster No. 7.

Rhode Island Cluster No. 8 Richmond (Figure 89)

This is a small, tightly packed oval cluster of thirty-three sites containing 783 structures in western Rhode Island, within an area of 19 square kilometers (density: 1.74 per square kilometer). Its main axis is north-south. It is entirely within the town of Richmond in Washington County, and is entirely within the Pawcatuck drainage. The sites in this cluster were all reported by Steve DiMarzo. The cluster has a VMR of 4.04 and a chi-square value of 76.80, and there is a 0.00 chance of its sites being randomly or uniformly distributed. The average NND is 0.11 km (range: 0.08–0.17 km). The average number of structures per site is rather high, 18.6 (range: 2–93), with an average of 3.9 types of structures per site. The distribution of types strongly favors rock piles (twenty-seven), split boulders (seventeen), balanced rocks (sixteen), stone rows (twelve), and enclosures (twelve). Chambers, standing stones, inscriptions, mounds, and unique structures do not occur in the cluster. The average stream rank is 1.5 (range: 1–2); the average slope is 11.7 percent (range: 4.0–25.0). The average elevation is 314.5 feet (range: 206–438 feet); the average distance to nearest water is 226.4 meters (range: 20–590 meters). The average distance to nearest fault is 2.09 km (range: 1.17–3.01 km); the average distance to the head-of-tide is 30.23 km (range: 29.53–31.18 km); the average distance to minor watershed boundary is 1.57 km (range: 0.84–2.10 km). There is a strong preference for sites with respect to swamps (seventeen), headwater streams (nine), and rivers (seven); and brooks, lakes, ponds, and the ocean were not utilized. Soil fertility is skewed in favor of sites in low fertility soils (twenty-seven), with smaller numbers in agriculturally productive soils (one) and naturally infertile soils (one), and none in pasture lands. The predominant environmental settings are on slopes (twenty-four), with smaller numbers in valleys (five) and on hilltops (four); no other environmental settings are used.

In Rhode Island, 25.8 percent of sites are outside of clusters (117; density: 0.03 per square kilometer). Most of these sites were reported by Steve DiMarzo, in the NEARA Archive, and at the Rhode Island Historic Preservation Commission. Smaller numbers were contributed by Charles Devine, David Cuneo, Doug Schwartz, Ed Lenik, Jim Porter, Joe Niernan, Nancy Hunt, Norman Muller, Peter Anick, Suzanne Tjoelker, Ted Ballard, Tim Fohl, Tim MacSweeney, and the author. These sites have an average number of 7.2 structures per site (range: 1–175), and an average of 1.8 types per site. With the

0	0	0	0
0	8	10	0
0	5	0	0
0	0	10	0
	0	0	0

Figure 89: Schematic of Rhode Island Cluster No. 8.

exception of mounds, all structure types are found outside of clusters in Rhode Island. The predominant types are rock piles (forty-four), stone rows (thirty-four), and balanced rocks (twenty-nine). Their average elevation is 231.1 feet (range: 0–771 feet); their average distance to water is 257.0 meters (range: 0–1,400 meters). Their average stream rank is 2.3 (range: 1–8); their average slope is 8.8 percent (range: 0.0–25.0). Their average distance to fault is 3.26 km (range: 0.02–28.77 km); the average distance to the head-of-tide is 15.22 km (range: 0.00–63.26 km); their average distance to minor watershed is 2.05 km (range: 0.01–8.83 km). Their average NND is 1.47 km (range: 0.09–7.04 km). All water types are utilized, but there is a predominance of sites near headwater streams (thirty-four), followed by named streams (twenty), swamps (nineteen), ponds (sixteen), and the ocean (eleven). Sites in low fertility soils predominate (forty-eight), followed by agriculturally productive soils (twenty-nine), pasture lands (twenty-four), and naturally infertile soils (sixteen). The predominant environmental settings are on slopes (forty-one), with nearly equal numbers on hilltops (twenty-five), in valleys (twenty-two), and on shores (nineteen); there are smaller numbers on plains (seven) and islands (three).

South Carolina Cluster No. 1 Northwestern McCormick County (Figure 90)

This is a small, irregularly-shaped cluster of twenty-four sites containing 103 structures in western South Carolina, within an area of 67 square kilometers (density: 0.36 per square kilometer). Its main axis is southeast to northwest. It is entirely located within McCormick County, and is entirely within the Savannah drainage, the flooded basin of the Savannah River forming its southwestern border. The sites in this cluster were all on file at the South Carolina Institute for Archaeology, and were filed by the U.S. Forest Service. The cluster has a VMR of 5.51 and a chi-square value of 363.72, and there is a 0.00 chance of its sites being randomly or uniformly distributed. The average NND is 0.55 km (range: 0.11–1.79 km). The average number of structures per site is slightly below the average of 5.5, 4.3 (range: 1–36), with an average of 1.0 types of structures per site. The distribution of types strongly favors rock piles (twenty-two). The only other types which occur in the cluster are cairns (two). The average stream rank is 2.8 (range: 1–6); the average slope is 8.1 percent (range: 0.0–27.5). The average elevation is 367.7 feet (range: 331–401 feet); the average distance to nearest water is 124.0 meters (range: 0–447 meters). The average distance to nearest fault is 6.26 km (range: 0.12–13.57 km); the average distance to the head-of-tide is 236.08 km (range: 230.39–240.83 km); the average distance to minor watershed boundary is 4.59 km (range: 0.29–10.34 km). There is a strong preference for sites with respect to headwater streams (twelve); and ponds, swamps, and the ocean were not utilized. Soil fertility is heavily skewed in favor of sites in agriculturally productive soils (twenty-eight), with small numbers in low fertility soils (three) and naturally infertile soils (one), and none in pasture lands. The predominant environmental settings are on hilltops (twelve) and slopes (seven), with smaller numbers on shores (three), islands and valleys (one each); there are none on plains.

0	0	0					
0	1	0	0	0	0		
0	0	1	1	5	0		
	0	0	2	0	0	0	
		0	0	1	1	0	
		0	3	0	0	0	0
	0	0	0	0	0	1	0
	0	2	1	0	1	0	0
	0	0	0	1	1	0	0	0
		0	0	0	0	1	0
			0	1	0	0
			0	0	0

Figure 90: Schematic of South Carolina Cluster No. 1.

South Carolina Cluster No. 2 Central McCormick County (Figure 91)

This is a small, oval cluster of eighteen sites containing ninety structures in western South Carolina, within an area of 33 square kilometers (density: 0.55 per square kilometer). Its main axis is east-southeast to west-northwest. It is entirely located within McCormick County, and is entirely within the Savannah drainage, the flooded Savannah River basin forming its southwestern border. The sites in this cluster were all on file at the South Carolina Institute for Archaeology, where they were reported by the U.S. Forest Service. The cluster has a VMR of 12.40 and a chi-square value of 396.90, and there is a 0.00 chance of its sites being randomly or uniformly distributed. The average NND is 0.43 km (range: 0.08–1.70 km). The average number of structures per site is slightly below the average of 5.5, 5.0 (range: 1–23), with an average of 1.0 types of structures per site. The distribution of types very strongly favors rock piles (eighteen), which is the only type to occur in the cluster. The average stream rank is 3.3 (range: 1–6); the average slope is 5.9 percent (range: 0–12.5). The average elevation is 372.6 feet (range: 342–400 feet); the average distance to nearest water is 165.2 meters (range: 0–423 meters). The average distance to nearest fault is 6.01 km (range: 3.48–8.27 km); the average distance to the head-of-tide is 224.76 km (range: 222.63–227.13 km); the average distance to minor watershed boundary is 2.85 km (range: 0.03–9.36 km). Site locations are about equally divided among lakes (seven), brooks (five), and headwater streams (six); and ponds, swamps, rivers, and the ocean were not utilized. Soil fertility is skewed in favor of sites in agriculturally productive soils (thirteen), with

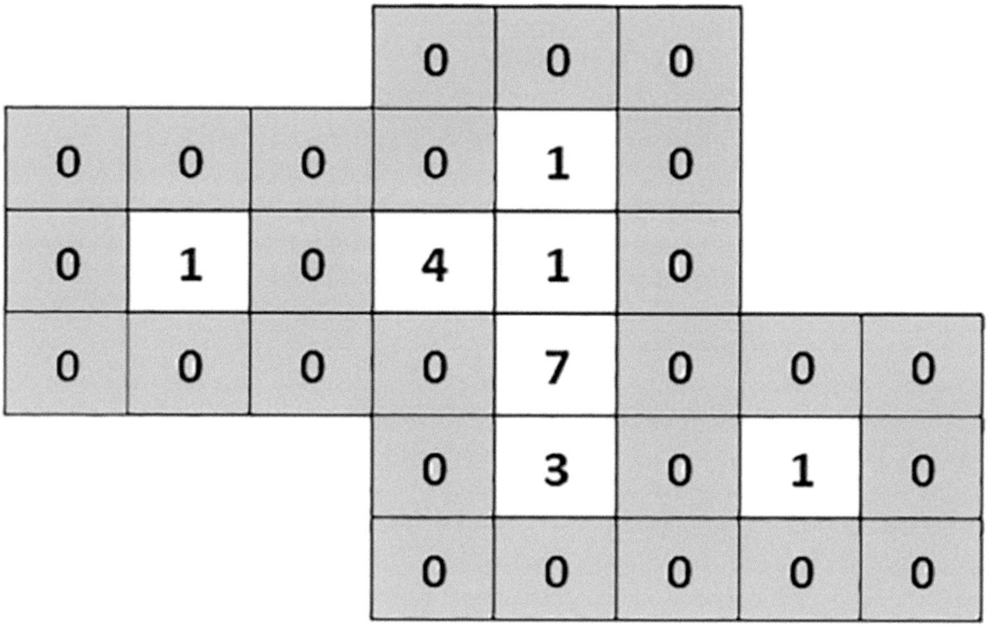

Figure 91: Schematic of South Carolina Cluster No. 2.

smaller numbers in naturally infertile soils (two), and none in low fertility soils and pasture lands. The predominant environmental settings are on slopes (eleven), with smaller numbers on hilltops (three), shores (two), islands and valleys (one each); there are none on plains.

South Carolina Cluster No. 3 Parksville (Figure 92, Plate 58)

This is a relatively linear cluster of thirty-five sites containing 275 structures in western South Carolina and eastern Georgia, within an area of 60 square kilometers (density: 0.58 per square kilometer). Its main axis is east to west. It is mostly located within McCormick County, but there are five sites in Lincoln County, Georgia, across the flooded basin of the Savannah River. It is entirely within the Savannah River drainage. That some of the sites are on islands in the river suggests that there may very well be submerged sites in the cluster which are not recorded. The sites in this cluster were all on file at either the South Carolina Institute for Archaeology, where they were reported by the U.S. Forest Service, or the University of Georgia Archaeology Laboratory, where they were reported by Carolina Archaeological Consultants, New South Associates, and Southeastern Archaeological Services. The cluster has a VMR of 6.59 and a chi-square value of 388.76, and there is a 0.00 chance of its sites being randomly or uniformly distributed. The average NND is 0.47 km (range: 0.10–1.89 km). The average number of structures per site is somewhat above the average of 5.5, 7.9 (range: 1–52), with an average of 1.0 types of structures per site. The only types present are cairns (twenty-six) and rock piles (nine). The average stream rank is 5.6 (range: 1–6); the average slope is 6.1 percent (range: 0.0–12.5). The average elevation is 351.9 feet (range: 331–417 feet); the average distance to nearest water is 108.8 meters (range: 0–385 meters). The average distance to nearest fault is 3.70 km (range: 0.04–12.63 km); the average distance to the head-of-tide is 220.15 km (range: 217.86–223.46 km); the average distance to minor watershed boundary is 4.75 km (range: 0.01–8.69 km). There is a strong preference for sites with respect to lakes (twenty-nine), due to the proximity of the cluster to the flooded basin of the Savannah River; and ponds, swamps, and the ocean were not utilized. Soil fertility is skewed in favor of sites in agriculturally productive soils (twenty-eight), with smaller numbers in naturally infertile soils (three), and none in low fertility soils or in pasture lands. The predominant environmental settings are on slopes (fourteen) and shores (ten), with smaller numbers on hilltops (seven), islands (three), and plains (one); there are none in valleys.

In South Carolina, 68.6 percent of sites are outside of clusters (157; density: 0.00 per square kilometer). Most of these sites were reported by the South Carolina Institute for Archaeology and Anthropology, with some petroglyph sites reported by Tommy Charles.[41] These sites have an average number of 5.1 structures per site (range: 1–200), and an average of 1.1 types per site. The predominant structure types outside of clusters in South Carolina are rock piles (seventy-seven), marked stones (thirty-five), petroglyphs (twenty-four), and cairns (twenty); U-shaped structures, chambers, split boulders, balanced rocks, inscriptions, mounds, platforms, enclosures, and niches are absent. Their average elevation is 672.5 feet (range: 0–2,835 feet); their average distance to water is 202.4 meters (range: 0–960 meters). Their average stream rank is 1.9 (range: 1–6); their average slope is 14.5 percent (range: 0.0–67.5). Their average distance to fault is 6.47 km (range: 0.04–55.36 km); the average distance to the head-of-tide is 277.44 km (range: 125.50–378.90 km); their average distance to minor watershed is 2.80 km (range: 0.01–10.34 km). Their average NND is 4.86 km (range: 0.19–19.77 km). There is a predominance of sites located near

							0	0	0		
							0	1	0		
	0	0	0		0	0	0	1	0	0	0
0	0	1	0	0	0	3	0	4	0	1	0
0	1	0	1	1	0	1	5	10	1	0	0
0	0	0	0	0	1	0	0	2	0	1	0
				0	0	0	0	0	0	0	0

Figure 92: Schematic of South Carolina Cluster No. 3.

headwater streams (ninety-seven) followed by named streams (forty-four). Swamps and the ocean were not utilized. Sites are predominantly in low fertility soils (sixty-eight), with relatively equal numbers in naturally infertile soils (thirty-five), agriculturally productive soils (twenty-nine), and pasture lands (twenty-five). The predominant environmental settings are on slopes (seventy-five), hilltops (forty-three), and in valleys (twenty-seven), with smaller numbers on plains (seven), shores (three), and islands (two).

Vermont Cluster No. 1 Pomfret (Figure 93)

This is a large, roughly oval cluster of eighty sites containing *c.* 303 structures in eastern Vermont, within an area of 132 square kilometers (density: 0.61 per square kilometer). Its main axis is north to south. It is entirely located within Windsor County, and it is entirely within the Connecticut drainage. The sites in this cluster were reported by Doug Schwartz, Norman Muller, and the NEARA Archive. The cluster has a VMR of 4.01 and a chi-square value of 525.28, and there is a 0.00 chance of its sites being randomly or uniformly distributed. The average NND is 0.50 km (range: 0.09–1.70 km). The average number of structures per site is somewhat below the average of 5.5, 3.8 (range: 1–22), with an average of 1.7 types of structures per site. The distribution of types strongly favors standing stones (thirty-five), petroglyphs (twenty-seven) stone rows (nineteen), and rock piles (eighteen). U-shaped structures, inscriptions, mounds, platforms, niches, and unique structures do not occur in the cluster. The average stream rank is 1.3 (range: 1–4); the average slope is

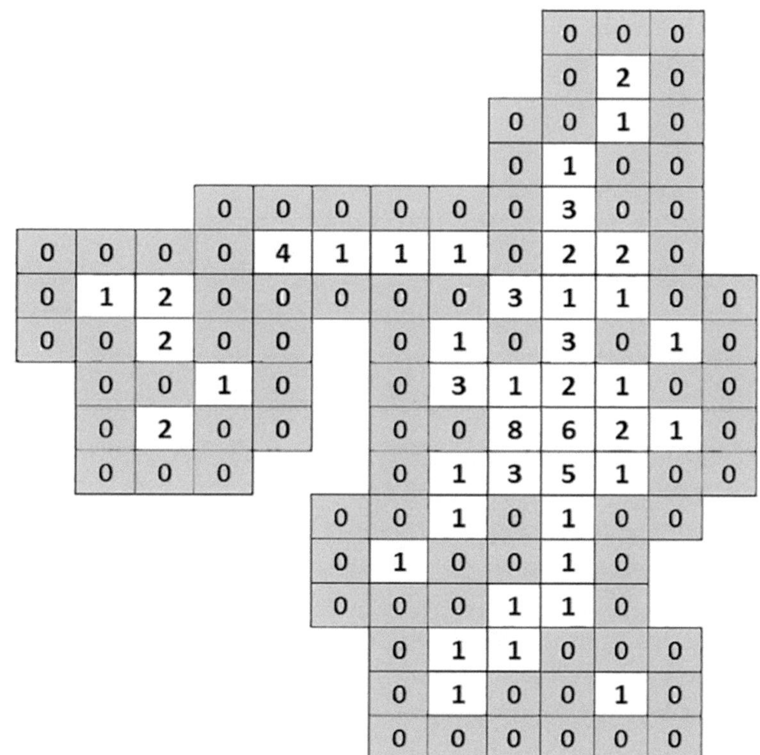

Figure 93: Schematic of Vermont Cluster No. 1.

24.8 percent (range: 2.5–47.5). The average elevation is 1,411.1 feet (range: 809–1,915 feet); the average distance to nearest water is 300.8 meters (range: 20–790 meters). The average distance to nearest fault is 17.22 km (range: 13.12–19.37 km); the average distance to the head-of-tide is 216.33 km (range: 208.99–223.34 km); the average distance to minor watershed boundary is 2.00 km (range: 0.05–6.53 km). There is a strong preference for sites with respect to headwater streams (fifty-three) and brooks (nineteen); and lakes and the ocean were not utilized. Soil fertility is skewed in favor of sites in low fertility soils (fifty) and naturally infertile soils (fourteen), with smaller numbers in agriculturally productive soils (two) and in pasture lands (three). The predominant environmental settings are on slopes (forty-six) and hilltops (twenty-three), with smaller numbers in valleys (eleven); no other environmental settings are used.

Vermont Cluster No. 2 Reading/Woodstock (Figure 94)

This is a small, roughly oval cluster of twenty-five sites containing *c.* ninety-six structures in eastern Vermont, within an area of 85 square kilometers (density: 0.29 per square kilometer). Its main axis is east-northeast to west-southwest. It is entirely located within Windsor County, and it is entirely within the Connecticut drainage. The sites in this cluster were reported by Doug Schwartz, Norman Muller, and in the NEARA Archive. The cluster has a VMR of 3.70 and a chi-square value of 310.90, and there is a 0.00 chance of its sites being randomly or uniformly distributed. The average NND is 0.85 km (range: 0.27–2.20 km). The average number of structures per site is somewhat below the average of 5.5, 3.8 (range: 1–16), with an average of 1.9 types of structures per site. The distribution of types strongly favors standing stones (ten), petroglyphs (nine), chambers (eight), and stone rows (six). Balanced rocks, inscriptions, mounds, platforms, niches, and unique structures do not occur in the cluster. The average stream rank is 1.2 (range: 1–2); the average slope is 21.7 percent (range: 4.0–47.5). The average elevation is 1,500.9 feet (range: 1,069–1,911 feet); the average distance to nearest water is 331.8 meters (range: 25–750 meters). The average distance to nearest fault is 12.36 km (range: 9.50–14.18 km); the average distance to the head-of-tide is 197.71 km (range: 193.44–202.04 km); the average distance to minor watershed boundary is 3.23 km (range: 0.52–8.22 km). There is a strong preference for sites with respect to headwater streams (sixteen) and brooks (nine); no other water types were utilized. Soil fertility is skewed in favor of sites in naturally infertile soils (twelve) and low fertility soils (eight), with smaller numbers in agriculturally productive soils (one) and in pasture lands (four). The predominant environmental settings are on slopes (sixteen), with smaller numbers in valleys (six) and hilltops (three); no other environmental settings are used.

Vermont Cluster No. 3 Royalton (Figure 95)

This is a small, roughly oval cluster of thirty-four sites containing *c.* 124 structures in eastern Vermont, within an area of 72 square kilometers (density: 0.47 per square kilometer). Its main axis is east-southeast to west-northwest. It is mostly located within Windsor County, but it overlaps into adjacent Orange County. It is entirely within the Connecticut drainage. The sites in this cluster were reported by Doug Schwartz, Norman Muller, and the NEARA Archive. The cluster has a VMR of 4.30 and a chi-square value

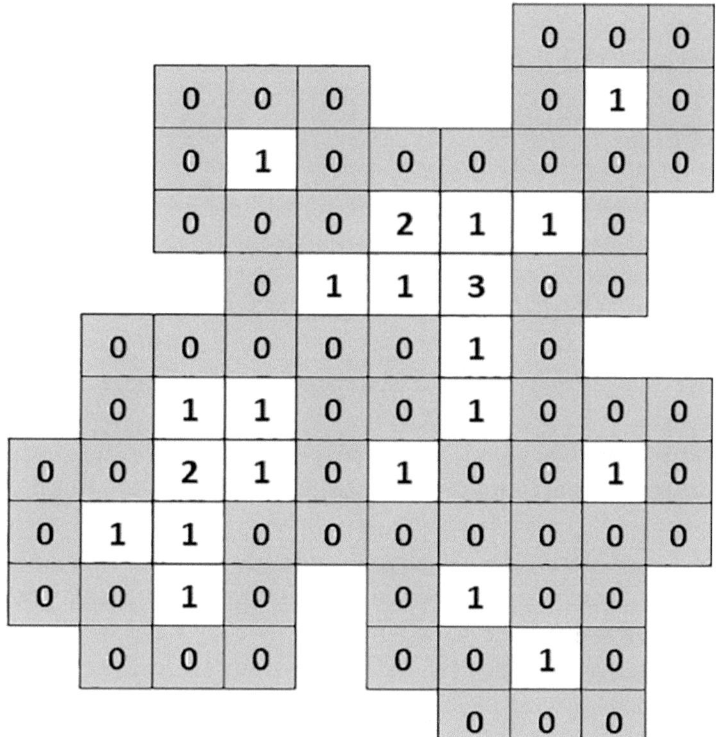

Figure 94: Schematic of Vermont Cluster No. 2.

Figure 95: Schematic of Vermont Cluster No. 3.

of 291.16, and there is a 0.00 chance of its sites being randomly or uniformly distributed. The average NND is 0.59 km (range: 0.13–1.44 km). The average number of structures per site is somewhat below the average of 5.5, 3.6 (range: 1–17), with an average of 1.8 types of structures per site. The distribution of types strongly favors chambers (seventeen) standing stones (eight), U-shaped structures (eight), and petroglyphs (seven). Inscriptions, mounds, platforms, enclosures, niches, and unique structures do not occur in the cluster. The average stream rank is 1.7 (range: 1–5); the average slope is 24.7 percent (range: 4.0–52.5). The average elevation is 954.4 feet (range: 495–1,601 feet); the average distance to nearest water is 274.9 meters (range: 25–890 meters). The average distance to nearest fault is 20.79 km (range: 18.10–23.91 km); the average distance to the head-of-tide is 232.57 km (range: 229.10–236.69 km); the average distance to minor watershed boundary is 2.93 km (range: 0.04–7.77 km). There is a strong preference for sites with respect to headwater streams (twenty-one); and lakes, swamps, and the ocean were not utilized. Soil fertility is skewed in favor of sites in naturally infertile soils (fourteen) and low fertility soils (ten), with smaller numbers in agriculturally productive soils (two), and none in pasture lands. The predominant environmental settings are on slopes (twenty-three), with smaller numbers in valleys (seven) and hilltops (four); no other environmental settings are used.

In Vermont, 60.4 percent of sites are outside of clusters (212; density: 0.01 per square kilometer). Most sites were reported by Doug Schwartz, Norman Muller, and in the NEARA Archive. Smaller numbers were contributed by Patrick Cooke and Barbara DeLong, Ed Lenik, Mary Stowe, Sarah Kohler, Tim Fohl, and Walter van Roggen.[42] These sites have an average number of 4.8 structures per site (range: 1–158), and an average of 1.4 types per site. Most structure types are found outside of clusters in Vermont, with the exception of inscriptions, mounds, and platforms. The predominant types are chambers (seventy-one), rock piles (sixty-three), cairns (thirty-six), stone rows (twenty-six), standing stones (twenty-five), and petroglyphs (twenty-two). Their average elevation is 1,214.5 feet (range: 111–3,712 feet); their average distance to water is 250.5 meters (range: 0–1,909 meters). Their average stream rank is 1.8 (range: 1–6); their average slope is 20.3 percent (range: 0.0–52.5). Their average distance to fault is 9.99 km (range: 0.01–34.88 km); the average distance to the head-of-tide is 191.24 km (range: 22.87–311.50 km); their average distance to minor watershed is 2.64 km (range: 0.00–8.14 km). Their average NND is 3.02 km (range: 0.15–35.01 km). There was a strong predominance of sites near headwater streams (120), followed by named streams (forty-seven); Vermont has no ocean frontage, so this setting is unavailable for use. Sites are predominantly in agriculturally productive soils (seventy-eight), followed by naturally infertile soils (sixty-four) and low fertility soils (fifty-one), and fewer in pasture lands (nineteen). The predominant environmental settings are slopes (108), followed by valleys (sixty-two) and hilltops (thirty), with smaller numbers on shores (seven), plains (four), and islands (one).

Virginia Cluster No. 1 Fairfax (Figure 96)

This is a small, tightly packed cluster of twenty-four sites containing 126 structures in northern Virginia, within an area of 16 square kilometers (density: 1.50 per square kilometer). Its main axis is east-northeast to west-southwest. It is entirely within the town of English Hills in Fairfax County, and is entirely within the Potomac drainage. Most of the sites in this cluster were reported in an article by Philip Mulford in the *Bulletin of the Virginia Archaeological Society*.[43] A few sites were on file at the Virginia State Historic Preservation Office, and one was reported by Tim MacSweeney.[44] The cluster has a VMR of 4.39 and a chi-square value of 65.83, and there is a 0.00 chance of its sites being randomly or uniformly distributed. The average NND is 0.14 km (range: 0.10–0.23 km). The average number of structures per site is close to the average of 5.5, 5.3 (range: 1–18), with an average of 1.0 types of structures per site. The only types present are rock piles (twenty-two) and cairns (two). The average stream rank is 2.2 (range: 1–5); the average slope is 19.0 percent (range: 0.0–57.5). The average elevation is 187.3 feet (range: 126–260 feet); the average distance to nearest water is 145.8 meters (range: 20–340 meters). The average distance to nearest fault is 3.49 km (range: 2.89–4.03 km); the average distance to the head-of-tide is 29.58 km (range: 28.81–30.25 km); the average distance to minor watershed boundary is 3.82 km (range: 3.26–4.23 km). There is a strong preference for sites with respect to headwater streams (seventeen) and rivers (seven); no other water types were utilized. Soil fertility is skewed in favor of sites in agriculturally productive soils (thirteen), with smaller numbers in naturally infertile soils (three), in low fertility soils (four), and in pasture lands (four). The predominant environmental settings are on slopes (seventeen), with smaller numbers on hilltops (five) and in valleys (two); no other environmental settings are used.

In Virginia, 64.2 percent of sites are outside of clusters (43; density: 0.00 per square kilometer). Most of these sites were reported by the Virginia State Historic Preservation Office or were in the writings of Gerard Fowkes. Smaller numbers were contributed by Dolores Elliott, Jack Hranicky, Kenneth Hill, Mary Green, Mike Futrell, Peter Anick, Peter Waksman, and Tim MacSweeney. A few sites were found in the writings of Thomas Jefferson and John Smith. These sites have an average number of 6.7 structures per site (range: 1–200), and an average of 1.2 types per site. Virginia has the most limited number of structure types outside of clusters: stone rows, U-shaped structures, standing stones, balanced rocks, inscriptions, effigies, mounds, platforms, enclosures, niches, and unique structures are absent. Rock piles predominate (twenty-five), followed by cairns (nine) and petroglyphs (nine). Their average elevation is 1,013.4 feet (range: 46–2,439 feet); their average distance to water is 244.2 meters (range: 25–810 meters). Their average stream

0	0	0	0
0	9	2	0
0	10	3	0
0	0	0	0

Figure 96: Schematic of Virginia Cluster No. 1.

rank is 2.6 (range: 1–7); their average slope is 16.6 percent (range: 1.0–37.5). Their average distance to fault is 5.14 km (range: 0.01–51.71 km); the average distance to the head-of-tide is 128.09 km (range: 7.70–261.07 km); their average distance to minor watershed is 2.51 km (range: 0.01–6.82 km). Their average NND is 1.0 km (range: 0.14–117.18 km). Sites are more often found near named streams (nineteen) and headwater streams (fourteen). Lakes, ponds, swamps, and the ocean were not utilized. There are relatively equal numbers of sites in naturally infertile soils (fourteen), agriculturally productive soils (twelve), low fertility soils (nine), and pasture lands (eight). The predominant environmental settings are on hilltops (fifteen); there were smaller numbers on slopes (eleven), in valleys (ten), on plains (six), and on shores (one); none are found on islands.

States Lacking Clusters

For the sake of completeness, below is a summary of the environmental and cultural parameters for the states and provinces that lacked clusters:

Delaware

There are a total of twelve sites in this state (density: 0.00 per square kilometer), most reported by the Delaware Valley Office of Archaeology and by local resident David Cuneo, with two reported by the Delaware State Historic Preservation Office. All are located in the Delaware drainage. The closest approximation to a cluster is a linear group of eight sites in Brandywine State Park, in an area of about 1.15 square kilometers. The average number of structures per site is 2.83 (range: 1–5); the average number of types is 1.0. The average elevation is 247.92 feet (range: 17–352 feet); the average distance to water is 317.92 meters (range: 10–1,410 meters). The average stream rank is 3.2 (range: 1–5); the average slope is 19.0 percent (range: 3.5–35.0). The average distance to nearest fault is 8.29 km (range: 1.87–33.60 km); the average distance to the head-of-tide is 84.18 km (range: 78.00–105.26 km); the average distance to minor watershed is 1.07 km (range: 0.25–2.77 km). Cairns were the most frequent structure type (six), the only others found being stone rows (three), rock piles (two), and split boulders (one). The average NND is 2.58 km (range: 0.12–10.18 km). All but one of the sites is located near a named stream (eleven); headwater streams, lakes, rivers, swamp, and the ocean were not utilized. Sites are predominantly in agriculturally productive soils (ten), with fewer in low fertility soils (two) and none in naturally infertile soils or pasture lands. The predominant environmental settings are slopes (seven), with fewer sites on hilltops and valleys (two each), or plains (one), and none on shores.

Maine

This state has the largest number of sites for a state without clusters (139; density: 0.00 per square kilometer). Most of them were reported by local residents Rob Sirois and Ros Strong, and the NEARA Archive. Smaller numbers were reported by local residents Don Wessel, Lee Hayes, Nan Millett, Scarlet Kinney, and Teig Tyrson, and by Ellen Cowie and James Petersen, Patrick Cooke and Barbara DeLong, Ed Lenik, Harvey Lipman,

James and Mary Gage, Peter Waksman, Steve DiMarzo, Valdimar Samuelson, Walter van Roggen, and the author.[45] The majority are located in coastal locations (twenty-seven), the Kennebec drainage (thirty-two), and the Saco drainage (twenty-nine), with smaller numbers in the Cromwell Brook, Damariscotta, Josias, Megunticook, Mousam, Nonesuch, Passagassawakeag, Pemaquid, Penobscot, Piscataqua, Presumpscott, Sheepscott, St. Croix, St. George, and Union drainages. The closest approximations to clusters are a group of four sites near Merrymeeting Bay in Bath, in an area of about 1.3 square kilometers; and a group of four sites near Mt. Hunger in Edgecomb, in an area of about 5.6 square kilometers. The average number of structures per site is 6.4 (range: 1–88); the average number of types is 1.6. The average elevation is 351.58 feet (range: 0–2,524 feet); the average distance to water is 248.56 meters (range: 0–1,680 meters). The average stream rank is 2.8 (range: 1–8); the average slope is 14.6 percent (range: 0.0–67.5). The average distance to nearest fault is 4.11 km (range: 0.01–22.47 km); the average distance to the head-of-tide is 32.70 km (range: 0.00–120.38 km); the average distance to minor watershed is 2.01 km (range: 0.01–8.16 km). With the exception of inscriptions and platforms, all structure types are present, but they are dominated by stone piles (fifty-one), cairns (thirty), stone rows (twenty-four), chambers (twenty-two), and balanced rocks (nineteen). The average NND is 5.23 km (range: 0.08–34.93 km). All water types are utilized, but there was near equal predominance for sites near headwater streams (forty-three) and named streams (thirty-eight). Sites are predominantly located in naturally infertile soils (fifty-nine) and agriculturally productive soils (fifty-two), with smaller numbers in low fertility soils (twenty-four) and in pasture lands (four). The predominant environmental settings are slopes (forty-nine), followed by valleys (thirty-three), hilltops (twenty-four), shores (fifteen), islands (twelve), and plains (six).

Maryland

There are a total of fifteen sites in this state (density: 0.00 per square kilometer), mostly reported by the Maryland State Historic Preservation Office, with smaller numbers reported in a location by C. A. Weslager and in the NEARA Archive.[46] The majority are in the Potomac drainage (ten), with the remainder in the Susquehanna drainage. The closest approximation to a cluster is a group of five sites, three in Maryland and two in West Virginia, on either side of the middle Potomac River near Cumberland, MD, in an area of about 30 square kilometers. The average number of structures per site is 2.3 (range: 1–9); the average number of types is 1.1. The average elevation is 681.87 feet (range: 7–2,223 feet); the average distance to water is 237.33 meters (range: 0–620 meters). The average stream rank is 3.7 (range: 1–7); the average slope is 15.0 percent (range: 0.0–50.0). The average distance to nearest fault is 14.76 km (range: 3.04–30.35 km); the average distance to the head-of-tide is 90.08 km (range: 7.38–182.58 km); the average distance to minor watershed is 2.19 km (range: 0.06–8.28 km). Site locations are most frequently adjacent to rivers (eight); and lakes, ponds, swamps, and the ocean were not utilized. More than half of the sites are in low fertility soils (eight), followed by soils in agriculturally productive soils (four) and naturally infertile soils (three); there are none in pasture lands. The predominant structure types are cairns (six) and petroglyphs (five); otherwise, only rock piles (three), stone rows (one), and stone circles (one) are present. The average NND is 2.22 km (range: 0.78–28.88 km). The predominant environmental settings are slopes (six), with fewer on islands (three), hilltops and plains (two each), and shores and valleys (one each).

New Brunswick

Nine sites were recorded (density: 0.00 per square kilometer), mostly by the New Brunswick Historic Tourism Office, with smaller numbers by Terry DeVeau and Ed Lenik.[47] All but one of the sites was in the St. John's drainage, the exception being in the St. Croix drainage. There are no groupings of more than two sites which approximate a cluster. The average number of structures per site is 11.7 (range: 1–65); the average number of types is 1.0. The average elevation is 354.00 feet (range: 15–1,296 feet); the average distance to water is 341.78 meters (range: 0–1,000 meters). The average stream rank is 2.4 (range: 1–5); the average slope could not be calculated. The average distance to nearest fault is 36.81 (range: 4.70–93.09 km); the average distance to the head-of-tide is 101.74 km (range: 13.81–180.32 km); the average distance to minor watershed could not be calculated due to problems accessing the Canadian data in GIS. The same problem applied to soil fertility assessment. The only structure types present are cairns (four), rock piles (three), stone rows (one), and petroglyphs (one). The average NND is 13.20 km (range: 0.51–31.77 km). There is a predominance of sites near rivers (four); and named streams, swamps, and the ocean were not utilized. The predominant environmental settings are plains (five), followed by slopes (two) and hilltops and valleys (one each); there are none on shores or on islands.

New Jersey

This state has the second highest total of sites which were not in clusters (81; density: 0.00 per square kilometer). The majority of sites are either in the Passaic (forty) or the Delaware (thirty-four) drainages, with small numbers in the Rahway, Raritan, and Hudson drainages. Most sites were reported by local resident Nancy Hunt, by the New Jersey State Historic Preservation Office, or in the NEARA archive, with smaller numbers reported by David Cuneo, Ed Lenik, Patrick Cooke and Barbara DeLong, Dolores Elliott, Norman Muller, and Frederick Werkheiser and Donald Repsher.[48] The closest approximation to a cluster is a group of six sites around Great Piece Meadows near North Caldwell, in an area of about 22 square kilometer. The average number of structures per site is 2.8 (range: 1–28); the average number of types is 1.2. The average elevation is 632.04 feet (range: 23–1,619 feet); the average distance to water is 263.46 meters (range: 3–970 meters). The average stream rank is 2.0 (range: 1–7); the average slope is 16.3 percent (range: 0.0–70.0). The average distance to nearest fault is 2.68 km (range: 0.12–14.20 km); the average distance to the head-of-tide is 50.72 km (range: 7.14–121.01 km); the average distance to minor watershed is 1.98 km (range: 0.01–5.30 km). Site locations are preferentially located with respect to headwater streams (twenty-eight), rivers (seventeen), brooks (fifteen), and swamps (thirteen); and no sites are adjacent to the ocean. The largest number of sites are in naturally infertile soils (thirty-eight), followed by sites in agriculturally productive soils (twenty-seven), low fertility soils (thirteen), and pasture lands (three). The predominant structure types are balanced rocks (twenty), marked stones (sixteen), and rock piles (eleven); inscriptions and platforms are absent from this state. The average NND is 3.63 km (range: 0.16–13.38 km). The predominant environmental settings are slopes (thirty-two), with about equal numbers on hilltops (sixteen) and in valleys (fifteen), and fewer on plains and shores (eight each), and only two on islands.

North Carolina

A total of eighteen sites were recorded for this state (density: 0.00 per square kilometer), mostly from the publications of Cyrus Thomas and Johannes Loubser.[49] Smaller numbers were recorded by Mike Harmon, Norman Muller, and Janice Ryalls. An equal number are from the Santee (eight) and PeeDee (eight) drainages, with one each in the Cape Fear and Roanoke drainages. There are no groupings of more than two sites which approximate a cluster. The average number of structures per site is 3.5 (range: 1–25); the average number of types is 1.0. The average elevation is 1,359.83 feet (range: 490–2,680 feet); the average distance to water is 198.72 meters (range: 0–445 meters). The average stream rank is 2.6 (range: 1–6); the average slope is 23.8 perfect (range: 1.5–70.0). The average distance to nearest fault is 9.42 km (range: 0.65–24.49 km); the average distance to the head-of-tide is 333.30 km (range: 185.38–381.49 km); the average distance to minor watershed is 2.92 km (range: 0.13–7.07 km). Site locations are preferentially near brooks (eight), headwater streams (five), and rivers (four); and ponds, swamps, and the ocean were not utilized. The majority of sites are in agriculturally productive soils (ten), followed by naturally infertile soils (six) and low fertility soils (two); no sites are located in pasture lands. The predominant structure types are cairns (eight) and petroglyphs (five); the only other structure types present are marked stones (three), U-shaped structures (one), and chambers (one). The average NND is 22.25 km (range: 0.10–104.32 km). The environmental settings are about equally divided among slopes (six), valleys (five), and hilltops (four), with fewer on shores (two) and plains (one), and none on islands.

Nova Scotia

There were twenty-one sites recorded for this province (density: 0.00 per square kilometer), mostly by local resident Terry DeVeau, Ed Lenik, or from the NEARA archive.[50] Additional sites were recorded by Gabriel Hrynick and on the website of the Mi'komaq Nation.[51] Most are located within the Mersey and Medway drainages or close to the coast, with small numbers in Grand, Clyde, and Sackville drainages. The closest approximation to a cluster is a group of four sites around Lake Kejimkujik, in an area of 16 square kilometers. The average number of structures per site is 6.9 (range: 1–42); the average number of types is 1.2. The average elevation is 207.33 feet (range: 0–759 feet); the average distance to water is 133.38 meters (range: 0–620 meters). The average stream rank is 3.8 (range: 1–8); the average slope could not be calculated. The average distance to nearest fault is not calculated due to difficulties in accessing Canadian data in GIS. The same problem applies to soil fertility assessment. The average distance to the head-of-tide is 18.88 km (range: 0.00–55.54 km); the average distance to minor watershed is 2.43 km (range: 0.12–4.01 km). Sites are preferentially located close to lakes (especially Lake Kejimkujik) (nine), followed by rivers (five) and the ocean (five); there are no sites adjacent to ponds or swamps. The predominant structure types are cairns (eight) and petroglyphs (seven); the only other structure types present are rock piles (three), stone rows (two), inscriptions (two), chambers (one), standing stones (one), and effigies (one). The average NND is 36.87 km (range: 0.41–305.21 km). The predominant environmental settings are shores (twelve), followed by slopes (five), plains and islands (two each); there are none on hilltops or in valleys.

Quebec

Only two sites were recorded for this vast province, only the portion south of the St. Lawrence River being included in this study. It was not possible to make contact with site file managers or antiquarians with information about other sites in the province. Both sites are from the NEARA archive (density: 0.00 per square kilometer). Both are in the St. Lawrence drainage. There are no groupings of more than two sites which approximate a cluster. The average number of structures per site is 3.00 (range: 2–4); the average number of types is 1.0. The average elevation is 983.5 feet (range: 895–1,072 feet); the average distance to water is 1,650.0 meters (range: 300–3,000 meters). The average stream rank is 2.5 (range: 2–3); the average slope could not be calculated. The average distance to nearest fault is 56.51 km (range: 55.83–57.19 km); the average distance to the head-of-tide is 17.80 km (same approximate distance for both sites); the average distance to minor watershed is not calculated due to difficulties in accessing the Canadian data on GIS. The same problem applies to soil fertility assessment. One site is close to a headwater stream, while the other is close to a lake. Cairns and rock piles are the only structure types present, one site for each. The two sites are nearest neighbors to each other, at 2.06 km apart. Both sites are on slopes.

West Virginia

A total of twenty-eight sites were recorded for this state (density: 0.00 per square kilometer), all in the Potomac drainage. Most were recorded in the publications of Gerard Fowke, or were supplied by the West Virginia State Historic Preservation Office.[52] One site was supplied by Philip Mulford. Aside from the group of five sites near Cumberland, Maryland mentioned above, the closest approximation of a cluster is a group of five sites in Hardy County, in an area of approximately 15 square kilometer. The average number of structures per site is 3.1 (range: 1–30); the average number of types is 1.1. The average elevation is 959.36 feet (range: 360–1,831 feet); the average distance to water is 229.25 meters (range: 50–631 meters). The average stream rank is 3.9 (range: 1–6); the average distance to minor watershed boundary is 2.00 km (range: 0.05–6.53 km). There is a strong preference for sites with respect to headwater streams (fifty-three) and brooks (nineteen); and lakes and the ocean were not utilized. Soil fertility is skewed in favor of sites in low fertility soils (fifty) and naturally infertile soils (fourteen), with smaller numbers in agriculturally fertile soils and pasture lands; the average slope is 22.5 percent (range: 1.5–50.0). The average distance to nearest fault is 11.54 km (range: 0.11–30.35 km); the average distance to the head-of-tide is 157.12 km (range: 87.76–208.16 km); the average distance to minor watershed is 3.51 km (range: 0.03–6.99 km). Site locations were preferentially close to rivers (thirteen) and brooks (twelve); lakes, ponds, swamps, and the ocean were not utilized. Types are dominated by cairns (fourteen) and rock piles (thirteen), with one each of petroglyphs, stone circles, and platforms.

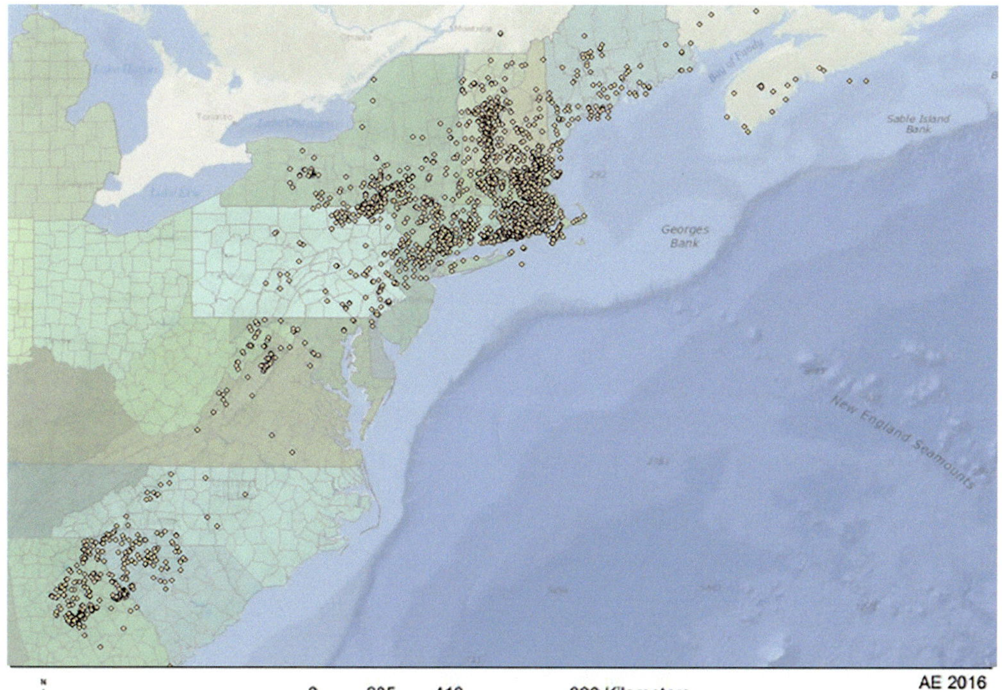

Above: Plate 1: Rock pile commemorating Thomas Mayhew, Jr., on Martha's Vineyard, MA. (*Photo by Bill Moody*)

Below: Plate 2: GIS Map of the total distribution of sites represented as 1-km circles.

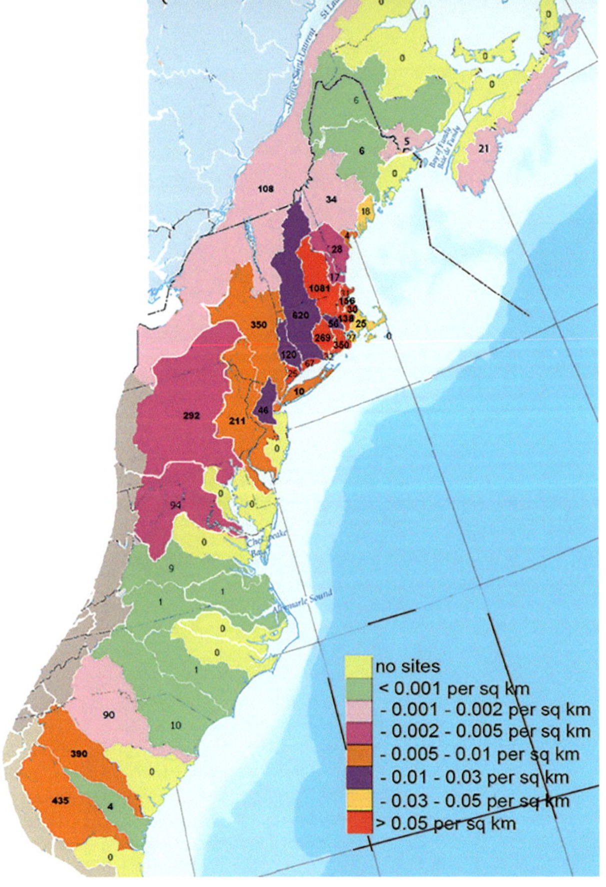

Plate 3: Distribution of sites by watershed.

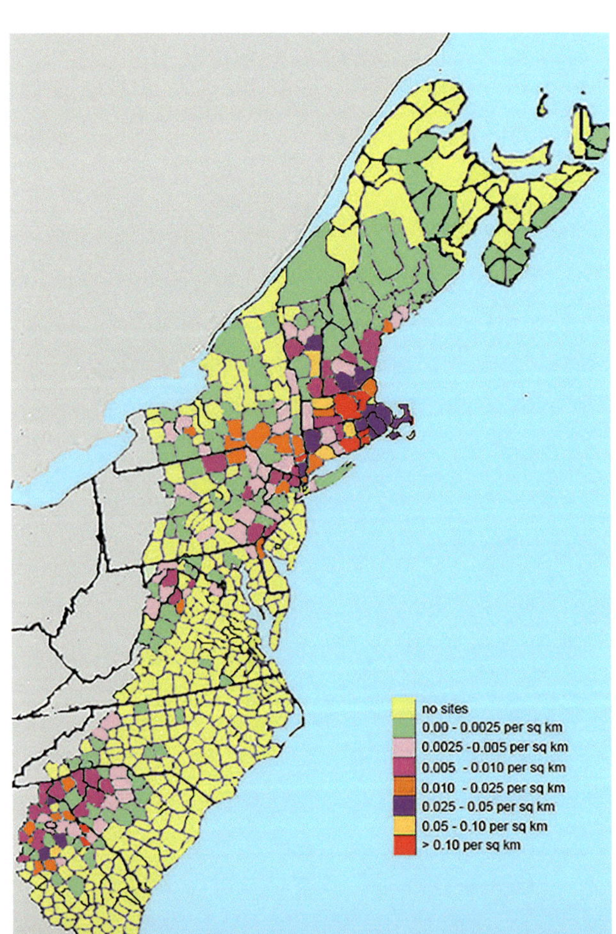

Plate 4: Distribution of sites by county.

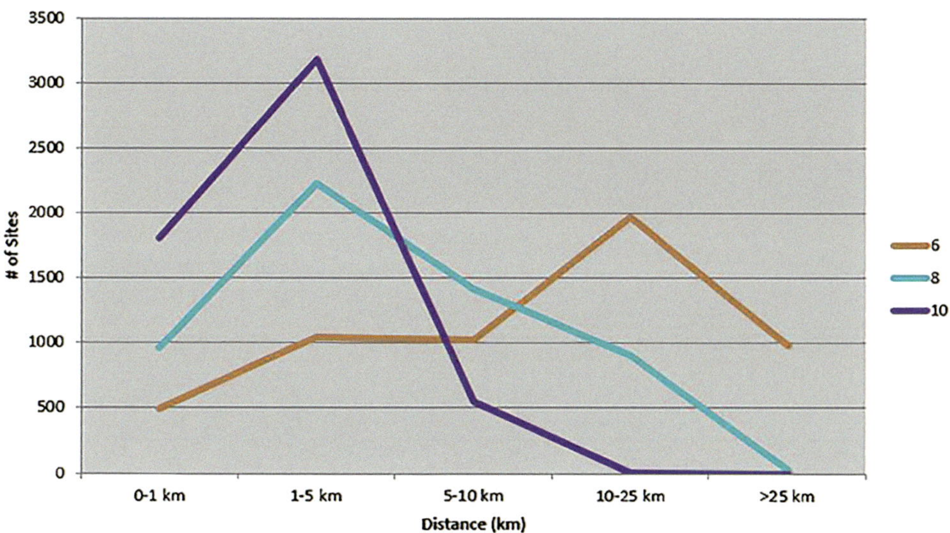

Above: Plate 5: Comparison of site distributions at level 6, 8, and 10 watersheds.

Below: Plate 6: Probability distribution for average nearest neighbors, all clusters.

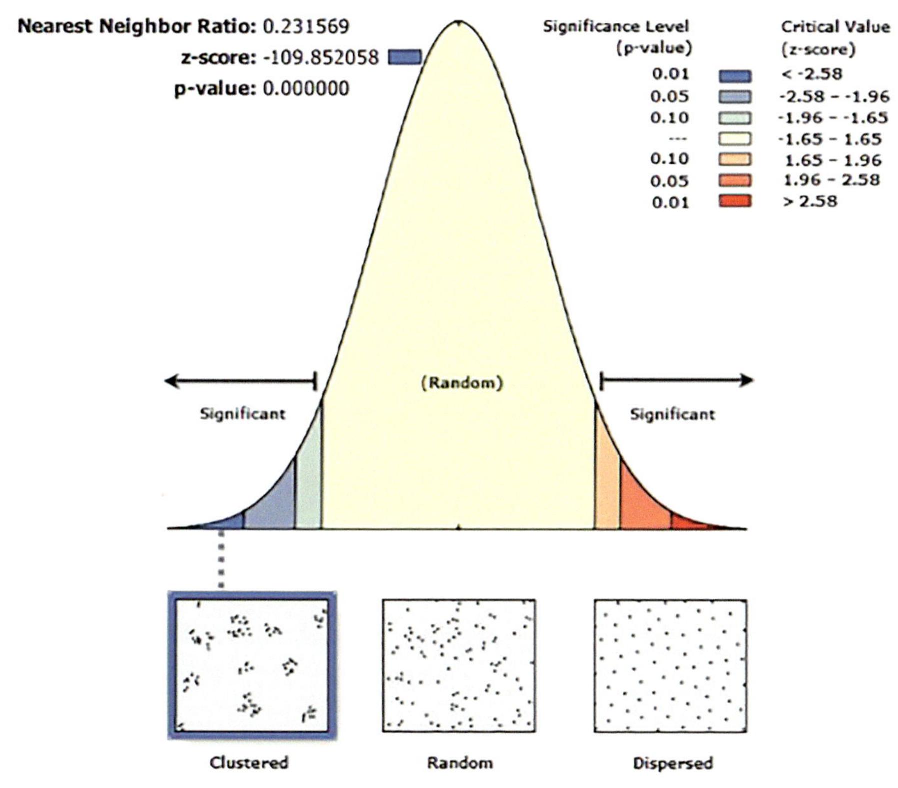

Given the z-score of -109.852057705, there is a less than 1% likelihood that this clustered pattern could be the result of random chance.

Plate 7: Rock pile, Ashland, MA. (*Photo by Gordon Bernstein*)

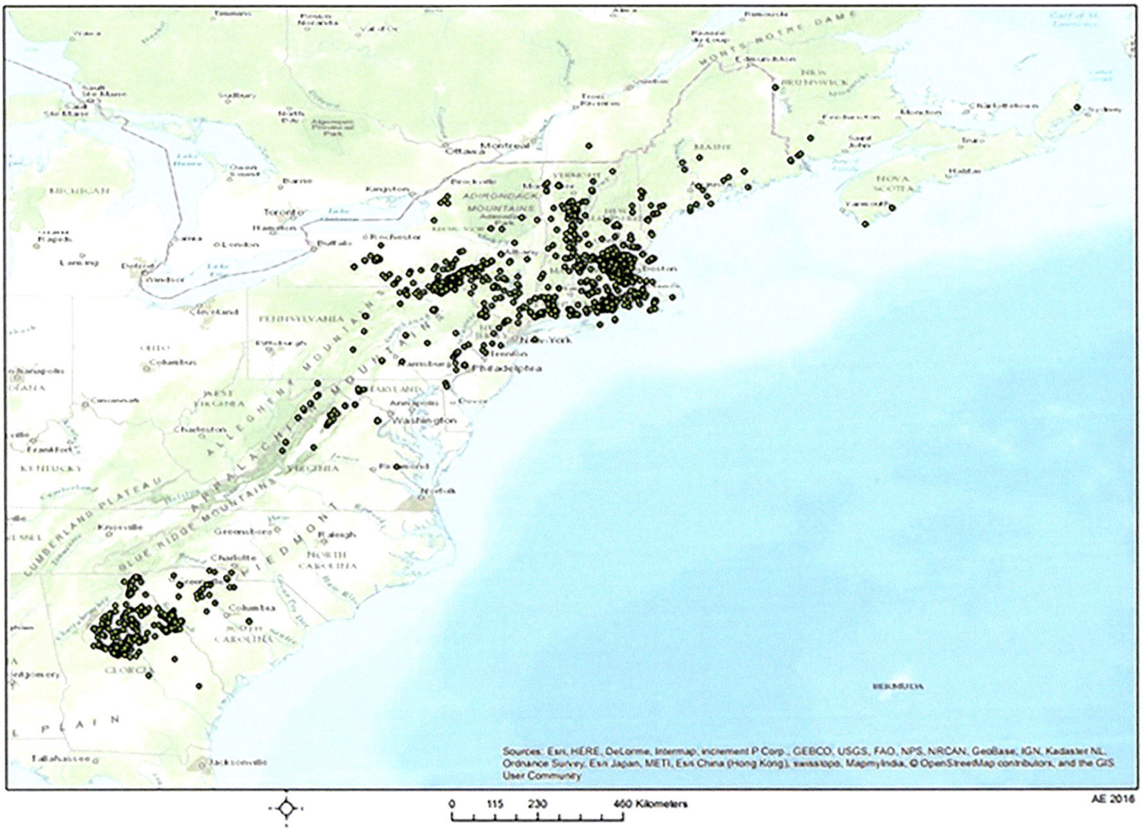

Plate 8: GIS map of the distribution of rock pile sites.

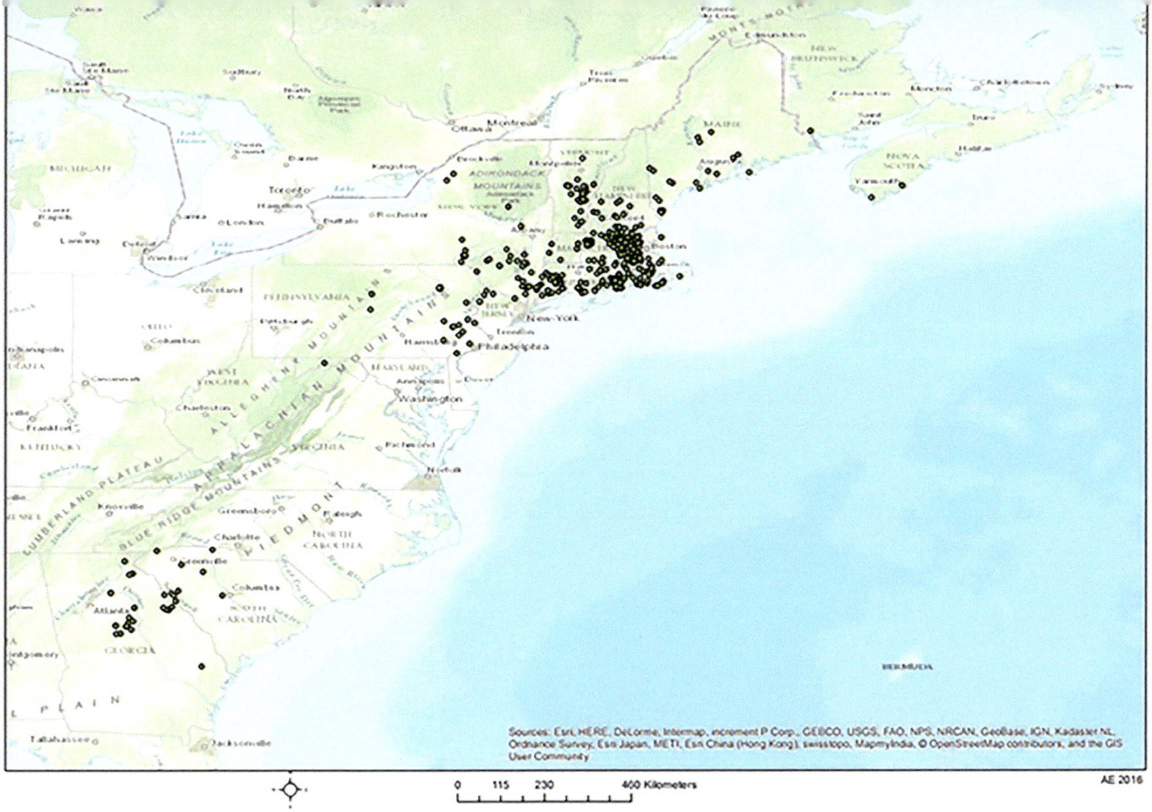

Above: Plate 9: GIS map of the distribution of stone row sites.

Right: Plate 10: Stone row, Ashland, MA. (*Photo by Gordon Bernstein*)

Plate 11: Cairn, Killingworth, CT. (*Photo by Tim Fohl*)

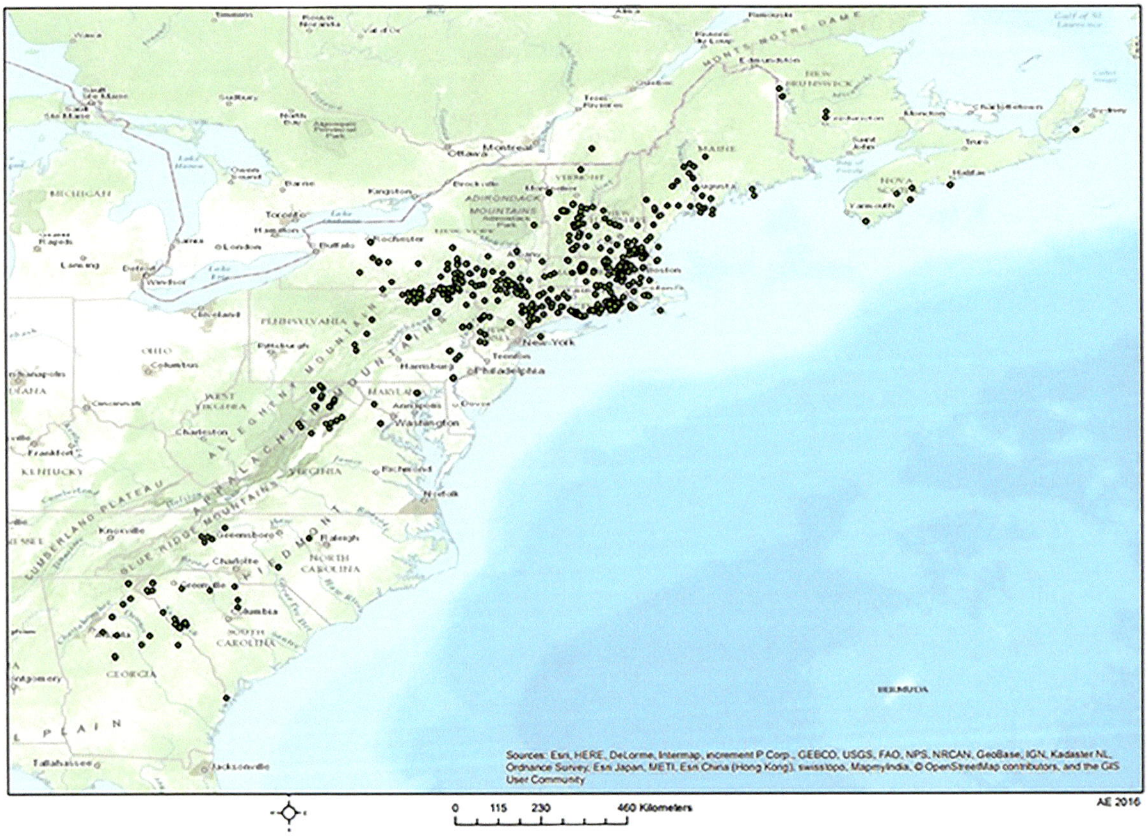

Plate 12: GIS map of the distribution of cairn sites.

Plate 13: Chamber, Upton, MA. (*Photo by Gordon Bernstein*)

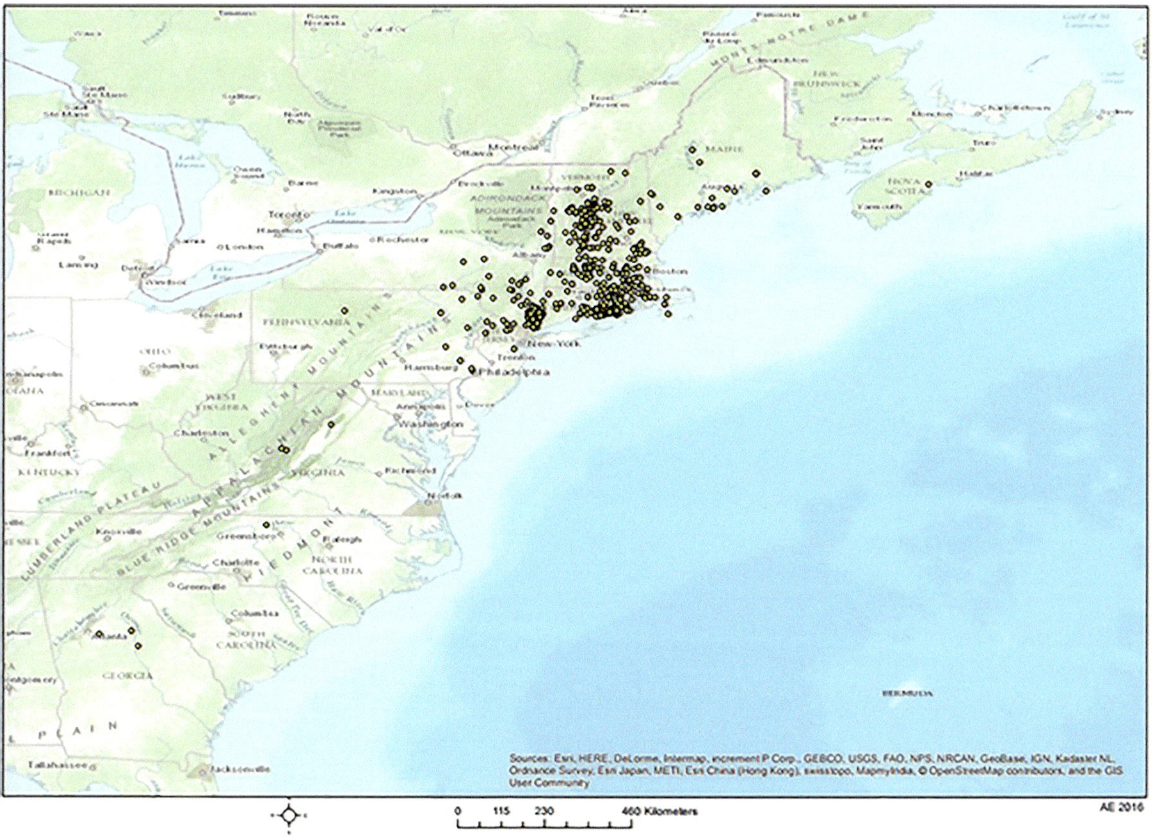

Plate 14: GIS map of the distribution of chamber sites.

Plate 15: Balanced rock, Ashland, MA. (*Photo by Gordon Bernstein*)

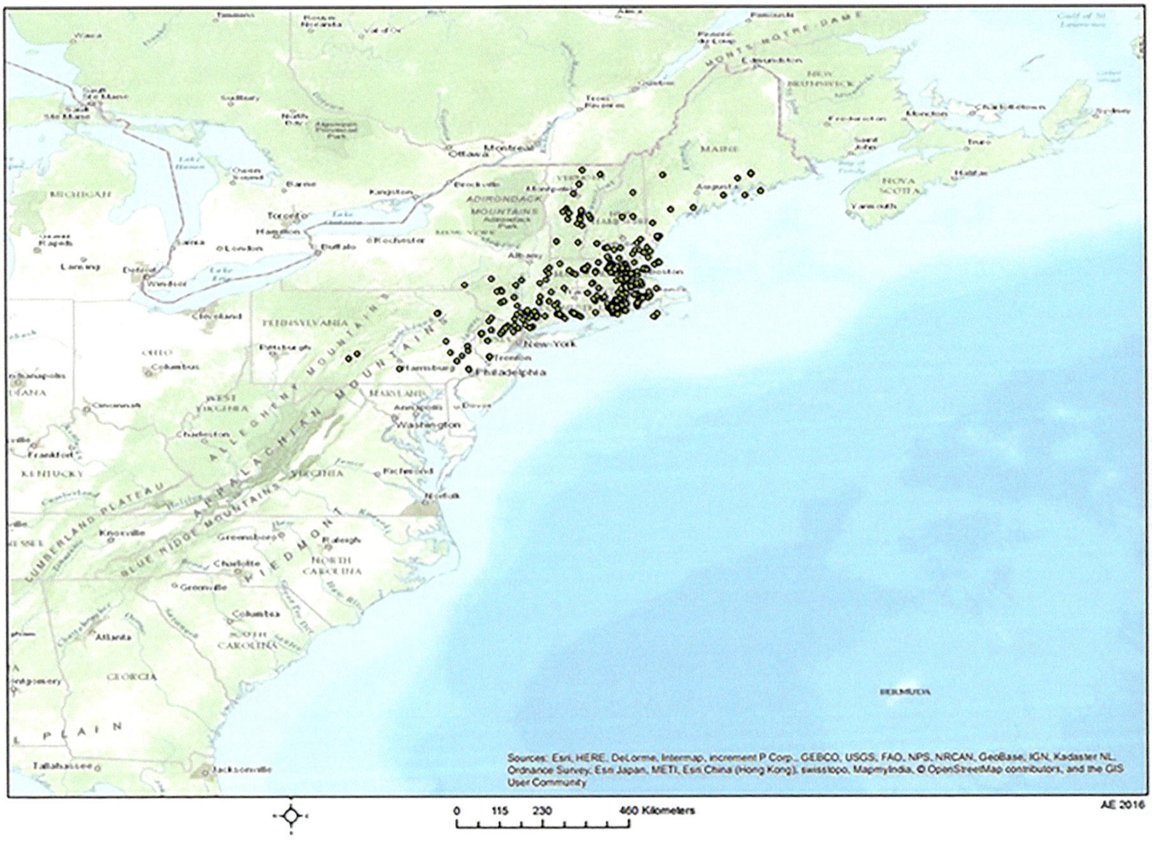

Plate 16: GIS map of the distribution of balanced rock sites.

Right: Plate 17: Marked stone, Ashland, MA. (*Photo by the author*)

Below: Plate 18: Fallen manitou stone, Ashland, MA. (*Photo by Gordon Bernstein*)

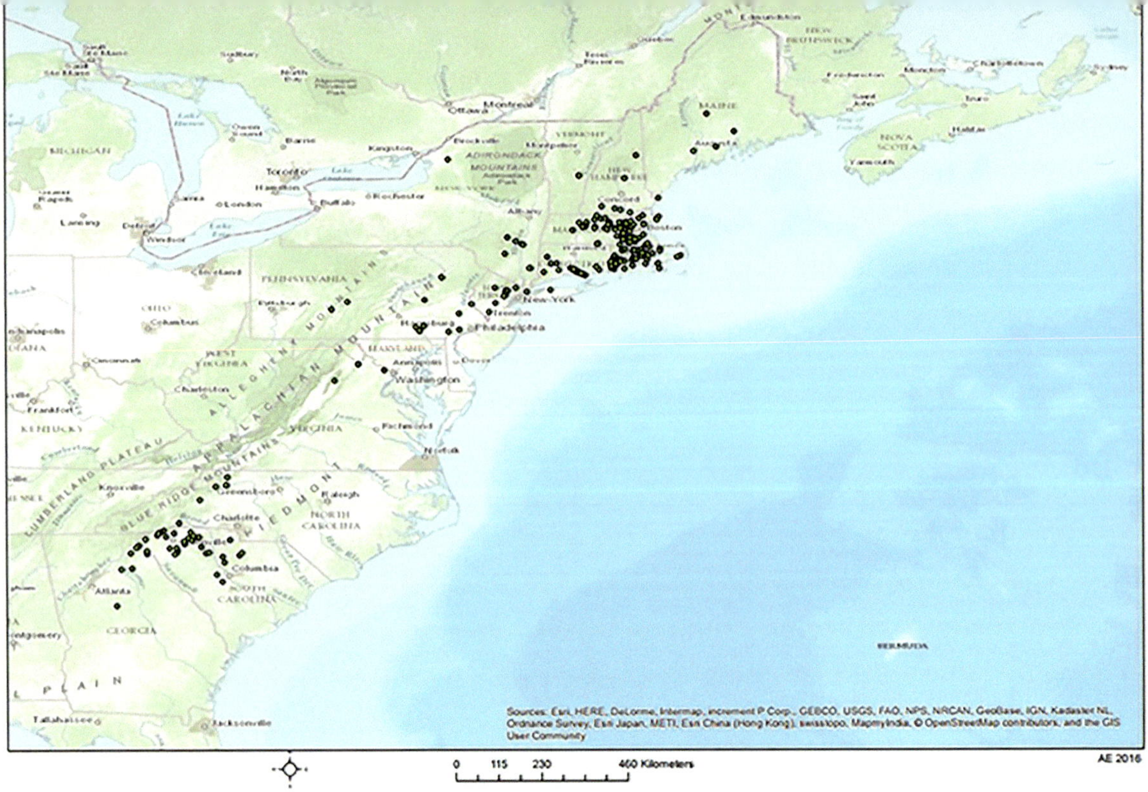

Above: Plate 19: GIS map of the distribution of marked stone sites.

Left: Plate 20: Split-filled boulder, Ashland, MA. (*Photo by Gordon Bernstein*)

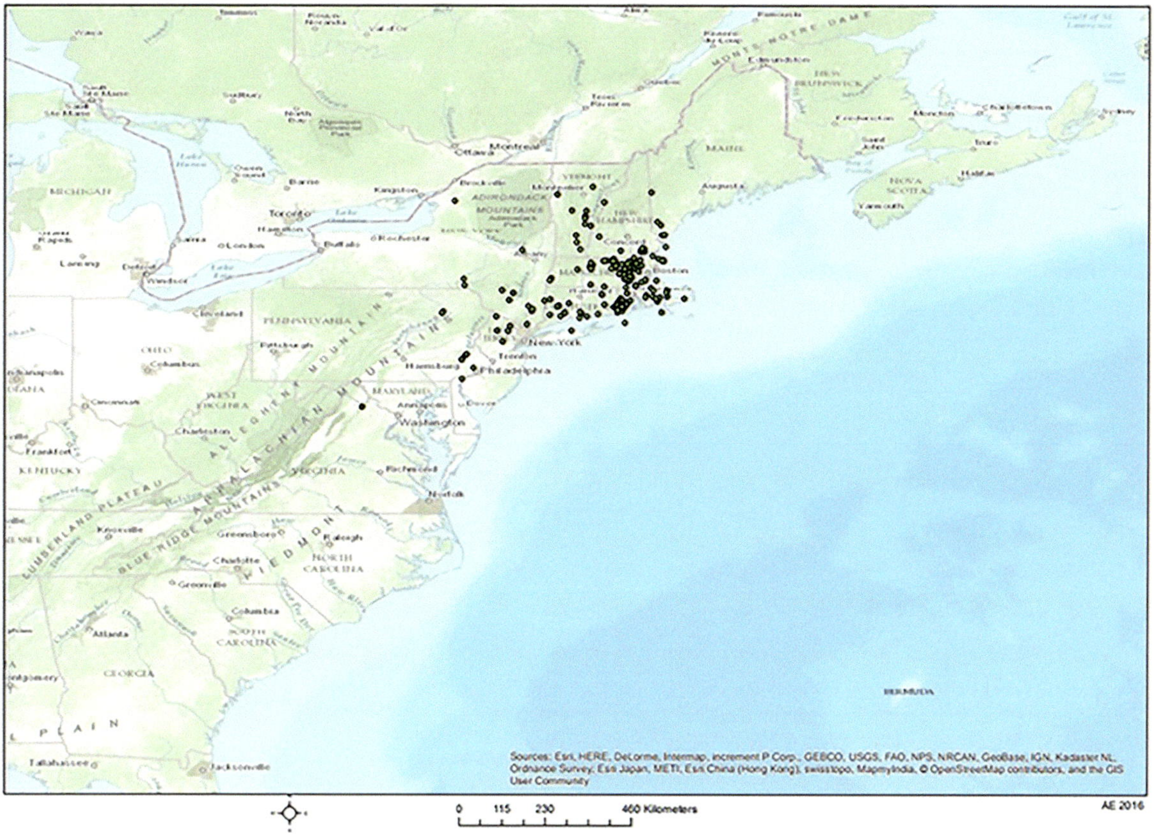

Plate 21: GIS map of the distribution of split-filled boulder sites.

Plate 22: Turtle effigy, Ashland, MA. (*Photo by Gordon Bernstein*)

Above: Plate 23: Serpent effigy, Ashland, MA. (*Photo by the Steve DiMarzo*)

Below: Plate 24: GIS map of the distribution of effigy sites.

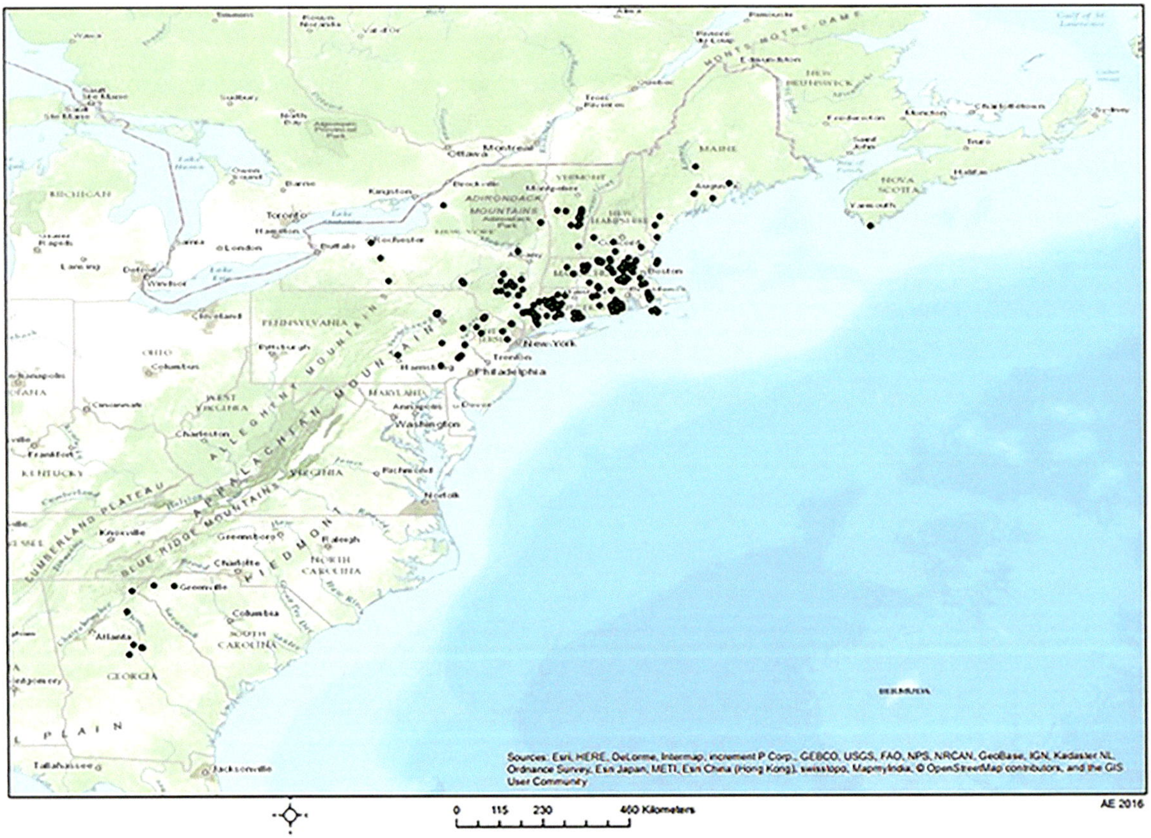

Above: Plate 25: Fallen standing stone, Ashland, MA. (*Photo by the author*)

Below: Plate 26: GIS map of the distribution of standing stone sites.

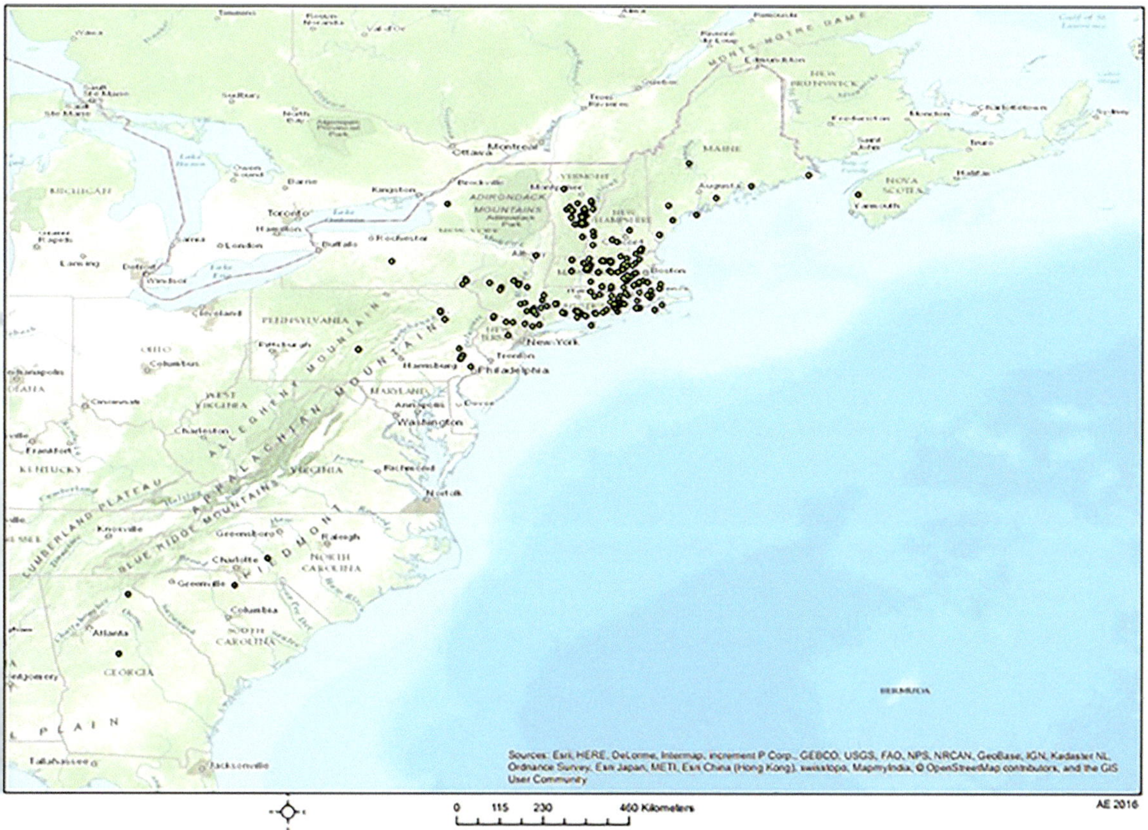

Above: Plate 27: U-shaped structure, Foxboro, MA. (*Photo by the author*)

Below: Plate 28: GIS map of the distribution of U-shaped structure sites.

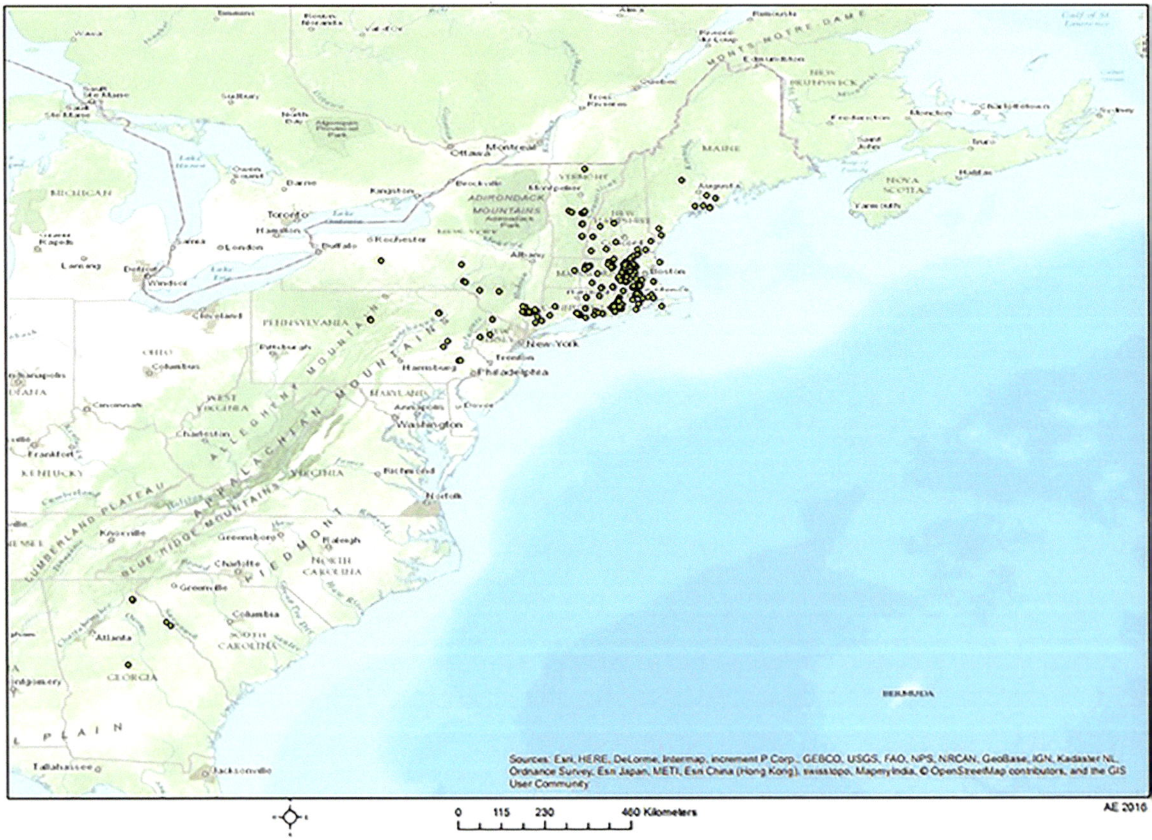

Above: Plate 29: Petroglyph, Bellows Falls, VT. (*Photo by Kristopher Radder, Bellows Falls News*)

Below: Plate 30: GIS map of the distribution of petroglyph sites.

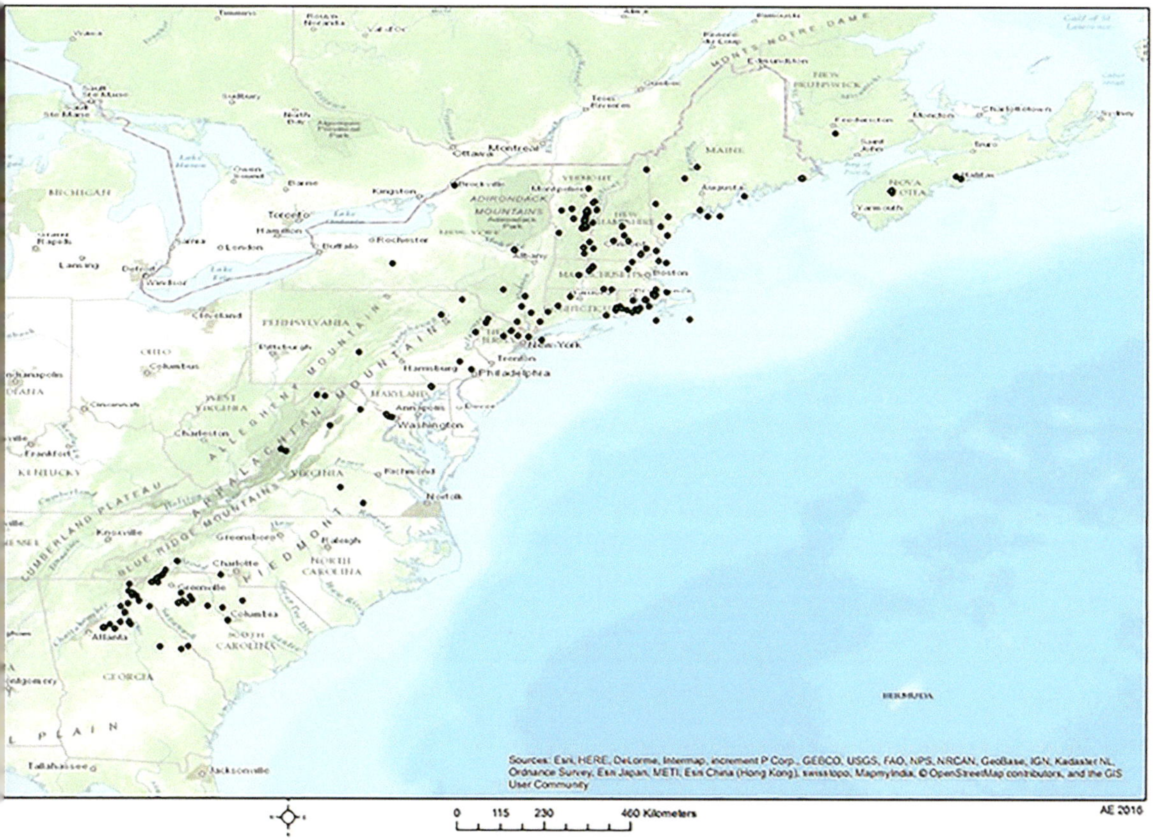

Plate 31: Enclosure, Ashland, MA. (*Photo by Gordon Bernstein*)

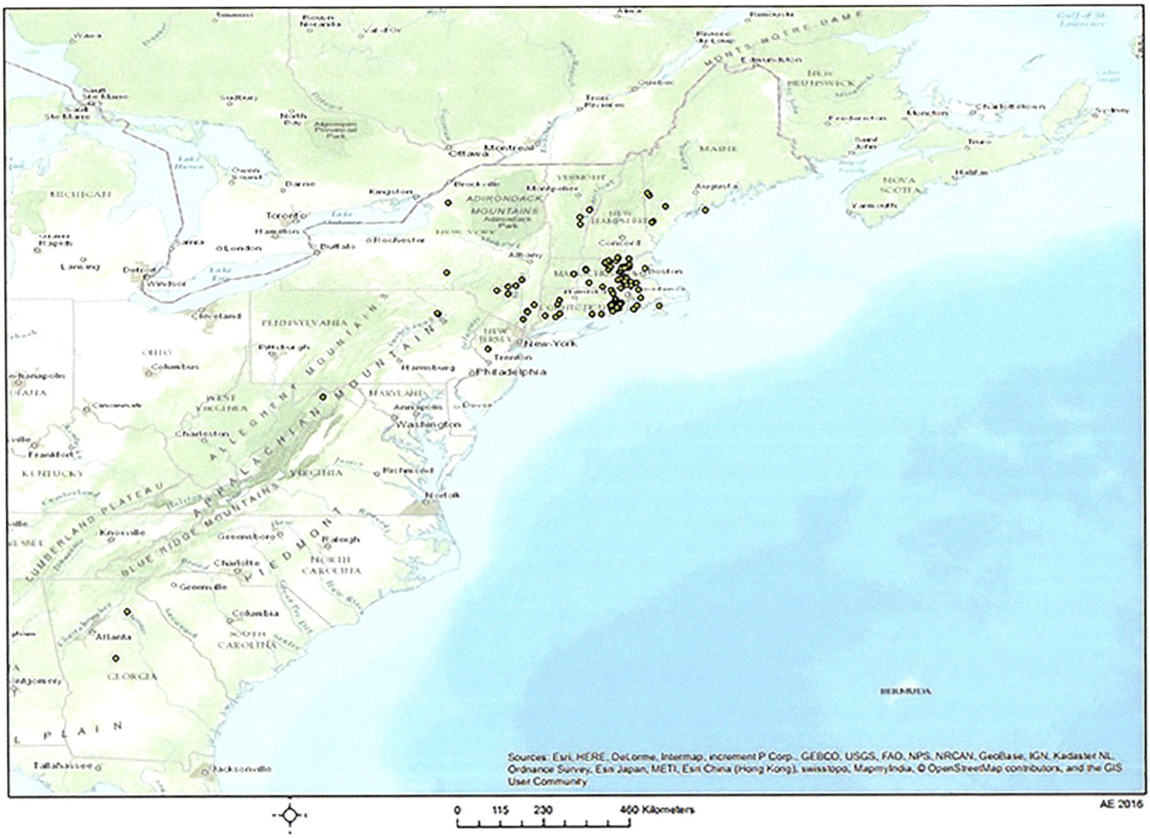

Plate 32: GIS map of the distribution of enclosure sites.

Plate 33: Stone circle, Ashland, MA. Note: standing stone and niche. (*Photo by Gordon Bernstein*)

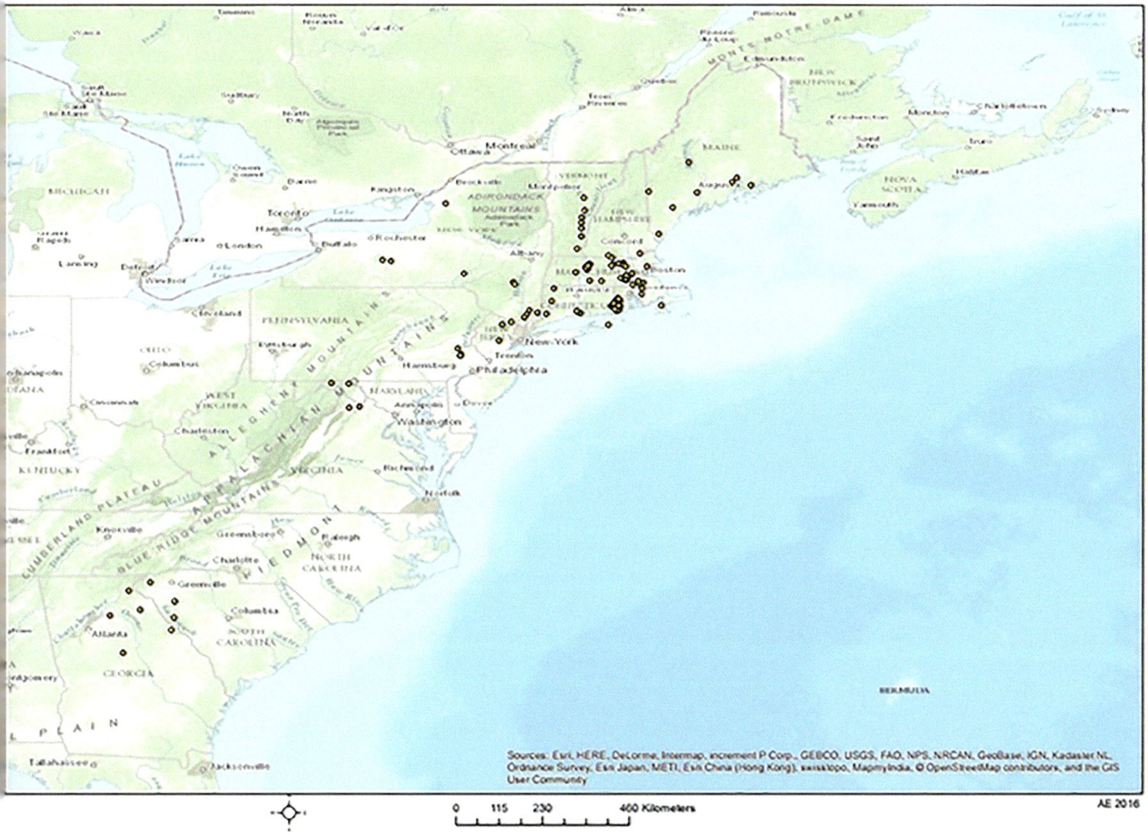

Plate 34: GIS map of the distribution of stone circle sites.

Above: Plate 35: Niches in complex stone structure, Ashland, MA. (*Photo by the author*)

Below: Plate 36: GIS map of the distribution of niche sites.

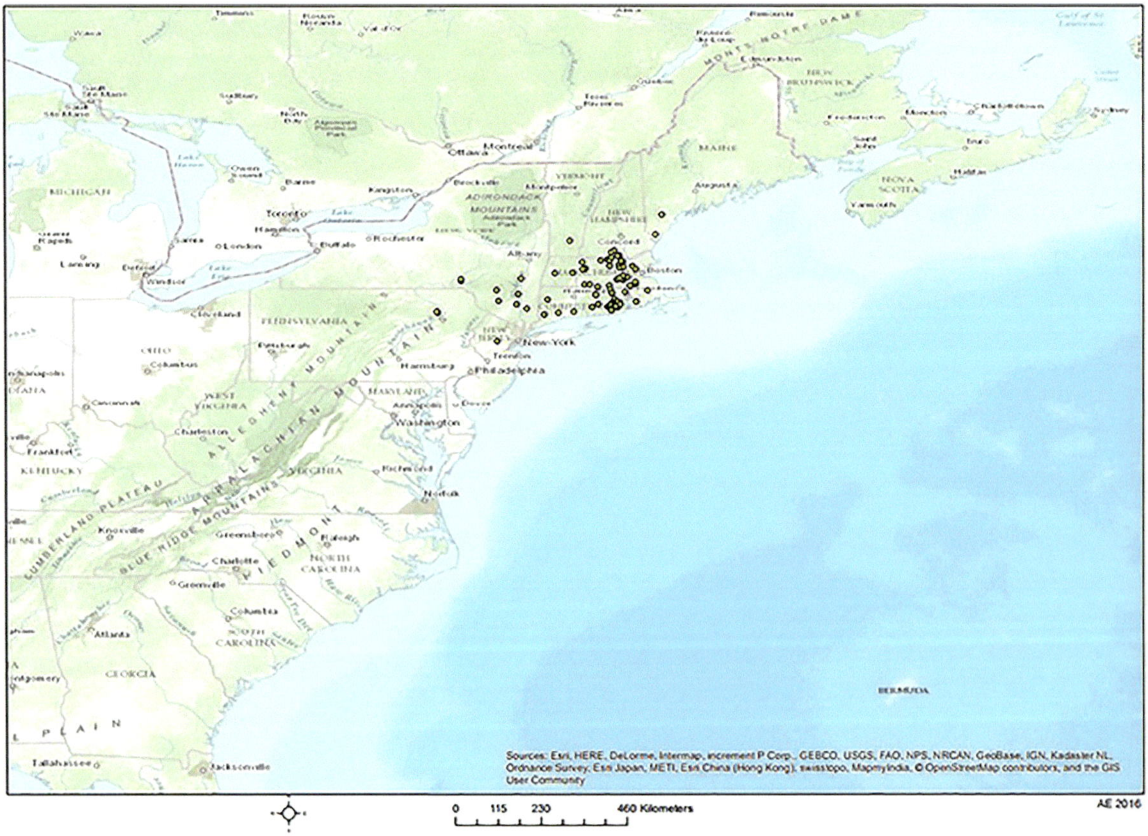

Above: Plate 37: Mound, Ashland, MA. (*Photo by Gordon Bernstein*)

Below: Plate 38: GIS map of the distribution of mound sites.

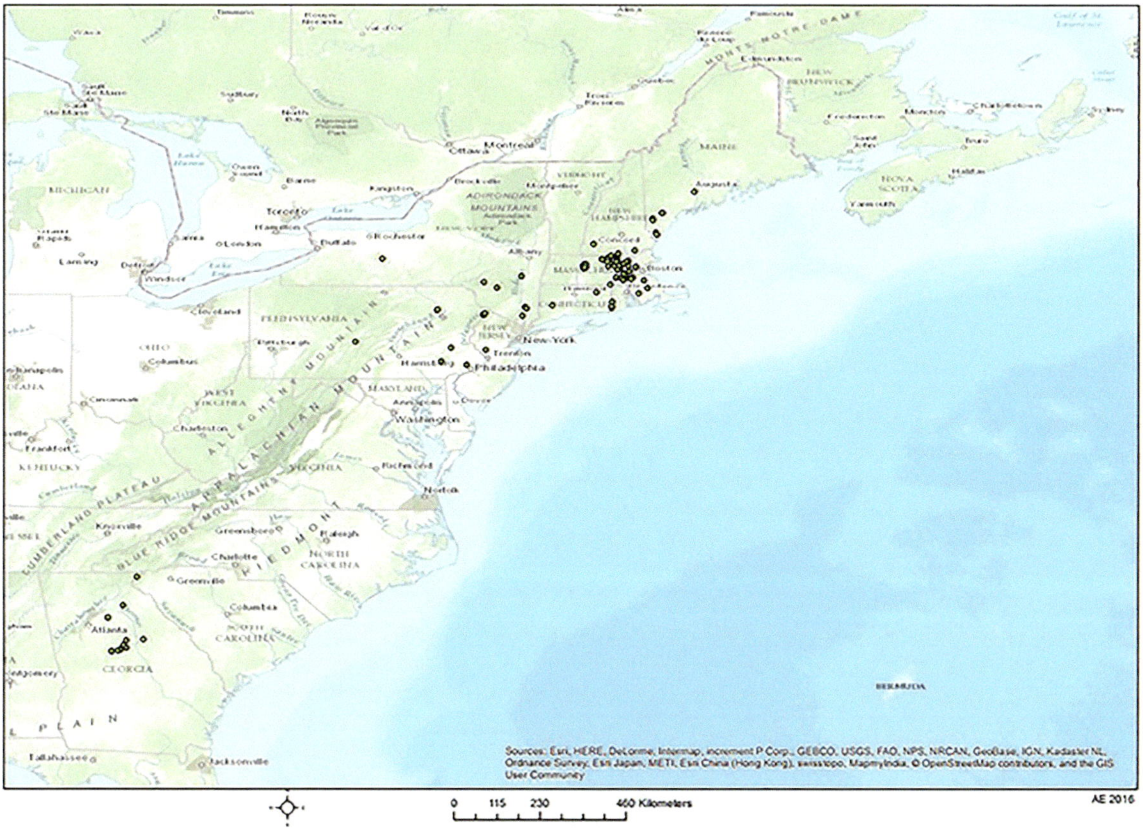

Plate 39: Unique structure (shrine), Ashland, MA. (*Photo by Gordon Bernstein*)

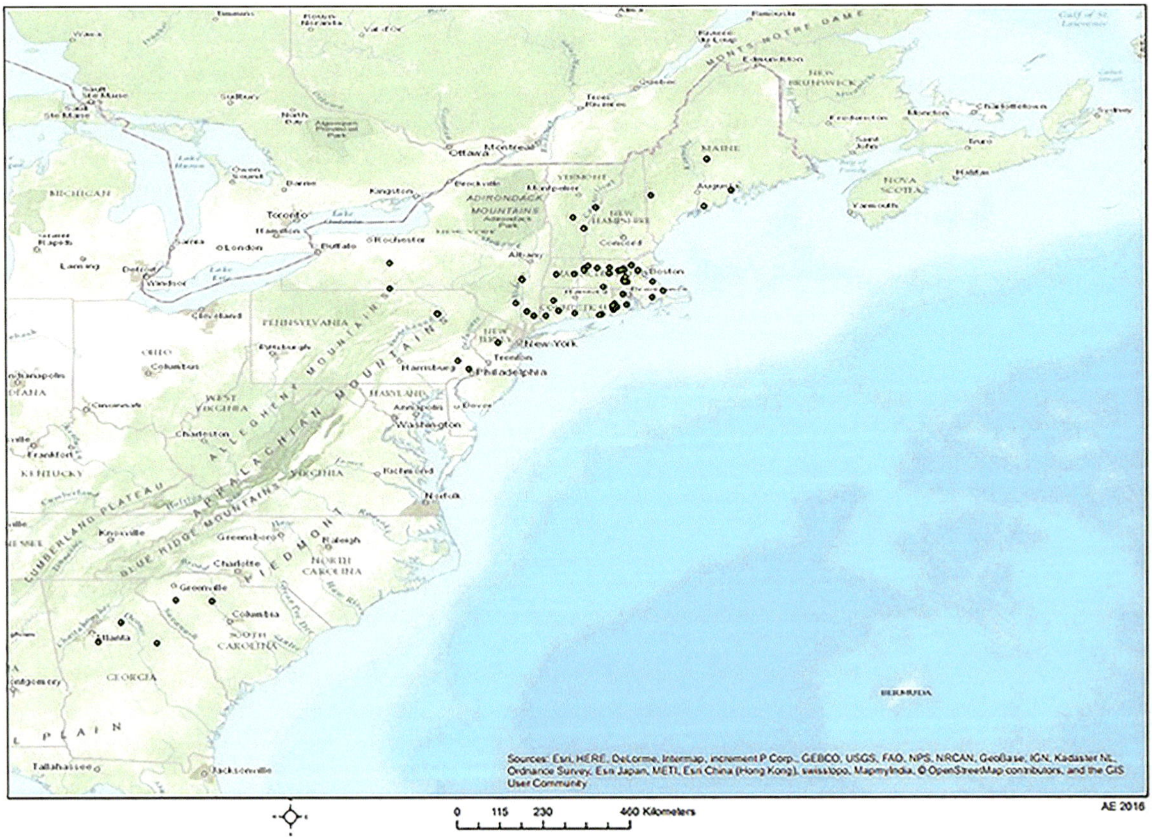

Plate 40: GIS map of the distribution of unique structure sites.

Above: Plate 41: Platform, Windham, NY. (*Photo by Peter Backes*)

Below: Plate 42: GIS map of the distribution of platform sites.

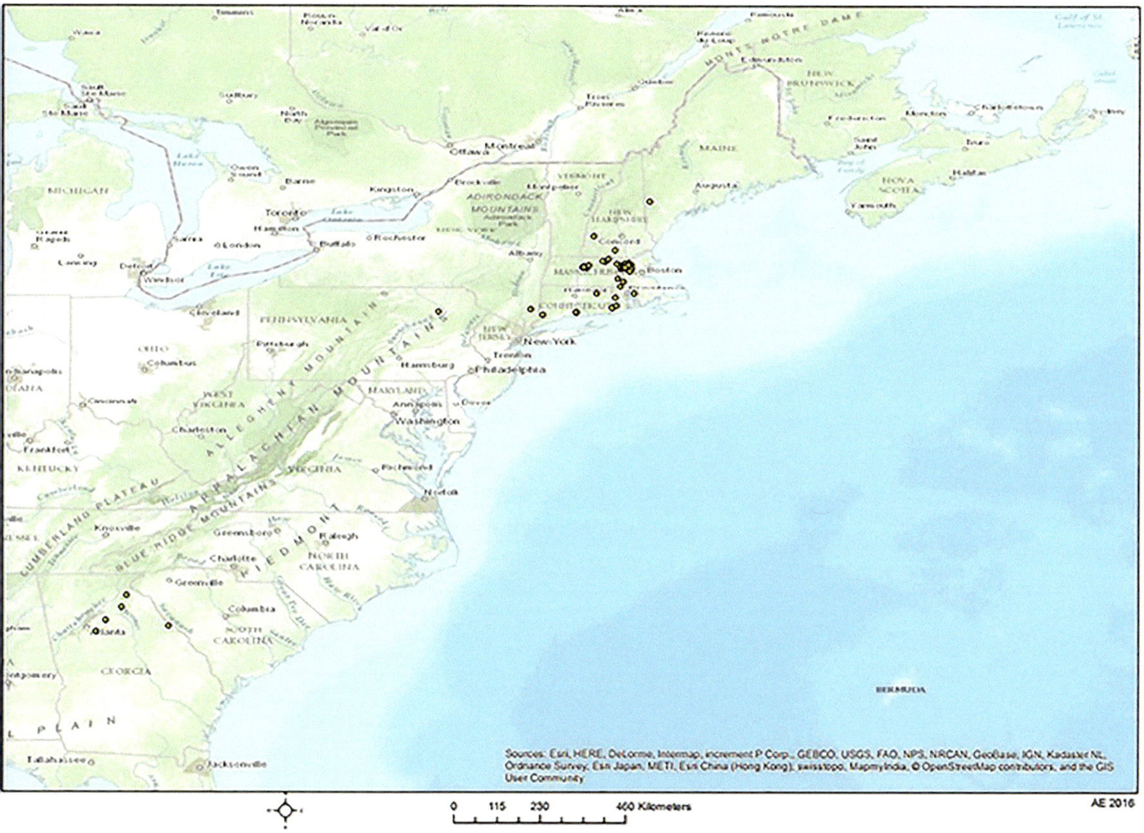

Plate 43: Inscription, North Kingston, MA. (*Photo by Steve DiMarzo*)

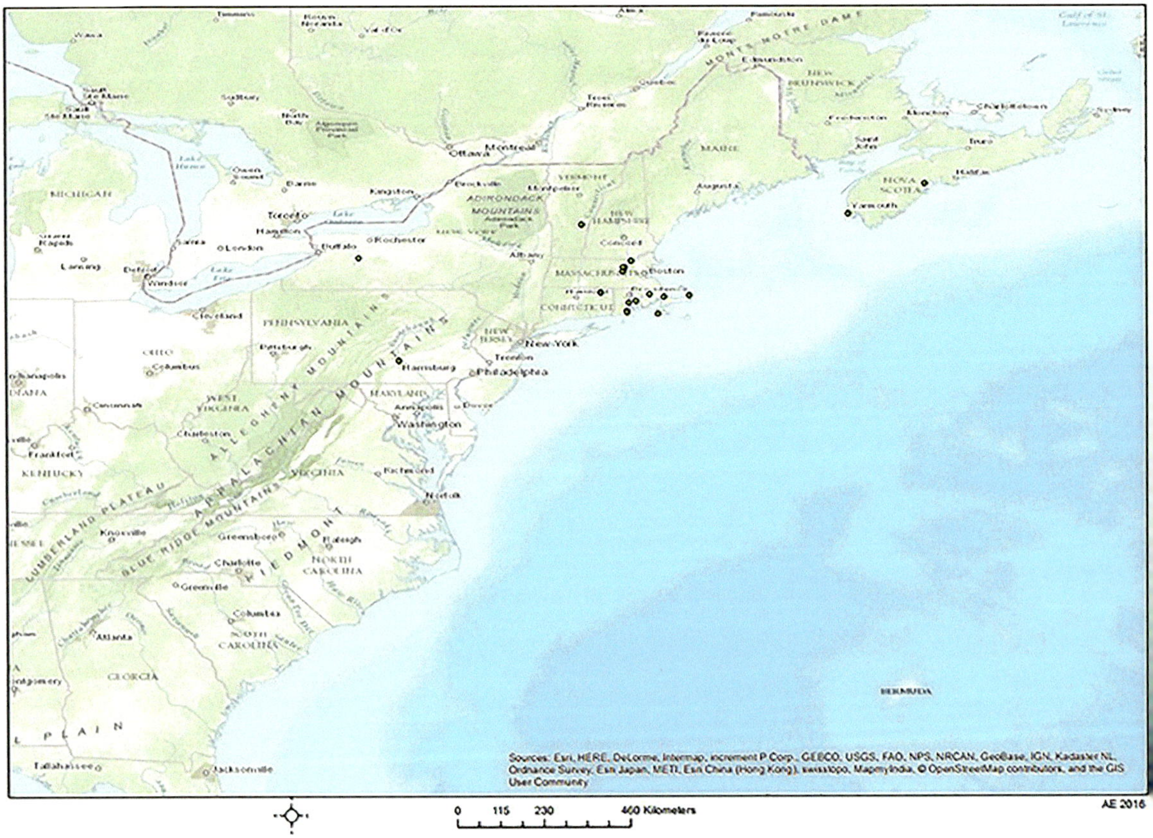

Plate 44: GIS map of the distribution of inscription sites.

Type	Cairn	Rock Pile	Stone Row	U-Shaped	Chamber	Standing Stone	Split Boulder	Balanced Rock	Marked Stone	Petroglyph	Inscription	Stone Circle	Effigy	Mound	Platform	Enclosure	Niche	Unique Structure
Cairn	X	241	185	74	46	76	80	73	79	18	0	40	89	26	9	47	44	12
Rock Pile	241	X	501	118	79	141	284	215	157	25	1	95	196	87	39	116	127	29
Stone Row	185	501	X	81	80	117	139	110	110	30	1	56	146	43	11	82	70	17
U-Shaped	74	118	81	X	26	34	56	53	37	4	0	20	31	6	3	27	28	4
Chamber	46	79	80	26	X	38	23	38	24	19	2	11	27	5	1	12	16	13
Standing Stone	76	141	117	34	38	X	50	55	53	29	0	29	50	16	3	25	27	11
Split Boulder	80	284	139	56	23	50	X	113	63	6	0	44	70	14	11	54	60	7
Balanced Rock	73	215	110	53	38	55	113	X	63	13	0	43	43	10	5	47	48	8
Marked Stone	79	157	110	37	24	53	63	63	X	15	3	26	55	12	7	28	36	11
Petroglyph	18	25	30	4	19	29	6	13	15	X	2	8	23	2	2	3	3	4
Inscription	0	1	1	0	2	0	0	0	3	2	X	0	1	0	2	0	0	0
Stone Circle	40	95	56	20	11	29	44	43	26	8	1	X	30	10	1	23	22	6
Effigy	89	196	146	31	27	50	70	43	55	23	0	30	X	19	9	34	47	8
Mound	26	87	43	6	5	16	14	10	12	2	0	10	19	X	6	12	16	4
Platform	9	39	11	3	1	3	11	5	7	2	2	1	9	6	X	6	4	0
Enclosure	47	116	82	27	12	25	54	47	28	3	0	23	34	12	6	X	39	9
Niche	44	127	70	28	16	27	60	48	36	3	0	22	47	16	4	39	X	8
Unique Structure	12	29	17	4	13	11	7	8	11	4	0	6	8	4	0	9	8	X

Above: Plate 45: Pairwise combinations of structure types.

Below: Plate 46: Three-way comparisons of types.

Type	Cairn	Rock Pile	Stone Row	U-Shaped	Chamber	Standing Stone	Split Boulder	Balanced Rock	Marked Stone	Petroglyph	Inscription	Stone Circle	Effigy	Mound	Platform	Enclosure	Niche	Unique Structure
Chamber • Effigy	5	12	6	4	X	6	3	4	2	2	5	1	X	0	0	1	4	0
Chamber • Inscription	4	3	5	2	X	5	1	0	1	1	X	1	5	0	0	0	1	0
Chamber • Standing Stone	4	9	13	4	X	X	2	7	2	5	4	1	5	1	0	2	2	2
Inscription • Effigy	5	9	7	2	5	5	1	1	1	1	X	1	X	0	1	0	1	0
Petroglyph • Effigy	6	9	10	3	4	7	2	4	3	X	0	4	X	0	0	2	3	2
Rock Pile • Balanced Rock	48	X	86	41	26	40	95	X	45	7	0	34	35	10	4	43	46	7
Rock Pile • Chamber	18	X	29	12	X	9	13	26	12	6	0	8	16	2	1	9	11	7
Rock Pile • Effigy	59	X	93	20	16	40	57	35	42	9	1	20	X	16	6	26	43	6
Rock Pile • Enclosure	31	X	68	23	9	21	45	43	26	1	0	22	26	9	6	X	36	7
Rock Pile • Mound	22	X	33	5	2	14	12	10	11	1	0	9	16	X	5	9	16	3
Rock Pile • Niche	37	X	65	24	11	26	53	46	34	2	0	19	43	16	4	36	X	5
Rock Pile • Platform	7	X	9	3	1	3	7	2	4	0	1	0	6	5	X	6	4	0
Rock Pile • Split Boulder	54	X	116	43	13	41	X	95	50	3	0	37	57	12	10	45	53	4
Rock Pile • Standing Stone	39	X	66	21	9	X	41	40	35	7	0	18	40	14	3	21	26	5
Rock Pile • Stone Circle	23	X	40	15	8	18	37	34	18	4	0	X	20	9	1	22	19	2
Rock Pile • Stone Row	90	X	X	53	29	66	116	86	73	9	0	40	93	33	9	68	65	11
Rock Pile • Unique	1	X	5	1	2	3	1	3	3	0	0	0	1	0	0	3	0	X
Rock Pile • U-shaped	38	X	53	X	12	21	43	41	23	1	0	15	20	5	3	23	24	2
Rock Pile • Petroglyph	7	X	9	1	6	7	3	7	8	X	0	4	9	1	0	1	1	1
RockPile • Marked Stone	43	X	73	23	12	35	50	45	X	8	0	18	42	11	6	26	34	8
Split Boulder • Balanced Rock	31	95	52	30	7	21	X	X	33	3	0	17	23	4	3	30	28	2
Stone Row • Balanced Rock	33	85	X	26	9	29	52	X	28	7	0	22	26	9	3	30	28	3
Stone Row • Chamber	25	29	X	9	X	10	9	10	7	4	0	5	11	2	0	6	6	3
Stone Row • Effigy	47	92	X	20	11	34	42	26	37	10	0	18	X	10	3	24	31	7
Stone Row • Enclosure	28	68	X	20	6	18	34	30	19	1	0	17	24	7	5	X	32	6
Stone Row • Marked Stone	39	73	X	19	7	31	33	28	X	5	0	14	37	8	5	19	19	5
Stone Row • Mound	11	33	X	5	2	9	9	9	8	1	0	5	10	X	2	7	11	2
Stone Row • Niche	27	65	X	17	6	17	33	28	19	1	0	15	31	11	3	32	X	5
Stone Row • Petroglyph	7	9	X	1	4	10	3	7	5	X	1	3	10	1	1	1	1	2
Stone Row • Split Boulder	43	116	X	28	9	27	X	52	33	3	0	17	42	9	6	34	33	4
Stone Row • Standing Stone	46	66	X	20	10	X	27	29	31	10	0	16	34	9	2	18	17	6
Stone Row • Stone Circle	23	40	X	10	5	16	17	22	14	3	0	X	18	5	1	17	15	4
Stone Row • Unique Structure	8	11	X	4	3	6	4	3	5	2	0	4	7	2	0	6	5	X
Stone Row • U-Shaped	37	53	X	X	9	20	28	26	19	1	0	10	20	5	2	20	17	4

Type	Cairn	Rock Pile	Stone Row	U-Shaped	Chamber	Standing Stone	Split Boulder	Balanced Rock	Marked Stone	Petroglyph	Stone Circle	Effigy	Mound	Platform	Enclosure	Niche	Unique Structure
Cairn • Rock Pile • Stone Row	X	X	X	24	14	25	33	28	27	4	15	34	10	3	23	23	5
Cairn • Stone Row • Chamber	X	14	X	4	X	2	7	8	4	1	4	5	1	0	5	5	3
Rock Pile • Balanced Rock • Marked Stone	18	X	23	15	6	21	28	X	X	2	8	17	4	3	20	19	3
Rock Pile • Chamber • Balanced Rock	8	X	7	6	X	5	7	X	6	3	3	4	1	0	6	5	5
Rock Pile • Chamber • Effigy	4	X	10	3	X	3	2	4	5	3	2	X	1	0	6	6	3
Rock Pile • Split Boulder • Balanced Rock	26	X	47	27	7	19	X	X	28	1	16	19	4	3	28	27	2
Rock Pile • Stone Row • Balanced Rock	28	X	X	23	7	23	47	X	25	4	18	22	9	3	28	28	3
Rock Pile • Stone Row • Chamber	14	X	X	6	X	3	8	7	6	2	3	10	1	0	5	6	3
Rock Pile • Stone Row • Effigy	34	X	X	14	10	28	34	22	30	5	13	X	9	2	21	21	6
Rock Pile • Stone Row • Enclosure	23	X	X	17	5	16	30	28	18	1	16	21	6	5	X	31	4
Rock Pile • Stone Row • Marked Stone	27	X	X	14	6	23	29	25	X	2	14	30	8	4	18	19	5
Rock Pile • Stone Row • Mound	10	X	X	4	1	7	7	9	8	0	5	9	X	1	6	11	2
Rock Pile • Stone Row • Platform	6	X	X	2	0	2	5	3	4	0	1	2	2	X	5	3	0
Rock Pile • Stone Row • Split Boulder	33	X	X	22	8	23	X	47	29	2	15	34	7	5	30	32	3
Rock Pile • Stone Row • Standing Stone	25	X	X	13	3	X	23	23	23	4	11	28	7	2	16	17	3
Rock Pile • Stone Row • Unique Structure	5	X	X	2	3	3	3	3	5	1	2	6	2	0	5	4	X
Rock Pile • Stone Row • U-shaped	24	X	X	X	6	13	22	23	14	1	8	14	4	2	17	17	2
Rock Pile • Stone Row • Niche	25	X	X	17	6	17	32	28	19	1	15	31	11	3	31	X	4
Rock Pile • Stone Row • Stone Circle	15	X	X	8	3	11	15	18	14	2	X	13	5	1	16	15	2
Stone Row • Petroglyph • Effigy	4	7	X	1	2	4	1	2	1	X	2	X	0	0	1	1	1

Above: Plate 47: Four-way comparisons of types.

Below: Plate 48: GIS map showing location of clusters.

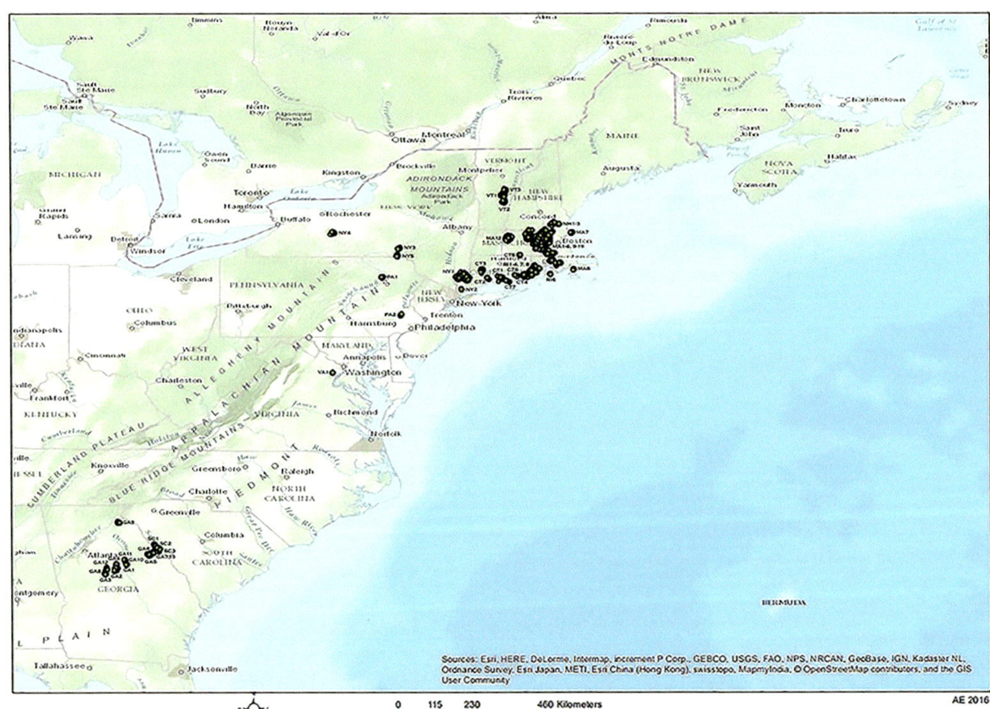

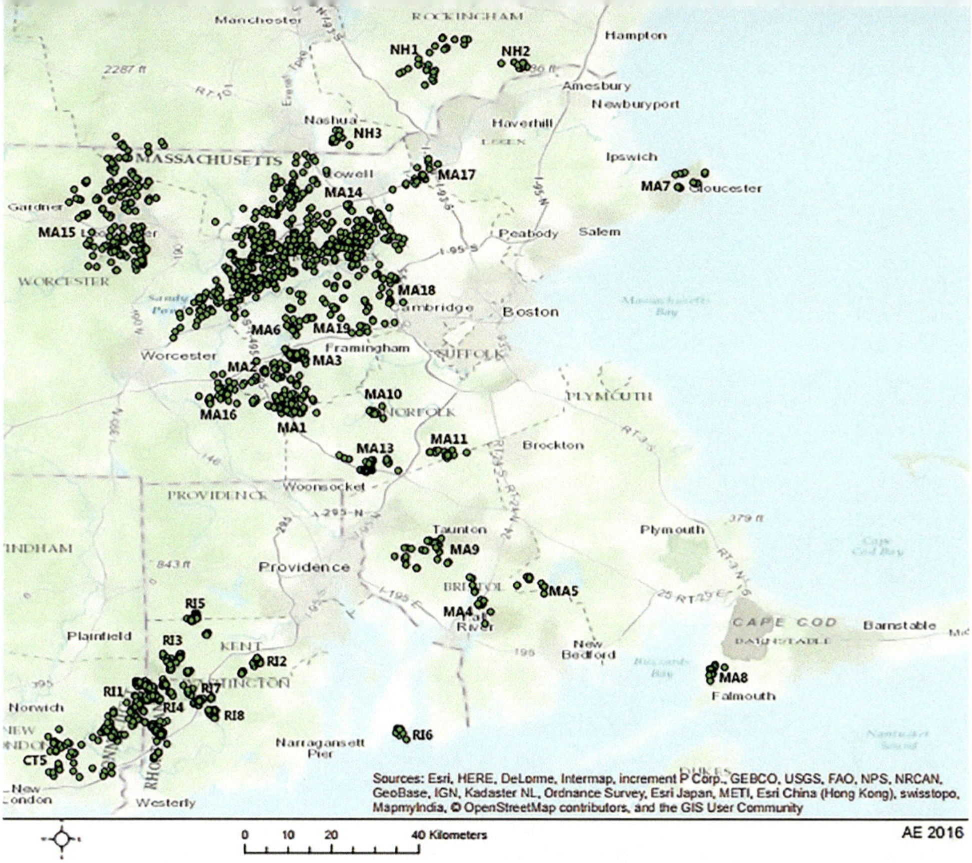

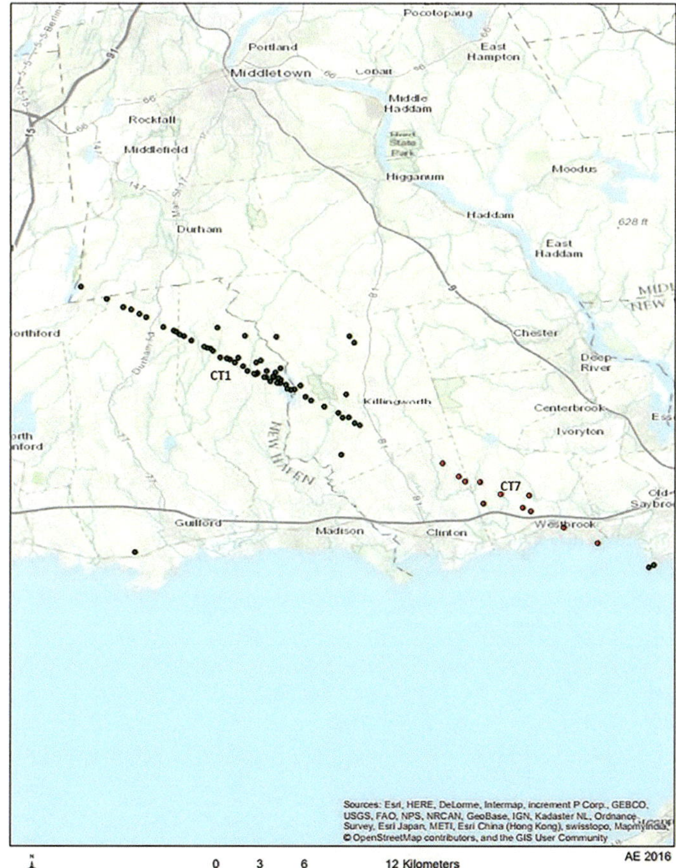

Above: Plate 49: GIS map showing locations of clusters in southeastern New England.

Right: Plate 50: GIS map showing Connecticut Clusters No. 1 and No. 7.

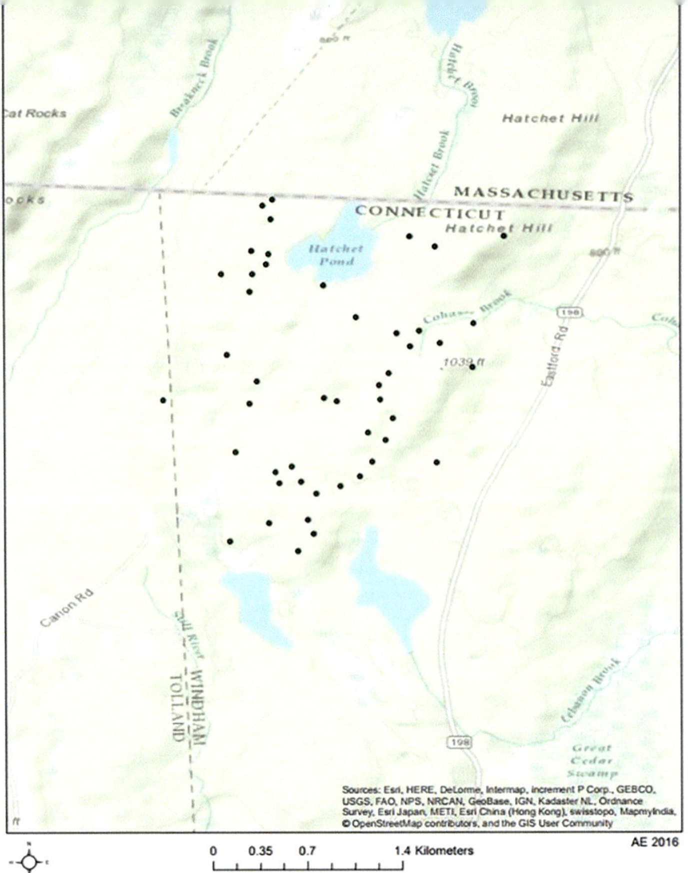

Plate 51: GIS map of Connecticut Cluster No. 5.

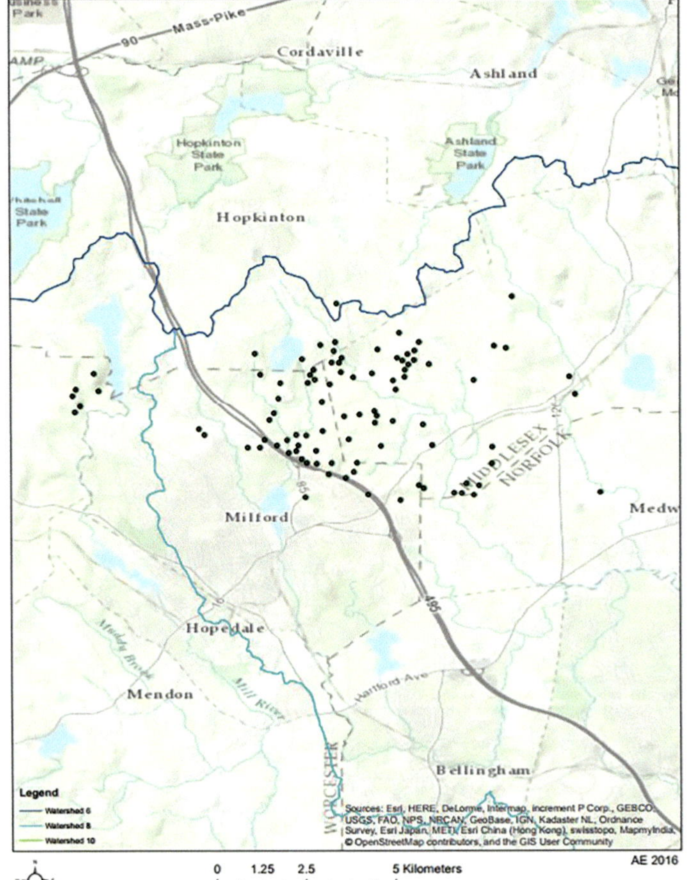

Plate 52: GIS map of Massachusetts Cluster No. 1 (north of dark blue line: Merrimack Drainage; west of blue-green line: Blackstone Drainage; remainder: Charles Drainage).

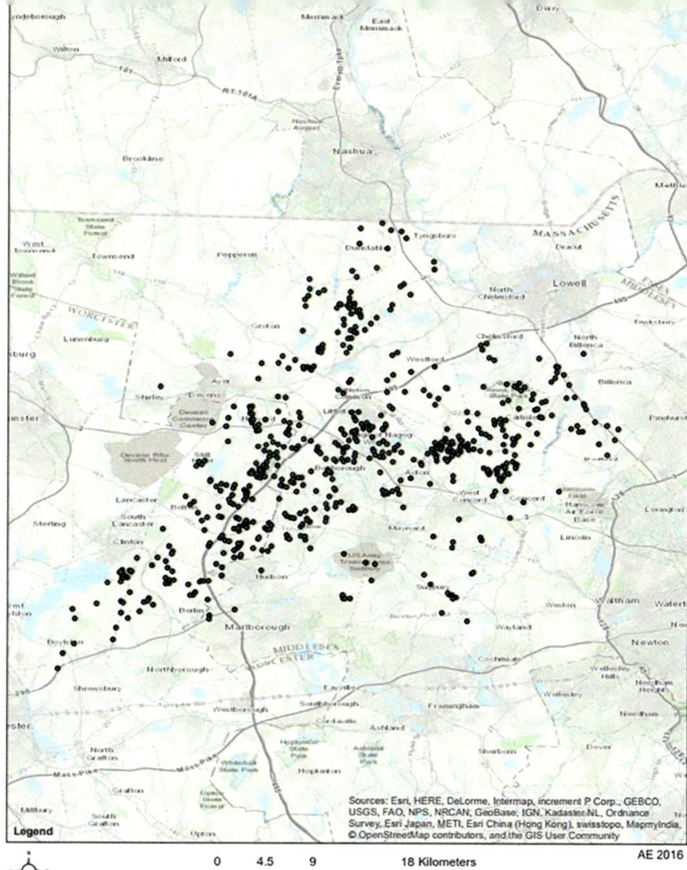

Plate 53: GIS map of Massachusetts Cluster No. 14.

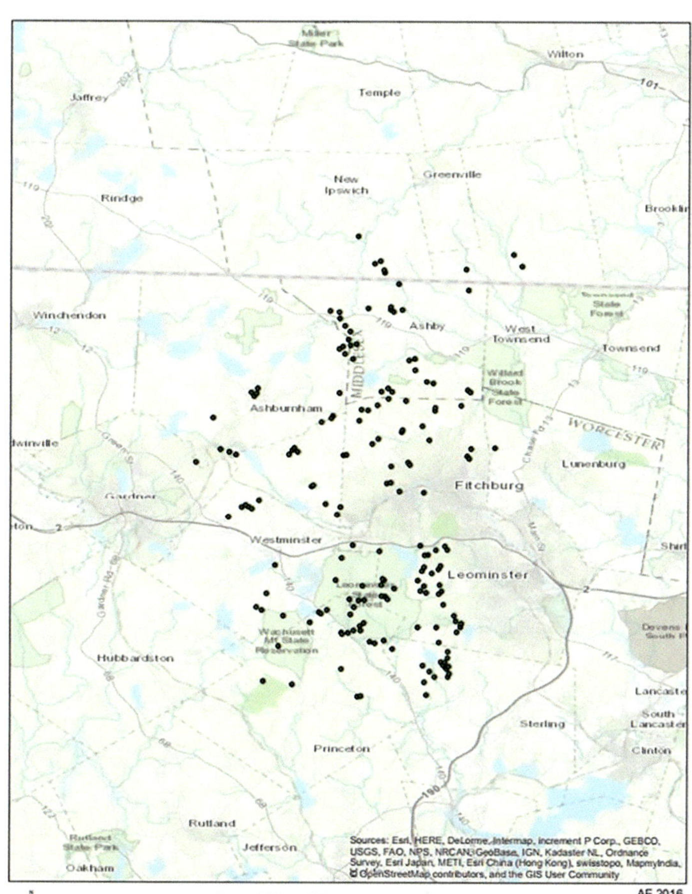

Plate 54: GIS map of Massachusetts Cluster No. 15.

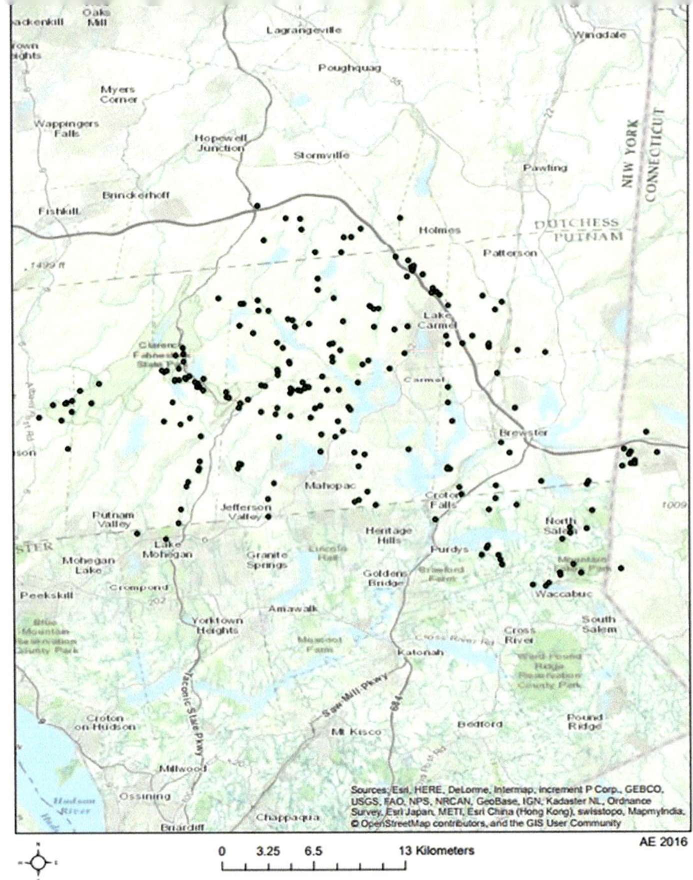

Plate 55: GIS map of New York Cluster No. 1.

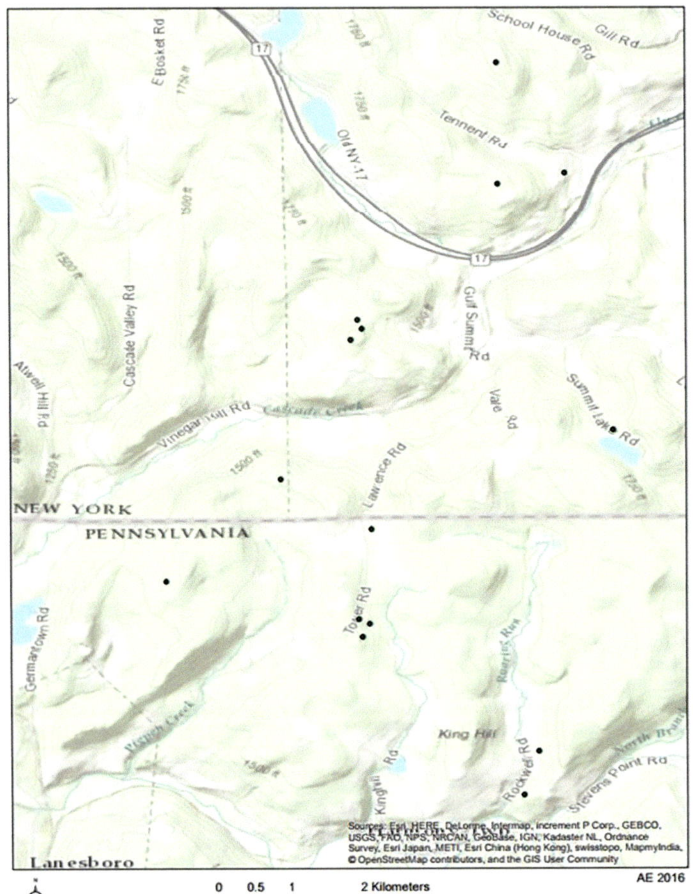

Plate 56: GIS map of New York Cluster No. 5.

Plate 57: GIS map of Rhode Island Cluster No. 1 (the blue line separates the Thames and Pawcatuck drainages).

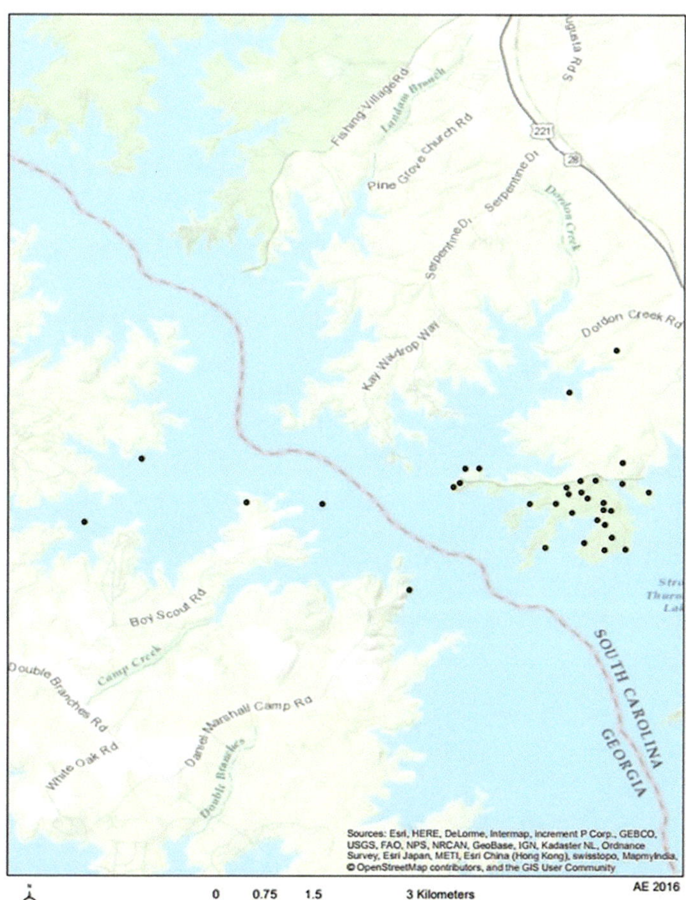

Plate 58: GIS map of South Carolina Cluster No. 3.

Above: Plate 59: Field clearing pile, Ashland, MA. (*Photo by Gordon Bernstein*)

Below: Plate 60: Probable Native American pile, Ashland, MA. (*Photo by the author*)

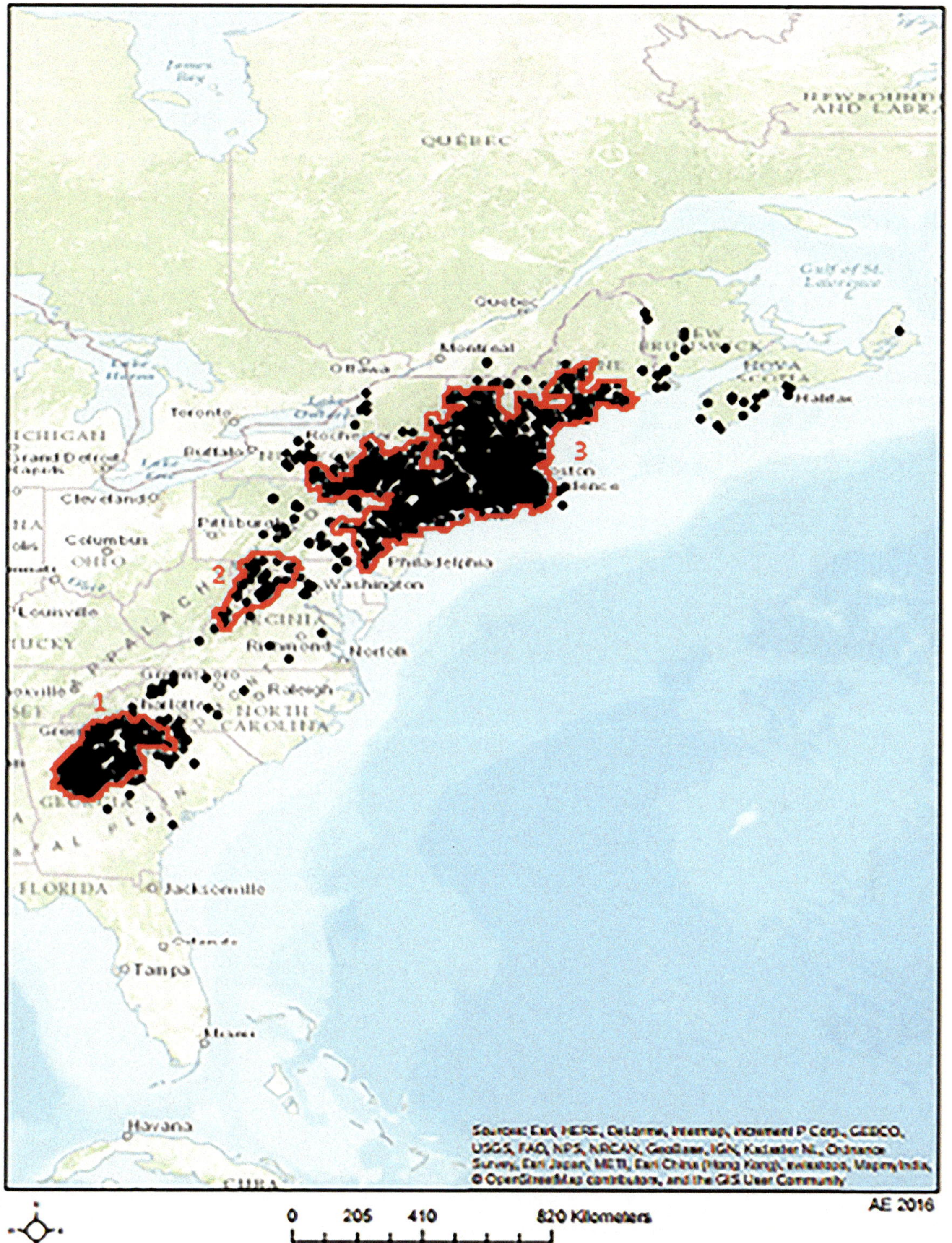

Plate 61: GIS map of the total distribution of sites, showing areas of concentration.

Type	Cairn	Rock Pile	Stone Row	U-Shaped	Chamber	Standing Stone	Split Boulder	Balanced Rock	Marked Stone	Petroglyph	Inscription	Stone Circle	Effigy	Mound	Platform	Enclosure	Niche	Unique Structure
Cairn	x	26	14	1	0	2	15	11	5	1	0	4	4	2	2	6	11	
Rock Pile	26	x	44	10	0	7	35	26	14	3	0	12	22	10	9	12	16	
Stone Row	14	44	x	6	0	5	18	13	7	0	0	9	16	2	2	6	12	
U-Shaped	1	10	6	x	0	0	3	2	1	1	0	0	2	2	1	0	3	
Chamber	0	0	0	0	x	0	0	0	0	1	0	0	0	0	0	0	0	
Standing Stone	2	7	5	0	0	x	3	2	0	0	0	2	1	0	0	4	4	
Split Boulder	15	35	18	3	0	3	x	20	6	2	0	7	9	1	2	6	13	
Balanced Rock	11	26	13	2	0	2	20	x	4	0	0	5	5	0	1	5	10	
Marked Stone	5	14	7	1	0	0	6	4	x	1	0	1	4	0	0	2	3	
Petroglyph	1	3	0	1	1	0	2	0	1	x	0	0	0	0	0	0	1	
Inscription	0	0	0	0	0	0	0	0	0	0	x	0	0	0	0	0	0	
Stone Circle	4	12	9	0	0	2	7	5	1	0	0	x	2	1	1	3	6	
Effigy	4	22	16	2	0	1	9	5	4	0	0	2	x	2	0	1	3	
Mound	2	10	3	2	0	0	1	0	0	0	0	1	2	x	2	0	0	
Platform	2	9	2	1	0	0	2	1	0	0	0	1	0	2	x	0	0	
Enclosure	6	12	6	0	0	4	6	5	2	0	0	3	1	0	0	x	5	
Niche	11	16	12	3	0	4	13	10	3	1	0	6	3	0	0	5	x	
Unique Structure	1	4	2	0	0	0	1	1	1	0	0	0	2	0	0	0	1	x
Total	105	250	157	32	1	30	141	105	49	10	0	53	73	22	20	50	88	

Plate 62: Pairwise combinations of structure types for newly documented sites (compare with Plate 45).

Conclusions

As noted in Chapter 6, the objectivity of this study may be questioned due to the fact that it relies so heavily upon informants who may be biased in favor of the areas where they reside. This may be a particularly important problem for clusters. As a check on this, the number of informants for each cluster was calculated. Only ten out of the sixty-four clusters (15.6 percent) had only one informant: Connecticut No. 3 (Tim MacSweeney), Connecticut No. 5 (Dennis Donais), Connecticut No. 7 (Tom Paul), New Hampshire No. 2 (Peter Waksman), Pennsylvania No. 1 (Heather Taylor), Rhode Island Nos. 6, 7, and 8 (Steve DiMarzo), and South Carolina Nos. 1 and 2 (U.S. Forest Service). All other clusters had at least two informants; the average was 3.8 per cluster, and the maximum was twenty-one informants for Massachusetts Cluster No. 14. The presence of multiple informants tends to cancel out any bias, which might be exhibited by a solitary informant.

The average ratio in all clusters of the number of sites to the cluster area was 0.59 sites per square kilometer, and the range was from 0.20 to 2.04 sites per square kilometer. Some single 1-square-kilometer cells within clusters contained as many as twenty-one sites. Outside of the clusters, no 1-square-kilometer cell in the study area contained more than seven sites, and there were only three areas that contained six sites. The average number of structures per site in a cluster was 8.26 (range: 1–681), while outside of clusters this average was 5.72 (range: 1–309). The average number of structure types per site in a cluster was 1.72, while outside of clusters this average was 1.42. The average minimum distance (NND) between sites in clusters was 0.48 km, while outside of clusters it was 4.07 km, more than eight times as distant. The overall average for the database was 2.07 km.

While clusters were comparable in terms of the close proximity between sites, especially as compared with sites outside of clusters, they were very diverse in terms of other parameters. There were three mega-clusters (Massachusetts No. 14, New York No. 1, and Rhode Island No. 1), which had extremely large numbers of sites—in excess of 200. Each of these contained smaller heavy concentrations of sites within them that might be considered as sub-clusters. Six additional clusters had large numbers of sites, between seventy-five and 200 (Georgia Clusters No. 2 and No. 5, Massachusetts Clusters No. 1, No. 12, and No. 15, and Vermont Cluster No. 1). These clusters did not, for the most part, contain recognizable sub-clusters. In addition to these large clusters, there were twenty-one clusters with moderate numbers of sites, between twenty-five and seventy-five, and thirty-four clusters with fewer than twenty-five sites.

It is possible that more data will eventually emerge that will either connect the sub-clusters to one another more tightly within the megaclusters or, alternatively, will argue for their disaggregation. Aggregation of clusters has actually been done within the course of this study: two of the large Massachusetts clusters (Nos. 12 and 15) had each previously been plotted as two separate clusters, until sites were reported (in Shutesbury for Cluster No. 12 and on the Leominster–Princeton border for Cluster No. 15), which allowed for them to be connected. Disaggregation has taken place with New York Cluster No. 1, which was originally combined with New York Cluster No. 2, but was later determined to be separated from it. It may also be the case that some of the clusters could be expanded to include areas not at present counted within the larger cluster. For example, Massachusetts Cluster No. 14 might merge with Massachusetts Clusters No. 18 and No. 19; Rhode Island Cluster No. 1 might merge with Connecticut Clusters No. 4 and/or No. 6. Finally, it is possible that additional sites may be found that would result in the identification of new, small clusters within the project area.

The frequency of types of structures within clusters was evaluated by comparing their percentages within the cluster to the average of sites with that structure type within clusters, calculating a standard deviation for each type, and finding how far above or below this mean the frequencies within clusters were for each structure type. When this was done, it became apparent that there were numerous instances in which a particular structure type dominated in a cluster, being found at a frequency at least as high as eight standard deviations away from the mean. The distribution for clusters is given in Figure 97 below. It should be obvious that all three of the mega-clusters (Massachusetts No. 14, New York No. 1, and Rhode Island No. 1) and four of the large clusters (Massachusetts No. 1, Massachusetts No. 12, Massachusetts No. 15, and Vermont No. 1) are overrepresented in this table. Despite this overrepresentation, it is possible to observe some general patterns. Most of the Georgia, South Carolina, and Virginia clusters have a very limited range of variation in structure types; they largely or entirely contain only rock piles. An overwhelming preponderance of chambers is found in New York Cluster No. 1, more than five times that found in any other cluster. Standing stones and petroglyphs are most common in the three Vermont clusters. Mounds are only commonly found in the Massachusetts clusters, while split boulders and niches are only common in the Massachusetts and Rhode Island clusters.

The same procedure was followed for sites outside of clusters, state by state. The results, shown in Figure 98, were less striking; for example, no state had any structure types more than seven standard deviations above the mean for types at sites outside of clusters, and, with three exceptions, all were within four standard deviations of the mean. However, there are some apparent similarities with the sites in clusters in the same areas. Like the sites in clusters in that state, Georgia sites outside of clusters had a high proportion of rock piles, and otherwise only mounds and platforms occurred there in excess of two standard deviations. The only structure type commonly found elsewhere in the southern states was petroglyphs, in South Carolina. These were most frequently found at higher elevations, while the three South Carolina clusters were located adjacent to the Savannah River, at lower elevations, and lacked petroglyphs. Standing stones were most prevalent in Vermont—as in the clusters in that state—and in Massachusetts. Mounds were most frequently found in Massachusetts, as they are in clusters in that state. It may be concluded that clusters are somewhat more specialized in terms of structure types than the areas outside of them, but that there are apparent regional vernacular styles.

σ > Mean	1	2	3	4	5	6	7	≥8
Cairn	MA1	NY1	PA1	NH1	CT5, MA6	SC3		CT1, MA12, MA14, RI1
Rock Pile	GA1, GA6, PA1, RI3			MA12			MA12	GA2. GA5, MA1, MA14, MA15, RI1
Stone Row	CT4, MA3, MA13, MA16, RI8	CT1	CT3, PA1, VT1	MA12, MA18		NY1		MA14, MA15, RI1
Prayer Seat/U-Shaped	RI5, RI8	VT3	MA13, MA15	CT1, MA1, MA12, NY1	MA11	MA9		MA14, RI1
Subterranean/Chamber/Cave	VT2	MA1, MA14, NY2		CT6	MA12, VT3			CT4, NY1, RI1
Standing Stone	PA1	MA3, RI3, VT3	NY1, VT2	CT1		MA1, RI1		MA12, MA14, VT1
Split Boulder	MA12, RI5	RI2	MA15	RI7	MA3, RI8			MA1, MA14, RI1, RI3
Balanced Rock	MA12	RI4	MA15, NY1, RI5, RI7	RI7	MA13, MA14, RI8			MA1, RI1, RI3
Marked Stone	MA15, RI3	CT7, VT1	CT5, MA3			MA12, MA14		CT1, RI1
Petroglyph				RI1	VT3	VT2	VT1	MA12
Inscription			RI1, VT2					MA14
Stone Circle	MA3, RI4	RI3			MA1, RI8			MA12, RI1
Effigy	MA1, MA3, NY1, PA1, VT1		MA1, MA3, NY1, PA1,	CT3		RI8	MA12	MA7, MA14, RI1
Mound			MA3, MA16	MA1				MA12, MA14, MA15
Platform	MA15, MA16	CT1, MA18			MA12			MA14
Enclosure		MA12, RI2, RI7	RI3, RI6	MA1		MA15	MA14, RI8	RI1
Niche	MA1	MA15, MA16, PA1, RI3, RI4	MA3, MA12, RI7			RI8	MA14	RI1
Unique Structure			PA1		MA12, RI1	MA1		MA14

Figure 97: Frequency of Structure Types in Clusters.

No. σ > Mean	1	2	3	4	5	7
Cairn		PA		NY		
Rock Pile			MA, NY	GA		
Stone Row	NH, RI		NY	CT		MA
Prayer Seat/U-Shaped	ME, NY	NH		MA		
Subterranean/Chamber/Cave	MA, NH, NY	VT	CT			
Standing Stone		CT, NY		VT	MA	
Split Boulder	RI					
Balanced Rock	CT, ME, NJ, NY	RI		MA		
Marked Stone	PA	RI				
Petroglyph	VT	SC				
Inscription		MA, RI				
Stone Circle		ME, NY			MA	
Effigy			NY	CT, MA		
Mound		GA, ME, PA		MA		
Platform	CT, NH	GA, MA				
Enclosure	CT, ME	NY	MA			
Niche	NH	CT, NY, RI	MA			
Unique Structure	NY	CT, ME			MA	

Figure 98: Frequency of Structure Types outside of Clusters.

In terms of their environmental locations, there are also some broad regional patterns that may be observed. The sites in the southeastern clusters tend to be located at higher stream ranks than average (2.7, as compared to the total average of 1.8). They tend to be located closer to rivers (the average being 3.9, compared to the total average of 2.6) and are rarely associated with ponds and never with swamps, although associations with these types of locations are common in the northeastern clusters. They are nowhere near the ocean, which is probably due to the lack of available stone in the coastal plain south of the glacial margin. They also are much more likely to be located in agriculturally productive soils on average (on average 23.4, compared to the total average of 16.1) and correspondingly much less likely to be located in low fertility soils (on average 1.6, compared to the total average of 15.1), naturally infertile soils (on average 1.4, compared to the total average of 14.5), or pasture lands (on average 0.1, compared to the total average of 2.8). With the exception of the avoidance of swamps and the ocean in the southeastern states, these trends are not reflected in the sites outside of clusters in the same states, when these parameters are averaged by state.

In conclusion, the clusters provide interesting insights into the distribution of stone structures throughout the study area, and present one of the strongest arguments for their construction by indigenous people. The fact that so many clusters cross post-Contact political boundaries strongly suggests that they are antecedent to the establishment of those boundaries, and, therefore, are more likely to be the work of indigenous people than of colonial farmers seeking to clear their fields. The one major exception to this, Connecticut Cluster No. 5, is associated with a post-Contact Native reservation that was established around the time that the Massachusetts–Connecticut boundary was established. This is an example of an exception that proves the rule, since it indicates that the Native tradition of building stone structures did not cease with Contact, even though by that time it was constrained by Euro-American ideas about territorial boundaries.

10

Evaluation of Hypotheses

The purpose of this chapter is to use the data accumulated in this study to evaluate the four hypotheses set forth in Chapter 3, on the basis of the test conditions posed for each hypothesis in that chapter. They will be evaluated along a seven-point Likert scale, using the following terms:

1. Disconfirmed: No cases satisfying the test condition were found.
2. Largely Disconfirmed: Very few cases satisfying the test condition were found.
3. Partially Disconfirmed: The majority of cases did not satisfy the test condition.
4. Neither Confirmed nor Disconfirmed: Either there was insufficient information, or the number of cases satisfying and not satisfying the test condition was relatively equal.
5. Partially Confirmed: The majority of cases satisfied the test condition.
6. Largely Confirmed: Very few cases not satisfying the test condition were found.
7. Confirmed: All cases for which data exists satisfied the test condition.

It should be noted that, as in any scientific study, nothing is ever absolutely confirmed or disconfirmed; the possibility that a single case might emerge that would satisfy, or not satisfy, the test condition in question must be held open. Using the Likert scale approach on such a large data set allows for this because, if this were to happen, it would simply move the evaluation into the "largely" category, while retaining the general positive or negative orientation of the rest of the data set.

The hypotheses, and their test conditions, are as follows:

A. The Structures are the Result of Colonial Farmers Clearing Agricultural or Pasturage Fields or for the Construction of Stone Walls

Test conditions for Hypothesis "A" are as follows:

1. Sites should be located close to or within agricultural fields, in either present or documented historical locations where farming took place. This hypothesis is partially disconfirmed. More than two-thirds of all sites (67.06 percent, 3,722) are located on hilltops or on slopes, and 25.71 percent (1,427) of all sites are on slopes in excess of

15 percent, which would not be preferred (or even possible) locations for farming activities. At most, these locations could have been used for grazing or timbering. Positioning of sites does not seem to have been based upon proximity to farm lands, though no documentary research has been done to prove this conclusively.

2. Sites should be in soils which are at least marginally suitable for farming. This is partially disconfirmed. While almost one-third of the sites (1,824) are located in agriculturally fertile land (especially in the Southeast, which contains 40.7 percent of them), nearly equal numbers of sites are in soils with low fertility (1,656), or in soils which are naturally infertile (1,617), including many on rock outcrops (53.9 percent of sites in naturally infertile soils), or in hydric soils or actually underwater (11.9 percent of sites in naturally infertile soils). It is simply the case that agriculturally fertile soils are more common in the unglaciated Southeast than in the glaciated Northeast. If the sites south of the Mason–Dixon line are subtracted from the total, the percentage of sites in agriculturally fertile soils drops from 32.9 percent to 23.9 percent.

3. Sites should be contained within the geopolitical boundaries (states, counties, or towns) established during the period of European settlement. This is largely disconfirmed. All but eight of the sixty-four site clusters identified in this study overlap town, county, or state boundaries. The integrity of these clusters is strongly confirmed by both VMR and nearest-neighbor analysis. In addition, of the 1,405 sites outside of clusters whose nearest neighbors were less than 2 kilometers away, there were fifteen sites whose nearest neighbors were across state boundaries: four between New Jersey and Pennsylvania; two each between Connecticut and Massachusetts, Maryland and West Virginia, and Georgia and South Carolina; and one each between Massachusetts and New Hampshire, Rhode Island and Connecticut, New Hampshire and Vermont, and New York and Connecticut. There were thirty sites whose nearest neighbors were across county boundaries: eight each in Massachusetts and Georgia, four in South Carolina, three in New York, two each in Connecticut and New Jersey, and one each in Maryland and West Virginia. There were 132 sites whose nearest neighbors were across town boundaries: twenty-nine in Massachusetts, seventeen in Georgia, fourteen in Connecticut, twelve in New Hampshire, ten each in New York, South Carolina, and Pennsylvania, eight in Vermont, seven in New Jersey, six in Maine, four in Rhode Island, two each in Nova Scotia and Virginia, and one in Delaware. This amounts to 12.6 percent of the sites outside of clusters whose nearest neighbors were less than two km away. When combined with the 2,864 sites in the clusters which overlap boundaries, the total is 3,041 sites, 68.2 percent of the total whose nearest neighbors were less than two km away across political boundaries. This strongly suggests that the majority of the sites were present on the landscape prior to the creation of those boundaries during the settlement period. It seems unlikely that individual Euro-American farmers would wish to pay taxes to two or more political jurisdictions.

4. Sites should be widely dispersed throughout the landscape wherever farming took place, and should not be clustered in particular locations. This is strongly disconfirmed. The sixty-four clusters, whose integrity has been confirmed by both VMR and nearest neighbor analysis, occupy only 0.5 percent of the study area, while

there are large areas which were farmed which appear to lack clusters. Any global explanation of these sites which claims that they are the result of farm activity must account for both the presence of clusters in certain areas and their absence in other areas. So far, aside from the absence of sites in the coastal plain south of the glacial margin, most likely due to the absence of stone there, no such explanation has been proposed, nor is it likely that any could be. Furthermore, there are many sites located in areas where farming would have been very difficult, if not impossible; for example, in the Catskills or the highlands of the southern Appalachians, or on bedrock outcrops or on slopes in excess of 15 percent.

5. Structures at most sites should reflect only simple piling of stones, or walls, rather than elaborate constructions. This is partially disconfirmed. While rock piles are by far the most common type of structure, accounting for 54.7 percent of the total (3,035), at nearly three-eighths of sites that contain them they are combined with other structures, especially stone rows. In fact, rock piles are not only the most common type, they are also the type most commonly combined with all other structures, with the exception of petroglyphs, which are more often combined with standing stones and stone rows; and inscriptions, which are more often combined with chambers, marked stones, petroglyphs, and platforms. The elaborate constructions include U-shaped structures, standing stones, split-filled boulders, balanced rocks, marked stones, petroglyphs, stone circles, effigies, mounds, platforms, enclosures, and niches, none of which has a clear association with colonial farming activities.

6. Where there are more elaborate constructions, there will be documentation to show that they are the result of "aesthetic farm maintenance." This is largely disconfirmed. A claim was made by Walwer to the effect that the stone cairns at the Killingworth site in Connecticut were the product of farm beautification efforts.[1] When investigating this, the author undertook historical research into so-called "stone bees"—occasions on which residents supposedly gathered, laced with grog, to construct aesthetically pleasing stone monuments to beautify farms and thus influence the younger generation to remain in New England's rocky landscape to perpetuate their elders' professions. In my response to Walwer's hypothesis, I stated:

> A Google© search on "stone bee" revealed eight references to this activity, most of them archival notes from outside of the region, and, with one exception, all later than 1865. The exception is a passing mention in James Fennimore Cooper's novel *The Wept of Wish-Ton-Wish*, which is set in the vicinity of Hartford in the seventeenth century and concerns relationships between colonists and Native Americans. The passage states that "the neighbors will not be backward at the stone-bee, or the raising," which relates this activity to house construction.[2] The only other detailed reference, in John Burroughs' *In the Catskills*, states that "… the farmers made 'bees' as they did a generation or two much more than they do now.…[3] There was the stone bee, the husking bee, the 'raising' the 'moving' etc." Once again, the bee is directly related to construction, rather than "aesthetic farm maintenance." We may conclude that, if stone bees were practiced in Killingworth, they were part of the process of manufacturing stone walls and house and barn foundations, and are unlikely to have produced decorative cairns. The one cairn

illustrated by Allport and said by her to have been constructed by a hired hand in the 1920s is not identified as to its location, nor do we know the ethnic identity of the hired hand—he could have been Native.[4] As an isolated example, it cannot be used to argue (as Walwer does) that "'beehive' stone piles similar to those of the study area … were made by some farmers to commemorate a person or event".[5] One is not some, and a hired hand is not a farmer.[6]

As Timothy Fohl has documented from his own experience as a farmhand, moving the rocks that crop up in New England's fields every spring is exhausting, time-consuming work, and farmers—a rather conservative group—would be unlikely to devote the time, energy, or interest to "doodle" in stone as Thorson has suggested.[7,8] It is, however, acknowledged that some landowners—perhaps only after farming became less viable as a profession in the New England uplands—may have created stone structures in their yards to amuse themselves. In some cases, these may have been cases of "copy-cat" activity, sparked by the presence of much older stone features on the premises. For example, Bob Miner, who owns a farm in southwestern Rhode Island, has admitted to constructing and maintaining some structures of this sort, but in conscious imitation of stone features on the same property which, as far as he and his father knew, had been there for "hundreds of years" prior to their occupancy.[9] Separating the copies out from the older structures is not always easy, but there are some observable differences. The behaviors involved in discarding unwanted objects produce different material signatures from those involved in creating deliberate monuments, and archaeologists regularly use patterning of the structure and contents of such features to discriminate between these two behaviors.[10] Stones in discard piles are not likely to be size-sorted and will tend to have a haphazard appearance to their configuration, in contrast to those in well-built, organized stone piles. For comparison, see Plates 59 and 60.

Moreover, one would expect that if the sort of "doodling" referred to by Thorsen were going on, it would be highly idiosyncratic to particular farms rather than there being widespread patterns of construction. Doodling might conceivably apply to the category of "unique structures" documented in this volume—but there are only sixty-eight such structures documented, while most other structure types are both far more numerous and more widely distributed.

7. The total number of structure types at sites should be limited. This is partially disconfirmed. While 69.7 percent of sites possess only a single type, and 16.7 percent possess only two types, there are numerous sites (754) with more than two types present. Some of the sites in the study have a great diversity of types of structure, as many as thirteen different types out of the total of eighteen defined in Chapter 5.

8. Structures should not be found in such quantities or in such close proximity at a site as to restrict the passage of the types of horse-drawn carts used by farmers to haul away stones. Partially disconfirmed. While 35.4 percent of sites have only one structure present, there are 113 sites with fifty or more structures, and thirty-four sites with 100 or more structures; the largest number present at any one site is 681. However, this study has not attempted to map each individual structure at a site, so the suggestion that the distance between structures may be too small for a cart

path must be considered to be anecdotal only. Tim Fohl has provided information on the size of stone-dragging carts, and at least at some sites I have visited with multiple structures, they are often much too closely spaced to allow the passage of such vehicles.[11]

9. Structures should not be situated at significantly higher elevations than the fields from which they are proposed to have been removed, or on slopes greater than *c.* 15 percent. Presumably, this is because farmers would not wish to take the effort to move stones uphill when they could move them downhill with the help of gravity.[12] Partially disconfirmed. As noted under item A1 above, more than 67 percent of sites are located on hilltops or on slopes; and where slope was defined, 25.7 percent were located on slopes more extreme than 15 percent. It would take considerable effort to remove those stones from fields and move them uphill. One exception to this appears to be chambers—especially isolated chambers without azimuths—which were more often located in valleys than on hilltops or slopes.

10. Walls, if present, should connect at right angles, should generally be straight, and should actually bound parcels. This has neither been confirmed nor disconfirmed in most cases. No study was made of the angles at which walls met, though, in general, if walls were perceived to meet at right angles, they were not included in the inventory. There were numerous examples of stone rows that were not straight, but curved or had a sinuous shape (either horizontally or, more rarely, vertically), which were considered to be serpent effigies. Some of these rows ended in marked stones, which had been shaped to resemble serpent heads. Also, in many cases, these rows did not meet other walls, but began and ended arbitrarily, sometimes adjacent to water bodies (lakes and swamps). No attempt was made in this study to examine the relationship of stone rows to property boundaries. It is possible that farmers who found pre-existing stone rows in their fields reused them as property boundaries. Anecdotally, I can relate one such boundary existing on the Bridgewater State University campus, which is marked by a discontinuous stone row at most one course high.[13] However, the orientation of this row is precisely on a summer solstice sunset alignment (this has been tested empirically), and a gap in the row allows viewing of the winter solstice sunset through a gap in a large split boulder downslope of the row.

11. Walls, if present, should be of sufficient height as to serve as boundaries that could keep domestic animals in, wild animals and trespassers out. Partially disconfirmed. Those sites that have stone rows (16.1 percent of the total) often do not exhibit the kinds of construction that would have been effective as walls, since many of them are only one or a few courses high, and often do not bound anything. However, there has been no attempt in this study (as there was in the earlier Killingworth study) to calculate the net weight of the stones in the rows, or their size or height; nor has any documentary research been done to show the relationships of these rows to actual field boundaries, as was done in Murray's study.[14]

12. Walls, if present, should not be associated with other types of stone structures. Partially disconfirmed. There is a total of 142 sites where walls or stone rows are not associated with other structures, representing 15.7 percent of the sites with stone rows. A comparison was made with the 760 sites (84.3 percent) where stone rows

are associated with other structure types (especially rock piles and cairns), in terms of location. While the two groups did not differ significantly in average slope (13.5 percent for associated rows, 13.7 percent for unassociated rows), elevation above sea level, or soil fertility, there were significant differences in terms of their presence within clusters (associated stone rows were more likely to be in clusters; the chi-square being 25.02, significant at p=.001); types of associated water resources (associated stone rows were more likely to be found near headwater streams; the chi-square being 23.70, significant at p=.001); environmental setting (associated stone rows were more likely to be found on slopes and less likely to be found on shores than unassociated rows; the chi-square being 35.67, significant at p=.001); distance to fault (unassociated rows were about twice as distant on average); and nearest neighbor (unassociated rows were more than twelve times as distant from other sites on average). Associated stone rows had a lower average stream rank (1.5, as compared with 2.1 for unassociated rows), a somewhat shorter distance to nearest watershed (0.13 km as compared with 0.16 km for unassociated rows), and a slightly shorter distance to head-of-tide (7.8 km as compared with 8.5 km for unassociated rows). This suggests the possibility that the unassociated stone rows may be significantly different from the associated rows, and perhaps are of post-Contact age, but that the associated stone rows are probably not.

13. Diagnostic artifacts and absolute dates associated with sites should never antedate the earliest European contact in the areas where the sites are located. Disconfirmed. As indicated in Figure 1, all twenty-two of the absolute dates that have been obtained from stone structures indicate that they are of pre-Contact age. Some sites are associated with pre-Contact artifacts as well, though this has not been studied quantitatively across the region. For example, a pit feature at the Call Site in Billerica, Massachusetts, contained a standing stone associated with artifacts of Transitional Archaic age, *c.* 4200–2900 B.P.[15] There are some structures that do contain post-Contact artifacts, but that does not necessarily mean that they were built by settlers.[16] Some post-Contact Native graves also contain post-Contact artifacts, and historical documentation cited in Chapter 2 strongly suggests that the indigenous practice of stone monument construction did not cease with European contact.[17]

14. There should be no preference for sites to be found in the vicinity of watershed boundaries and fault lines. Disconfirmed. There is a strong preference for sites to be located adjacent to Rank One streams (64.5 percent, 3,577), within 2 kilometers of a fault (49.4 percent, 2,706), and within 2 kilometers of a level ten watershed (53.7 percent, 2,974).

15. Sites should not be located in areas with topographic place names that indicate deliberate avoidance by colonial farmers, such as names associated with Native Americans or with the Devil. Disconfirmed. As noted above in Chapter 6, 313 sites (5.6 percent) have names that are associated with either Native Americans or with the Devil. In addition, two sites in New York Cluster No. 4 are located within Clark's Gully, which the traditions of the Seneca Nation identify as the place of their emergence from the earth.[18]

16. There should be colonial names for the different types of structures, and an absence of indigenous terminology for them. Partially disconfirmed. Thirteen out of the eighteen

structure types appear to have indigenous names. There is evidence suggesting that two of the types that do not have such names, inscriptions and unique structures, may not be indigenous constructions.

17. There should be colonial names for individual sites. Largely disconfirmed. Only twenty-seven sites (0.4 percent) have colonial names, far fewer than those noted in point 16 above, which are related to indigenous people or to ritual avoidance. This is remarkable when one considers the extent to which colonists renamed locations after places and persons from their own culture. At the state/province level, only three jurisdictions retained their Native names: Connecticut, Massachusetts, and Quebec. As Figure 99 shows, only about 10.0 percent of counties and 4.8 percent of towns in the study area have Native names.

These figures were compared with the density of sites in each state/province (see Figure 5), using the Spearman Rank-Order test. For counties, there was actually a strong negative correlation of -0.42; for towns there was a very small positive correlation of 0.04. When the numbers of counties and towns were combined, there was a very small negative correlation of -0.08. This indicates that there is no

State	# Native Counties	Total #	% Native	# Native Towns	Total #	% Native
Connecticut	0	7	0.0%	2	169	1.2%
Delaware	0	3	0.0%	1	57	1.8%
Georgia	1	91	1.1%	10	221	4.5%
Maine	6	16	37.5%	20	455	4.4%
Maryland	2	21	9.5%	2	142	1.4%
Massachusetts	1	14	7.1%	18	351	5.1%
New Brunswick	2	15	13.3%	4	26	15.4%
New Hampshire	2	10	20.0%	3	221	1.4%
New Jersey	1	21	4.8%	37	565	6.5%
New York	15	57	26.3%	54	781	6.9%
North Carolina	8	88	9.1%	14	487	2.9%
Nova Scotia	0	18	0.0%	0	263	0.0%
Pennsylvania	5	46	10.9%	39	518	7.5%
Quebec	9	55	16.4%	5	23	21.7%
Rhode Island	0	5	0.0%	3	39	7.7%
South Carolina	2	46	4.3%	12	269	4.5%
Vermont	0	14	0.0%	1	255	0.4%
Virginia	8	84	9.5%	10	172	5.8%
West Virginia	0	7	0.0%	11	99	11.1%
TOTAL	62	618	10.0%	246	5113	4.8%

Figure 99: Percentage of Counties and Towns with Native Names.

relationship between the number of sites in a state/province and the number of retained indigenous names. The combined figures do show a fairly strong positive correlation of 0.55 with the total area within the state/province; this is significant at the 0.25 confidence interval with 19 degrees of freedom. This simply points to the widespread erasure of indigenous place names across the study area. The twenty-seven counties in which stone structures were found that had retained their indigenous names actually had a lower number of sites (the average being 7.19) than the 229 counties with stone structures with non-indigenous names (the average being 23.19). This suggests that there is no relationship between the colonial practice of renaming places and the existence of these sites—which further suggests that the colonists were largely unaware of them. For some reason, river names have not been subject as thoroughly to this renaming process; fully 60.6 percent of those within the study area retain indigenous names.

18. Any archaeoastronomical alignments should reflect the belief systems of the colonizing English culture, or should be demonstrated to be random orientations. Disconfirmed. English colonists—who inhabited all of the study area, except for Quebec and Nova Scotia—may have been among the last literate people on earth to use the Julian calendar, up until 1752, because the more accurate Gregorian calendar, adopted by the Catholic Church in 1583, was perceived as part of a Papist plot to return the breakaway Anglican Church to the Catholic fold.[19] At the point when it was finally abandoned, the Julian calendar was out of alignment with the solar year by ten days, which is the reason that we used to celebrate the birthday of George Washington—who was born in 1732—on February 21. The actual timing of the calendar could easily have been corrected had the colonists set up stone markers in alignment with winter or summer solstice sunrise. That the correction was not made until the mid-eighteenth century, on the basis of a proclamation by the British crown rather than by local calibration, is strong evidence that such markers were not in use by English colonists.[20] As for the supposed randomness of the orientations, as claimed on the MHC website, this is disconfirmed by the fact that 50.9 percent of the sites for which azimuths were obtained were oriented towards either winter or summer solstice directions.[21] This can hardly be considered random placement. A total of seventy-six of these sites were isolated chambers (18.4 percent of the total), and an additional forty-nine chambers with azimuths had additional structure types present (11.9 percent).

B. The Structures are Natural Features of a Glaciated Landscape, or of Downslope Erosion

Test conditions for Hypothesis "B" are as follows:

1. Sites should not be found south of the glacial margin. This is strongly disconfirmed: 1,159 sites, 20.9 percent of the total, lie south of the glacial margin. All sites in Delaware, Maryland, Virginia, West Virginia, North Carolina, South Carolina, and Georgia, plus ninety-three sites in Pennsylvania, eighteen sites in New Jersey, and seven sites in New York are south of the Wisconsinan terminal moraine.[22]

2. The distribution of sites north of the glacial margin should be essentially random on the small scale, or reflect glacial movement on the large scale. This is disconfirmed by the presence of sixty-four discrete site clusters, both north and south of the glacial margin. In fact, there are three times as many clusters north of the glacial margin (forty-eight) as south of it (sixteen).

3. No evidence of human alteration of stones should be present. With the possible exception of balanced rocks (see point B5 below), this is disconfirmed. All of the other structures are clearly altered by human agency (unless one wishes to believe Frank Vento's claim that the rocks rolled downhill and self-organized into piles). While this study has not looked at the balanced rocks in detail, quantitatively, the author has observed at least one balanced rock in Maine that does appear to have been altered, and which is furthermore associated with several other types of structures.

4. With the exception of balanced rocks, structures should be found downslope from higher elevations. This is disconfirmed: 67.0 percent of sites were found on hilltops or on slopes. Balanced rocks were slightly more common in these two environmental settings (76.8 percent) than the rest of the site types, but they occurred in all other settings as well.

5. If balanced rocks are present, they should not be accompanied by other types of structures. This is largely disconfirmed, since at 301 of the sites containing balanced rocks (61.8 percent) they are accompanied by other structure types. The remaining 170 sites with isolated balanced rocks are widely scattered through the Northeast, with six of them south of the glacial margin (three each in Pennsylvania and New Jersey). Moreover, seventy-one of the isolated balanced rocks are found within site clusters (thirty-eight in Massachusetts, nineteen in Rhode Island, twelve in New York, and one each in Connecticut and Vermont). There remains the possibility that the sixty-five isolated balanced rock sites which are located north of the glacial margin and outside of clusters are natural formations and are not associated with cultural activity.

6. If structures are associated with dates, they should be prior to human occupation of the region. Disconfirmed. There are not many associations with absolute dates (see Figure 1), but those that there are all postdate the arrival of Paleo-Indians in the eastern U.S. and Canada by at least 8,000 years.

C. The Structures Represent the Work of pre-Columbian non-Native Peoples, either as Navigational Markers or Archaeoastronomical Placements

Test conditions for Hypothesis "C" are as follows:

1. Structures should be primarily located along the coast or close to major river transportation corridors, possibly radiating out from these locations to hinterlands. This is largely disconfirmed. Only 1.3 percent of sites (seventy-one) are located close to the ocean, and only 7.4 percent of sites (341) are located near the shores of the ocean, rivers, or lakes. Only 9.5 percent of sites (525) are within 10 km of the head-of-tide; the average distance to head-of-tide is 113.2 km. One significant exception to this is

the location of inscriptions, which had a higher than average proximity to the ocean (six out of eighteen) and tended to be closer to head-of-tide locations (the average distance being 12.3 km). Also, chambers have a stronger tendency to be located in valleys than do other structure types (217; 31.0 percent), but the valleys were not necessarily those of navigable rivers. In fact, only fifteen chambers (6.9 percent) were in the valleys of rivers of Rank Four or above. Only three of the sixty-four clusters, Massachusetts Nos. 7 and 8 and Rhode Island No. 6, are located near the ocean. All of the other clusters are located well inland.

2. If located close to major river corridors, sites should not be upstream of fall lines that would render the river unnavigable to the type of watercraft used by the incoming culture. This is largely disconfirmed. While no specific attempt was made in this study to identify fall lines, the three Vermont clusters—for which numerous claims have been made of Phoenician origin—are well upstream of Turner's Falls, the major falls in the Connecticut River, Massachusetts, a drop of 18 meters in half a kilometer of river distance.[23] This would certainly have been impossible for Phoenician triremes to navigate! In addition, the preponderance of sites at Rank One stream locations (3,577; 64.5 percent), at elevations above 500 feet above sea level (2,461; 44.3 percent), on slopes of 15 percent or more (1,427; 28.5 percent) and within 2 km of a level ten watershed (2,974; 53.7 percent) all strongly indicate that they were not accessible by ocean-going watercraft.

3. Artifactual evidence of specific non-Native cultural materials should be present at the sites that would allow identification of the specific cultures involved—as at L'Anse aux Meadows. Disconfirmed. As far as I am aware, no pre-seventeenth-century portable artifacts of non-Native origin have ever been found at any of the stone structure sites in the study area or, for that matter—with the sole exception of the Norse penny from the Goddard site in Maine—from any sites whatsoever south of Newfoundland.[24] The only exceptions to this may be petroglyphs and inscriptions (which are not portable), for which see point C5 below.

4. Any archaeoastronomical alignments should reflect the belief systems of the invasive non-Native culture. Neither confirmed nor disconfirmed, since this would require specialized knowledge of what those belief systems were and to what degree they differed from those of indigenous peoples. Many people throughout the world have observed key times in the annual cycle, such as solstices and equinoxes, and have erected monuments to mark and celebrate them. For example, there was considerable interest, in the sixteenth-century Catholic Church, in fixing the date of the spring equinox, since the scheduling of the Easter celebration is contingent upon it—on the first Sunday after the first full moon after the equinox—and Europeans during the Age of Exploration certainly constructed monuments in their cathedrals to capture this date.[25] While the winter solstice was also important for the scheduling of Christmas, there was less attention paid to summer solstice in Europe and certainly very little to August 13. Winter solstice does not require as elaborate constructions to capture it as does the equinox, since the sun sets at about the same point for two days on either side of the actual date. The contention that only Europeans recognized these times (or even that they may have introduced them to indigenous people) should be

recognized, as noted in Chapter 2, as a holdover from colonial attempts at the erasure of indigenous culture.[26]

5. Any representational structures—petroglyphs, pictographs, or effigies—should also be consonant with the belief systems and material culture of the non-Native culture. This is largely disconfirmed, with support for it on the basis of only two coastal sites that appear to have engraved images of European material culture: Dighton Rock in Massachusetts and Ship Rock in Maine. The late Dr. Manuel da Silva argued for many years that the equal-armed crosses at Dighton Rock represent a 1511 voyage by the Portuguese explorer Miguel Cortereal.[27] Other researchers have attributed its carvings, variously, to Norse or Native people, and it is possible that these explanations are not mutually exclusive.[28] I was informed of the Ship Rock carving, which appears to represent a sailing ship, by Valdemar Samuelsson, who has tried to claim that all the stonework in New England was the work of his own Viking ancestors, as noted in Chapter 1. However, it is difficult to believe that the Norse—who had been Christianized by the time of the establishment of the Vinland colony—would have created stone effigies of serpents. Even in pre-Christian Norse religion, the Midgard serpent was perceived as a negative entity.[29] Nor do turtles figure prominently in any European belief systems, though they are of paramount importance to eastern Algonquian Native peoples, and—like the serpents—are commonly represented in effigies as well as on portable art.[30]

6. If the non-Native peoples were literate, sites may contain inscriptions in their languages. Partially disconfirmed. Claims have been made—most notably by Barry Fell—that the vertical marks found on numerous rocks in the study area represent Ogham scripts in a variety of languages, from Celtic to Ibero-Punic.[31] Many of them consist of three vertical marks that Fell interpreted as the letter combination B-L, which he felt represented the common Semitic god Bel or Ba'al. Yet the name of this god contains an additional consonant, an 'ayin, not present in European languages, but which no Northwest Semitic speaker would have left out. There is no reason to suppose that these marks are attempts to convey language at all; they may simply be glacial striae, or tally marks made by Native people for one reason or another. This is especially likely for those at the Vermont sites, which, as noted under point C2, lie upstream of a major fall line in the Connecticut River and would thus have been inaccessible to hypothetical Phoenician navigators. Accordingly, while the information I was provided about these sites identified them as inscriptions, I have recoded them as petroglyphs. The claim for an ancient Egyptian inscription at the Gilmore Hill site in Southborough, Massachusetts has been dealt with—as an example of pseudoscience—in Chapter 1.[32]

There remain a small number of sites (eighteen, 0.3 percent of the total), mostly along the coast from Nova Scotia to Narragansett Bay, which contain inscriptions for which extra-continental origin has been claimed, mostly in Norse runes, but two in Latin. I do not wish to judge the authenticity of these, although Alice Beck Kehoe, a respected archaeologist, has argued strongly for the authenticity of the Kensington Rune Stone in Minnesota.[33] Since most of these inscriptions in this study are on the coast, and since they share few environmental characteristics with any of the other types of structures in this study, I am willing to consider the possibility that Norse mariners from L'Anse aux Meadows on Newfoundland explored down the coast and left some graffiti behind—but not that they penetrated into the interior.[34]

D. The Structures are the Result of Repetitive Ritual Usage by Native Americans, either pre- or post-Contact

Test conditions for Hypothesis "D" are as follows:

1. Site locations should reflect patterns of indigenous settlement, though not necessarily be congruent with those patterns. This is partially confirmed. All of the clusters are situated within, or on the boundaries of tribal homelands, as shown in Figure 101. Sources for this information are a variety of tribal websites. (Please note that tribal names for Algonquian groups are given with the -og gentilic suffix rather than the more familiar -ett locative suffix, according to the preference of tribal members.)

    However, the distribution pattern of stone structure sites does not necessarily conform to indigenous habitation site patterns. Figure 100 compares the locations of stone structure sites in the Sudbury–Assabet–Concord watershed—which is on the boundary between Nipmuck, Massaschuseog, and Pawcatuck tribal territories, mostly within Massachusetts Clusters Nos. 2, 3, 6, and 14—with the location of known habitation sites, mapped at the 10-square-kilometer scale.[35] There is a clear separation in terms of preferred site location, with the habitation sites being in lower-lying areas and the stone structures being at higher elevations. A Spearman Rho comparison of the two distributions provided a value of 0.269, which is well below the critical value of 0.414 with 17 degrees of freedom at the .05 confidence interval. This indicates no correlation between the two distributions.

2. Site locations should not be constrained by post-Contact geopolitical boundaries, unless there is evidence that the site was constructed by post-Contact Native Americans. This

Stone Structures

			4	23
		57	40	16
	60	108	76	15
9	39	40	17	
2	5	15	6	
	14	28		

Habitation Sites

			1	9
		3	17	34
	3	33	117	6
5	55	102	169	
0	99	45	48	
	2	2		

Figure 100: Comparison of Stone Structure Sites with Habitation Sites, SuAsCo Watershed.

Cluster Name	Cluster #	Tribal Homeland
Hammonasset - West	CT1	Hammonasseog
Woodbridge	CT2	Paugusseog
Nonewaug	CT3	Paugusseog
Pequot	CT4	Mashantucket Pequot
Hatchet Pond	CT5	Wabaquasseog
Montville	CT6	Mohegan
Hammonasset - East	CT7	Hammonasseog
Greene County West	GA1	Oconee
Southwestern Putnam County	GA2	Oconee
Ocmulgee	GA3	Ocmulgee
Western Putnam County	GA4	Oconee
McDuffie County	GA5	Coweta
Lincoln County #1	GA6	Coweta
Lincoln County #2	GA7	Coweta
Gladesville	GA8	Oconee
Stephens County	GA9	Cherokee
Lawrence Shoals	GA10	Oconee
Richland Creek	GA11	Oconee
McElheneys Crossroads	GA12	Oconee
Elbert County	GA13	Coweta
College Rock	MA1	Massachuseog, Nipmuck
Hopkinton State Forest	MA2	Massachuseog, Nipmuck
Ashland Town Forest	MA3	Massachuseog, Nipmuck
Fall River	MA4	Sakonneog
Lakeville Ponds	MA5	Nemaskeog
Nobscot Hill	MA6	Massachuseog, Nipmuck
Cape Ann	MA7	Naumkeag
Falmouth	MA8	Sakonneog
Dighton-Rehoboth	MA9	Herring Pond Wampanoag
Noon Hill	MA10	Ponkapoag
King Philip's Rock	MA11	Neponseog
Leverett-New Salem	MA12	Sokoki, Pocumtuck

uster Name	Cluster #	Tribal Homeland
rentham	MA13	Neponseog
etro-West	MA14	Massachuseog, Nipmuck
tchburg-Wachusett	MA15	Nashaway Nipmuck
oton	MA16	Hassanamisco Nipmuck
ndover	MA17	Pawcatuck
ncoln	MA18	Massachuseog
eston	MA19	Massachuseog
ew Hampshire Border #1	NH1	Pennacook
ew Hampshire Border #2	NH2	Pennacook
ew Hampshire Border #3	NH3	Pennacook
utnam County	NY1	Mahican
ensico	NY2	Mahican
pper Susquehanna #1	NY3	Susquehannock
-Tor	NY4	Cayuga
pper Susquehanna #2	NY5	Susquehannock
ke Catalpa	PA1	Susquehannock
ami-Hacking	PA2	Susquehannock
chaug-Beach Pond	RI1	Narraganseog
rr's Pond	RI2	Narraganseog
ickaboxet	RI3	Narraganseog
rber Road	RI4	Narraganseog
ventry	RI5	Narraganseog
elson Pond	RI6	Cowisseog
fft Hill	RI7	Narraganseog
chmond	RI8	Narraganseog
orthwestern McCormick County	SC1	Euchee
uthwestern McCormick County	SC2	Euchee
rksville	SC3	Euchee
irfax	VA1	Powhatan
mfret	VT1	Pennacook
ading/Woodstock	VT2	Pennacook
yalton	VT3	Pennacook

Figure 101: Association of Clusters with Tribal Homelands.

is confirmed. As noted under point A3, all but eight of the sixty-four site clusters identified in this study overlap town, county, or state boundaries. The overlap with state and county boundaries, which includes twenty-four of the sixty-four clusters (37.5 percent), is shown in Figure 102 below. This strongly suggests that the sites were present on the landscape prior to the creation of those boundaries during the settlement period. The one obvious exception to this, for clusters, is Connecticut Cluster No. 5, which coincides with the late eighteenth- to early nineteenth-century Wabaquassett Reservation, created around the time of the final delineation of the Massachusetts–Connecticut border. Other clusters that do not overlap town boundaries are Georgia Cluster No. 12, in McElheney's Crossing; Massachusetts Cluster No. 8, in Falmouth; Rhode Island Clusters Nos. 2 and 3, in West Greenwich; Rhode Island Cluster No. 6, in Middletown; Rhode Island Cluster No. 8, in Richmond; and Virginia Cluster No. 1, in English Hills. In addition, as noted in point A3, there are numerous cases outside of clusters where the nearest neighbor to a site is across a political boundary—state, county, or town. These cases are also shown in Figure 102 below.

These distributions were compared to the total number of sites per state (dividing the cross-state pairs by two), and a Spearman Rank-Order statistic gave a value of 0.896, which is significant at the 0.002 confidence level.[36] Thus, the distribution of cross-border sites outside of clusters is directly proportional to the number of sites per state. This strongly indicates that most, if not all of the sites both within and outside of clusters antedate the creation of the boundaries.

Cluster Name	Cluster no.	State(s)	No. of counties	Counties
Hammonasset—West	CT1	CT	2	Middlesex, New Haven
Southwestern Putnam County	GA2	GA	2	Jones, Putnam
Stephens County	GA9	GA	2	Habersham, Stephens
Elbert County	GA13	GA	3	Elbert, Lincoln, Wilkes
College Rock	MA1	MA	3	Middlesex, Norfolk, Worcester
Ashland Town Forest	MA3	MA	2	Middlesex, Worcester
Lakeville Ponds	MA5	MA	2	Bristol, Plymouth
King Philip's Rock	MA11	MA	2	Bristol, Norfolk
Metro—West	MA14	MA	2	Middlesex, Worcester
Fitchburg-Wachusett	MA15	MA, NH	3	Middlesex, Worcester, Hillsborough
Upton	MA16	MA	2	Middlesex, Worcester

Andover	MA17	MA	2	Essex, Middlesex
New Hampshire Border No. 2	NH2	NH	2	Hillsborough, Rockingham
Putnam County	NY1	CT, NY	4	Dutchess, Putnam, Westchester, Fairfield
Upper Susquehanna No. 1	NY3	NY	3	Broome, Chenango, Delaware
Hi-Tor	NY4	NY	2	Ontario, Yates
Upper Susquehanna No. 2	NY5	NY, PA	2	Broome, Susquehanna
Lake Catalpa	PA1	PA	2	Luzerne, Wyoming
Unami-Hacking	PA2	PA	2	Bucks, Montgomery
Pachaug-Beach Pond	RI1	CT, RI	3	New London, Washington, Kent
Coventry	RI5	RI	2	Kent, Providence
Parksville	SC3	GA, SC	2	Lincoln, McCormick
Royalton	VT3	VT	2	Orange, Windsor

Figure 102: Clusters that Overlap State and County Boundaries

3. Sites should have no particular relationship to lands favored by colonial settlers for agricultural activities. This is partially confirmed. As noted above, 59.3 percent of sites (3,273) are located in either naturally infertile or low fertility soils. The former include 880 sites on bedrock outcrops and 194 sites in wet soils. No matter how desperate eighteenth-century farmers may have been, there is no way that they could have made productive use of these sites for agriculture or pasturage—at most, they could have served as woodlots.[37] Of the 33.0 percent of sites (1,824) that are located in agriculturally productive soils, 40.8 percent (774) are in the southeast. This most likely simply reflects the higher proportion of productive soils in that region.

4. Site configurations should be highly clustered, in line with the idea of repetitive usage. This is strongly confirmed. A total of 3,057 sites (59.8 percent) were found in sixty-four discrete clusters throughout the study area. The strongest concentrations of these are in piedmont Georgia and adjacent South Carolina; in southern New York and northeastern Pennsylvania; and in New England, as far north as UTM 4840000, the latitude of Hanover, NH. These clusters are confirmed by both VMR and nearest neighbor analysis and take up only 0.51 percent of the land area within the study area.

5. The variability of structure types at sites should not be constrained. This is largely confirmed. While 69.7 percent of sites contained only one structure type, the

remaining 30.1 percent had between two and thirteen types present. Sites within clusters were considerably more likely to have multiple structure types, as shown in Figure 103. However, there are a number of structure types that have a greater tendency to occur as solitaries, as shown in Figure 30. In descending order of frequency, these are chambers (69.3 percent), inscriptions (55.6 percent), petroglyphs (42.6 percent), and balanced rocks (34.9 percent). All other types are present as solitaries in less than one-third of cases. No attempt has been made in this study to examine whether there are structural differences between the chambers, which are combined with other types and those which are not. As chambers and inscriptions are so often found as solitaries and also are located in environmental settings that are rather divergent from most other sites, this suggests that many of the chambers may be unrelated to the other structure types and may indeed be colonial root cellars, as claimed long ago by Neudorffer for Vermont chambers.[38] However, the fact that 30.7 percent of the chambers are associated with other structure types further suggests that some of them may be indigenous after all. In addition, eighty-one of the isolated chambers (16.7 percent) have significant azimuths recorded for them. Despite MHC's claims (n.d.) that these might be due to random chance, the data in this study suggest that these were deliberate placements and unlikely to be related to post-Contact farm activities. Chambers associated with other structures have a somewhat higher frequency of recorded azimuths (fifty-five out of 215, or 25.6 percent).

As shown in Figure 103, 172 (42.5 percent) of the 405 solitary chambers without azimuths fall within clusters. If they were removed from the inventory, three of the clusters—Connecticut No. 6, New Hampshire No. 3, and New York No. 2—would fall below the threshold of ten sites per cluster and would have to be eliminated. Some of the other clusters—notably Connecticut No. 4, New York No. 1, and Vermont No. 3—would be somewhat reduced in total area but not eliminated, as shown in Figures 105, 106, and 107. For Connecticut Cluster No. 4, this would increase the VMR from 5.15 to 6.20, and reduce the chi-square value from 644.2 to 365.8—still well within the 0.00 probability range. It should be noted that I was informed of the existence of many more sites within both of the two Connecticut clusters, but the two chief informants for that area of the state were either unable or unwilling to provide me with information about any sites other than the chambers, so the

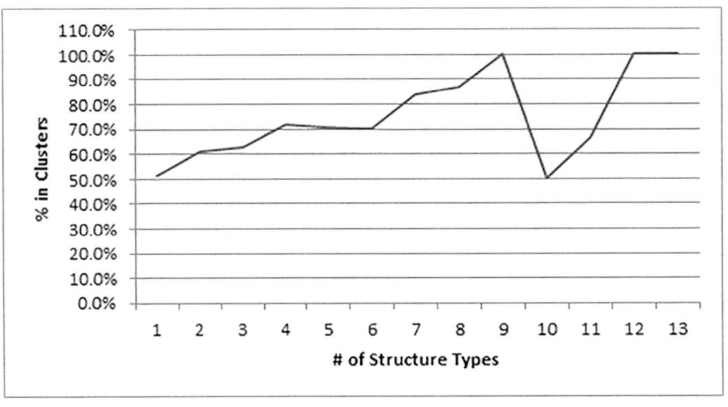

Figure 103: Percentage of Multiple Structure Types in Clusters.

actual impact of eliminating or reducing these clusters in those clusters could be mitigated. In the case of New York Cluster No. 1, all of the sites on the Connecticut side of the state border would be eliminated, but the cluster would still extend into both Dutchess and Westchester Counties. This would decrease the cluster's VMR from 6.75 to 5.14, and reduce the chi-square value from 5,985.5 to 2,072.1—still well within the 0.00 probability range. For Vermont Cluster No. 3, removing the solitary chambers would reduce the VMR from 4.10 to 3.68, and the chi-square value from 291.2 to 246.8—again, within the 0.00 probability range. In none of the other clusters would the removal of solitary chambers have any significant effects.

Cluster no.	No. of solitary chambers	No. of sites	Percentage	Cluster effects
CT3	1	32	3.1%	
CT4	26	41	63.4%	reduced
CT6	12	17	70.6%	fails
MA1	1	94	1.1%	
MA9	3	29	10.3%	
MA11	1	20	5.0%	
MA12	13	129	10.1%	
MA14	7	613	1.1%	
MA15	3	177	1.7%	
NH1	1	26	3.8%	
NH3	2	11	18.2%	fails
NY1	73	220	33.2%	reduced
NY2	7	10	70.0%	fails
RI1	11	252	4.4%	
RI5	1	31	3.2%	
VT1	2	80	2.5%	
VT2	2	25	8.0%	
VT3	6	34	17.6%	reduced

Figure 104: The Effect of Removing Isolated Chambers from Clusters.

				0	0	0		
0	0	0	0	0	1	0		
0	1	0	1	0	0	0		
0	1	0	0	1	0	0	0	
0	0	0	0	5	1	3	0	
0	1	0	0	0	1	0	0	0
0	0	0	0	2	0	0	1	0
0	1	0	0	0	0	0	0	0
0	1	0						
0	0	0						

Figure 105: Schematic of Connecticut Cluster No. 4 with Isolated Chambers Removed (compare with Figure 36).

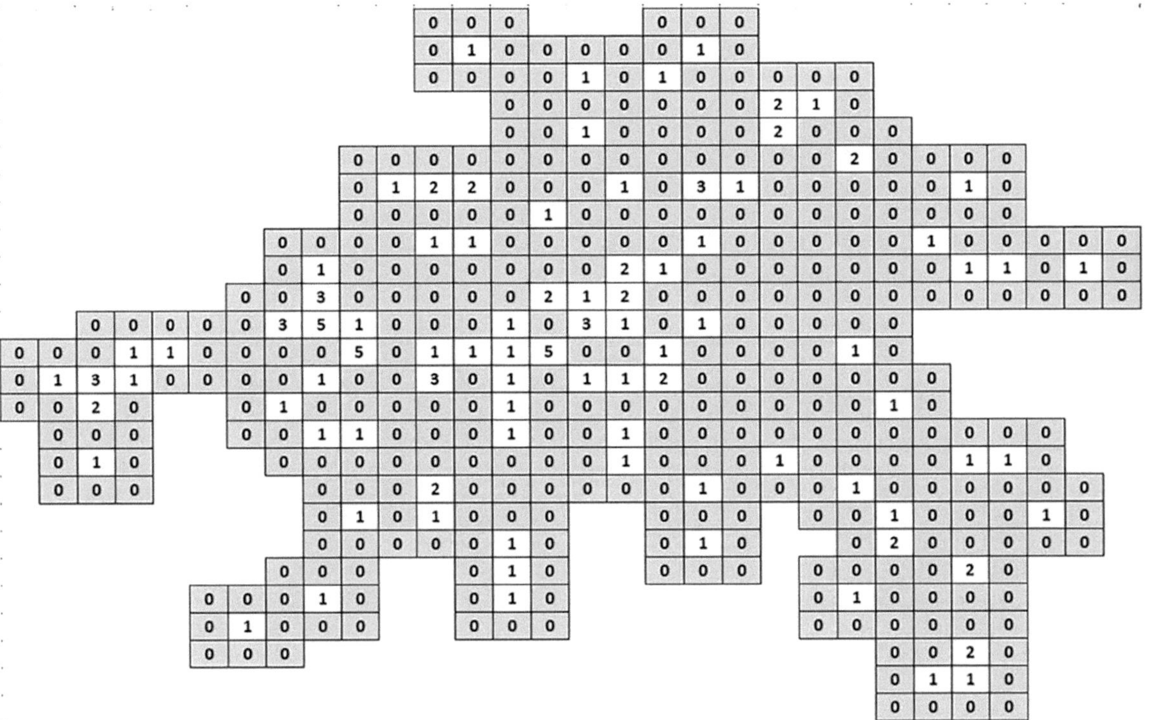

Figure 106: Schematic of New York Cluster No. 1 with Isolated Chambers Removed (compare with Figure 75).

		0	0	0					
		0	1	0	0				
		0	1	1	0	0	0	0	0
		0	1	0	2	0	1	1	0
		0	0	0	0	3	2	0	0
			0	0	0	2	0	0	
	0	0	0	1	1	2	1	0	
0	0	1	0	0	0	4	1	0	
0	1	0	0		0	0	1	0	
0	0	0				0	0	0	

Figure 107: Schematic of Vermont Cluster No. 3 with Isolated Chambers Removed (compare with Figure 95).

In the case of inscriptions, only three sites with inscriptions occur in clusters: two in Massachusetts Cluster No. 14 and one in Vermont Cluster No. 2. Removing these from the inventory would not affect either cluster significantly. As the average location of inscriptions also differs significantly from that of other structure types, most of them were found close to the coast. These may be evidence of Viking exploratory expeditions, as noted above.

For solitary balanced rocks, there are sixty-five sites out of a total of 170 (38.2 percent) that fall within clusters. As Figure 108 shows, these are more dispersed than the solitary chambers. Only one cluster, Massachusetts No. 5, would fall below the threshold of ten sites if these sites were removed from the inventory. Of the remainder, only Rhode Island Cluster No. 2 would lose more than 10 percent of its sites, and the effect would not change the size of the cluster. The effect of removing the isolated balanced rocks from clusters would therefore not be very significant. However, the fact that 219 of the remaining balanced rocks (45.0 percent) occur in clusters in association with other structure types suggests that indigenous peoples venerated these impressive "erratic boulders" and—whether or not they performed any alterations on them—that they tended to position other stone structures in their vicinity.[40] Sites in clusters with solitary balanced rocks have an average NND of 0.48 km, while those in clusters with balanced rocks combined with other structures have an average NND of 0.24 km, both well below the average NND within clusters of 0.59 km. This suggests that it might not be appropriate to remove the solitary balanced rocks in clusters from the inventory. For solitary balanced rocks outside of clusters, the average NND is 4.50 km, while that for balanced rocks combined with other structure types it is 2.22 km. This suggests that it might be appropriate to remove the 103 sites that have isolated balanced rocks outside of clusters from the inventory.

Cluster #	# solitary balanced rocks	# sites	%	Cluster effects
CT3	1	32	3.1%	
MA1	3	94	3.2%	
MA3	2	46	4.3%	
MA4	1	15	6.7%	
MA5	2	10	9.5%	fails
MA6	1	21	7.7%	
MA7	1	13	3.4%	
MA9	3	29	2.3%	
MA12	2	129	4.8%	
MA13	5	42	0.8%	
MA14	6	613	1.0%	
MA15	9	177	5.1%	
MA16	1	39	2.6%	
NY1	11	220	5.0%	
RI1	7	252	2.8%	
RI2	3	21	14.3%	reduced
RI3	3	41	7.3%	
RI4	1	17	5.9%	
RI5	2	31	6.5%	
VT1	1	80	1.3%	

Figure 108: The Effect of Removing Isolated Balanced Rocks from Clusters.

The situation with petroglyphs is more complicated. There are only sixteen sites with solitary petroglyphs that occur in clusters: seven in Vermont Cluster No. 1; two in Massachusetts Cluster No. 4; and one each in Massachusetts Clusters No. 12 and No. 14, New Hampshire Cluster No. 1, Rhode Island Clusters No. 1 and No. 6, and Vermont Clusters No. 2 and No. 3. The remaining eighty-two solitary petroglyphs occur outside of clusters. However, there are forty-one petroglyph sites that contain multiple petroglyphs with no other structure types present, and four of these sites that were in clusters were uncombined with other structure types: two in Rhode Island Cluster No. 1 and one each in Vermont Clusters No. 1 and No. 2. The remaining thirty-seven uncombined petroglyphs were outside of clusters. The average NND for sites in clusters containing only petroglyphs was 0.60 km, very close to the average of

0.59. The average NND for sites outside of clusters containing petroglyphs uncombined with other structure types was 6.89 km. Like chambers, petroglyphs had a somewhat higher probability of being found in valleys (fifty-four) than on slopes (thirty-nine), but the difference is not as extreme as it is for chambers. For solitary petroglyphs, this tendency is much more marked, as is the tendency for them to be located on islands and on shores, as shown in Figure 109, below. This suggests that the isolated petroglyphs might be removed from the inventory, but there is good reason to think of petroglyphs in general as being part of the indigenous cultural repertoire, as Lenik has illustrated.[41]

Setting	Solitary	Combined
Hilltop	21	18
Island	11	1
Plain	6	3
Shore	23	3
Slope	43	47
Valley	35	19

Figure 109: Environmental Settings for Petroglyphs.

If the four types of isolated structures as described above were removed from the inventory, the total number of sites that remain would still be very high, 4,905 sites (88.4 percent of the original total). This indicates that the overwhelming majority of the sites satisfy test condition D5.

6. The total number of structures at sites should also not be constrained. Also largely confirmed. While 35.4 percent of sites had only one structure present, the largest number of structures at any one site was 681. Of the thirty-six sites with at least 100 structures present, twenty-four (66.7 percent) were in clusters. Of the seventy-eight sites with between fifty and 100 structures present, fifty-one (65.4 percent) were in clusters. Of the 191 sites with between twenty-five and fifty structures present, 126 (66.0 percent) were in clusters. As shown in Figure 29, there is a strong correlation between the number of structures and the number of types at sites.

7. Artifacts and absolute dates associated with sites should include pre-Contact evidence for the particular location of the site, though post-Contact dates and artifacts may also be encountered. Largely confirmed. As Figure 1 shows, there are twenty-two absolute dates associated with stone structures that antedate European settlement. I know of two sites from my own excavations that have stone structures, which are associated with pre-Contact artifacts, but these tend to be infrequent.[42] When I asked my Native informants about this, they observed that Euro-Americans are as unlikely to leave trash in their churches as their people are to leave trash in their sacred spaces. I am also aware of some stone structures that have iron objects

embedded within them, but no quantitative study has been done of these.[43] While this evidence must be considered anecdotal only, it may indicate an ongoing utilization of the structures by indigenous people after the arrival of European settlers. It does not necessarily indicate that these structures were the product of Euro-American trash disposal.

8. Sites should be found throughout the entire study area, without regard for the glacial margin—though they should also be absent from areas lacking in stone materials, such as the coastal plain south of the glacial margin. This is confirmed. As noted above in Test B1, 1,159 sites, 20.9 percent of the total, lie south of the glacial margin. There is a significant gap in the distribution in North Carolina and southern Virginia, and no clusters between the three South Carolina clusters in McCormick County on the Savannah River and the one Virginia cluster in Fairfax County on the Potomac River. This may indicate the presence of separate, but distantly related cultural traditions. This is further suggested by the relatively smaller inventory of structure types in the Southeast: balanced rocks, niches, and inscriptions are entirely absent; and chambers, U-shaped structures, split boulders, effigies, standing stones, enclosures, stone circles, platforms, and unique structures are rare. The only structure types that occur with comparable frequencies in both regions are rock piles, stone rows, cairns, petroglyphs, and marked stones. South of the glacial margin, sites are notably absent from the coastal plain, with very few exceptions. Despite these differences, stone structures are clearly found considerably to the north and south of the glacial margin.

9. If walls are present, they should not meet at right angles, or run straight, and may be associated with water features rather than field boundaries. Partially confirmed. No attempt was made in this study to measure the angles at which walls met, or to investigate whether they marked field boundaries or were associated with water features. In general, if I encountered instances of walls meeting at apparent right angles in the absence of other structures, I did not include them in the inventory—but this is anecdotal. However, there were a significant number of walls that did not run straight, and 131 of these had either a horizontal or (more rarely) vertical undulating or zig-zag pattern. The latter were reinterpreted as serpent effigies, and some of them (again, anecdotally) had large stones at one end, which had been selected and/or shaped to resemble serpent heads.[44]

10. If walls are present, they should not be high enough to bar access or exit. Neither confirmed nor disconfirmed. No quantitative data was collected on the height of stone rows/walls. Anecdotally, many walls were noted to be only one or two courses high, which would fit this condition, while others were considerably higher and could have served to bar access or exit. Also, some stone rows were discontinuous, and could not have served as barriers, except perhaps in a symbolic sense.

11. There should be a preference for sites to be found in the vicinity of watershed boundaries and fault lines—and, possibly, head-of-tide locations. This statement, based upon a hint given by the late Narragansett Tribal Medicine Woman Ella Seketau, to the effect that her people liked to construct these monuments "where water flows in two directions," is largely confirmed. A total of 3,577 sites (64.5 percent) are located

adjacent to Rank One streams; 4,984 of them (89.9 percent) are within 5 kilometers of a level ten watershed boundary; and 3,964 of them (72.3 percent) are located within 5 kilometers of a fault. However, relatively few sites (283, 5.1 percent) are located within 100 meters of a watershed boundary, a distance at which it might actually be perceived that "water flows in two directions," and an even smaller number (180, 3.2 percent) are located within 100 meters of a fault. Figure 110 below, plotted at 100-meter increments, shows that the number of sites from 0–2 kilometers from level ten watersheds and from faults tends to decline as the distance increases, with the steepest decline being between sites within 100 meters of the watershed and those 100–200 meters from it, beyond which the decline is very gradual. The trend line for distance to faults is similar, without the sharp decline from 0–100 meters to locations further away. Twenty-two of the sixty-four site clusters (34.4 percent) extend across watershed boundaries, as shown in Figure 111. Seven of these clusters extend into more than two watersheds. The tendency to cross watershed boundaries appears to be limited to clusters in the northeast, particularly in southern New York and southern New England. All of the southeastern clusters and the three Vermont clusters are confined to a single watershed. This may be indicative of regional differences. The most obvious example of an overlap is Rhode Island Cluster No. 1, shown in Figure 82. Many of its sites lie very close to the Pawcatuck–Thames watershed, on either side of it.

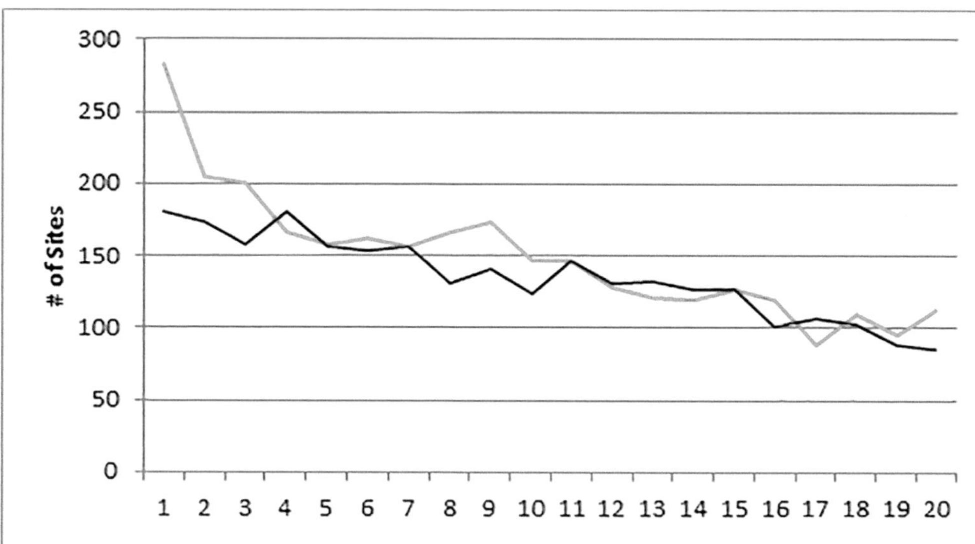

Figure 110: Distribution of Sites within 2 km of a Level 10 Watershed (grey) or a Fault (black).

Cluster Name	Cluster no.	No. of watersheds	Watersheds
Hammonasset—West	CT1	5	East, Farm, Hammonasset, Indian, West
Pequot	CT4	4	Mystic, Pawcatuck, Poquonock, Thames
Montville	CT6	2	Connecticut, Thames
Hammonasset—East	CT7	3	Menunkeetesuck, Patchogue, Coastal
College Rock	MA1	3	Blackstone, Charles, Merrimack
Hopkinton State Park	MA2	2	Charles, Merrimack
Fall River	MA4	2	Taunton, Westport
Cape Ann	MA7	2	Annisquam, coastal
Dighton-Rehoboth	MA9	2	Taunton, Warren
King Philip's Rock	MA11	2	Neponset, Taunton
Wrentham	MA13	3	Charles, Neponset, Taunton
Upton	MA16	2	Blackstone, Merrimack
Lincoln	MA18	2	Charles, Merrimack
Weston	MA19	2	Charles, Merrimack
New Hampshire Border No. 1	NH1	2	Merrimack, Piscataqua
New Hampshire Border No. 3	NH3	2	Merrimack, Piscataqua
Putnam County	NY1	4	Housatonic, Hudson, Rippowam, Saugatuck
Kensico	NY2	3	Bronx, Mamaroneck, Hudson
Upper Susquehanna No. 1	NY3	2	Delaware, Susquehanna
Pachaug-Beach Pond	RI1	2	Pawcatuck, Thames
Carr's Pond	RI2	2	Pawcatuck, Pawtuxet
Coventry	RI5	2	Pawcatuck, Pawtuxet

Figure 111: Clusters Which Cross Watershed Boundaries.

The head-of-tide parameter is less clear, with only 525 sites (9.5 percent) within 10 kilometers of the tidal limit, and the highest percentages of these were found in Nova Scotia (ten, 47.6 percent), Connecticut (180, 32.7 percent), Maine (thirty-nine, 28.1 percent), and Rhode Island (ninety-seven, 21.4 percent). In all other states and provinces the percentage was below 15 percent. There were only 129 sites (2.3 percent) found within 100 meters of a head of tide. As shown in Figure 19, there is a tendency for this parameter to be more evident from about the longitude of the Poquonock River in eastern coastal Connecticut eastwards.

All three of these indicators—distance to fault, distance to watershed, and distance to head-of-tide—show that the claim by indigenous informants that sites are located "where water flows in two directions" is at least partially corroborated by the data.

12. Sites may be located in environmental settings unsuitable for agriculture, such as bedrock outcrops, hilltops, steep slopes, and swamps. This is partially confirmed. A total of 3,722 sites (67.0 percent) were located on hilltops and slopes; and a total of 1,664 (36.7 percent) were located on slopes of 15 percent or more. There were 868 sites on bedrock outcrops. A total of 673 (12.1 percent) were associated with swamps. However, there were also large numbers of sites in valleys (1,148, 20.7 percent), on shorelines (409, 7.4 percent), on plains (195, 3.5 percent), and on islands (seventy-six, 1.4 percent). There were also 1,887 sites (41.7 percent) at slopes between 5 and 15 degrees, and 977 sites (21.6 percent) on shallow slopes of less than 5 degrees. This suggests that while hilltops, slope, and swamps were favored for stone monuments, as they would certainly not have been favored for agricultural purposes, they were not the only types of environmental settings in which these sites might be located. As noted above in point D5, solitary inscriptions, chambers, and petroglyphs diverge from this pattern.

13. If structures that may have resulted from glacial action are present (such as balanced rocks), they should be accompanied by structures of other types. This is partially confirmed, as noted above in point D5. More than one-third of all balanced rocks in the inventory are solitaries, and are unaccompanied by structures of other types. However, more than one-third of the solitary balanced rocks are found in site clusters, so this may indicate that they are part of the cultural repertoire represented by those clusters. The fact that nearly two-thirds of balanced rocks are associated with other structure types suggests that even if their original placement was due to glacial action, they were observed by indigenous peoples, were assigned sacred status, and served as foci for the placement of additional structures around them.

14. Structures should show human alteration, either by the placement of their stones or by evidence of actual alterations to individual stones. This is largely confirmed, with the exception of some of the balanced rocks, as noted above. Sites with balanced rocks make up only 8.8 percent of the total (487), and at 301 of the sites where they occur, other structure types were present. No systematic study of deliberate alterations to balanced rocks was undertaken in this study. For all other types, their stones were altered either by shaping (especially for marked stones and petroglyphs) or deliberate placement.

15. The iconography of representational structures—petroglyphs/pictographs, marked stones, and effigies—should be consonant with the belief systems of the Native cultures involved. This is largely confirmed. Figure 112 gives the distribution by (attributed) image for these three types of structures, in descending order of frequency. It should be noted that only 21.7 percent of petroglyphs (230), 28.9 percent of marked stones (415), and 83.4 percent of effigies (379) were identified as to what they ostensibly represented, and that the marked stones also included fifty-one

Type	Petro-glyphs	Marked Stones	Effigies	Total
turtle	2		144	146
serpent	1	1	131	133
manitou		82		82
cupule/dot	1	30		31
bird	4		11	15
human	2		7	9
hand	7		1	8
circle	6			6
face	1	1	4	6
fern	6			6
eye	3		1	4
feline		1	3	4
foot	2		2	4
X/cross	4			4
fish	1		2	3
whale			3	3
arrow	1	1		2
boat	1		1	2
butterfly	1	1		2
line	2			2
scallop		1	1	2
spiral	1	1		2
alligator			1	1
atl-atl	1			1
bear			1	1
elephant			1	1
frog			1	1
horned head	1			1
map	1			1
phallus	1			1
triangle		1		1
wolf			1	1

Figure 112: Representations in Structures.

in-ground mortars (12.3 percent), which may have been strictly utilitarian. Thus, it is possible—especially for the petroglyphs and marked stones—that the sample is not representative of the total. It would be necessary to revisit each of the sites with indefinite representations to clarify this, and that is beyond the scope of this study. The two most common representations are of turtles and snakes, both of which are prominent in the indigenous stories of many of the eastern tribes. Many indigenous peoples refer to the North American continent as "Turtle Island," with Florida and the northeast states and Maritimes forming the lower and upper right flippers of the turtle.

For example, in *Picture Rocks,* Lenik related the following creation story of the Lenape people:

> At the beginning of time, the world was made up of water with a tortoise lying in it. The tortoise raised its back above the water, the water ran off its shell, and dry land was created.[45]

Similarly, an Iroquois creation legend relates:

> … when there was yet no land, but all was on extensive lake … one duck offered to dive to see if there might be some bottom to their lake which might be brought up … at last a muskrat made the attempt … with a little earth in his claw … which they placed, at the suggestion of their chief, on the back of an immense turtle who was willing to become the foundation of an island for them.[46]

James Mooney recounted the following Cherokee story about a giant turtle:

> … an immense turtle which lived in its vicinity in ancient times. This turtle was particularly famous for its repelling power, having been known not to be at all injured by a stroke of lightning. Nothing on earth had power to annihilate the creature, but, on account of the many attempts made to take its life, when it was known to be a harmless and inoffensive creature, it became disgusted with this world, and burrowed its way into the middle of the earth, where it now lives in peace.[47]

As for serpents, recounted an early seventeenth-century story told to Edward Winslow by two Massachuseog Indians about the empowerment of shamans (pauwaus):

> … if any of the Indians fall into any strange dream wherein Chepian appears unto them as a serpent, then the next day they tell the other Indians of it, whereupon the others dance and rejoice for what they tell them about this Serpent, and so they become their Powwows.[48]

There is a well-known Iroquois legend about the Peacemaker, Hionwatha, who is said to have confronted the Onondaga chief Atotarho and healed him by combing the snakes out of his hair.[49] The Malecite tell the following Gluskap story, which involves both a snake transformation and the creation of Tobique Rocks, one of the New Brunswick stone structure sites in the inventory:

He had one enemy and he was called the "Beaver," whose name was Gwabid. One day they had a big battle at Grand Falls which is called Gupsquick. The Kluskap was trying to catch the beaver on the riverbank. Since the beaver lived on water he could travel faster than Kluskap. He gave up trying to keep up with him, and went to the riverbank and picked up a large rock and threw it at the beaver, thinking that if he hit him he would kill him on the spot. After he threw it he found out that the beaver was farther away than he had thrown the rock. The rock landed at the mouth of the Tobique River. When Kluskap saw that, he picked up another rock and threw it with more force, only this time the rock was much bigger. The rock is still at the mouth of the river. The Indians still believe that it is the very rock Kluskap had thrown at the Gwabid.

He gave up trying to get the beaver with a rock and decided to call upon the powers that he possessed and try to catch him by jumping along the riverbank. The jump he took was one-half mile long, so it took him fifty-four jumps along the riverbank. Finally he was on the other side of the river and the beaver was in the water. He jumped in the river and went to the bottom. When he got his hand on the beaver he turned himself into another beaver, and they fought like beavers until they got tired. That didn't prove anything, because their strength was evenly matched, so the first beaver decided to turn himself into a snake, thinking he could choke the other beaver. When the other beaver saw he had turned himself into a snake, he also decided to turn himself into a snake. They fought until they were tired. Neither one could overpower the other. When they could not get the best of each other, the first one turned himself into a Budeb, an Indian name for some kind of monster. When the second one saw this he turned himself into a Budeb, and they fought for four weeks. The pool of water where they fought is so muddy now and the underneath keeps boiling up. We don't know who won the battle, because people still think that they are still fighting.[50]

Mooney cited a Cherokee informant who stated that "Thunder is a horned snake, and lightning its tongue, and it lives with water and rains."[51] He also stated:

[Among the Cherokee,] the generic name for snakes is inadu. They are all regarded as anida'wehi, "supernaturals," having an intimate connection with the rain and thunder gods, and possessing a certain influence over the other animal and plant tribes.… The feeling toward snakes is one of mingled fear and reverence, and every precaution is taken to avoid killing or offending one, especially the rattlesnake.[52]

The third most common type of representation is the so-called Manitou stone.[53] These stones are vaguely shaped in the form of the upper half of a human torso and head, consisting of a central, rounded, raised portion and "shoulders" usually symmetrical on either side. One is shown in Plate 18. These were first described by Ezra Stiles as "god stones," and according to his account, some of them appear to have been hidden away in caves by seventeenth-century Native people who were concerned about their desecration by Euro-American Christian zealots—including the same caves used by the judges who ordered the execution of Charles I and who fled to New England upon the restoration of the monarchy.[54] Stiles also observed indigenous people worshipping at these stones.

16. If archaeoastronomical alignments are present, they should also accord with indigenous belief systems. This is partially confirmed. As Howard Russell wrote: "To the Indian the celestial powers were very real. Because they held his fate so fully in their hands, he did his best to cooperate with them, and did not fail to seek their blessing with elaborate ritual."[55] This belief extended to astronomical observations; as Roger Williams noted of the Narragansett:

> They are punctuall in measuring their Day by the Sunne, and their Night by the Moon and the Starres, and their lying much abroad in the ayre; and so living in the open fields, occasioneth even the youngest amongst them to be very observant of those Heavenly Lights.... By occasion of their frequent lying in the Fields and Woods, they much observe the Starres, and their very children can give Names to many of them, and observe their Motions.... And know their Course and therein doe Excell the English tame.[56]

One of the most important rituals for indigenous people in the Northeast is nikkomo, "I give away," scheduled at the time of the first full moon after the winter solstice.[57] This corresponds to the time when the sun sets at its furthest point south on the horizon, and Roger Williams referred to it as "their kind of Christmas."[58] Another important celebration, called schemitzun among the Pequot, takes place in mid-August.[59] In other areas, it is referred to as the Green Corn Ceremony.[60] It corresponds to the time of the Perseid meteor shower, from August 13–15. This timing is also related to the idea that the Milky Way appears to descend to Earth at this time of year, and it is regarded by many Native peoples as the "path of souls."[61]

While only a relatively small number of sites in the inventory (494, 8.9 percent) have recorded azimuths, there is a strong correlation with some of these key points in the astronomical year: winter solstice sunrise (seventy-five) and sunset (sixty-two), followed by equinox sunrise (sixty-two), summer solstice sunset (fifty-three), equinox sunset (fifty-one), and summer solstice sunrise (thirty-five), account for 68.4 percent (338) of the recorded azimuths. An additional seventy-nine are oriented towards geographic north–south, and fifteen are related to August 13 sunrise or sunset. Altogether, these account for 87.4 percent of all recorded azimuths. This suggests that there was a deliberate placement of these structures, as suggested by Ballard.[62] In addition, eleven of the site clusters have their main axes oriented towards either winter solstice sunset/summer solstice sunrise (Georgia Clusters Nos. 7 and 8, Massachusetts Clusters Nos. 6, 16, 17, and 19) or winter solstice sunrise/summer solstice sunset (Connecticut Clusters Nos. 1, 6, and 7, Georgia Clusters Nos. 3 and 4). The southern edge of Massachusetts Cluster No. 14 also aligns closely with winter solstice sunset/summer solstice sunrise. While the intentionality of these cluster orientations may be questioned in some cases, the orientation of the Hammonassett Line (Connecticut Clusters Nos. 1 and 7) is highly focused on a single line, as shown in Plate 50, and it furthermore aligns with other sites further afield to the west-northwest in the Catskills, and to a stone structure to the east-southeast near Montauk Point on Long Island.[63] All of this indicates that there is a correlation between these sites and the principal orientations of the indigenous calendrical system.

17. Inscriptions in non-indigenous scripts should be absent from sites, as should artifacts of non-indigenous origin. If sites are post-Contact, however, they may include some items obtained in trade from Euro-American settlers. This is largely confirmed. There are only eighteen sites that have alleged inscriptions, and their locations differ substantially from that of all other structure types, nor are they often combined with other structure types. These inscriptions have not been demonstrated to be genuine beyond the shadow of a doubt, unlike the sites further to the north in Newfoundland and the Elizabethan Archipelago, which are accepted by archaeologists as indisputable evidence of Norse activity, not on the basis of inscriptions but of items of material culture. These kinds of items appear to be lacking from the inscription sites within the study area. Also, as noted above in point D7, anecdotally there are some stone structures that have iron objects embedded within them, which certainly represent post-Contact deposits, but these were not necessarily deposited by European settlers. Other than this, post-Contact artifacts are absent from structures.

18. Sites may be located in areas with topographic place names that are associated in Euro-American folk traditions with indigenous peoples, or which indicate deliberate avoidance by colonial farmers, such as names associated with the Devil. This is confirmed. As noted above, 313 sites (5.6 percent) have names that are associated with either Native Americans or with the Devil. While there are many other such place names throughout the continent (a search for geographic place names associated with the Devil in the states within the study area using Topo!© found 212 of them), the fact that so many stone structure sites have these associations suggests strongly that such places are not locations that settlers would frequent or utilize for agricultural activities. These names may have been assigned to further effect the erasure of indigenous religious practices, and/or to deter non-conformist colonists like Thomas Morton from engaging in them.[64]

19. Sites should be absent, or very infrequent, in areas that are identified as places of deliberate avoidance by indigenous people, based upon their traditions. This is confirmed. There is a remarkable absence of sites from the Adirondacks in northern New York State. Only eleven sites are reported from that region, all but two of them from around its margins, in an area of *c.* 53,000 square kilometers (density: 0.0002 sites per square km). This is an area that is identified in Iroquois beliefs as the final resting place of Tawiskaron, the evil twin, who was vanquished and turned to stone by his older brother.[65] I am informed by Rolf Cachat-Schilling that there is a Munsee term for prohibited places: *gwëtëlásu* or *gwëthigásu*.[65] I am not aware of any comparable beliefs among the Western or Eastern Abenaki with regard to the northern sections of the Green Mountains or the White Mountains, or in northern Maine, but sites are also quite rare in those areas. It is certainly not an issue of a general indigenous avoidance of mountainous areas. The Catskills, while not as rugged as the Adirondacks, contain sixty-seven sites within an area of *c.* 9,600 square kilometers (density: 0.007 sites per square km, 34.7 times as high as for the Adirondacks). These sites are too diffusely scattered to be considered to be in a cluster, and each cell in the Figure 113 below represents 100 square kilometers (10 km by 10 km) rather than 1 square kilometer as in the other schematic cluster diagrams. But sites are certainly present there, in some cases even on mountain peaks, whereas they are notably absent from the Adirondacks. Some of the South Carolina sites in the southern Appalachians are also at fairly high elevations.

				0	0	0	0			
			0	0	2	1	0	0	0	
			0	1	0	0	0	4	0	
			0	1	0	9	1	0	0	
		0	0	0	1	5	7	0	0	0
		0	2	5	1	1	0	1	1	0
	0	0	0	0	0	1	2	2	0	0
0	0	1	0	0	1	0	3	1	0	
0	1	0	0	2	1	1	1	0	0	
0	0	1	0	0	0	0	0	1	0	
	0	0	1	0			0	0	0	
	0	1	0	0						
	0	0	0							

Figure 113: Schematic of Distribution of Sites in the Catskills.

Another possible example of deliberate avoidance may be the outer portion of Cape Cod. Ramona Peters, the Mashpee Wampanoag Tribal Historic Preservation Officer, has often asserted that "our people never built these structures," and in fact there are only four such sites reported east of Massachusetts Cluster No. 8 in Falmouth. There are some other areas that appear largely to lack this type of site, including most of Long Island, New York, and Nantucket Island. However, while this may simply be due to the lack of available rock in those areas, as is the case on the coastal plain south of New York City, it is certainly not true of the Adirondacks, nor is it the case in the Virginia piedmont east of the Blue Ridge. I am informed by Dr. Jeffrey Hantman—an archaeologist in the University of Virginia Anthropology Department—that local archaeologists consider that the "stone mound" culture of the Shenandoah and James watersheds west of the Blue Ridge does not extend very far east of the mountains.[67]

20. Indigenous terminology for specific types of structures should exist. This is largely confirmed; thirteen out of the eighteen structure types (and some sub-types) have indigenous names in Algonquian languages, at least for New England and adjacent New York State. In addition, we have John Smith's account of 1624, which includes an indigenous name for one type of Virginia stone structures, and Roger Williams' 1643 dictionary, which provides a Narragansett name for another type. It seems unlikely that they would have such designations if they had been built exclusively by colonial settlers.

Conclusions

Figure 114 summarizes the results of testing. As noted at the beginning of this chapter, whenever the results were clearly positive or negative in all cases, the test condition was described as "confirmed" or "disconfirmed," respectively. When they were clearly positive or negative in all but a few cases, the test condition was described as "largely confirmed" or "largely disconfirmed." When they were clearly positive or negative in the majority of cases, the test condition was described as "partially confirmed" or "partially disconfirmed." When the data were unclear or where there was a relatively equal balance between positive and negative results, the test condition was described as "neither confirmed nor disconfirmed."

Hypothesis:	"A"	"B"	"C"	"D"
Disconfirmed	5	5	1	0
Largely Disconfirmed	3	1	2	0
Partially Disconfirmed	9	0	2	0
Neither Confirmed nor Disconfirmed	1	0	1	1
Partially Confirmed	0	0	0	6
Largely Confirmed	0	0	0	8
Confirmed	0	0	0	5

Figure 114: Results of Testing.

As in the Killingworth study, the first three hypotheses did not fare well in this testing.[68] Nearly one-third of the test conditions for Hypothesis "A"—that the structures were built by colonial farmers—were outright disconfirmed, as were five of the six test conditions for Hypothesis "B"—that the structures were the result of natural deposition. The remaining test condition for Hypothesis "B," as well as three of the remaining test conditions for Hypothesis "A," were largely disconfirmed. Nine of the remaining test conditions for Hypothesis "A" were partially disconfirmed. The best case for Hypothesis "A," test condition 10, could neither be confirmed nor disconfirmed. Hypothesis "C"—that the structures were built by pre-Columbian European voyagers—fared a little better than Hypotheses "A" and "B," but a third of its test conditions were largely disconfirmed, a third were partially disconfirmed, and it had one test condition each in the disconfirmed and the neither confirmed nor disconfirmed category. None of these three hypotheses had any test conditions that fell into any of the confirmed categories. By contrast, the most equivocal test condition for Hypothesis "D"—that the structures were built by indigenous people—was test condition 10, which could neither be confirmed nor disconfirmed. The main reason for this was that the parameter of wall heights was not systematically measured in this study. All other test conditions were either outright confirmed (five), largely confirmed (eight), or partially confirmed (six).

This provides strong, quantitative and qualitative support for Hypothesis "D" and permits the rejection, in large part, of Hypotheses "A," "B," and "C." It should be emphasized that this does not reject these hypotheses altogether. There are certainly examples of colonial field clearing piles, walls, and chambers; of glacially deposited balanced rocks; and of a few possibly exogenous inscriptions. But even if the isolated chambers, balanced rocks, stone rows, and inscriptions were removed from the inventory, they would reduce the total by only 633 sites (11.4 percent of the total). Contrary to statements made by some historical commissions and researchers that Native sacred sites, or what are now being termed Ceremonial Stone Landscapes, are non-existent or rare, this would leave over 4,900 sites in the category of probable indigenous constructions.[69, 70]

11

Conclusions and Future Prospects

While it must again be acknowledged (as I did in the introductory chapter) that we are just at the outset of the scientific study of stone structures in the eastern Woodlands, this study has provided a number of quantitatively based conclusions that hopefully will be applied to future research.

Conclusions

First, contrary to the claims of some State Historic Preservation Offices that indigenous people never, or only rarely, constructed stone monuments, either prior to or subsequent to European settlement, it is my contention—based upon the robust evidence provided by this study as well as abundant documentary evidence from the early Contact period onwards—that the overwhelming majority of stone structure sites (but probably not all of them) were in fact constructed by Native Americans, in most cases as expressions of deeply held religious/spiritual beliefs.[1] As shown in the preceding chapter, the data argue strongly for the outright refutation of the three other competing hypotheses: that they were the result of colonial farm activities; that they are natural deposits; or that they were produced by pre-Columbian European explorers—at least in the overwhelming majority of cases. This conclusion has important implications for policy decisions made by State Historic Preservation Offices regarding their statutory responsibilities to preserve these sites wherever "prudent and feasible."[2] If it is acknowledged that most of these sites are indeed both indigenous in origin and functionally associated with indigenous sacrality, a number of federal and state/provincial laws regarding such sites will immediately be applicable to them. We are already seeing examples in which Tribal Historic Preservation Offices are presenting legal arguments in court, or before the President's Advisory Council for Historic Preservation, using this legislation as a foundation for their arguments, in some cases with successful outcomes.[3]

Some Massachusetts towns, in the absence of any acknowledgement by the Massachusetts Historical Commission of the importance of these sites, have begun to take steps on their own to protect them, with input from local THPOs, especially the Narragansett Tribal Historic Preservation Office. For example, in Massachusetts the Town of Acton's Historical

Commission, in the heart of Massachusetts Cluster No. 14, took the call for tribes to partner with towns in the first of the USET resolutions (see Chapter 2) very seriously, and established a committee to inventory and protect the stone structures in their town, which in my inventory number sixty-five. The town of Sharon, Massachusetts, faced with the prospect of a planned housing development that would have destroyed the important King Philip's Rocks site in Massachusetts Cluster No. 11, voted in Town Meeting in 2001 to purchase the property, at a cost of $500,000, to protect it from development.[4] I was informed that the argument which won the day was voiced in the following terms: "We have a dozen churches, three synagogues, and a mosque in this town. Why can't we have a sacred place for Native Americans?"[5] Similarly, the residents of Hopkinton, Rhode Island, voted to purchase a 14-acre parcel containing a large concentration of structures within Rhode Island Cluster No. 1, and my own hometown of Ashland, Massachusetts, has recently voted to purchase a 38-acre parcel to add to its Town Forest, which contains several stone structure sites within Massachusetts Cluster No. 3.[6, 7] The presence of stone structure sites was one rationale for the citizens to vote overwhelmingly in favor of the purchase.

However, citizens should expect that there will be push-back against these efforts from the development community, which can at times be quite rancorous. The town of Shutesbury, Massachusetts, recently voted down, by only two votes on a secret ballot, a resolution similar to Acton's to inventory and protect indigenous sacred sites in that town—which I have sixty-nine listed in my inventory. The attorney for a developer used his influence to sway the vote, in response to local efforts to allow indigenous representatives to observe a threatened site in the town.[8] The same developer has now peremptorily banned all Native Americans from trespassing on any of their properties in the state, amounting to over 100,000 acres. Despite protests by indigenous people and concerned citizens of the town of Sandisfield, Massachusetts, the Federal Energy Regulatory Commission (FERC) has insisted on putting a natural gas pipeline through a state forest in that town, which has destroyed as many as seventy-three stone structures. FERC claimed that they would put the structures back together after they disassembled them. The response from Doug Harris to this was, "Then you will have created an artistic representation of a sacred site, after having destroyed the sacred site."[9]

Second, there is a very obvious gap in the distribution of sites between the northeast and the southeast. This distribution is shown in Plate 61, where Area One is the southeast, Area Two is the Shenandoah and Middle Potomac Valley, and Area Three is the northeast. These three areas include all but two of the sixty-four clusters: New York Cluster No. 4 and Virginia Cluster No. 1 appear to be isolated away from these three areas. There are also some clear differences in the sites in these three regions. Sites in the southeast tend to have a much lower variability of structure types, with a higher percentage of them containing only stone piles than in other regions. They tend to be located on agriculturally productive soils much more than do their counterparts in the northeast. They are for the most part located within major river systems rather than on their peripheries, having higher stream ranks and greater mean distances to the nearest minor watershed. They are also located significantly further from head-of-tide than are sites further north. These differences are likely to reflect divergent cultural expressions and environmental parameters within the broad area of the eastern seaboard.

Third, in a few cases it has been possible to ascertain the ages of the structures in question. Figure 1 provides a listing of twenty-two radiocarbon and OSL dates associated with structures that are pre-Contact in age. In addition, there are some structures at sites (e.g. the Call site in Billerica, Massachusetts), and the Flagg Swamp Rockshelter in Marlborough, Massachusetts that have associations with artifacts, whose typology provides a relative age for the structures.[10, 11] So far as I am aware, there are no structures whose ages based on either of these two measures precede the latter part of the Late Archaic period (c. 6000–4000 B.P.), but of course this does not preclude the possibility that earlier structures may be discovered in the future. At least from this time period onwards, there is evidence for indigenous construction. In the southeast, most of the structures are regarded by local archaeologists as being Hopewellian in origin (c. 1500–1000 B.P.) in age, and the general absence of Hopewell sites east of the Appalachians and north of South Carolina has been suggested by Steve Claggett, North Carolina State Archaeologist (personal communication 2012) as the reason for the gap mentioned above. In the northeast, and also in Virginia, most of the dates are Late Woodland in age, a time when many peoples in the region adopted horticulture, for which they might have needed more precise calendrical systems. The stone monuments, mostly located away from horticultural fields, may have served this purpose, among others.

Fourth, there is conclusive evidence, both ethnohistoric and anecdotal, to suggest that the practice of building or adding to stone monuments did not cease with European contact. The sites in Connecticut Cluster No. 5 are associated with a late seventeenth- to early eighteenth-century Indian reservation, and, unlike other clusters located adjacent to state boundaries, they do not cross the border into Massachusetts. Local informants in Connecticut Cluster No. 1 have indicated that a "strange man" visits the Killingworth site there each year to pray—though we do not know his ethnicity.[12] I have been present at Native visits to sites in that cluster and in Massachusetts Clusters No. 3, No. 12, and No. 14 and Rhode Island Cluster No. 1. I have also personally observed alterations of previously documented stone structures in Massachusetts Clusters No. 3, No. 12, and No. 14, which suggests that enhancements of these structures are ongoing in the present day. In one case, at the Benfield "A" site in Carlisle, Massachusetts, Tim Fohl, Doug Harris, and I carefully mapped each structure.[13] Subsequently, Doug invited the members of the United South and Eastern Tribes, who were holding their annual meeting in the area, to visit the site. At some time after this, Fohl, who lives adjacent to the site, observed that there were new piles at the site that we had not documented.[14] John Brown, the Narragansett Tribal Historic Preservation Officer, has indicated that he knows of three locations, including one in Massachusetts Cluster No. 12, where such sites exist and are still being visited by tribal members for ceremonial purposes.[15]

Conversely, as noted in Chapter 10, Ramona Peters, the Tribal Historic Preservation Officer of the Mashpee Band of the Wampanoag Nation, claims that her people never built such structures, except perhaps under duress from colonial authorities.[16] This may indeed be true of the Mashpee; outside of Massachusetts Cluster No. 8, located on the extreme western edge of Barnstable County, there are only four sites in the inventory reported from Cape Cod: two in Yarmouth, one in Dennis, and one in Eastham. However, stone structures are certainly not infrequent in southeastern Massachusetts outside of Cape Cod. This may indicate a cultural difference. Kerrie Helme, of the Aquinnah Band of the Wampanoag Nation, which has been active in preserving stone structures both on Martha's Vineyard and elsewhere in the state, told me that "I argue with Ramona all the time about this."[17] There is no reason why different bands, even within the same tribal nation, should not have differing practices which are reflected in these opinions.

Fifth, the environmental data clearly indicates that the overwhelming majority of stone structure sites are located in upland areas rather than in proximity to indigenous villages. This correlates very well with indigenous land use practices, which regarded these areas as "open" or "sacred" lands subject to strong restrictions on their use:

> The final land use type is *Ehenda tauwundín*, which means "burial place," derived from *tauwatawík*, "uninhabited, wilderness," *tauwunasu*, "to bury someone," *tauwundowagan*, "a funeral, internment" (Zeisberger 2002: 159–160. *wakan/(w)agan*—a process, state or property, *viz. tauwwunnuw*, "opening," Mahheakanneuw, Miles 2015:61; Nipmeuw, *wagan*, similar to Lënapeuw application, as in *môskwelendamôwangan*, "anger," Gustafson 2000:34). A duality of meaning occurs because the wilderness is open, as opposed to closed in with houses, or closed by allotment to a given clan, while a grave is physically opened ground. *Ehenda* applies here because non-sacred activity is forbidden.[18]

Sixth, it will likely be as rewarding to consider where stone structures are absent as it is to consider where they are present. Peter Waksman speculated that, at least in the eastern portion of Massachusetts Cluster No. 14, stone structures tend to be absent from lands that could have been useful for either indigenous or colonial agriculture.[19] My analysis confirms this for much of the study area. Yet stone structure sites also appear to be much less frequent at major watershed boundaries than at minor watershed boundaries. One possible explanation for this might be the mid-range archaeological theory of river-basin territoriality: that tribal groups considered major watershed boundaries to be the edges of their maintained territory.[20] This might have affected their choices of the placement of sacred places: well within their boundaries, but still at a remove from sites used for more utilitarian purposes. This might also be a reason why so many of these sites have survived the ravages of Euro-American development until recently: they are located in areas in which it is difficult either to farm or to build housing developments. As noted in Chapter 10, sites are also absent from areas of documented indigenous avoidance; in particular, from the Adirondacks.

Recommendations

In terms of future prospects, there is obviously a great deal of work that can be done to elucidate the distribution and functions of stone monuments throughout the eastern seaboard. Despite its strong conclusions, this study has been explicitly broad-brush in its approach, looking primarily at the distribution of sites throughout the landscape. It has not attempted to detail distributions at the individual site level, beyond counting the number of structures and types of structures present. However, some researchers are working at a much finer scale to delineate the configuration of structures within sites, and even of stones within individual structures. For example, Rolf Cachat-Schilling has developed a method for documenting sites, which allows for calculations such as average, minimum, and maximum NNDs between structures, as well as the number of courses of stone in certain structure types.[21] He is also looking at configurations of stones with multiple azimuths within the same site, and the relationship of certain structure types within sites to water bodies and slopes. He has found an impressive degree of uniformity among the sites in the Shutesbury, Massachusetts, area he has studied. Similarly, Steve DiMarzo and Todd Carden have meticulously documented each individual structure at numerous sites in Rhode Island over the past several years, providing multiple photographic images for each structure as well as GPS points for them.[22] Mary and James Gage have taken this information and used it to create site maps for many of the sites (for example, see Figure 115).

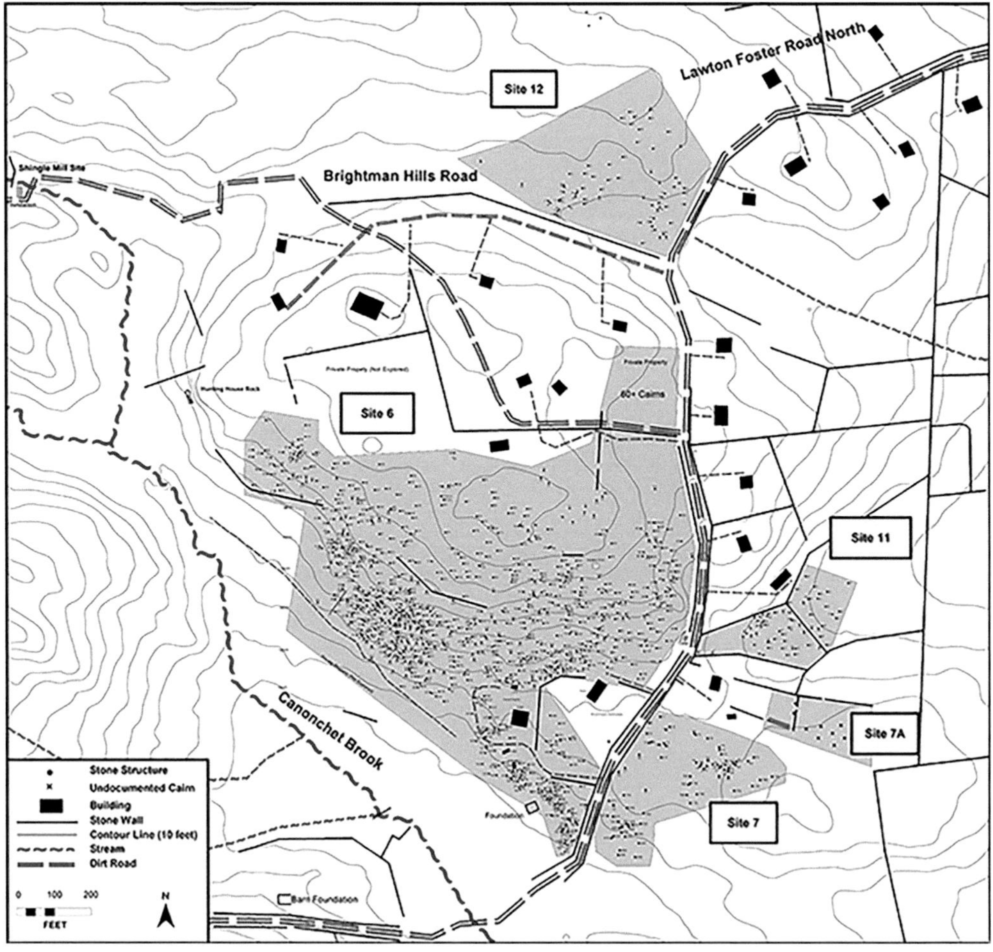

Figure 115: Distribution Map of Stone Structures within Part of Rhode Island Cluster No. 1. (*Courtesy James Gage*)

The Gages have recently produced a very detailed publication of this site complex, which includes over 1,000 monuments.[23] (I have inventoried these as five separate sites based upon the parameters discussed in Chapter 5.) The book includes an exhaustive title trace for the property, proving that the lands to the northwest of the road were never used for agricultural purposes, *contra* Ives.[24] One of the results of detailed studies of this type throughout the study area may be the recognition of vernacular patterns of expression, which differ between areas. These approaches are going to be necessary if we are to discern the patterns on the landscape in greater detail, but they are well beyond the scope of the present study.

Additional studies that could be useful for this level of investigation include the use of LIDAR (especially at the more accurate 1-meter resolution), which can identify stone structures even in forested areas, to scan for additional sites. There are also several innovative dating methods based upon the succession of lichen communities, upon optically stimulated luminescence (OSL), and upon pollen analysis of samples taken from soils beneath or within structures. OSL can provide absolute dates supposedly more accurate than radiocarbon, while lichen dating of structures within the same site can give relative ages, and pollen analysis can indicate the presence or absence of European-introduced species, allowing for a determination of pre- or post-Contact age—though we should also keep in mind the probability (as noted in Chapter 2) that the tradition of Native stonework did not cease upon European contact.[25]

An important way of exploring sites in more detail will be exhaustive searches through archival records, including deeds, probate records, genealogies, church registers, historical maps, town histories, and contemporary accounts of individual landowners and travelers. These will be important to establish the patterns of land use subsequent to the establishment of written record-keeping in the Contact period. For example, Mary Gage has discovered an eighteenth-century farmer's diary from New London, Connecticut, spanning some forty-seven years, in which the farmer detailed his actual use of stone on a day-to-day basis.[26] She concluded that there was no evidence that he created stone monuments of the sort covered in this study. Her most recent study, co-authored by James Gage, provides a complete set of archival records for the family whose property is shown in Figure 115.[27] The authors concluded that while much of the stonework there may post-date European contact, the Foster family who lived there in the eighteenth century may themselves have been Native descendants living on lands traditionally used by Narragansett tribal members for ceremonial purposes, and that they were actively engaged in reviving traditional ceremonies.[28] Even if this claim cannot be demonstrated conclusively, it is at least possible that the Fosters permitted local indigenous people to use their property for this purpose. While the land may have been useful for grazing or timbering before it was dedicated to ceremony, the creation of so many monuments would have made such uses increasingly impossible.

Parameters not included in this study, which would be useful to measure, include the distance of structures to houses, cemeteries, roads, or other obvious Euro-American standing structures, and measurements of angles formed by adjoining stone rows. It will also be instructive to map the relationship between structures and what are likely colonial stone walls. Just as clusters of sites that overlap political boundaries provide strong evidence for their structures having been in place prior to the creation of those boundaries, clusters of structures at individual sites that overlap field boundaries may provide evidence that they antedate those boundaries.[29]

For example, at the Middleborough Little League site, during the 2016 field season, we found a stone row containing quartz stones adjoining a second row that contained concrete blocks. At first, both were considered to be post-Contact, but the angle between them was 97 degrees, not a right-angle, and the orientation of the first row is 227 degrees east of magnetic north (212 degrees true), which corresponds closely to winter solstice sunset/summer solstice sunrise. Furthermore, the first row ends only 25 meters away from its junction with the second row. These characteristics are all typical of stone rows in this study, but the clincher was the discovery of a small rock pile a few meters away from the row.[30] As noted in Chapter 8, combinations between stone rows and rock piles are the most frequent combinations in the study area. This location is about 850 meters from the nearest colonial era house, and about 350 meters from a late nineteenth-century Japan Works factory.[31] This suggests that it is not associated with post-Contact farming or industrial activities. This discovery further suggests that more attention needs to be paid to azimuths. It has been suggested to me by some Native people that large clusters of stone monuments in a restricted area may in fact map star locations. Only with the level of detailed mapping such as provided in Figure 115 will we be able to confirm or disconfirm this interesting idea.

We should also be paying more attention to the contents of individual structures. Several of my informants have noted, as have I, the presence of quartz or other white rocks in prominent positions within structures. One of the more striking Pennsylvania sites I have visited contains a stone row entirely comprised of white quartz. However, I have also seen some sites—for example, Massachusetts Cluster No. 1—which have a black rock placed prominently in each of the structures. What we may be looking at here is the expression of an indigenous system of color symbolism, such as has been adduced for the Iroquois by George Hammell.[32] The use of the colors white, black, red, and a fourth color (which may be yellow, blue, or green) is widespread among North American tribal groups. White, black, red, and yellow are associated with the four directions, four seasons, and various other tetrads in the tribal shield of the Assonet Band of the Wampanoag Nation, and clays of these four colors are found at Gay Head on Martha's Vineyard, the home of the Aquinnah Band of the Wampanoag Nation.[33] In addition, we should pay attention to the sizes and types of stones used to construct the monuments. My study of the Killingworth site revealed that many of the stones in the piles were far too small for their removal from fields to have served any useful agricultural purpose.[34] This was confirmed for me by Rolf Cachat-Schilling during a recent site visit to Massachusetts Cluster No. 3, and it conforms to what he has found in Massachusetts Cluster No. 12.

The overwhelming majority of the sites recorded in this study have been located through antiquarian research: through individuals (myself included) going out to likely locations and seeking sites there. It is no surprise that we have found them in those locations, but this does not accord well with modern archaeological sampling strategy, which requires us to search for sites both in expected and unexpected locations.[35] Despite the large number of sites involved, this means that the sample is potentially biased in favor of locations that contain stone monuments and against areas that are not thought to have them. The classic archaeological way to offset this type of bias would be to conduct random surveys of areas that lie adjacent to known clusters to see if the clusters in fact extend beyond their reported dimensions. For example, I have proposed making use of Connecticut Clusters No. 1 and No. 7, which have a distinctly linear configuration, for an experiment in which researchers would walk perpendicular to the Hammonassett Line at intervals in both directions, recording what they find (if anything), out to at least 1 km away from the line. This would allow the testing of a pair of falsifiable, quantifiable, competing hypotheses:

H_0: The Hammonassett Line is the product of antiquarian speculation, by a researcher who has only looked for sites along it, in which case other sites should be distributed at random distances from the line throughout the landscape around it; or

H_1: The Hammonassett Line is a real phenomenon, intentionally created by indigenous people in its particular alignment, in which case the frequency of stone monuments should be inversely proportional to their distance from the line.

Ideally, this testing should be done as a double-blind, without the researchers who conduct the survey being aware of the hypotheses in question, and simply being asked to record the GPS positions of every stone structure they encounter. While this method is particularly applicable to the Hammonasset clusters, it could also potentially be applied to any of the other clusters in this study.

In addition, the environmental parameters developed for stone structure sites in this book may be used by cultural resource managers and other preservationists as a loose predictive model when undertaking survey operations, as some archaeologists are already doing.[36] This will be particularly important for large-scale cross-country projects such as gas pipelines and powerlines. Locating stone structures early, well in advance of such projects, may allow for rerouting so as to avoid damaging the sites. This is already being done in some cases.[37] This would very much be the preference of indigenous groups, who consider preserving these sites and their general configuration to be a sacred duty, one which is important to maintaining their (and our) relationship with the earth.

Another parameter not studied for this study is site size. Anecdotally, there is a great deal of variability in the raw number of structures per site, ranging from one to 681, but this variability does not reflect how tightly clustered the structures are, except as noted in Chapter 5, where structures further apart than 75 meters were arbitrarily considered to be in separate sites. A detailed study of internal site size and configuration may permit the establishment of a typology of sites, at least in terms of general size categories (small, medium, large) as has been done by Cachat-Schilling for the Shutesbury sites.[38] This, in turn, may bring us closer to a better understanding of site function. Understandably, many Native people are reluctant to allow non-Natives to explore this subject, which is for them highly sacred. I have found, however, that they sometimes do drop hints about this, and they also at times will confirm conclusions that I, and other researchers, have reached independently.

The geographical scope of this study has been limited to the Eastern Seaboard, but as noted in Chapter 5, there have been some parallel studies done of stone structures in the southeast and the Ohio Valley.[39, 40] The methodologies developed here could be applied productively to these regions, as well as beyond them. Moore and Weiss have established that stone structures are documented from all of the states in the continental U.S.[41]

240

A final suggestion for future research would be to engage in some non-destructive experimental archaeology. The historical documentation discussed in Chapter 2 indicates that some stone structures were accretional—that is, they were added to stone by stone by individuals over time. It would be interesting to know how many man-hours it takes, using only human labor, to construct a carefully built stone monument. Obviously, some monuments that consist of the simple placement of a single rock upon another could be created very quickly, but others—for example, the elaborate cairns at the Killingworth site (see Plate 11)—would require much more investment of time. If we knew how much, it would be possible to generate estimates of how many individuals, or over how long a span of time, it would take to create a complex such as that shown in Figure 115. This could help to determine whether it is realistic to suppose that three generations of the Foster family, on their own, could have accomplished this task, in addition to whatever else they were doing to make a living.

New Sites

Although I closed the inventory in September 2016 in order to compile the results and conduct the analyses presented in Chapters 6–9 of this volume, additional sites continue to be reported to me. At the time of publication, there are 218 of these, from eight states, containing 2,317 structures. While these could not be included in the GIS analysis, it is useful to present some information about them here. Figure 116 presents their distribution by state, both within and outside of existing clusters; 64.8 percent of the new sites are within clusters.

Cluster no:	1	2	3	7	8	9	12	14	15	16	18	20	Non-Cluster	Total
State:														
Connecticut		1	2	1									13	17
Maine													4	4
Maryland													2	2
Massachusetts	2	2	28				9	23	12	2	3	3	16	99
New Hampshire													13	13
New York													15	15
Rhode Island	9		2		25	23							2	61
Virginia													7	7
Total	11	3	32	1	25	23	9	23	12	2	3	3	72	218

Figure 116: Recently Reported Stone Structure Sites.

These new sites have added one new Rhode Island Cluster, No. 9, whose distribution is shown in Figure 117. The new cluster, designated as the Maxwell-Mays Cluster, consists of twenty-three sites containing 610 structures within a roughly circular area of 15 square kilometers in the Pawtuxet watershed in the town of Coventry in Kent County. One of these sites had previously been identified by Tim MacSweeney; the rest were reported by Steve DiMarzo. Their average elevation is 545.6 feet; their average distance to water is 226.3 meters. All sites are at Rank One streams, with eleven at headwater streams, six at swamps, and four at ponds. Fourteen of the sites are on slopes, four are on hilltops, four are at shores, and one is in a valley. Average slope, soil fertility, distance to fault, distance to head-of-tide, and distance to watershed were not calculated. Distance to nearest neighbor was 0.27 km. The VMR was 4.99, with a chi-square value of 69.85, which means that there is a 0.00 chance that the distribution is random. The average number of structures was 22.6; the average number of types was 3.33. Types were dominated by rock piles (twenty-two sites), with smaller numbers of balanced rocks (twelve sites), split boulders (nine sites), stone rows (eight sites), niches (eight sites); cairns (six sites), enclosures (five sites); stone circles (three sites), standing stones, manitous, U-shaped structures, and turtle effigies (two sites each); and a snake effigy.

0	**0**	**0**	
0	**11**	**0**	**0**
0	**10**	**3**	**0**
0	**0**	**0**	**0**

Figure 117: Schematic of Rhode Island Cluster No. 9.

These new sites have added one new Massachusetts Cluster, No. 20, whose distribution is shown in Figure 118. The new cluster, designated as the Winchendon Cluster, consists of eleven sites containing 239 structures within a roughly linear area of 40 square kilometers in the Connecticut watershed, very close to the boundary between it and the Merrimack watershed, in the town of Winchendon and the city of Gardner. Seven of the sites were reported by Paul Kachinsky, and four by Peter Waksman. Their average elevation is 1,037.3 feet; their average distance to water is 230.0 meters. All but one of the sites are at Rank One streams, with one at a Rank Two stream; the average stream rank is 1.2. Five sites are at swamps, three are at headwater streams, two are at brooks, and one is at a river. Four of the sites are on hilltops, four are on slopes, two are in valleys, and one is on a shore. Average slope, soil fertility, distance to fault, distance to head-of-tide, and distance to watershed were not calculated. Distance to nearest neighbor was 0.78 km. The VMR was 3.30, with a chi-square value of 128.60, which means that there is a 0.00 chance that the distribution is random. The average number of structures was 21.73; the

0	0	0	0	0	0	0			
0	1	0	1	0	1	0			
0	0	0	0	0	1	0	0	0	0
				0	1	2	1	1	0
				0	0	0	1	1	0
						0	0	0	0

Figure 118: Schematic of Massachusetts Cluster No. 20.

average number of types was 3.03. Types were dominated by rock piles (ten sites) and effigies (six sites), with smaller numbers of stone rows (four sites); split boulders (three sites); marked stones (three sites); mounds (two sites); and platforms, standing stones, and niches (one site each). Effigies included two turtles, three birds, and an eagle.

The new sites have also significantly changed the distribution of sites in Rhode Island Cluster No. 8, as shown in Figure 119. All of the new sites were reported by Steve DiMarzo. All are within the Pawcatuck drainage in the town of Richmond in Washington County. The cluster now has fifty-seven sites in an area of 20 square kilometers. The VMR is now 3.32, and the chi-square value is 63.08, which means there is still a 0.00 probability that the cluster is randomly distributed. The average elevation is 310.9 feet; the average distance to water is 215.9 meters; the average stream rank is 1.4. Average slope, soil fertility, distance to fault, distance to head-of-tide, and distance to watershed were not calculated. Distance to nearest neighbor was calculated using Topo!©'s ruler tool rather than GIS; it is 0.13 kilometers. The average number of structures per site is 21.7; the average number of types is 3.7. The twenty-five new sites are located adjacent to swamps (eleven), rivers (eight), and headwater streams (five). Their environmental settings are on slopes (eighteen), hilltops (four) shores (two), and valleys (one). Structure types include stone piles (twenty-five sites), split boulders (fourteen sites), balanced rocks and enclosures (six sites each), cairns, stone rows, and stone circles (four sites each), U-shaped structures and niches (three sites each), standing stones (two sites), and turtle effigies (one site).

The new sites have slightly altered the concentrations, but not the configuration, of Massachusetts Cluster No. 3 (see Figure 121). The VMR is now 5.76, and the chi-square value is 213.25, which means there is still a 0.00 probability that the cluster is randomly distributed. All of the new sites are in the Merrimack drainage in Middlesex County, and were reported by Harvey Lipman and by the author. All are on Rank One streams. Seventeen are on slopes; eight are on hilltops; one is on a shore; one is on a plain; and

0	0	0	0
0	12	18	0
0	6	0	0
0	3	10	0
0	0	0	0

Figure 119: Schematic of Rhode Island Cluster No. 8, Updated (compare with Figure 89).

one is in a valley. Fifteen are closest to headwater streams; seven are closest to ponds; four are closest to named streams, and two are closest to swamps. The average elevation for the entire cluster is now 349.5 feet above sea level; the average distance to water is 218.0 meters; the average stream rank is 1.07; and the average distance to nearest neighbor is now 0.20 kilometers. The sites have an average of 9.61 structures per site and an average of 2.30 structure types per site. Structure types include sixteen rock piles, seven stone rows, four balanced rocks, four split boulders, three standing stones, two marked stones, two enclosures, one cairn, one effigy (serpent), one stone circle, one mound, and one niche.

The new sites have somewhat altered the configuration of sites in Massachusetts Cluster No. 12, as shown in Figure 120. The VMR is now 7.60, and the chi-square value is 1,763.53, which means there is still a 0.00 probability that the cluster is randomly distributed. All nine of the new sites are in Shutesbury and were reported by Rolf Cachat-Schilling. All are at Rank One streams in the Connecticut drainage. Six of the new sites are on brooks, and three at headwater streams. Five sites are on slopes, two on hilltops, and one each at shores and in valleys. The average elevation of the entire cluster is now 963.5 feet; the average distance to water is 313.5 meters; the average stream rank is 1.23. The average distance to nearest neighbor (calculated using Topo!©'s ruler tool) is 0.48 kilometers. The VMR is now 4.61, with a chi-square of 1,102.0, still indicating a 0.00 chance that the distribution is random. The average number of structures per site is 11.6; the average number of types is 2.1. Structure types include seven rock piles, three cairns, two split boulders, two stone circles, and one each of stone rows, marked stones, effigies, enclosures, niches, and unique structures.

The new sites have slightly altered the concentrations, as well as the configuration, of Massachusetts Cluster No. 14 (see Figure 122). The VMR is now 3.91 and the chi-square value is 3379.62, which means there is still a 0.00 probability that the cluster is randomly distributed. All of the new sites are in the Merrimack drainage in Middlesex and Worcester Counties, and were reported by Peter Waksman and David Guthrod. All but four are on Rank One streams, with two at Rank Two and two at Rank Three streams. Five are on hilltops; eight are on shores; ten are on slopes; and one is in a valley. Eight are closest to swamps; eight are closest to headwater streams; five are closest to ponds; and three are closest to brooks. Structure types include twenty-one with rock piles, ten with

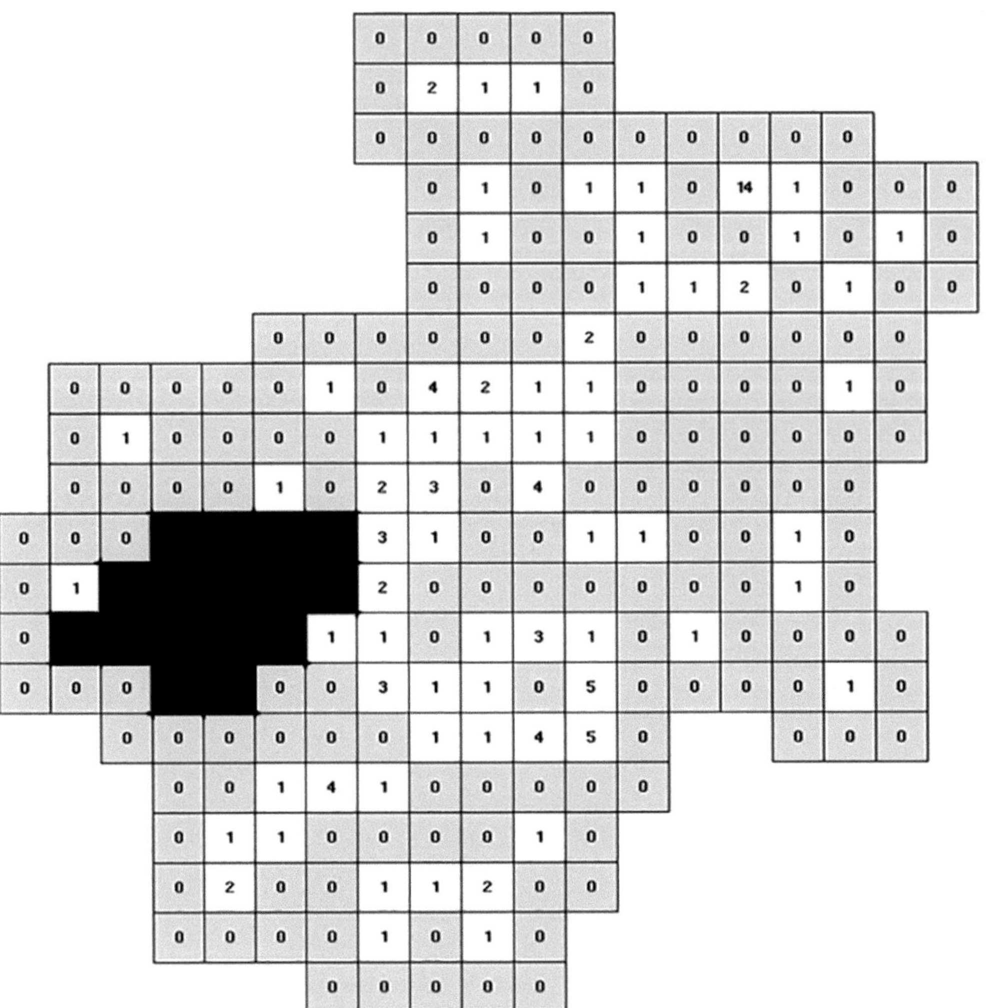

Figure 120: Schematic of Massachusetts Cluster No. 12, Updated (compare with Figure 64).[42]

0	0	0	0	0	0	0
0	1	2	0	1	1	0
0	1	4	23	9	0	0
0	0	9	8	3	3	0
	0	0	0	1	1	0
			0	0	0	0

Figure 121: Schematic of Massachusetts Cluster No. 3, Updated (compare with Figure 55).

Figure 122: Schematic of Massachusetts Cluster No. 14, updated (compare with Figure 66).

stone rows, three with split boulders, two each with cairns and niches, and one each of U-shaped structures, stone circles, mounds, platforms, enclosures, and unique structures (a causeway). The average elevation is 220.7 meters; the average stream rank is 1.38; and the average distance to nearest neighbor is now 0.51 kilometers. The sites have an average of 6.14 structures per site and an average of 1.54 structure types per site.

The new sites have slightly altered both the concentrations and the configuration of Massachusetts Cluster No. 15 (see Figure 123). The VMR is now 3.58 and the chi-square value is 1353.78, which means there is still a 0.00 probability that the cluster is randomly distributed. All of the new sites are in the Merrimack drainage in Middlesex and Worcester Counties, and all were reported by Peter Waksman. All but two are on Rank One streams, the exceptions being at Rank Three and Rank Two stream. Five are on slopes; four are on hilltops, two are on shores, and one is on a plain. Seven are closest to headwater streams; two are closest to swamps; two are near named brooks; and one is closest to a pond. Structure types include six with rock piles, three with mounds, one with an enclosure, one

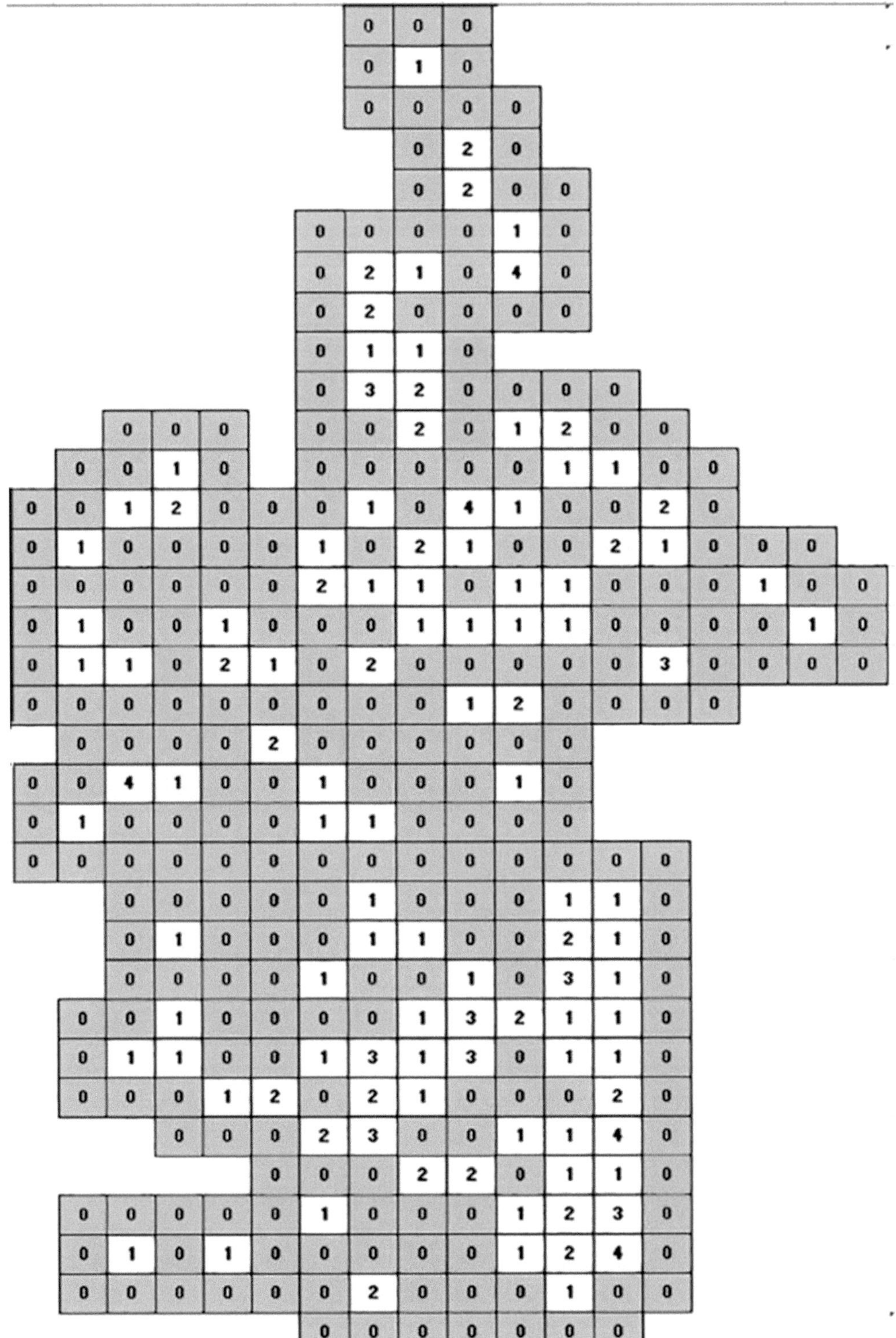

Figure 123: Schematic of Massachusetts Cluster No. 15, updated (compare with Figure 67).

with a stone row, and one with a split boulder. The average elevation is now 936.6 feet above sea level; the average distance to water is 260.9 meters; the average stream rank is 1.21; and the average distance to nearest neighbor is now 0.48 kilometers. The sites have an average of 4.86 structures per site and an average of 1.62 structure types per site.

The new sites have slightly altered the concentrations, but not the configuration, of Rhode Island Cluster No. 1 (see Figure 124). The VMR is now 5.51 and the chi-square value is 1,235.1, which means there is still a 0.00 probability that the cluster is randomly distributed. All of the new sites are in the Pawcatuck drainage in Washington County, and all were reported by Steven DiMarzo. All but one are on Rank Two streams, the exception being at a Rank One stream. Three are on slopes; two are on hilltops; two are on shores; one is in a valley; and one is on a plain. Seven are near named brooks; and two are closest to swamps. Structure types include nine with rock piles, six with split boulders, six with balanced rocks, four with cairns, three with mounds, four with stone rows, five with effigies (two possible human figures, a turtle, and three serpents) two with standing stones, three with manitou stones, two with niches, one with an enclosure, one with a stone circle, one with a U-shaped structure, and one with a star-shaped petroglyph. The average elevation for the entire cluster is now 352.8 feet above sea level; the average distance to water is 259.4 meters; the average stream rank is 1.24; and the average distance to nearest neighbor is now 0.21 kilometers. The sites have an average of 23.70 structures per site and an average of 2.67 structure types per site.

Changes to the other seven clusters are minimal and do not affect the results significantly. The new sites in Connecticut Clusters Nos. 2, 3, and 7 were reported by Tim MacSweeney; the new sites in Massachusetts Clusters Nos. 1, 16, and 18 were reported by Peter Waksman; and the new sites in Rhode Island Cluster No. 3 were reported by Steve DiMarzo.

The new sites in Connecticut outside of clusters were reported by Tim MacSweeney, K. Pat Thorne, Steve DiMarzo, and the author; five of them are in the Housatonic drainage, three in coastal Connecticut, and one each are in the Thames, Greenwich Creek, Poquonock, Fort Hill Brook, and Menunkeetesuck drainages. The new sites in Maine outside of clusters were reported by James Porter, Edward Bourne, Ken King, and Samuel Penhallow; three are on the Atlantic Ocean and one is in the Saco drainage.[43] The new sites outside of clusters in Massachusetts were reported by Peter Waksman, Don Duffy, Emily Brunelle, Alan Smith, Mike Coughlin, Rachel Mulroy, Chris Pittman, Gin Keating, Joanna Delaney, and the author. They are in the Merrimack (five), Connecticut (five), Taunton (four), and Housatonic (one) drainages and on the coast (one). The new sites in New Hampshire were reported by Marty Dudek and the New Hampshire Cultural Historic Preservation Commission.[44] They are in the Connecticut, Merrimack, and Lamprey drainages. The new sites outside of clusters in New York were reported by Frank Speck, James Porter, Lockwood Barr, Peter Backes, and Rolf Cachat-Schilling.[45] They are in the Hudson (seven), Hutchinson, and St. Lawrence drainages (one each) and on Long Island Sound (one). The new sites in Virginia were reported by Jack Hranicky.[46] They are in the James (three), Potomac (one), Chowan (one), and, for the first time, the Rappahannock (two) drainages. The new sites in Maryland were reported Robert Stephenson and Alice Ferguson.[47] Both are in the Potomac drainage.

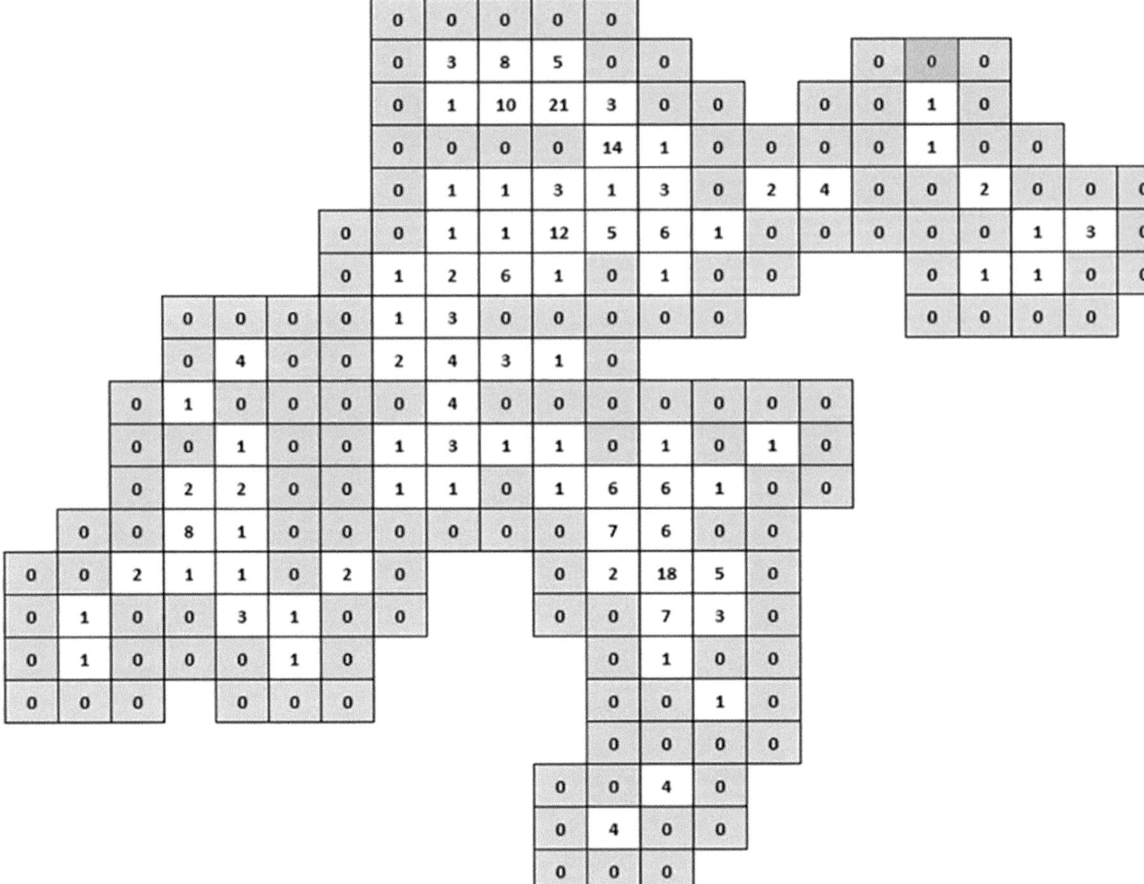

Figure 124: Schematic of Rhode Island Cluster No. 1, updated (compare with Figure 82).

The new sites in Rhode Island outside of clusters were reported by Mike Cavanagh and by C. J. Hall; one is in the Woonasquacket drainage and the other is in the Thames drainage.

If, as suggested in the preceding chapter, the isolated chambers without azimuths and the isolated balanced rocks, stone rows, and inscriptions (633 sites in total) are removed from the inventory, and the 218 new sites are added in, the percentage of sites with multiple types of structures is increased to 35.2 percent, close to 5 percent above the original figure, as Figure 125 below shows. (Note: Figures 120–124 have had the above-mentioned isolated structures removed.) All eighteen structure types are represented at the new sites: 154 have rock piles, fifty-two have stone rows, fifty-one have split-filled boulders, forty have cairns, thirty-six have balanced rocks, twenty-nine have effigies, twenty-one have enclosures, twenty-one have niches, twenty-one have marked stones, sixteen have stone circles, twelve have standing stones, eleven have mounds, ten have platforms, ten have U-shaped structures, seven have petroglyphs, seven have unique structures, and one each have inscriptions and chambers. A Spearman Rho comparison of the frequency of these types and that in the rest of the data, with the isolated chambers, balanced rocks, and inscriptions eliminated, gave a value of 0.75, which is significant at the .01 confidence interval. Thus, the changes to the inventory do not change the distribution of types significantly. Seventy-nine of the new sites are at headwater streams; fifty-one are at swamps; thirty-one are at ponds; thirty are at named brooks; sixteen are at rivers; five are at the ocean, and three are at lakes. A total of 101 are on slopes; fifty-four are on hilltops; thirty-five are on shores; fifteen are in valleys; seven are on plains; and three are on islands. Only fourteen of the new sites have recorded azimuths: nine to winter solstice sunrise/summer solstice sunset, three to winter solstice sunset/summer solstice sunrise, and two to equinox sunrise/sunset.

The major differences between the new data set and the previous data set in terms of structure types are the relative scarcity of marked stones, U-shaped structures, and chambers; and the relative abundance of platforms, enclosures and niches in the new data set. Subtracting the solitary chambers, balanced rocks, and inscriptions results in a marked increase in the average number of structures per site and a slight increase in the average number of types per site, but otherwise the averages for the quantifiable parameters for sites (number of structures per site; number of types per site; elevation; distance to water; and nearest neighbor) are very comparable, as shown in Figure 126, below.

The distribution of nearest water types and of environmental settings is also very similar, as shown in Figure 127 below. There are slightly more sites in the revised data set that are adjacent to swamps and ponds and slightly fewer adjacent to named streams than in the previous data set. There are slightly more sites on slopes and on hilltops in the revised data set, and slightly fewer sites in valleys than in the previous data set.

# of types	total	%
1	3342	64.8%
2	991	19.2%
3	420	8.1%
4	182	3.5%
5	97	1.9%
6	55	1.1%
7	23	0.4%
8	28	0.5%
9	7	0.1%
10	3	0.1%
11	3	0.1%
12	1	0.0%
13	2	0.0%
Total	5154	35.2%

Figure 125: Distribution of Sites by Number of Types Present (compare with Figure 28).

 Stone Prayers

Parameter:	Old Set	New Set
Structures/Site	4.60	8.03
Types/Site	1.50	1.68
Elevation	624.30	622.90
D to Water	250.80	249.81
Stream Rank	1.80	1.78
Nearest Neighbor	2.07	1.97

Figure 126: Comparison of Average Values between the Old and New Data Sets.

	old set		new set	
Setting	# of sites	%	# of sites	%
hilltop	1212	21.8%	1143	22.2%
slope	2510	45.2%	2371	46.0%
valley	1148	20.7%	992	19.2%
plain	195	3.5%	115	2.2%
shore	409	7.4%	456	8.8%
island	76	1.4%	77	1.5%
total	5550		5154	

	old set		new set	
Water Type	# of sites	%	# of sites	%
headwater stream	2320	41.8%	2149	41.7%
named stream	1193	21.5%	1083	21.0%
river	456	8.2%	361	7.0%
pond	529	9.5%	506	9.8%
swamp	673	12.1%	721	14.0%
lake	308	5.5%	269	5.2%
ocean	71	1.3%	65	1.3%
total	5550		5154	

Figure 127: Comparison of Water Types and Environmental Settings between the Old and New Data Sets.

Pairwise combinations of structures for the new sites are shown on Plate 62. As in Plates 45–47, the color coding is as follows:

Values $\geq 2\sigma$ above the mean are shown in red;
Values $\geq 1\sigma$ but $<2\sigma$ above the mean are shown in orange;
Values between 1σ above the mean and 1σ below the mean are shown in yellow;
Values $>1\sigma$ below the mean but $<2\sigma$ below the mean are shown in green;
Values $\geq 2\sigma$ below the mean are shown in blue.

As in Plate 45, rock piles are most often combined above 2σ, but split boulders, balanced rocks, and stone rows are frequently combined above 1σ. Inscriptions are not combined, and chambers are combined only with petroglyphs. This further suggests the congruence of the new data with the old.

Final Words

Following the publication of this book, I am committed to continuing to update this inventory and to distributing the information to the THPO and SHPO offices. Readers who are interested in contributing sites to this effort are encouraged to contact me at teximus@comcast.net. Please provide specific locational information about the sites (UTM coordinates, latitudinal and longitudinal coordinates, or street addresses with accompanying information on how to reach the sites from the street); and also an indication of how many structures of which types are present at the site, and azimuths if these are taken. Photographs of structures are also welcome.

There remains one important issue to be discussed. Until quite recently, as noted in Chapter 2, most archaeologists in the region have conducted their research in a kind of intellectual vacuum, without reference to the beliefs and sensitivities of the indigenous peoples whose ancestors' sites they were excavating. The passage of the NAGPRA law essentially forced the archeological community to deal with Tribal Historic Preservation Offices, at least with regard to burials.[48] As noted in Chapter 2, indigenous people throughout the study area—indeed, across the continent and even beyond have now found ways to voice their views in the public forum, and these views very definitely include calls for the preservation of what they consider to be their sacred places.[49] Even archaeologists who believe that the majority of stone structures are the result of Euro-American farming activities have had to pay at least lip service to strongly voiced indigenous concerns. For example, in his attempt to fabricate a forgotten eighteenth-century farm use for stone structures in Rhode Island, Ives stated:

It is important to emphasize that no disrespect is intended toward Native American Tribes who may ascribe sacred value to cairnfields within the context of Ceremonial Stone Landscapes [*sensu* United South and East Tribes 2007]. The existence of such landscapes is not in question, nor are the assumptions that they may integrate natural and artificial stone features and that they may occupy the same physical spaces as do historic farmsteads.

Rather, this paper presents a modest contribution toward the shared goal of distinguishing ceremonial stonework from that of farmers in a region where a variety of mutually influential cultural traditions render stone piles and cairns meaningful.[50]

Despite this, he concluded:

… cairnfields were once ordinary landscape elements on many New England farms, particularly on rocky slopes maintained as pasture. Though popular memory has not inherited this sensibility, we realize that the prosaic practices of rural people may elude historical documentation and that their material signatures may appear mysterious to subsequent generations.[51]

However, it is my opinion that if researchers really intend to function as good anthropologists, they need to do much more than this: they need to take more seriously the statements of indigenous communities regarding these structures and the need to preserve them, and this will have important implications for cultural resource management policies. As shown in Chapter 2, there is simply much more historical evidence for a "forgotten" tradition of indigenous stonework than there is for a "forgotten" tradition of this practice on colonial farmsteads. The USET Resolutions (see Chapter 2) also make it quite clear that this tradition has not at all been "forgotten" by the descendants of the peoples who constructed (and, in some cases, continue to construct) the monuments. They have had, at least until recently, what they considered to be good reasons to conceal this knowledge from their non-Native neighbors. At least, to his credit, Ives makes sure to record all reported stonework sites in the Rhode Island Historical Preservation and Heritage Commission's site inventory. This is preferable to the policy of his Massachusetts counterparts, who still hold to their dogmatic position that these structures are "invariably" the work of New England farmers and will not list them in their inventory, thereby depriving them of any protection from development.

There are some recent signs that this change in attitude is beginning to take hold within the archaeological community. Both in Georgia and Connecticut professional archaeologists have sponsored conferences devoted to the subject of stone structures, which have featured both archaeologists and indigenous speakers. The American Cultural Resources Association, a national organization, has recently held a webinar on this subject. In Massachusetts, the Division of Conservation and Recreation has recently adopted a forward-looking policy that allows for the delineation and preservation of stone structure sites, which are not specifically identified as either historic or pre-European but "other." That, at least, is an advance over the Massachusetts Historical Commission's continued assertions that all such structures have nothing to do with Native Americans. Four of the southern New England Federally recognized tribes—the Narragansetts, the Aquinnah Wampanoags, the Mashantucket Pequots, and the Mohegans—have banded together to form a Sacred Landscapes consortium to argue for the preservation of these sites. The National Park Service now recognizes Ceremonial Stone Landscapes (CSLs) as a category potentially eligible for nomination to the National Register of Historic Places.[52] It would be possible to nominate all of the site clusters identified in this book to the National Register as CSLs, and thereby provide them with a greater measure of protection from development.

To conclude, this study has demonstrated that there is substantial and widespread evidence for the assignment of the overwhelming majority of stone structures to the work of many generations of indigenous peoples throughout the Eastern Seaboard. Given four centuries of oppression and persecution that these peoples have suffered at the hands of the dominant Euro-American immigrants, the descendant communities are understandably reluctant to share very much about what the function of these sites were, and are, for their way of life, beyond the statement that they constitute "stone prayers." Beyond this, researchers should not seek to inquire without their explicit permission. Nor should archaeologists endeavor to explore this subject by the excavation of the structures without their permission—this is clearly identified in USET Resolution 2007:037 as "the sacrilege of archaeological dissection." There are, however, as noted above, a number of relatively non-invasive techniques that can substitute for excavation. I would recommend that any such studies be done with full permission of local Tribal Historic Preservation Offices.

It is my considered opinion—based upon all of the information presented in this volume— that these monuments are worthy of preservation, and I encourage all of the state and provincial historic preservation offices in the region to include them in their inventories (as many already do) and to provide the same measure of protection to them, under the National Historic Preservation Act of 1966 and its parallel legislative acts at the state/provincial and local levels, that is currently afforded to standing structures and buried archaeological sites. To this end, I am supplying each State Historic Preservation Office and each Tribal Historic Preservation Office with a copy of the pertinent sections of the inventory, complete with locational information. This information will be available only on a need-to-know basis exempt from the provisions of the Freedom of Information Act, as is the case with other site locational data, but it should provide the Historic Preservation Offices, both state/provincial and tribal, with the information that they need to protect these sites in the future.

The main goal of this study has been to use an explicitly scientific methodology to dispel the scientistic, increasingly unsupportable, and racially biased notion of some segments of the professional and avocational archaeological community that pre-Contact Native Americans were incapable of constructing stone monuments. This is not an entirely new idea: if anything, in this pursuit, I have followed Nietzsche's way of the Lion—"the creation of freedom for oneself to create new values."[53] If I have succeeded in doing this, it may pave the way for what Black-Eagle Sun, in his introduction to this volume, has called for: an affective approach to these stone sites, through which we can begin to appreciate not only the quantitative aspect of these monuments, but also their qualitative, aesthetic properties. As stone prayers that continue to play a role in indigenous cultures today, these monuments are not merely objects on a landscape stripped of its sacred associations by four centuries of Euro-American erasure. Like the Wintu excerpt quoted at the opening of Chapter 2, they are poems, each with its own diction and meter. If we can view them from this perspective, perhaps even those of us who were not raised in an indigenous cultural context can now begin to appreciate them more and thereby work to overcome our collective Nature Deficit Disorder.

Endnotes

Preface

1. Cajete, G., *Look to the Mountain: An Ecology of Indigenous Education* (Kivaki Press, Skyland NC, 1994).
2. Louv, R., *Last Child in the Woods: Saving Children from Nature Deficit Disorder* (Algonquian Books, Chapel Hill NC, 2005).

Chapter 1

1. National Historic Preservation Act of 1966, as amended through 2006 (with annotations), www.achp.gov/docs/nhpa%202008-final.pdf (2006); Determination of Eligibility Notification, The Turners Falls Sacred Ceremonial Hill Site, www.achp.gov/docs/TurnerFallsDOEDecision-Redacted1.pdf (2008).
2. www.massarchaeology.org.
3. Ballard, E. C., and Mavor, Jr., J., "A Case for the Use of Above-Surface Stone Constructions in a Native American Ceremonial Landscape in the Northeast," *Bulletin of the Massachusetts Archaeological Society* 71(1):8-26 (2010); Fohl, T., "Integrated Wetland-Dry Land Features with Astronomical Associations," *Bulletin of the Massachusetts Archaeological Society* 71(1):44-56 (2010), Leonard, Jr., K. C., "Identification and Preliminary Analysis of a Late Woodland Ceremonial Site in Southeastern Massachusetts," *Bulletin of the Massachusetts Archaeological Society* 71(1):26–44 (2010); Waksman, P., "A Context for Studying Rock Piles in Massachusetts," *Bulletin of the Massachusetts Archaeological Society* 73(2):68–75 (2012); Gage, M., "New England Native American Spirit Structures," *Bulletin of the Massachusetts Archaeological Society* 74(1):25-33 (2013); Ballard, E. C., "It's About Time and the Paradigm," *Bulletin of the Massachusetts Archaeological Society* 75:13-21 (2014); Gage, M., "Testing the Stockpiling and Field Stone Clearing Theories," *Bulletin of the Massachusetts Archaeological Society* 76(1):2-27 (2015); Lepionka, M. E., and Carlotto, M., "Evidence of a Native American Solar Observatory on Sunset Hill in Gloucester, Massachusetts," *Bulletin of the Massachusetts Archaeological Society* 76(1):27–43 (2015); Henry, J. M., "The Westford Pseudo-Knight," *Bulletin of the Massachusetts Archaeological Society* 76(2):71–81 (2015); and Lenik, E. J., "The Human Hand in Northeastern Rock Art: Communicating with the Spirits," *Bulletin of the Massachusetts Archaeological Society* 77(1):1–12 (2016).
4. Tylor, E., *Primitive Culture: Research into the Development of Mythology, Philosophy, Religion, Language, Art, and Custom* (John Murray, London, 1871).
5. E.g. Ballard, E. C., "For Want of a Nail: An Analysis of the Function of Some Horseshoe or 'U'-shaped Stone Structures," *Bulletin of the Massachusetts Archaeological Society* 60(2):39–54 (1999); Leveillee, A., "When Worlds Collide: Archaeology in the New Age: The Conant Parcel Stone Piles," *Bulletin of the Massachusetts Archaeological Society* 58(1):24–30 (1997a);

"Archaeological Investigations of Stone Pile Features within the Orchard Valley Estates Subdivision, Cranston, Rhode Island," *Bulletin of the Massachusetts Archaeological Society* 58(1):15–24 (1997b); "Public Archaeology: The New Age, and Local Truths," *Bulletin of the Massachusetts Archaeological Society* 62(1):23–28 (2001); Leveillee, A., and Lance, M., "On the Archaeology of Stone Piles and a Late Archaic Date," *Bulletin of the Massachusetts Archaeological Society* 69(2):58–64 (2008); Taylor, W. B., "Thunderbirds in Southeast MA," *Bulletin of the Massachusetts Archaeological Society* 69(2):64–68 (2008) (all prior to my editorship).

6. Grey, D. R., (ed.), *Critical Engagements with Fringe Science* (Cognella, San Diego CA, 2016), p. 4.

7. *Ibid.*

8. McGee, W. J., "Man and the Glacial Period," *American Anthropologist* v. A6(1): 85–95 (1893), p. 85.

9. Haisch, B., *The God Theory* (Weiser Books, San Francisco CA, 2006), p. 146.

10. Kimmerer, R. W., *Braiding Sweetgrass: Indigenous Wisdom, Scientific Knowledge, and the Teachings of Plants* (Milkweed Editions, Minneapolis MN, 2013), p. 345.

11. "The Last Word: Debunking the Myth of Stone Walls, Piles, and Chambers," *Terra Firma*, Massachusetts Division of Conservation Resources, v. 5:14 (2005).

12. Archaeological Intensive Survey of Terrace 2, Middleborough Little League Site, Middleborough, Massachusetts (2017). On file at the Massachusetts Historical Commission, Boston MA.

13. Ives, T., "Cairnfields in New England's Forgotten Pastures," *Archaeology of Eastern North America* 43:119–132 (2015).

14. Moore, C., and Weiss, M. V., "The Continuing 'Stone Mound Problem': Identifying and Interpreting the Ambiguous Rock Piles of the Upper Ohio Valley," *Journal of Ohio Archaeology* 4:39–71 (2016), p. 45.

15. Vieira, J., Stone Builders, Mound Builders, and the Giants of Ancient North America. TEDx Talk (subsequently withdrawn from the TEDx website—see tedxshelburnefalls.wordpress. com/2012/12/14/jim-vieiras-talk-removed-from-internet/) (2012).

16. Samuelson, V., Personal communications regarding Viking contacts with New England (2014–15).

17. Crandall, W., Jonasch, J. J., and Keller, R., "A Massachusetts Patterned Mound Complex," in Cook, W., (ed.), *Ancient Vermont* (Academy Books, Rutland VT, 1978), pp. 39–41.

18. Heyerdahl, T., *The Ra Expeditions* (Flamingo Publishing, New York, 1993).

19. Walwer, G., and Walwer, D. N., Phase I Archaeological Reconnaissance Survey Report of the Ridges at Deer Lake Housing Development (Phase III) in the town of Killingworth CT (2003). Manuscript filed with the State Historic Preservation Office, Hartford CT.

20. Grinnell, J. B., *Men and Events of Forty Years* (D. Lothrop and Company, Boston MA, 1891).

21. Taylor, H., Personal communication regarding Frank Vento's characterization of stone piles in the Lake Catalpa PA area (2015).

22. Adams, D., *Mostly Harmless* (Ballantine Books, New York, 2009).

Chapter 2

1. White, T. D., Toth, N., Chase, P. G., Clark, G. A., Conrad, N. J., Cook, J., d'Errico, F., Donahue, R. E., Gargett, R. H., Giacobini, G., Pike-Tay, A., and Turner, A., "The Question of Ritual Cannibalism at Grotta Guattari," *Current Anthropology* 32(2):118–138 (1991).

2. Coles, J. M., and Higgs, E. S., *The Archaeology of Early Man* (Frederick A. Praeger, New York, 1969), pp. 286–287.

3. Wagner, G., *Age Determination of Young Rocks and Artifacts: Physical and Chemical Clocks in Quaternary Geology and Archaeology* (Springer Verlag, Berlin, 1995), p. 43.

4. For a comprehensive overview, please see Carmichael, D., Hubert, J., Reeves, B., and Schance, A., (eds.) *Sacred Sites, Sacred Places. One World Archaeology* 23 (Routledge, London, 1997).

5. Theodoratus, D., and LaPena, F., "Wintu Sacred Geography of Northern California," in Carmichael, D., Hubert, J., Reeves, B., and Schance, A., (eds.), *Sacred Sites, Sacred Places: One World Archaeology* 23 (Routledge, London, 1997) pp. 24–26

6. Rudolph, J. H., "An Ancient Solar Observatory at Willow Creek, California," in Gilmore, D., and McElroy, L., (eds.), *Across Before Columbus? Evidence for Transoceanic Contact with the Americas before 1492* (Mercantile Printing Company, Worcester MA, 1998), p. 71.

7. Ferrero, P., *Hopi: Songs of the Fourth World* (video) (New Day Films, Blooming Grove NY, 1983).

8. Southwest Traditions, The Hopi, www.southwesttraditions.com/The_Hopi/the_hopi.html (2017).

9. Price, N., "Tourism and the Bighorn Medicine Wheel: How Multiple Use Does Not Work for Sacred Land Sites," in Carmichael, D., Hubert, J., Reeves, B., and Schance, A., (eds.), *Sacred Sites, Sacred Places: One World Archaeology* 23 (Routledge, London, 1997), p. 260.

10. Reeves, B., "Ninaistakis—The Nitsitapii's Sacred Mountain: Traditional Native Religious Activities and Land Use/Tourism Conflicts," in Carmichael, D., Hubert, J., Reeves, B., and Schance, A., (eds.), *Sacred Sites, Sacred Places: One World Archaeology* 23 (Routledge, London, 1997), pp. 278–279.

11. Graburn, N., "Inuksuk: Icon of the Inuit of Nunavut," *Etudes/Inuit/Studies* 28(1):69-82 (2004).

12. Stites, S. H., *Economics of the Iroquois* (The New Era Printing Company, Lancaster PA, 1905), p. 127.

13. Elvas, F. de, *True Relation of the Hardships Suffered by Governor Hernando de Soto and Certain Portuguese Gentlemen during the Discovery of the Province of Florida* (Alexander Robertson, trans. Florida Historical Society, Deland FL, 1933 [1577]).

14. Mahan, J., *Identification of the Tsoyaha Waeno, Builders of Temple Mounds* (Doctoral Dissertation. University Microfilm, Ann Arbor MI, 1970), pp. 40–51.

15. Smith, J., *The Generall Historie of Virginia, New England, and the Summer Isles* (Reprinted by the Wisconsin Historical Society, Document No. AJ-082. Madison WI, 2003 [1624]), p. 580.

16. Beverley, R., *The History and Present State of Virginia* (New Edition, University of North Carolina Press, Chapel Hill NC, 2013 [1722]), pp. 168–169.

17. Williams, R., *A Key into the Language of America* (Wayne State University Press, Detroit MI, 1935 [1643]), p. 197.

18. Norton, H. F., *History of Martha's Vineyard* (Henry Franklin Norton and Robert Emmett Pyne, Tisbury MA, 1923), pp. 3–4.

19. *Ibid*, pp. 4–6.

20. Ruttenber, E. M., *Indian Tribes of Hudson's River, 1700–1850*, v. 2 (Hope Farm Press, Saugerties NY, 1922 [1872]), pp. 391–393.

21. O'Callaghan, MD, E. B., *The Documentary History of the State of New York* (Weed, Parsons & Co., Albany NY, 1850), p. 375.

22. Penhallow, S., *The History of the Wars of New-England with the Eastern Indians, or a Narrative of Their Continued Perfidy and Cruelty* (J. Harpel, Cincinnati OH, 1859), p. 16.

23. Bourne, E., *The Ancient History of Kennebunk, Maine* (Star Press, Clintonville CT, 1970 [1831]), pp. 48–49.

24. Mahan, J., *North American Sun Kings: Keepers of the Flame* (ISAC Press, Columbus GA, 1992), p. 87.

25. Mahan, J., *The Secret: America in World History before Columbus* (Joseph Mahan, Columbus GA, 1983), pp. 38–39.

26. Lepore, J., *The Name of War: King Philip's War and the Origins of American Identity* (Alfred A. Knopf, New York, 1998).

27. Gookin, D., *Historical Collections of the Indians in New England* (Towtaid, Leicester MA, 1970 [1674]), p. 37.

28. Geake, R., *A History of the Narragansett Tribe of Rhode Island: Keepers of the Bay* (The History Press, Charlestown SC, 2011).

29. Hawley, G., Letter containing an account of his services among the Indians of Massachusetts and New York, and a narrative of his journey to Onohoghgwage, *Collections of the Massachusetts Historical Society* series 1, vol. 4 (1835 [1794]), p. 60.

30. Stiles, E., *Extracts from the Itineraries and Other Miscellanies of Ezra Stiles, D.D., LL.D., 1755-1794, with a Selection from His Correspondence* (Franklin Bowditch Dexter, ed. Yale, University Press, New Haven CT 1916 [1762]), pp. 161–162.

31. Mahan, J., *Identification of the Tsoyaha Waeno, Builders of Temple Mounds* (Doctoral Dissertation. University Microfilm, Ann Arbor MI, 1970), p. 15.

32. Mavor, Jr., J., and Dix, B., *Manitou: The Sacred Landscape of New England's Native Civilization* (Inner Traditions International, Rochester VT, 1989), p. 172.

33. Stiles, E., *Literary Diaries of Ezra Stiles*, Vol. I: 1767–1775 (Scribners & Sons, New York 1901 [1794]).

34. Williams, R., *A Key into the Language of America* (Wayne State University Press, Detroit MI, 1935 [1643]), pp. 127–128.

35. Geake, R., Known Land, Foreign Tongue: Early European Attempts to Navigate the Algonquian Language, rifootprints.com/2012/03/23/known-land-foreign-tongue-early-european-attempts-to-navigate-the-algonquian-language (2012).

36. Whitfield, H., *The Light Appearing More and More towards the Perfect Day: Massachusetts Historical Society Collections*, 3rd Series, Vol. 4 (Cambridge, MA, 1814), p. 134.

37. MacLeod, M., "Great Sachem of the Nashaways, Part 2," *Archaeological Quarterly of the W. Elmer Ekblaw Chapter of the Massachusetts Archaeological Society* 8(3):1–22 (1986), p. 14.

38. Shurtleff, N., (ed.), *Records of the Governor and Company of the Massachusetts Bay in New England* (William White, Boston MA, 1853), p. 177.

39. Empire of Laws, New England (1787–1833): The End of State Religion. Empire of Laws: The Legal History of the 50 American States, www.statelegalhistory.com, Section 1.2.1 (n.d.).

40. Hornburg, A.-C., *Mi'Kmaq Landscapes: From Animism to Sacred Ecology* (Ashgate Publishing Company, Burlington VT, 2008), p. 44.

41. Porter, J. D., *Strengthened Resolve: Secrecy, Oppression, and Indigenous Stonework in Early America* (Unpublished ms, 2017), pp. 5–6.

42. Stiles, E., *Literary Diaries of Ezra Stiles*, Vol. I: 1767–1775 (Scribners & Sons, New York 1901 [1794]), p. 386.

43. Kittredge, G. L., "Some Notes on Witchcraft," *Proceedings of the American Antiquarian Society*, new series 18 (1907), pp. 195–196.

44. Cronon, W., *Changes in the Land: Indians, Colonists, and the Ecology of New England* (Hill and Wang, New York, 2003).

45. Amherst, J., Letter to Henry Louis Bouquet, 16 July 1763 (1763). Cited in Gill, Jr., H., Colonial Germ Warfare, *Colonial Williamsburg Journal*, Spring 2004.

46. Mooney, J., *Myths of the Cherokee: Bureau of American Ethnology* 19 (1) (Smithsonian Institution, Washington DC, 2006 [1891]), pp. 350–351.

47. *Ibid*, p. 541.

48. Barber, J. W., *Connecticut Historical Collections, Containing a General Collection of Interesting Facts, Traditions, Biographical Sketches, Anecdotes, &c., Relating to the History and Antiquities of Every Town in Connecticut, with Geographical Descriptions* (A. Willard, New Haven CT, 1836), p. 199; cited in Porter, J. D., *Strengthened Resolve: Secrecy, Oppression, and Indigenous Stonework in Early America* (Unpublished ms, 2017), p. 136.

49. Niles, G. G., *The Hoosac Valley: Its Legends and Its History* (G. P. Putnam's Sons, New York, 1912), p. 107; cited in Porter, J. D., *Strengthened Resolve: Secrecy, Oppression, and Indigenous Stonework in Early America* (Unpublished ms, 2017), p. 38.

50. Weston, T., *History of the Town of Middleboro Massachusetts* (Houghton and Mifflin, Boston MA and New York, 1906).

51. Silverberg, R., *Mound Builders of Ancient America: The Archaeology of a Myth* (New York Graphic Society, New York, 1968).

52. Adair, J., Esq., *The History of the American Indians: Particularly Those Nations Adjoining to the Mississippi, East and West Florida, Georgia, South and North Carolina, and Virginia* (London: Edward and Charles Dilly, 1777), pp. 184–185.

53. Wheeler, M., *Archaeology from the Earth* (Oxford University Press, Oxford, Great Britain, 1954).

54. Riffe, J., and Burdeau, G., (directors), *Who Owns the Past?* (video) (Saul Zaentz Film Center, Berkeley CA, 2000).

55. Chari, S., and Lavallee, J., (eds.), *Accomplishing NAGPRA: Perspectives on the Intent, Impact, and*

Future of the Native American Graves Protection and Repatriation Act (Oregon State University Press, Corvallis OR, 2015).

56. Speck, F. G., "The Memorial Brush Heap in Delaware and Elsewhere," *Bulletin of the Archaeological Society of Delaware* 4:17–23 (1945), pp. 19–20.
57. Thomas, C., "Report on the Mound Explorations of the Bureau of Ethnology," *Twelfth Annual Report of the Bureau of American Ethnology* (Washington, D.C., 1894).
58. Goodwin, W., *The Ruins of Great Ireland in New England* (Meador Publishing, Boston MA, 1946).
59. Feldman, M., *The Mystery Hill Story* (Mystery Hill Press, North Salem NH, 1977).
60. New England Antiquities Research Association (NEARA), NEARA Supports a Wide Range of Interests and Disciplines, www.neara.org/index.php/interests-menu (2017).
61. *Ibid.*
62. Ingstad, H., and Ingstad, A. S., *The Viking Discovery of America: The Excavation of a Norse Settlement at L'Anse Aux Meadows, Newfoundland* (Checkmark Books, New York, 2001).
63. Parcak, S., Potential Viking Site found in Newfoundland, www.cbc.ca/news/canada/ newfoundland-labrador/vikings-newfoundland-1.3515747 (2016).
64. Pringle, H., Evidence of Viking Outpost Found in Canada, news.nationalgeographic.com/ news/2012/10/121019-viking-outpost-second-new-canada-science-sutherland/ (2012).
65. Kehoe, A. B., *The Kensington Runestone: Approaching a Research Question Holistically* (Waveland Press, Long Grove IL, 2004).
66. Cole, J., Western Massachusetts "Monks Caves": 1979 University of Massachusetts Field Research, *Man in the Northeast* 24:37–57 (1982), p. 39.
67. *Ibid*, p. 52.
68. *Ibid*, p. 53.
69. *Ibid*, pp. 44, 47.
70. Walwer, G., "Stone Piles: A Tale of Two Towns," *Bulletin of the Archaeological Society of Connecticut* 77:111–121 (2015).
71. E.g. *Terra Firma*, 2008.
72. E.g. U.S. Department of Interior, 2008.
73. Ojibwa, Native American Ceremonial Landscape Sites in the Northeast, nativeamericannetroots. net/diary/tag/ceremonial-stone-landscape-sites (2015).

Chapter 3

1. Fohl, T., Harris, D., Hoffman, C., and Waksman, P., Survey Report of Indian Ceremonial Structures on Benfield Parcel "A" Property in Carlisle, Massachusetts. Report submitted to the Carlisle Board of Selectmen (2005).
2. Murray, W. F., Investigation of Stone Structures in Eastern Massachusetts. Senior Honors Thesis, Bridgewater State College, Bridgewater MA (2003).
3. Walwer, G., and Walwer, D. N., Phase I Archaeological Reconnaissance Survey Report of the Ridges at Deer Lake Housing Development (Phase III) in the town of Killingworth CT (2003). Manuscript filed with the State Historic Preservation Office, Hartford CT.
4. Hoffman, C., On file at the Massachusetts Historical Commission, Boston MA; "A Quantitative Analysis of Stone Features at the Buell Hill Site in Killingworth, Connecticut," *Bulletin of the Archaeological Society of Connecticut* 77:123–150 (2015).
5. Walwer, G., "Stone Piles: A Tale of Two Towns," *Bulletin of the Archaeological Society of Connecticut* 77:111–121 (2015).

Chapter 4

1. Timreck, T., *The Great Falls: Discovery, Destruction, and Preservation in a Massachusetts Town* (video) (Bullfrog Films, Oley PA, 2012).
2. Lenik, E. J., *Picture Rocks: American Indian Rock Art in the Northeast Woodlands* (University

Press of New England, Hanover NH, 2002); Mulford, P. B., "Fountainhead Regional Park Light-Colored Stone Mounds, Fairfax County, Virginia: The Mulford Mounds," *Archaeological Society of Virginia Quarterly Bulletin* 69(2):116–132 (2014); Mavor, Jr., J., and Dix, B., *Manitou: The Sacred Landscape of New England's Native Civilization* (Inner Traditions International, Rochester VT, 1989); Fowke, G., *Archeological Investigations. Bureau of American Ethnology Bulletin* 76 (Smithsonian Institution, Washington, D.C., 1922); DeLong, B., and Cooke, P., "Secrets of the Stones" www.barbaradelong.com/special-projects/secrets-of-the-stones/secret-of-the-stones-maps/ (n.d.); Bua, M., *Talking Walls: Casting out the Post-Contact Stone-Wall Building Myth* (Publication Studio Hudson, Catskill NY, 2015); Werkheiser, F., and Repsher, D., *Documentary Evidence of Aboriginal Stonework in the American Northeast: A Collection of Documents Referencing Amerindian Stone Building Tradition, Spiritual Expression and Art* (Werkheiser and Repsher, New York, 2005); Gardner, R., (Great Moose), "Anthropomorphic and Fertility Stone-works of Southeastern New England: A Native Interpretation," *Bulletin of the Massachusetts Archaeological Society* 59(2):57-65 (1994); Ballard, E. C., "For Want of a Nail: An Analysis of the Function of Some Horseshoe or 'U'-shaped Stone Structures," *Bulletin of the Massachusetts Archaeological Society* 60(2):39–54 (1999); and Ballard, E. C., and Mavor, Jr., J., "A Case for the Use of Above-Surface Stone Constructions in a Native American Ceremonial Landscape in the Northeast," *Bulletin of the Massachusetts Archaeological Society* 71(1):8-26 (2010).

3. Smith, J., *The Generall Historie of Virginia, New England, and the Summer Isles* (Reprinted by the Wisconsin Historical Society, Document No. AJ-082. Madison WI, 2003 [1624]); Stiles, E., *Literary Diaries of Ezra Stiles*, Vol. I: 1767–1775 (Scribners & Sons, New York 1901 [1794]); Jefferson, T., *Notes on the State of Virginia*, edited with an introduction by William Peden (W. W. Norton & Company, Inc., New York, 1972 [1800]); Agassiz, L., *Contributions to the Natural History of the United States of America* (Little, Brown, Boston MA, 1857–62); Ruttenber, E. M., *Indian Tribes of Hudson's River, 1700–1850*, v. 2 (Hope Farm Press, Saugerties NY, 1922 [1872]); Butler, E., "The Brush or Stone Memorial Heaps of Southern New England," *Bulletin of the Connecticut Archaeological Society* 4:9 (1946); Weslager, C. A., *The Delaware Indians: A History* (Rutgers University Press, New Brunswick NJ, 1990 [1946]); Pohl, F. J., "Further Proof of Vikings at Follins Pond, Cape Cod," *Bulletin of the Massachusetts Archaeological Society* 21(3–4):48–53 (1960); Robbins, M., *Wapanucket: An Archaeological Report* (Massachusetts Archaeological Society, Attleboro MA, 1980); Huntington, F., "Preliminary Report on the Excavation of Flagg Swamp Rockshelter." Institute for Conservation Archaeology, Peabody Museum of Archaeology and Ethnography, Harvard University, Cambridge MA (1982); Gresham, T., "Historic Patterns of Rock Piling and the Rock Pile Problems," *Early Georgia* 18(1/2):1-40 (1990); Cowie, E. R., and Petersen, J. B., Archaeological Phase II Survey and Testing of the Bonny Eagle Project (FERC No. 2529), Cumberland and York Counties, Maine. Report on file with the Maine Historic Preservation Commission, Augusta ME (1990); Mahan, J., *North American Sun Kings: Keepers of the Flame* (ISAC Press, Columbus GA, 1992); Hranicky, W. J., and Collins, L. D., "Short Mountain Petroglyph Site, Shenandoah County, Virginia," *Archaeological Society of Virginia Quarterly Bulletin* 60(3):125–132 (2005); *Virginia Fixed and Portable Artworks* (Virginia Rock Art Survey, Alexandria VA, 2015); Winter, E., "An Atlantic Phase Mortuary Feature at the Call Site, Billerica, MA," *Bulletin of the Massachusetts Archaeological Society* 67(2):42–47 (2006); Leveillee, A., and Lance, M., "On the Archaeology of Stone Piles and a Late Archaic Date," *Bulletin of the Massachusetts Archaeological Society* 69(2):58–64 (2008); Charles, T., *Discovering South Carolina's Rock Art* (University of South Carolina Press, Columbia SC, 2010); Goodby, R., Tremblay, S., and Bouras, E., "The Swanzey Fish Dam: A Large, Precontact Native American Stone Structure in Southwestern New Hampshire," *Northeast Anthropology* 81/82:1-22 (2014); Flynn, E., and Doucette, D., Community Connections from Archaic to Present in Southeastern Massachusetts: Insights from Halls Swamp and Beyond. Paper given at the 2015 Annual Meeting of the Society for American Archaeology, core.tdar.org/collection/29613/new-research-on-the-archaic-period-in-the-northeast-the-past-20-years (2015); and Loubser, J., "Betwixt and Between: Petroglyph Boulders on Liminal Locations in the Southeastern Mountains," core.tdar.org/browse/other-keyword/134154/rock-art (2016).

Chapter 5

1. E.g. Holtstein, H., "A Preliminary Archaeological Investigation of the Morton Hill Stone Structure Complex, 1CA671, Calhoun County, Alabama," *Jacksonville State University Archaeological Research Laboratory, Research Series #5*, Jacksonville FL (2010); e.g. Romain, W. F., *An Archaeology of the Sacred: Adena-Hopewell Astronomy and Landscape Archaeology* (The Ancient Earthworks Project, Olmsted Township OH, 2015).
2. Hallendy, N., *Tukiliit: An Introduction to Inuksuit and Other Stone Figures of the North* (Douglas & McIntyre and University of Alaska Press, Vancouver, BC, 2009), p. 60.
3. Cassedy, D., Phase I Archaeological Survey of the Constitution Pipeline Project. Prepared by: AECOM, Burlington, NJ. Prepared for: Constitution Pipeline Company, LLC, Houston, TX (2014).
4. www.nrcan.gc.ca/earth-sciences/geography/topographic-information/maps/97650.
5. E.g. Gage, M., and Gage, J., *A Guide to New England Stone Structures: Stone Cairns, Stone Walls, Standing Stones, Chambers, Foundations, Wells, Culverts, Quarries, and Other Structures* (Powwow River Books, Amesbury MA, 2012) and *Land of a Thousand Cairns: Revival of Old-Style Ceremonies* (Powwow River Books, Amesbury MA, 2017); Waksman, P., "A Context for Studying Rock Piles in Massachusetts," *Bulletin of the Massachusetts Archaeological Society* 73(2):68–75 (2012); and Ives, T., "Cairnfields in New England's Forgotten Pastures," *Archaeology of Eastern North America* 43:119–132 (2015).
6. Harris, D., and Robinson, P., "The Ancient Ceremonial Landscape and King Philip's War Battlefields of Nipsachuck," *Northeast Anthropology* 83/84:133–149 (2015) and Cachat-Schilling, R., "A Quantitative Assessment of Stone Relics in a Western Massachusetts Town," *Bulletin of the Massachusetts Archaeological Society* 77(2):37–55 (2016).
7. Ives, T., "Cairnfields in New England's Forgotten Pastures," *Archaeology of Eastern North America* 43:119–132 (2015).
8. Waksman, P., Rockpiles, rockpiles.blogspot.com/ (2009–2016).
9. Allport, S., *Sermons in Stone: The Stone Walls of New England and New York* (W. W. Norton & Sons, New York, 1990) and Thorson, R. M., *Stone by Stone: The Magnificent History in New England's Stone Walls* (Walker and Company, New York, 2002).
10. E.g. Ballard, E. C., "For Want of a Nail: An Analysis of the Function of Some Horseshoe or 'U'-shaped Stone Structures," *Bulletin of the Massachusetts Archaeological Society* 60(2):39–54 (1999).
11. Davis, J., Personal communication regarding the function of split-filled boulders (2003).
12. Agassiz, L., *Contributions to the Natural History of the United States of America* (Little, Brown, Boston MA, 1857–62).
13. E.g. Bell, E., "Discerning Placemaking: Archaeology and Native Histories of the Den Rock Area, Lawrence and Andover, MA," *Bulletin of the Massachusetts Archaeological Society* 73(2):42-63 (2012).
14. Mavor, Jr., J., and Dix, B., *Manitou: The Sacred Landscape of New England's Native Civilization* (Inner Traditions International, Rochester VT, 1989).

Chapter 6

1. Holtstein, H., "A Preliminary Archaeological Investigation of the Morton Hill Stone Structure Complex, 1CA671, Calhoun County, Alabama," *Jacksonville State University Archaeological Research Laboratory, Research Series #5*, Jacksonville FL (2010).
2. Rice, O. K., and Brown, S. W., *West Virginia: A History* (University Press of Kentucky, Lexington KY, 1985), p. 7.
3. Speck, F. G., "The Memorial Brush Heap in Delaware and Elsewhere," *Bulletin of the Archaeological Society of Delaware* 4:17–23 (1945), p. 19.
4. E.g. Mather, I., *A Brief Historie of the Warr with the Indians in New England* (John Foster, Boston MA, 1676).

Chapter 7

1. E.g. Hoffman, C., and Edwards, A., "The SuAsCo Watershed Archaeological Inventory Project: Exploring the Cultural Resources of a Suburban Area" (2002). On file at the Massachusetts Historical Commission, Boston MA.
2. *Ibid.*
3. *Ibid.*
4. Hays, W. L., *Statistics for Psychologists* (Holt, Rinehart & Winston, New York, 1963), pp. 643–647.
5. E.g. Hoffman, C., and Edwards, A., "The SuAsCo Watershed Archaeological Inventory Project: Exploring the Cultural Resources of a Suburban Area" (2002). On file at the Massachusetts Historical Commission, Boston MA.
6. McGrew, J. C., and Monroe, C. B., *An Introduction to Statistical Problem Solving in Geography* (William C. Brown, Dubuque IA, 1993), pp. 215–224.
7. Hays, W. L., *Statistics for Psychologists* (Holt, Rinehart & Winston, New York, 1963), pp. 675–676.
8. Waksman, P., Rockpiles, rockpiles.blogspot.com/ (2009–2016).

Chapter 8

1. Cachat-Schilling, R., "A Quantitative Assessment of Stone Relics in a Western Massachusetts Town," *Bulletin of the Massachusetts Archaeological Society* 77(2):37–55 (2016) and personal communication.
2. Harris, D., and Robinson, P., "The Ancient Ceremonial Landscape and King Philip's War Battlefields of Nipsachuck," *Northeast Anthropology* 83/84:133–149 (2015).
3. E.g. Gage, M., and Gage, J., *A Guide to New England Stone Structures: Stone Cairns, Stone Walls, Standing Stones, Chambers, Foundations, Wells, Culverts, Quarries, and Other Structures* (Powwow River Books, Amesbury MA, 2012); Waksman, P., "A Context for Studying Rock Piles in Massachusetts," *Bulletin of the Massachusetts Archaeological Society* 73(2):68–75 (2012); and Ives, T., "Cairnfields in New England's Forgotten Pastures," *Archaeology of Eastern North America* 43:119–132 (2015).
4. Williams, R., *A Key into the Language of America* (Wayne State University Press, Detroit MI, 1935 [1643]).
5. Mavor, Jr., J., and Dix, B., *Manitou: The Sacred Landscape of New England's Native Civilization* (Inner Traditions International, Rochester VT, 1989).
6. Winter, E., "Skug River: The Meaning of a Landscape Name in Andover, Massachusetts," *Bulletin of the Massachusetts Archaeological Society* 71(1):79–87 (2010)

Chapter 9

1. MacSweeney, T., "Waking up on Turtle Island," wakinguponturtleisland.blogspot.com (2009–2016).
2. *Ibid.* and Waksman, P., Rockpiles, rockpiles.blogspot.com/ (2009–2016).
3. MacSweeney, T., "Waking up on Turtle Island," wakinguponturtleisland.blogspot.com (2009–2016).
4. Jones, B., "Interpreting Cultural Stone Landscapes in Southeastern Connecticut," *Bulletin of the Archaeological Society of Connecticut*, No. 77 (2015) and Waksman, P., Rockpiles, rockpiles. blogspot.com/ (2009–2016).
5. Paine, H. D., (ed.), *A Journal of Genealogical and Biographical Information Respecting the American Families of Payne, Paine, Payn, &c* Volume I (New York, 1880), p. 186 and Hiscox, O. A.," The Last of the Wabaquassets," In Lincoln, A. B., (ed.), *A Modern History of Windham County, Connecticut* (S. J. Clarke Publishing Company, Chicago IL, 1920) pp. 60–62.
6. MacSweeney, T., "Waking up on Turtle Island," wakinguponturtleisland.blogspot.com (2009–2016).
7. Howes, M., Ceremonial Stoneworks of the Northeast, nativenewenglandstones.blogspot.

com/2015/03/looking-at-rock-piles-in-holliston-ma.html (2015–2016); Waksman, P., Rockpiles, rockpiles.blogspot.com/ (2009–2016); and personal communications.

8. Howes, M., Ceremonial Stoneworks of the Northeast, nativenewenglandstones.blogspot. com/2015/03/looking-at-rock-piles-in-holliston-ma.html (2015–2016); Waksman, P., Rockpiles, rockpiles.blogspot.com/ (2009–2016); and Hoffman, C., Howe Street Regional Water Treatment Facility Locational Archaeological Survey. Draft Report (1997).

9. Howes, M., Ceremonial Stoneworks of the Northeast, nativenewenglandstones.blogspot. com/2015/03/looking-at-rock-piles-in-holliston-ma.html (2015–2016) and Waksman, P., Rockpiles, rockpiles.blogspot.com/ (2009–2016).

10. Ballard, E. C., "For Want of a Nail: An Analysis of the Function of Some Horseshoe or 'U'-shaped Stone Structures," *Bulletin of the Massachusetts Archaeological Society* 60(2):39–54 (1999); "It's About Time and the Paradigm," *Bulletin of the Massachusetts Archaeological Society* 75:13-21 (2014) and DiMarzo, S., Personal communications about sites in Rhode Island (2014–2017).

11. Leonard, Jr., K. C., "Identification and Preliminary Analysis of a Late Woodland Ceremonial Site in Southeastern Massachusetts," *Bulletin of the Massachusetts Archaeological Society* 71(1):26–44 (2010) and Mavor, Jr., J., and Dix, B., *Manitou: The Sacred Landscape of New England's Native Civilization* (Inner Traditions International, Rochester VT, 1989).

12. Waksman, P., Rockpiles, rockpiles.blogspot.com/ (2009–2016).

13. Lepionka, M. E., and Carlotto, M., "Evidence of a Native American Solar Observatory on Sunset Hill in Gloucester, Massachusetts," *Bulletin of the Massachusetts Archaeological Society* 76(1):27–43 (2015); Gage, M., and Gage, J., *A Guide to New England Stone Structures: Stone Cairns, Stone Walls, Standing Stones, Chambers, Foundations, Wells, Culverts, Quarries, and Other Structures* (Powwow River Books, Amesbury MA, 2012); and Hoffman, C., Howe Street Regional Water Treatment Facility Locational Archaeological Survey. Draft Report (1997).

14. Mavor, Jr., J., *Stones to the Sun* (James Mavor, Woods Hole MA, 1993).

15. Ballard, E. C., "For Want of a Nail: An Analysis of the Function of Some Horseshoe or 'U'-shaped Stone Structures," *Bulletin of the Massachusetts Archaeological Society* 60(2):39–54 (1999) and Lenik, E. J., *Picture Rocks: American Indian Rock Art in the Northeast Woodlands* (University Press of New England, Hanover NH, 2002).

16. Waksman, P., Rockpiles, rockpiles.blogspot.com/ (2009–2016).

17. MacSweeney, T., "Waking up on Turtle Island," wakinguponturtleisland.blogspot.com (2009–2016).

18. Ballard, E. C., "For Want of a Nail: An Analysis of the Function of Some Horseshoe or 'U'-shaped Stone Structures," *Bulletin of the Massachusetts Archaeological Society* 60(2):39–54 (1999).

19. Cachat-Schilling, R., "A Quantitative Assessment of Stone Relics in a Western Massachusetts Town," *Bulletin of the Massachusetts Archaeological Society* 77(2):37–55 (2016) and Timreck, T., *The Great Falls: Discovery, Destruction, and Preservation in a Massachusetts Town* (video) (Bullfrog Films, Oley PA, 2012).

20. DeLong, B., and Cooke, P., "Secrets of the Stones" www.barbaradelong.com/special-projects/ secrets-of-the-stones/secret-of-the-stones-maps/ (n.d.); Waksman, P., Rockpiles, rockpiles. blogspot.com/ (2009–2016); and Howes, M., Ceremonial Stoneworks of the Northeast, nativenewenglandstones.blogspot.com/2015/03/looking-at-rock-piles-in-holliston-ma.html (2015–2016).

21. Ballard, E. C., "For Want of a Nail: An Analysis of the Function of Some Horseshoe or 'U'-shaped Stone Structures," *Bulletin of the Massachusetts Archaeological Society* 60(2):39–54 (1999) and Hoffman, C., Howe Street Regional Water Treatment Facility Locational Archaeological Survey. Draft Report (1997).

22. Some cells redacted due to landowner concerns; *vide supra* p. 233.

23. Waksman, P., Rockpiles, rockpiles.blogspot.com/ (2009–2016) and Timreck, T., *The Great Falls: Discovery, Destruction, and Preservation in a Massachusetts Town* (video) (Bullfrog Films, Oley PA, 2012).

24. Waksman, P., Rockpiles, rockpiles.blogspot.com/ (2009–2016) and Fohl, T., "Integrated

Wetland-Dry Land Features with Astronomical Associations," *Bulletin of the Massachusetts Archaeological Society* 71(1):44-56 (2010).

25. Ballard, E. C., "For Want of a Nail: An Analysis of the Function of Some Horseshoe or 'U'-shaped Stone Structures," *Bulletin of the Massachusetts Archaeological Society* 60(2):39–54 (1999); Huntington, F., "Preliminary Report on the Excavation of Flagg Swamp Rockshelter." Institute for Conservation Archaeology, Peabody Museum of Archaeology and Ethnography, Harvard University, Cambridge MA (1982); Winter, E., "An Atlantic Phase Mortuary Feature at the Call Site, Billerica, MA," *Bulletin of the Massachusetts Archaeological Society* 67(2):42–47 (2006); and Mavor, Jr., J., and Dix, B., *Manitou: The Sacred Landscape of New England's Native Civilization* (Inner Traditions International, Rochester VT, 1989).

26. Waksman, P., Rockpiles, rockpiles.blogspot.com/ (2009–2016).

27. Gage, M., and Gage, J., *A Guide to New England Stone Structures: Stone Cairns, Stone Walls, Standing Stones, Chambers, Foundations, Wells, Culverts, Quarries, and Other Structures* (Powwow River Books, Amesbury MA, 2012); DeLong, B., and Cooke, P., "Secrets of the Stones" www.barbaradelong.com/special-projects/secrets-of-the-stones/secret-of-the-stones-maps/ (n.d.); MacSweeney, T., "Waking up on Turtle Island," wakinguponturtleisland.blogspot.com (2009–2016) and Mavor, Jr., J., and Dix, B., *Manitou: The Sacred Landscape of New England's Native Civilization* (Inner Traditions International, Rochester VT, 1989).

28. Waksman, P., Rockpiles, rockpiles.blogspot.com/ (2009–2016) and Hoffman, C., Howe Street Regional Water Treatment Facility Locational Archaeological Survey. Draft Report (1997).

29. Waksman, P., Rockpiles, rockpiles.blogspot.com/ (2009–2016) and Timreck, T., *The Great Falls: Discovery, Destruction, and Preservation in a Massachusetts Town* (video) (Bullfrog Films, Oley PA, 2012).

30. Waksman, P., Rockpiles, rockpiles.blogspot.com/ (2009–2016).

31. Waksman, P., Rockpiles, rockpiles.blogspot.com/ (2009–2016) and Fohl, T., Personal communication concerning additions to the Benfield A site (2009); "Integrated Wetland-Dry Land Features with Astronomical Associations," *Bulletin of the Massachusetts Archaeological Society* 71(1):44-56 (2010).

32. Gage, M., and Gage, J., *A Guide to New England Stone Structures: Stone Cairns, Stone Walls, Standing Stones, Chambers, Foundations, Wells, Culverts, Quarries, and Other Structures* (Powwow River Books, Amesbury MA, 2012).

33. Feldman, M., *The Mystery Hill Story* (Mystery Hill Press, North Salem NH, 1977).

34. Waksman, P., Rockpiles, rockpiles.blogspot.com/ (2009–2016).

35. Gage, M., and Gage, J., *A Guide to New England Stone Structures: Stone Cairns, Stone Walls, Standing Stones, Chambers, Foundations, Wells, Culverts, Quarries, and Other Structures* (Powwow River Books, Amesbury MA, 2012).

36. DeLong, B., and Cooke, P., "Secrets of the Stones" www.barbaradelong.com/special-projects/secrets-of-the-stones/secret-of-the-stones-maps/ (n.d.); Waksman, P., Rockpiles, rockpiles.blogspot.com/ (2009–2016); and MacSweeney, T., "Waking up on Turtle Island," wakinguponturtleisland.blogspot.com (2009–2016).

37. Cassedy, D., Phase I Archaeological Survey of the Constitution Pipeline Project. Prepared by: AECOM, Burlington, NJ. Prepared for: Constitution Pipeline Company, LLC, Houston, TX (2014).

38. *Ibid.*

39. Gage, M., and Gage, J., *A Guide to New England Stone Structures: Stone Cairns, Stone Walls, Standing Stones, Chambers, Foundations, Wells, Culverts, Quarries, and Other Structures* (Powwow River Books, Amesbury MA, 2012).

40. *Ibid.*

41. Charles, T., *Discovering South Carolina's Rock Art* (University of South Carolina Press, Columbia SC, 2010).

42. DeLong, B., and Cooke, P., "Secrets of the Stones" www.barbaradelong.com/special-projects/secrets-of-the-stones/secret-of-the-stones-maps/ (n.d.); Waksman, P., Rockpiles, rockpiles.blogspot.com/ (2009–2016); Lenik, E. J., *Picture Rocks: American Indian Rock Art in the*

Northeast Woodlands (University Press of New England, Hanover NH, 2002); and Fohl, T., "Integrated Wetland-Dry Land Features with Astronomical Associations," *Bulletin of the Massachusetts Archaeological Society* 71(1):44-56 (2010).

43. Mulford, P. B., "Fountainhead Regional Park Light-Colored Stone Mounds, Fairfax County, Virginia: The Mulford Mounds," *Archaeological Society of Virginia Quarterly Bulletin* 69(2):116–132 (2014).

44. MacSweeney, T., "Waking up on Turtle Island," wakinguponturtleisland.blogspot.com (2009–2016).

45. Cowie, E. R., and Petersen, J. B., Archaeological Phase II Survey and Testing of the Bonny Eagle Project (FERC No. 2529), Cumberland and York Counties, Maine. Report on file with the Maine Historic Preservation Commission, Augusta ME (1990); DeLong, B., and Cooke, P., "Secrets of the Stones" www.barbaradelong.com/special-projects/secrets-of-the-stones/secret-of-the-stones-maps/ (n.d.); Lenik, E. J., *Picture Rocks: American Indian Rock Art in the Northeast Woodlands* (University Press of New England, Hanover NH, 2002); Gage, M., and Gage, J., *A Guide to New England Stone Structures: Stone Cairns, Stone Walls, Standing Stones, Chambers, Foundations, Wells, Culverts, Quarries, and Other Structures* (Powwow River Books, Amesbury MA, 2012); Waksman, P., Rockpiles, rockpiles.blogspot.com/ (2009–2016) and Hoffman, C., Howe Street Regional Water Treatment Facility Locational Archaeological Survey. Draft Report (1997).

46. Weslager, C. A., *The Delaware Indians: A History* (Rutgers University Press, New Brunswick NJ, 1990 [1946]).

47. Lenik, E. J., *Picture Rocks: American Indian Rock Art in the Northeast Woodlands* (University Press of New England, Hanover NH, 2002).

48. Lenik, E. J., *Picture Rocks: American Indian Rock Art in the Northeast Woodlands* (University Press of New England, Hanover NH, 2002); DeLong, B., and Cooke, P., "Secrets of the Stones" www.barbaradelong.com/special-projects/secrets-of-the-stones/secret-of-the-stones-maps/ (n.d.); and Werkheiser, F., and Repsher, D., *Documentary Evidence of Aboriginal Stonework in the American Northeast: A Collection of Documents Referencing Amerindian Stone Building Tradition, Spiritual Expression and Art* (Werkheiser and Repsher, New York, 2005).

49. Thomas, C., "Report on the Mound Explorations of the Bureau of Ethnology," *Twelfth Annual Report of the Bureau of American Ethnology* (Washington, D.C., 1894) and Loubser, J., "Betwixt and Between: Petroglyph Boulders on Liminal Locations in the Southeastern Mountains," core. tdar.org/browse/other-keyword/134154/rock-art (2016).

50. Lenik, E. J., *Picture Rocks: American Indian Rock Art in the Northeast Woodlands* (University Press of New England, Hanover NH, 2002); "The Human Hand in Northeastern Rock Art: Communicating with the Spirits," *Bulletin of the Massachusetts Archaeological Society* 77(1):1–12 (2016).

51. Googoo, M., Protecting Mi'kmaq Petroglyphs in Bedford, Kejimkujik National Park, www. kukukwes.com/2015/08/26 (2015).

52. Fowke, G., *Archeological Investigations. Bureau of American Ethnology Bulletin* 76 (Smithsonian Institution, Washington, D.C., 1922).

Chapter 10

1. Walwer, G., and Walwer, D. N., Phase I Archaeological Reconnaissance Survey Report of the Ridges at Deer Lake Housing Development (Phase III) in the town of Killingworth CT (2003). Manuscript filed with the State Historic Preservation Office, Hartford CT.

2. Cooper, J. F., *The Wept of Wish-Ton-Wish* (Reprint Services Corporation, Irvine CA, 1829), p. 423.

3. Burroughs, J., *In the Catskills* (Houghton Mifflin, Boston and New York, 1910).

4. Allport, S., *Sermons in Stone: The Stone Walls of New England and New York* (W. W. Norton & Sons, New York, 1990), pp. 78–79.

5. Walwer, G., and Walwer, D. N., Phase I Archaeological Reconnaissance Survey Report of the Ridges at Deer Lake Housing Development (Phase III) in the town of Killingworth CT (2003). Manuscript filed with the State Historic Preservation Office, Hartford CT.

6. Hoffman, C., Analysis of Stone Features: The Ridges at Deer Lake Housing Development Property, Killingworth, Connecticut. On file at the Connecticut Historical Commission, Hartford CT (2004).

7. Fohl, T., "Confessions of a Former Professional Rock Popper," *New England Antiquities Research Association Journal* 37(2):15 (2003).

8. Thorson, R. M., *Stone by Stone: The Magnificent History in New England's Stone Walls* (Walker and Company, New York, 2002).

9. Miner, personal communication with the author, 2017.

10. Hoffman, C., "Caches or Offerings? Ceremonial Objects from the First Terrace at the Middleborough Little League Site (19-PL-520)," *Bulletin of the Massachusetts Archaeological Society* 77(2):61–68 (2016), p. 63.

11. Fohl, T., "Confessions of a Former Professional Rock Popper," *New England Antiquities Research Association Journal* 37(2):15 (2003).

12. *Ibid.*

13. Hoffman, C., South Brook Archaeological Survey, Bridgewater, Massachusetts (2006). On file at the Massachusetts Historical Commission, Boston MA.

14. Murray, W. F., Investigation of Stone Structures in Eastern Massachusetts. Senior Honors Thesis, Bridgewater State College, Bridgewater MA (2003).

15. Winter, E., "An Atlantic Phase Mortuary Feature at the Call Site, Billerica, MA," *Bulletin of the Massachusetts Archaeological Society* 67(2):42–47 (2006).

16. Walwer, G., "Stone Piles: A Tale of Two Towns," *Bulletin of the Archaeological Society of Connecticut* 77:111–121 (2015).

17. E.g. Kraft, H., "Late Woodland Cultures of the Upper Delaware Valley," in Custer, J., (ed.), *Late Woodland Cultures of the Middle Atlantic Region* (University of Delaware Press, Newark DE, 1986), p. 114.

18. Parker, A. C., *Nundawao and the Coming of the Senecas* (Nundawaga Society for History and Folklore, (Naples(?)NY, 1955).

19. Duncan, D. E., *Calendar: Humanity's Epic Struggle to Determine a True and Accurate Year* (HarperCollins, New York, 1999).

20. Hoffman, C., Howe Street Regional Water Treatment Facility Locational Archaeological Survey. Draft Report (1997). On file at the Massachusetts Historical Commission, Boston MA.

21. www.sec.state.ma.us/mhc/ (2016).

22. Antevs, E., Correlation of Wisconsin Glacial Maxima. *Daly Volume* 1–85 (1945). earth.geology.yale.edu/~ajs/1945A/1.pdf.

23. E.g. Fell, H. B., "Vermont's Ancient Sites and the Larger Picture of Trans-Atlantic Visitations to America, B.C.," in Cook, W., (ed.), *Ancient Vermont* (Academy Books, Rutland VT, 1978) pp. 70–84.

24. Seaby, P., "The First Datable Norse Find from North America?" *Seaby Coin and Medal Bulletin* (December 1978).

25. Heilbron, J. L., *The Sun in the Church: Cathedrals as Solar Observatories* (Harvard University Press, Cambridge MA, 2001).

26. Feldman, M., *The Mystery Hill Story* (Mystery Hill Press, North Salem NH, 1977).

27. Da Silva, M., *Portuguese Pilgrims and Dighton Rock* (Published by the author, 1971).

28. E.g. Goudsward, D., *Ancient Stone Sites of New England and the Debate over Early European Exploration* (McFarland & Co., Jefferson NC, 2006) and Hunter, D., *The Place of Stone: Dighton Rock and the Erasure of America's Indigenous Past* (University of North Carolina Press, Chapel Hill NC, 2017).

29. Sturluson, S., *Prose Edda*, Brodeur, A. G., (transl.), (The American-Scandinavian Foundation, New York, 1916).

30. Fowler, W. S., "Ceremonial and Domestic Products of Aboriginal New England," *Bulletin of the Massachusetts Archaeological Society* 27(3/4):33-68 (1966), pp. 43–45.

31. Fell, H. B., *America, B.C.: Ancient Settlers in the New World* (Quadrangle Books, New York, 1976).

32. Crandall, W., Jonasch, J. J., and Keller, R., "A Massachusetts Patterned Mound Complex," in Cook, W., (ed.), *Ancient Vermont* (Academy Books, Rutland VT, 1978), pp. 39–41.

33. Kehoe, A. B., *The Kensington Runestone: Approaching a Research Question Holistically* (Waveland Press, Long Grove IL, 2004).

34. Ingstad, H., and Ingstad, A. S., *The Viking Discovery of America: The Excavation of a Norse Settlement at L'Anse Aux Meadows, Newfoundland* (Checkmark Books, New York, 2001).

35. Hoffman, C., and Edwards, A., "The SuAsCo Watershed Archaeological Inventory Project: Exploring the Cultural Resources of a Suburban Area" (2002). On file at the Massachusetts Historical Commission, Boston MA.

36. Hays, W. L., *Statistics for Psychologists* (Holt, Rinehart & Winston, New York, 1963), pp. 643–647.

37. Ives, T., "Cairnfields in New England's Forgotten Pastures," *Archaeology of Eastern North America* 43:119–132 (2015), p. 120.

38. Neudorffer, G., "A Preliminary Analysis of Vermont's Stone Chambers" in Cook, W. L., (ed.), *Ancient Vermont* (Academy Books, Rutland VT, 1977), pp. 9–13.

39. www.sec.state.ma.us/mhc/ (2017).

40. Bell, E., "Discerning Placemaking: Archaeology and Native Histories of the Den Rock Area, Lawrence and Andover, MA," *Bulletin of the Massachusetts Archaeological Society* 73(2):42-63 (2012), p. 48.

41. Lenik, E. J., *Picture Rocks: American Indian Rock Art in the Northeast Woodlands* (University Press of New England, Hanover NH, 2002).

42. Hoffman, C., South Brook Archaeological Survey, Bridgewater, Massachusetts (2006). On file at the Massachusetts Historical Commission, Boston MA and Archaeological Intensive Survey of Terrace 2, Middleborough Little League Site, Middleborough, Massachusetts (2017). On file at the Massachusetts Historical Commission, Boston MA.

43. E.g. Walwer, G., "Stone Piles: A Tale of Two Towns," *Bulletin of the Archaeological Society of Connecticut* 77:111–121 (2015).

44. MacSweeney, T., "Waking up on Turtle Island," wakinguponturtleisland.blogspot.com (2009-2016), *passim.*

45. Lenik, E. J., *Picture Rocks: American Indian Rock Art in the Northeast Woodlands* (University Press of New England, Hanover NH, 2002), p. 177.

46. Converse, H. M., and Parker, A. C., *Myths and Legends of the New York State Iroquois* (New York State Museum, Albany NY, 1906), p. 184.

47. Mooney, J., *Myths of the Cherokee: Bureau of American Ethnology* 19 (1) (Smithsonian Institution, Washington DC, 2006 [1891]), p. 475.

48. Simmons, W. S., *Spirit of the New England Tribes: Indian History and Folklore* (University Press of New England, Hanover NH, 1986), p. 41.

49. Houston, J., and Rubin, M., *Manual for the Peacemaker: An Iroquois Legend to Heal Self and Society* (Quest Books, Wheaton IL, 1997), p. 86.

50. Speck, F. G., "Malecite Tales," *The Journal of American Folklore* 30(118):479–485 (1917), pp. 479–480.

51. Mooney, J., *Myths of the Cherokee: Bureau of American Ethnology* 19 (1) (Smithsonian Institution, Washington DC, 2006 [1891]), p. 481.

52. *Ibid*, p. 294.

53. Mavor, Jr., J., and Dix, B., *Manitou: The Sacred Landscape of New England's Native Civilization* (Inner Traditions International, Rochester VT, 1989), p. 100.

54. Stiles, E., *A History of Three of the Judges of King Charles I* (Elisha Babcock, Hartford CT, 1795).

55. Russell, H. S., *Indian New England before the Mayflower* (University Press of New England, Hanover NH, 1980), p. 165.

56. Williams, R., *A Key into the Language of America* (Wayne State University Press, Detroit MI, 1935 [1643]), pp. 62, 80–81.

57. Narragansett Indian Tribe, "*Nikkomo*—I Give Away," artways.libsyn.com/podcast/episode-3-nikkomo (2016).

58. Williams, R., *A Key into the Language of America* (Wayne State University Press, Detroit MI, 1935 [1643]).

59. Pequot Tribal Nation, Schemitzun: Feast of Green Corn and Dance, schemitzun.mptn-nsn.gov/uploadedFiles/Shemitzun_brochure_2016.pdf (2016).

60. Russell, H. S., *Indian New England before the Mayflower* (University Press of New England, Hanover NH, 1980), p. 170.

61. Ballard, E. C., and Mavor, Jr., J., "A Case for the Use of Above-Surface Stone Constructions in a Native American Ceremonial Landscape in the Northeast," *Bulletin of the Massachusetts Archaeological Society* 71(1):8-26 (2010).

62. Ballard, E. C., "For Want of a Nail: An Analysis of the Function of Some Horseshoe or 'U'-shaped Stone Structures," *Bulletin of the Massachusetts Archaeological Society* 60(2):39–54 (1999); "It's About Time and the Paradigm," *Bulletin of the Massachusetts Archaeological Society* 75:13-21 (2014).

63. Paul, C. T., The Hammonassett line, Chapter 1: A Summer Solstice Sunset Line, www.neara.org/images/pdf/Hammonasset01.pdf (2001).

64. New England Historical Society, The Maypole That Infuriated the Puritans, www.newenglandhistoricalsociety.com/maypole-infuriated-puritans/ (2015).

65. Beauchamp, W. M., *The Iroquois Trail, or, Footprints of the Six Nations* (Published by the author, Fayetteville NY, 1892).

66. Cachat-Schilling, R., personal communications with the author (2017).

67. Hantman, Dr. J., personal communication with the author (2017).

68. Hoffman, C., Archaeological Intensive Survey of Terrace 2, Middleborough Little League Site, Middleborough, Massachusetts (2017). On file at the Massachusetts Historical Commission, Boston MA.

69. (National Park Service 2017)

70. www.sec.state.ma.us/mhc/ (2017); Ives, T., "Cairnfields in New England's Forgotten Pastures," *Archaeology of Eastern North America* 43:119–132 (2015); Porter, J. D., *Strengthened Resolve: Secrecy, Oppression, and Indigenous Stonework in Early America* (Unpublished ms, 2017); and National Park Service, National Register of Historic Places—Traditional Cultural Properties (TCPs): A Quick Guide for Preserving Native American Cultural Resources, www.nps.gov/history/tribes/Documents/TCP.pdf (2017)

Chapter 11

1. www.sec.state.ma.us/mhc/ (2017) and Ives, T., "Cairnfields in New England's Forgotten Pastures," *Archaeology of Eastern North America* 43:119–132 (2015).

2. www.sec.state.ma.us/mhc/ (n.d.).

3. E.g. United States Department of Interior, Determination of Eligibility Notification, The Turners Falls Sacred Ceremonial Hill Site, www.achp.gov/docs/TurnerFallsDOEDecision-Redacted1.pdf (2008).

4. malegislature.gov/Laws/GeneralLaws/

5. Martin, F., Personal communication regarding the preservation of the King Philip's Rocks site (2004).

6. Gage, M., and Gage, J., *Land of a Thousand Cairns: Revival of Old-Style Ceremonies* (Powwow River Books, Amesbury MA, 2017).

7. Town of Ashland, Massachusetts, Warrant Articles, Information, and Recommendations of the Finance Committee for the November 14, 2017 Special Town Meeting, Ashland High School (2017).

8. Cachat-Schilling, R., personal communications with the author (2017).

9. Bellow, H., "Narragansetts Blame FERC for Problems on Pipeline Path," *Berkshire Eagle*, April 28 (2017). www.berkshireeagle.com/stories/narragansetts-blame-ferc-for-problems-on-pipeline-path,505862.

10. Winter, E., "An Atlantic Phase Mortuary Feature at the Call Site, Billerica, MA," *Bulletin of the Massachusetts Archaeological Society* 67(2):42–47 (2006).

11. Blancke, S., and Spiess, A. E., "The Flagg Swamp Rockshelter, Marlborough, MA: A Summary," *Bulletin of the Massachusetts Archaeological Society* 67(1):2-24 (2006).

12. McDermott, K., Personal communication concerning ongoing ritual use of the Buell Hill site (2007).

13. Fohl, T., Harris, D., Hoffman, C., and Waksman, P., Survey Report of Indian Ceremonial Structures on Benfield Parcel "A" Property in Carlisle, Massachusetts. Report submitted to the Carlisle Board of Selectmen (2005).

14. Fohl, T., Personal communication concerning additions to the Benfield A site (2009).

15. Timreck, T., *The Great Falls: Discovery, Destruction, and Preservation in a Massachusetts Town* (video) (Bullfrog Films, Oley PA, 2012).

16. Peters, R., Personal communication regarding the absence of stone structure sites on Cape Cod (2014).

17. Helme, K., Personal communication concerning her dispute with Ramona Peters about the origin of stone structures (2015).

18. Cachat-Schilling, R., personal communications with the author (2017).

19. Waksman, P., "A Context for Studying Rock Piles in Massachusetts," *Bulletin of the Massachusetts Archaeological Society* 73(2):68–75 (2012).

20. E.g. Dincauze, D. F., "An Introduction to the Archaeology of the Greater Boston Area," *Archaeology of Eastern North America* 2(1):39–67 (1974).

21. Cachat-Schilling, R., "A Quantitative Assessment of Stone Relics in a Western Massachusetts Town," *Bulletin of the Massachusetts Archaeological Society* 77(2):37–55 (2016).

22. DiMarzo, S., Personal communications about sites in Rhode Island (2014–2017).

23. Gage, M., and Gage, J., *Land of a Thousand Cairns: Revival of Old-Style Ceremonies* (Powwow River Books, Amesbury MA, 2017).

24. Ives, T., "Cairnfields in New England's Forgotten Pastures," *Archaeology of Eastern North America* 43:119–132 (2015).

25. Mahan, S., Martin, F., and Carlson, C., "Construction Ages of the Upton Stone Chamber: Preliminary Findings and Suggestions for Future Luminescence Research," *Quaternary Geochronology* 30:422–430 (2015).

26. Gage, M., "Testing the Stockpiling and Field Stone Clearing Theories," *Bulletin of the Massachusetts Archaeological Society* 76(1):2-27 (2015).

27. Gage, M., and Gage, J., *Land of a Thousand Cairns: Revival of Old-Style Ceremonies* (Powwow River Books, Amesbury MA, 2017), pp. 217–245.

28. *Ibid*, p. 5.

29. E.g. Murray, W. F., Investigation of Stone Structures in Eastern Massachusetts. Senior Honors Thesis, Bridgewater State College, Bridgewater MA (2003).

30. Hoffman, C., Archaeological Intensive Survey of Terrace 2, Middleborough Little League Site, Middleborough, Massachusetts (2017). On file at the Massachusetts Historical Commission, Boston MA, pp. 30–33.

31. Maddigan, M., Japan Works: A History of the George H. Shaw Company Site, East Grove Street, Middleborough. Manuscript prepared for the Middleborough Historical Commission, Middleborough MA (1996).

32. Hammell, G., "The Iroquois and the World's Rim: Speculations on Color, Culture, and Contact," *American Indian Quarterly* 16(4):451–469 (1992).

33. Wampanoag Tribe, www.wampanoagtribe.net/Pages/index (2017).

34. Hoffman, C., Analysis of Stone Features: The Ridges at Deer Lake Housing Development Property, Killingworth, Connecticut. On file at the Connecticut Historical Commission, Hartford CT (2004).

35. E.g. Mueller, J., *Sampling in Archaeology* (University of Arizona Press, Tucson AZ, 1975).

36. E.g. Cassedy, D., Phase I Archaeological Survey of the Constitution Pipeline Project. Prepared by: AECOM, Burlington, NJ. Prepared for: Constitution Pipeline Company, LLC, Houston, TX (2014).

37. E.g. Dudek, M., Phase IA Archaeological Sensitivity Assessment, Eversource's Line L-163 Storm Hardening Project, Hillsborough, Antrim, Stoddard, Nelson, and Sullivan, New Hampshire. Commonwealth Heritage Group, Littleton MA (2016).

38. Cachat-Schilling, R., "A Quantitative Assessment of Stone Relics in a Western Massachusetts Town," *Bulletin of the Massachusetts Archaeological Society* 77(2):37–55 (2016).

39. E.g. Holtstein, H., "A Preliminary Archaeological Investigation of the Morton Hill Stone Structure Complex, 1CA671, Calhoun County, Alabama," *Jacksonville State University Archaeological Research Laboratory, Research Series #5*, Jacksonville FL (2010).

40. E.g. Romain, W. F., *An Archaeology of the Sacred: Adena-Hopewell Astronomy and Landscape Archaeology* (The Ancient Earthworks Project, Olmsted Township OH, 2015).

41. Moore, C., and Weiss, M. V., "The Continuing 'Stone Mound Problem': Identifying and Interpreting the Ambiguous Rock Piles of the Upper Ohio Valley," *Journal of Ohio Archaeology* 4:39–71 (2016).

42. Some cells redacted due to landowner concerns; *vide supra* p. 233.

43. Porter, J. D., *Strengthened Resolve: Secrecy, Oppression, and Indigenous Stonework in Early America* (Unpublished ms, 2017); Bourne, E., *The Ancient History of Kennebunk, Maine* (Star Press, Clintonville CT, 1970 [1831]); and Penhallow, S., *The History of the Wars of New-England with the Eastern Indians, or a Narrative of Their Continued Perfidy and Cruelty* (J. Harpel, Cincinnati OH, 1859).

44. Dudek, M., Phase IA Archaeological Sensitivity Assessment, Eversource's Line L-163 Storm Hardening Project, Hillsborough, Antrim, Stoddard, Nelson, and Sullivan, New Hampshire. Commonwealth Heritage Group, Littleton MA (2016).

45. Speck, F. G., "The Memorial Brush Heap in Delaware and Elsewhere," *Bulletin of the Archaeological Society of Delaware* 4:17–23 (1945), p. 11; Porter, J. D., *Strengthened Resolve: Secrecy, Oppression, and Indigenous Stonework in Early America* (Unpublished ms, 2017); Barr, L., *A Brief but Most Complete & True Account of the Settlement of the Ancient Town of Pelham, Westchester County, State of New York, Known One Time Well & Favourably as the Lordshipp & Mannour of Pelham; Also the Story of the Three Modern Villages Called the Pelhams* (The Dietz Press, Richmond, VA, 1946); and Cachat-Schilling, R., "A Quantitative Assessment of Stone Relics in a Western Massachusetts Town," *Bulletin of the Massachusetts Archaeological Society* 77(2):37–55 (2016).

46. Hranicky, W. J., and Collins, L. D., *Virginia Fixed and Portable Artworks* (Virginia Rock Art Survey, Alexandria VA, 2015).

47. Stephenson, R., and Ferguson, A. L. L., *The Accokeek Creek Site: A Middle Atlantic Seaboard Culture Sequence* (University of Michigan, Ann Arbor MI, 1963).

48. Chari, S., and Lavallee, J., (eds.), *Accomplishing NAGPRA: Perspectives on the Intent, Impact, and Future of the Native American Graves Protection and Repatriation Act* (Oregon State University Press, Corvallis OR, 2015).

49. Carmichael, D., Hubert, J., Reeves, B., and Schance, A., (eds.) *Sacred Sites, Sacred Places. One World Archaeology* 23 (Routledge, London, 1997).

50. Ives, T., "Cairnfields in New England's Forgotten Pastures," *Archaeology of Eastern North America* 43:119–132 (2015), p. 119.

51. *Ibid.*, p. 127.

52. United States Department of Interior, Determination of Eligibility Notification, The Turners Falls Sacred Ceremonial Hill Site, www.achp.gov/docs/TurnerFallsDOEDecision-Redacted1.pdf (2008).

53. Nietzsche, F. W., *Also Sprach Zarathustra: Ein Buch fuer Alle und Keinen* (Phillip Reclam, Stuttgart, Germany 1966), p. 20.

Bibliography

Adair, J., Esq., *The History of the American Indians: Particularly Those Nations Adjoining to the Mississippi, East and West Florida, Georgia, South and North Carolina, and Virginia* (London: Edward and Charles Dilly, 1777)

Adams, D., *Mostly Harmless* (Ballantine Books, New York, 2009)

Agassiz, L., *Contributions to the Natural History of the United States of America* (Little, Brown, Boston MA, 1857–62)

Allport, S., *Sermons in Stone: The Stone Walls of New England and New York* (W. W. Norton & Sons, New York, 1990)

Amherst, J., Letter to Henry Louis Bouquet, 16 July 1763 (1763). Cited in Gill, Jr., H., Colonial Germ Warfare, *Colonial Williamsburg Journal*, Spring 2004, www.history.org/foundation/journal/spring04/warfare.cfm

Antevs, E., Correlation of Wisconsin Glacial Maxima. *Daly Volume* 1–85 (1945). earth.geology.yale.edu/~ajs/1945A/1.pdf.

Ballard, E. C., "For Want of a Nail: An Analysis of the Function of Some Horseshoe or 'U'-shaped Stone Structures," *Bulletin of the Massachusetts Archaeological Society* 60(2):39–54 (1999);

"It's About Time and the Paradigm," *Bulletin of the Massachusetts Archaeological Society* 75:13-21 (2014)

Ballard, E. C., and Mavor, Jr., J., "A Case for the Use of Above-Surface Stone Constructions in a Native American Ceremonial Landscape in the Northeast," *Bulletin of the Massachusetts Archaeological Society* 71(1):8-26 (2010)

Barber, J. W., *Connecticut Historical Collections, Containing a General Collection of Interesting Facts, Traditions, Biographical Sketches, Anecdotes, &c., Relating to the History and Antiquities of Every Town in Connecticut, with Geographical Descriptions* (A. Willard, New Haven CT, 1836)

Barr, L., *A Brief but Most Complete & True Account of the Settlement of the Ancient Town of Pelham, Westchester County, State of New York, Known One Time Well & Favourably as the Lordshipp & Mannour of Pelham; Also the Story of the Three Modern Villages Called the Pelhams* (The Dietz Press, Richmond, VA, 1946)

Beauchamp, W. M., *The Iroquois Trail, or, Footprints of the Six Nations* (Published by the author, Fayetteville NY, 1892)

Bell, E., "Discerning Placemaking: Archaeology and Native Histories of the Den Rock Area, Lawrence and Andover, MA," *Bulletin of the Massachusetts Archaeological Society* 73(2):42-63 (2012)

Bellow, H., "Narragansetts Blame FERC for Problems on Pipeline Path," *Berkshire Eagle*, April 28 (2017). www.berkshireeagle.com/stories/narragansetts-blame-ferc-for-problems-on-pipeline-path,505862

Beverley, R., *The History and Present State of Virginia* (New Edition, University of North Carolina Press, Chapel Hill NC, 2013 [1722])

Blancke, S., and Spiess, A. E., "The Flagg Swamp Rockshelter, Marlborough, MA: A Summary," *Bulletin of the Massachusetts Archaeological Society* 67(1):2-24 (2006).

Bourne, E., *The Ancient History of Kennebunk, Maine* (Star Press, Clintonville CT, 1970 [1831])

Bua, M., *Talking Walls: Casting out the Post-Contact Stone-Wall Building Myth* (Publication Studio Hudson, Catskill NY, 2015)

Burroughs, J., *In the Catskills* (Houghton Mifflin, Boston and New York, 1910)

Butler, E., "The Brush or Stone Memorial Heaps of Southern New England," *Bulletin of the Connecticut Archaeological Society* 4:9 (1946)

Cachat-Schilling, R., "A Quantitative Assessment of Stone Relics in a Western Massachusetts Town," *Bulletin of the Massachusetts Archaeological Society* 77(2):37–55 (2016)

Éli Luweyok Kikayunkahke—So Said the Departed Elders. Paper presented at the 84th Annual Meeting of the Eastern States Archaeological Federation, New London CT (2017)

Cajete, G., *Look to the Mountain: An Ecology of Indigenous Education* (Kivaki Press, Skyland NC, 1994)

Carmichael, D., Hubert, J., Reeves, B., and Schance, A., (eds.) *Sacred Sites, Sacred Places. One World Archaeology* 23 (Routledge, London, 1997)

Cassedy, D., Phase I Archaeological Survey of the Constitution Pipeline Project. Prepared by: AECOM, Burlington, NJ. Prepared for: Constitution Pipeline Company, LLC, Houston, TX (2014)

Chari, S., and Lavallee, J., (eds.), *Accomplishing NAGPRA: Perspectives on the Intent, Impact, and Future of the Native American Graves Protection and Repatriation Act* (Oregon State University Press, Corvallis OR, 2015)

Charles, T., *Discovering South Carolina's Rock Art* (University of South Carolina Press, Columbia SC, 2010)

Claggett, S., Personal communication concerning the age of stone pile sites in North Carolina (2012)

Cole, J., Western Massachusetts "Monks Caves": 1979 University of Massachusetts Field Research, *Man in the Northeast* 24:37–57 (1982)

Coles, J. M., and Higgs, E. S., *The Archaeology of Early Man* (Frederick A. Praeger, New York, 1969)

Converse, H. M., and Parker, A. C., *Myths and Legends of the New York State Iroquois* (New York State Museum, Albany NY, 1906)

Cooper, J. F., *The Wept of Wish-Ton-Wish* (Reprint Services Corporation, Irvine CA, 1829)

Cowie, E. R., and Petersen, J. B., Archaeological Phase II Survey and Testing of the Bonny Eagle Project (FERC No. 2529), Cumberland and York Counties, Maine. Report on file with the Maine Historic Preservation Commission, Augusta ME (1990)

Crandall, W., Jonasch, J. J., and Keller, R., "A Massachusetts Patterned Mound Complex," in Cook, W., (ed.), *Ancient Vermont* (Academy Books, Rutland VT, 1978), pp. 39–41

Cronon, W., *Changes in the Land: Indians, Colonists, and the Ecology of New England* (Hill and Wang, New York, 2003)

Da Silva, M., *Portuguese Pilgrims and Dighton Rock* (Published by the author, 1971)

Davis, J., Personal communication regarding the function of split-filled boulders (2003)

DeLong, B., and Cooke, P., "Secrets of the Stones" www.barbaradelong.com/special-projects/secrets-of-the-stones/secret-of-the-stones-maps/ (n.d.)

DiMarzo, S., Personal communications about sites in Rhode Island (2014–2017)

Dincauze, D. F., "An Introduction to the Archaeology of the Greater Boston Area," *Archaeology of Eastern North America* 2(1):39–67 (1974)

Donta, C., Wendt, J., Barker, T., and Medina, A., Archaeological Intensive (Locational) and Site Examination Surveys of the Muttock-Pauwating Native American Site, 19-PL-292, Middleborough, Massachusetts (2013). On file at Massachusetts Historical Commission, Boston MA

Dudek, M., Phase IA Archaeological Sensitivity Assessment, Eversource's Line L-163 Storm Hardening Project, Hillsborough, Antrim, Stoddard, Nelson, and Sullivan, New Hampshire. Commonwealth Heritage Group, Littleton MA (2016).

Duncan, D. E., *Calendar: Humanity's Epic Struggle to Determine a True and Accurate Year* (HarperCollins, New York, 1999)

Elvas, F. de, *True Relation of the Hardships Suffered by Governor Hernando de Soto and Certain Portuguese Gentlemen during the Discovery of the Province of Florida* (Alexander Robertson, trans. Florida Historical Society, Deland FL, 1933 [1577])

Empire of Laws, New England (1787–1833): The End of State Religion. Empire of Laws: The Legal History of the 50 American States, www.statelegalhistory.com, Section 1.2.1 (n.d.)

Feldman, M., *The Mystery Hill Story* (Mystery Hill Press, North Salem NH, 1977)

Fell, H. B., *America, B.C.: Ancient Settlers in the New World* (Quadrangle Books, New York, 1976); "Vermont's Ancient Sites and the Larger Picture of Trans-Atlantic Visitations to America, B.C.," in Cook, W., (ed.), *Ancient Vermont* (Academy Books, Rutland VT, 1978) pp. 70–84; *Saga America* (Times Books, New York, 1980); *Bronze Age America* (Little, Brown, & Co., New York, 1982)

Ferrero, P., *Hopi: Songs of the Fourth World* (video) (New Day Films, Blooming Grove NY, 1983)

Flynn, E., and Doucette, D., Community Connections from Archaic to Present in Southeastern Massachusetts: Insights from Halls Swamp and Beyond. Paper given at the 2015 Annual Meeting of the Society for American Archaeology, core.tdar.org/collection/29613/new-research-on-the-archaic-period-in-the-northeast-the-past-20-years (2015); Archaeological Site Examination and Data Recovery Program, Halls Swamp Site (19-PL-1067), Kingston, Massachusetts, Volume I. The Public Archaeology Laboratory, Inc. No. 2880.01. Submitted to Kingston Historical Commission, Kingston, MA (2016)

Fohl, T., "Confessions of a Former Professional Rock Popper," *New England Antiquities Research Association Journal* 37(2):15 (2003); Personal communication concerning additions to the Benfield A site (2009); "Integrated Wetland-Dry Land Features with Astronomical Associations," *Bulletin of the Massachusetts Archaeological Society* 71(1):44-56 (2010)

Fohl, T., Harris, D., Hoffman, C., and Waksman, P., Survey Report of Indian Ceremonial Structures on Benfield Parcel "A" Property in Carlisle, Massachusetts. Report submitted to the Carlisle Board of Selectmen (2005)

Fournier, C., A Locational Analysis of Sacred Sites in Southern New England. Senior Honors Thesis, Anthropology Department Bridgewater State University, Bridgewater MA (2013)

Fowke, G., *Archeological Investigations. Bureau of American Ethnology Bulletin* 76 (Smithsonian Institution, Washington, D.C., 1922)

Fowler, W. S., "Ceremonial and Domestic Products of Aboriginal New England," *Bulletin of the Massachusetts Archaeological Society* 27(3/4):33-68 (1966)

Gage, M., "New England Native American Spirit Structures," *Bulletin of the Massachusetts Archaeological Society* 74(1):25-33 (2013); "Testing the Stockpiling and Field Stone Clearing Theories," *Bulletin of the Massachusetts Archaeological Society* 76(1):2-27 (2015)

Gage, M., and Gage, J., *A Guide to New England Stone Structures: Stone Cairns, Stone Walls, Standing Stones, Chambers, Foundations, Wells, Culverts, Quarries, and Other Structures* (Powwow River Books, Amesbury MA, 2012); "How to Identify and Distinguish Native American Ceremonial Stone Structures from Historic Farm Structures," *Bulletin of the Archaeological Society of Connecticut* 77:17-40 (2015); *Land of a Thousand Cairns: Revival of Old-Style Ceremonies* (Powwow River Books, Amesbury MA, 2017)

Gardner, R., (Great Moose), "Anthropomorphic and Fertility Stone-works of Southeastern New England: A Native Interpretation," *Bulletin of the Massachusetts Archaeological Society* 59(2):57-65 (1994)

Geake, R., *A History of the Narragansett Tribe of Rhode Island: Keepers of the Bay* (The History Press, Charlestown SC, 2011); Known Land, Foreign Tongue: Early European Attempts to Navigate the Algonquian Language, rifootprints.com/2012/03/23/known-land-foreign-tongue-early-european-attempts-to-navigate-the-algonquian-language (2012)

Goodby, R., Tremblay, S., and Bouras, E., "The Swanzey Fish Dam: A Large, Precontact Native American Stone Structure in Southwestern New Hampshire," *Northeast Anthropology* 81/82:1-22 (2014)

Goodwin, W., *The Ruins of Great Ireland in New England* (Meador Publishing, Boston MA, 1946)

Googoo, M., Protecting Mi'kmaq Petroglyphs in Bedford, Kejimkujik National Park, www.kukukwes.com/2015/08/26 (2015)

Gookin, D., *Historical Collections of the Indians in New England* (Towtaid, Leicester MA, 1970 [1674])

Goudsward, D., *Ancient Stone Sites of New England and the Debate over Early European Exploration* (McFarland & Co., Jefferson NC, 2006)

Graburn, N., "Inuksuk: Icon of the Inuit of Nunavut," *Etudes/Inuit/Studies* 28(1):69-82 (2004)

Gresham, T., "Historic Patterns of Rock Piling and the Rock Pile Problems," *Early Georgia* 18(1/2):1-40 (1990)

Grey, D. R., (ed.), *Critical Engagements with Fringe Science* (Cognella, San Diego CA, 2016)

Grinnell, J. B., *Men and Events of Forty Years* (D. Lothrop and Company, Boston MA, 1891)

Haisch, B., *The God Theory* (Weiser Books, San Francisco CA, 2006)

Hallendy, N., *Tukiliit: An Introduction to Inuksuit and Other Stone Figures of the North* (Douglas & McIntyre and University of Alaska Press, Vancouver, BC, 2009)

Hammell, G., "The Iroquois and the World's Rim: Speculations on Color, Culture, and Contact," *American Indian Quarterly* 16(4):451–469 (1992)

Hantman, Dr. J., personal communication with the author (2017).

Harris, D., Personal communication regarding the deliberations of the Narragansett Tribal Council regarding sacred sites (2008)

Harris, D., and Robinson, P., "The Ancient Ceremonial Landscape and King Philip's War Battlefields of Nipsachuck," *Northeast Anthropology* 83/84:133–149 (2015)

Hawley, G., Letter containing an account of his services among the Indians of Massachusetts and New York, and a narrative of his journey to Onohoghgwage, *Collections of the Massachusetts Historical Society* series 1, vol. 4 (1835 [1794]), pp. 57–60

Hays, W. L., *Statistics for Psychologists* (Holt, Rinehart & Winston, New York, 1963)

Heilbron, J. L., *The Sun in the Church: Cathedrals as Solar Observatories* (Harvard University Press, Cambridge MA, 2001)

Helme, K., Personal communication concerning her dispute with Ramona Peters about the origin of stone structures (2015)

Henry, J. M., "The Westford Pseudo-Knight," *Bulletin of the Massachusetts Archaeological Society* 76(2):71–81 (2015)

Heyerdahl, T., *The Ra Expeditions* (Flamingo Publishing, New York, 1993)

Hiscox, O. A.," The Last of the Wabaquassets," In Lincoln, A. B., (ed.), *A Modern History of Windham County, Connecticut* (S. J. Clarke Publishing Company, Chicago IL, 1920) pp. 60–62

Hoffman, C., Howe Street Regional Water Treatment Facility Locational Archaeological Survey. Draft Report (1997). On file at the Massachusetts Historical Commission, Boston MA; Analysis of Stone Features: The Ridges at Deer Lake Housing Development Property, Killingworth, Connecticut. On file at the Connecticut Historical Commission, Hartford CT (2004); South Brook Archaeological Survey, Bridgewater, Massachusetts (2006). On file at the Massachusetts Historical Commission, Boston MA; "A Quantitative Analysis of Stone Features at the Buell Hill Site in Killingworth, Connecticut," *Bulletin of the Archaeological Society of Connecticut* 77:123–150 (2015); "Caches or Offerings? Ceremonial Objects from the First Terrace at the Middleborough Little League Site (19-PL-520)," *Bulletin of the Massachusetts Archaeological Society* 77(2):61–68 (2016); Archaeological Intensive Survey of Terrace 2, Middleborough Little League Site, Middleborough, Massachusetts (2017). On file at the Massachusetts Historical Commission, Boston MA

Hoffman, C., and Edwards, A., "The SuAsCo Watershed Archaeological Inventory Project: Exploring the Cultural Resources of a Suburban Area" (2002). On file at the Massachusetts Historical Commission, Boston MA

Holtstein, H., "A Preliminary Archaeological Investigation of the Morton Hill Stone Structure Complex, 1CA671, Calhoun County, Alabama," *Jacksonville State University Archaeological Research Laboratory, Research Series* #5, Jacksonville FL (2010)

The Holy Bible, *A Reader's Guide to the Holy Bible, King James Version* (Thomas Nelson, Publishers, Nashville TN, 1972)

Hornburg, A.-C., *Mi'Kmaq Landscapes: From Animism to Sacred Ecology* (Ashgate Publishing Company, Burlington VT, 2008)

Houston, J., and Rubin, M., *Manual for the Peacemaker: An Iroquois Legend to Heal Self and Society* (Quest Books, Wheaton IL, 1997)

Howes, M., Ceremonial Stoneworks of the Northeast, nativenewenglandstones.blogspot.com/2015/03/looking-at-rock-piles-in-holliston-ma.html (2015–2016)

Hranicky, W. J., and Collins, L. D., "Short Mountain Petroglyph Site, Shenandoah County, Virginia," *Archaeological Society of Virginia Quarterly Bulletin* 60(3):125–132 (2005); *Virginia Fixed and Portable Artworks* (Virginia Rock Art Survey, Alexandria VA, 2015)

Hunter, D., *The Place of Stone: Dighton Rock and the Erasure of America's Indigenous Past* (University of North Carolina Press, Chapel Hill NC, 2017)

Huntington, F., "Preliminary Report on the Excavation of Flagg Swamp Rockshelter." Institute for Conservation Archaeology, Peabody Museum of Archaeology and Ethnography, Harvard University, Cambridge MA (1982)

Ingstad, H., and Ingstad, A. S., *The Viking Discovery of America: The Excavation of a Norse Settlement at L'Anse Aux Meadows, Newfoundland* (Checkmark Books, New York, 2001)

Ives, T., "Cairnfields in New England's Forgotten Pastures," *Archaeology of Eastern North America* 43:119–132 (2015)

Jefferson, T., *Notes on the State of Virginia*, edited with an introduction by William Peden (W. W. Norton & Company, Inc., New York, 1972 [1800])

Jones, B., "Interpreting Cultural Stone Landscapes in Southeastern Connecticut," *Bulletin of the Archaeological Society of Connecticut*, No. 77 (2015)

Kehoe, A. B., *The Kensington Runestone: Approaching a Research Question Holistically* (Waveland Press, Long Grove IL, 2004)

Kimmerer, R. W., *Braiding Sweetgrass: Indigenous Wisdom, Scientific Knowledge, and the Teachings of Plants* (Milkweed Editions, Minneapolis MN, 2013)

Kittredge, G. L., "Some Notes on Witchcraft," *Proceedings of the American Antiquarian Society*, new series 18 (1907), pp. 148–212

Kraft, H., "Late Woodland Cultures of the Upper Delaware Valley," in Custer, J., (ed.), *Late Woodland Cultures of the Middle Atlantic Region* (University of Delaware Press, Newark DE, 1986), pp. 103–115

Lenik, E. J., *Picture Rocks: American Indian Rock Art in the Northeast Woodlands* (University Press of New England, Hanover NH, 2002); "The Human Hand in Northeastern Rock Art: Communicating with the Spirits," *Bulletin of the Massachusetts Archaeological Society* 77(1):1–12 (2016)

Leonard, Jr., K. C., "Identification and Preliminary Analysis of a Late Woodland Ceremonial Site in Southeastern Massachusetts," *Bulletin of the Massachusetts Archaeological Society* 71(1):26–44 (2010)

Lepionka, M. E., and Carlotto, M., "Evidence of a Native American Solar Observatory on Sunset Hill in Gloucester, Massachusetts," *Bulletin of the Massachusetts Archaeological Society* 76(1):27–43 (2015)

Lepore, J., *The Name of War: King Philip's War and the Origins of American Identity* (Alfred A. Knopf, New York, 1998)

Leveillee, A., "When Worlds Collide: Archaeology in the New Age: The Conant Parcel Stone Piles," *Bulletin of the Massachusetts Archaeological Society* 58(1):24–30 (1997a); "Archaeological Investigations of Stone Pile Features within the Orchard Valley Estates Subdivision, Cranston, Rhode Island," *Bulletin of the Massachusetts Archaeological Society* 58(1):15–24 (1997b); "Public Archaeology: The New Age, and Local Truths," *Bulletin of the Massachusetts Archaeological Society* 62(1):23–28 (2001)

Leveillee, A., and Lance, M., "On the Archaeology of Stone Piles and a Late Archaic Date," *Bulletin of the Massachusetts Archaeological Society* 69(2):58–64 (2008)

Loubser, J., "Betwixt and Between: Petroglyph Boulders on Liminal Locations in the Southeastern Mountains," core.tdar.org/browse/other-keyword/134154/rock-art (2016)

Louv, R., *Last Child in the Woods: Saving Children from Nature Deficit Disorder* (Algonquian Books, Chapel Hill NC, 2005)

MacLeod, M., "Great Sachem of the Nashaways, Part 2," *Archaeological Quarterly of the W. Elmer Ekblaw Chapter of the Massachusetts Archaeological Society* 8(3):1–22 (1986)

MacSweeney, T., "Waking up on Turtle Island," wakinguponturtleisland.blogspot.com (2009–2016)

Maddigan, M., Japan Works: A History of the George H. Shaw Company Site, East Grove Street, Middleborough. Manuscript prepared for the Middleborough Historical Commission, Middleborough MA (1996)

Mahan, J., *Identification of the Tsoyaha Waeno, Builders of Temple Mounds* (Doctoral Dissertation. University Microfilm, Ann Arbor MI, 1970); *The Secret: America in World History before Columbus* (Joseph Mahan, Columbus GA, 1983); *North American Sun Kings: Keepers of the Flame* (ISAC Press, Columbus GA, 1992)

Mahan, S., Martin, F., and Carlson, C., "Construction Ages of the Upton Stone Chamber: Preliminary Findings and Suggestions for Future Luminescence Research," *Quaternary Geochronology* 30:422–430 (2015)

Mails, T. E., *The Mystic Warriors of the Plains* (Mallard Press, New York, NY, 1991)

Martin, F., Personal communication regarding the preservation of the King Philip's Rocks site (2004)

Massachusetts General Laws, An Act Relative to the Transfer of Land in the Town of Sharon, malegislature.gov/Laws/SessionLaws/Acts/2002/Chapter249 (2002)

Massachusetts Historical Commission, Review and Compliance, www.sec.state.ma.us/mhc/mhcrevcom.revcomidx.htm (2017); "What to Do When Human Burials Are Accidentally Uncovered," *KnowHow* #4, www.sec.state.ma.us/mhc/mhcpdf/knowhow4.pdf (n.d.)

Mather, I., *A Brief Historie of the Warr with the Indians in New England* (John Foster, Boston MA, 1676)

Mavor, Jr., J., *Stones to the Sun* (James Mavor, Woods Hole MA, 1993)

Mavor, Jr., J., and Dix, B., *Manitou: The Sacred Landscape of New England's Native Civilization* (Inner Traditions International, Rochester VT, 1989)

McDermott, K., Personal communication concerning ongoing ritual use of the Buell Hill site (2007)

McGaa, E. E., *Native Wisdom: Perceptions of the Natural Way* (Council Oaks Books, Tulsa OK, 1995)

McGee, W. J., "Man and the Glacial Period," *American Anthropologist* v. A6(1):85–95 (1893)

McGrew, J. C., and Monroe, C. B., *An Introduction to Statistical Problem Solving in Geography* (William C. Brown, Dubuque IA, 1993)

Miner, personal communication with the author, 2017.

Mooney, J., *Myths of the Cherokee: Bureau of American Ethnology* 19 (1) (Smithsonian Institution, Washington DC, 2006 [1891])

Moore, C., and Weiss, M. V., "The Continuing 'Stone Mound Problem': Identifying and Interpreting the Ambiguous Rock Piles of the Upper Ohio Valley," *Journal of Ohio Archaeology* 4:39–71 (2016)

Mueller, J., *Sampling in Archaeology* (University of Arizona Press, Tucson AZ, 1975)

Mulford, P. B., "Fountainhead Regional Park Light-Colored Stone Mounds, Fairfax County, Virginia: The Mulford Mounds," *Archaeological Society of Virginia Quarterly Bulletin* 69(2):116–132 (2014)

Murray, W. F., Investigation of Stone Structures in Eastern Massachusetts. Senior Honors Thesis, Bridgewater State College, Bridgewater MA (2003)

Narragansett Indian Tribe, "*Nikkomo*—I Give Away," artways.libsyn.com/podcast/episode-3-nikkomo (2016)

National Park Service, National Register of Historic Places—Traditional Cultural Properties (TCPs): A Quick Guide for Preserving Native American Cultural Resources, www.nps.gov/history/tribes/Documents/TCP.pdf (2017)

Neudorffer, G., "A Preliminary Analysis of Vermont's Stone Chambers" in Cook, W. L., (ed.), *Ancient Vermont* (Academy Books, Rutland VT, 1977), pp. 9–13

New England Antiquities Research Association (NEARA), NEARA Supports a Wide Range of Interests and Disciplines, www.neara.org/index.php/interests-menu (2017)

New England Historical Society, The Maypole That Infuriated the Puritans, www.newenglandhistoricalsociety.com/maypole-infuriated-puritans/ (2015)

Nietzsche, F. W., *Also Sprach Zarathustra: Ein Buch fuer Alle und Keinen* (Phillip Reclam, Stuttgart, Germany 1966)

Niles, G. G., *The Hoosac Valley: Its Legends and Its History* (G. P. Putnam's Sons, New York, 1912)

Norton, H. F., *History of Martha's Vineyard* (Henry Franklin Norton and Robert Emmett Pyne, Tisbury MA, 1923)

O'Callaghan, MD, E. B., *The Documentary History of the State of New York* (Weed, Parsons & Co., Albany NY, 1850)

Ojibwa, Native American Ceremonial Landscape Sites in the Northeast, nativeamericannetroots.net/diary/tag/ceremonial-stone-landscape-sites (2015)

Paine, H. D., (ed.), *A Journal of Genealogical and Biographical Information Respecting the American Families of Payne, Paine, Payn, &c* Volume I (New York, 1880)

Parcak, S., Potential Viking Site found in Newfoundland, www.cbc.ca/news/canada/newfoundland-labrador/vikings-newfoundland-1.3515747 (2016)

Parker, A. C., *Nundawao and the Coming of the Senecas* (Nundawaga Society for History and Folklore, (Naples(?)NY, 1955)

Paul, C. T., The Hammonassett line, Chapter 1: A Summer Solstice Sunset Line, www.neara.org/images/pdf/Hammonasset01.pdf (2001)

Penhallow, S., *The History of the Wars of New-England with the Eastern Indians, or a Narrative of Their Continued Perfidy and Cruelty* (J. Harpel, Cincinnati OH, 1859)

Pequot Tribal Nation, Schemitzun: Feast of Green Corn and Dance, schemitzun.mptn-nsn.gov/uploadedFiles/Schemitzun_brochure_2016.pdf (2016)

Peters, R., Personal communication regarding the absence of stone structure sites on Cape Cod (2014)

Pohl, F. J., "Further Proof of Vikings at Follins Pond, Cape Cod," *Bulletin of the Massachusetts Archaeological Society* 21(3–4):48–53 (1960)

Porter, J. D., *Strengthened Resolve: Secrecy, Oppression, and Indigenous Stonework in Early America* (Unpublished ms, 2017)

Price, N., "Tourism and the Bighorn Medicine Wheel: How Multiple Use Does Not Work for Sacred Land Sites," in Carmichael, D., Hubert, J., Reeves, B., and Schance, A., (eds.), *Sacred Sites, Sacred Places: One World Archaeology* 23 (Routledge, London, 1997), pp. 259–264

Pringle, H., Evidence of Viking Outpost Found in Canada, news.nationalgeographic.com/news/2012/10/121019-viking-outpost-second-new-canada-science-sutherland/ (2012)

Reader's Digest, "Through Indian Eyes: The Untold Story of Native American Peoples," (Reader's Digest Association, Scarsdale NY, 1995)

Reeves, B., "Ninaistakis—The Nitsitapii's Sacred Mountain: Traditional Native Religious Activities and Land Use/Tourism Conflicts," in Carmichael, D., Hubert, J., Reeves, B., and Schance, A., (eds.), *Sacred Sites, Sacred Places: One World Archaeology* 23 (Routledge, London, 1997), pp. 265–290

Rice, O. K., and Brown, S. W., *West Virginia: A History* (University Press of Kentucky, Lexington KY, 1985)

Riffe, J., and Burdeau, G., (directors), *Who Owns the Past?* (video) (Saul Zaentz Film Center, Berkeley CA, 2000)

Robbins, M., *Wapanucket: An Archaeological Report* (Massachusetts Archaeological Society, Attleboro MA, 1980)

Romain, W. F., *An Archaeology of the Sacred: Adena-Hopewell Astronomy and Landscape Archaeology* (The Ancient Earthworks Project, Olmsted Township OH, 2015)

Rudolph, J. H., "An Ancient Solar Observatory at Willow Creek, California," in Gilmore, D., and McElroy, L., (eds.), *Across Before Columbus? Evidence for Transoceanic Contact with the Americas before 1492* (Mercantile Printing Company, Worcester MA, 1998), pp. 71–84

Russell, H. S., *Indian New England before the Mayflower* (University Press of New England, Hanover NH, 1980)

Ruttenber, E. M., *Indian Tribes of Hudson's River, 1700–1850*, v. 2 (Hope Farm Press, Saugerties NY, 1922 [1872])

Samuelson, V., Personal communications regarding Viking contacts with New England (2014–15).

SCWA Environmental Consultants, Supplement to Phase Ia Archaeological Pedestrian Survey, Town of Shutesbury, Franklin County, Massachusetts. Report submitted to Lake Street Development Partners, Chicago IL (2016)

Seaby, P., "The First Datable Norse Find from North America?" *Seaby Coin and Medal Bulletin* (December 1978)

Seketau, E., Personal communication concerning location of stone structure sites (2003)

Shurtleff, N., (ed.), *Records of the Governor and Company of the Massachusetts Bay in New England* (William White, Boston MA, 1853)

Silverberg, R., *Mound Builders of Ancient America: The Archaeology of a Myth* (New York Graphic Society, New York, 1968)

Simmons, W. S., *Spirit of the New England Tribes: Indian History and Folklore* (University Press of New England, Hanover NH, 1986)

Smith, J., *The Generall Historie of Virginia, New England, and the Summer Isles* (Reprinted by the Wisconsin Historical Society, Document No. AJ-082. Madison WI, 2003 [1624])

Snow, D., *The Archaeology of New England* (Academic Press, New York, 1980)

Southwest Traditions, The Hopi, www.southwesttraditions.com/The_Hopi/the_hopi.html (2017). Originally posted by the Museum of Northern Arizona, Flagstaff AZ (www.musnaz.org)

Speck, F. G., "Malecite Tales," *The Journal of American Folklore* 30(118):479–485 (1917); "The Memorial Brush Heap in Delaware and Elsewhere," *Bulletin of the Archaeological Society of Delaware* 4:17–23 (1945)

Stephenson, R., and Ferguson, A. L. L., *The Accokeek Creek Site: A Middle Atlantic Seaboard Culture Sequence* (University of Michigan, Ann Arbor MI, 1963)

Stiles, E., *A History of Three of the Judges of King Charles I* (Elisha Babcock, Hartford CT, 1795); *Literary Diaries of Ezra Stiles*, Vol. I: 1767–1775 (Scribners & Sons, New York 1901 [1794]); *Extracts from the Itineraries and Other Miscellanies of Ezra Stiles, D.D., LL.D., 1755–1794, with a Selection from His Correspondence* (Franklin Bowditch Dexter, ed. Yale, University Press, New Haven CT 1916 [1762])

Stites, S. H., *Economics of the Iroquois* (The New Era Printing Company, Lancaster PA, 1905)

Storm, H., *Seven Arrows* (Ballantine Books, New York NY, 1972); *Lightningbolt* (Ballantine Books, New York NY, 1994)

Sturluson, S., *Prose Edda*, Brodeur, A. G., (transl.), (The American-Scandinavian Foundation, New York, 1916)

Taylor, W. B., "Thunderbirds in Southeast MA," *Bulletin of the Massachusetts Archaeological Society* 69(2):64–68 (2008)

Taylor, H., Personal communication regarding Frank Vento's characterization of stone piles in the Lake Catalpa PA area (2015)

"The Last Word: Debunking the Myth of Stone Walls, Piles, and Chambers," *Terra Firma*, Massachusetts Division of Conservation Resources, v. 5:14 (2005)

Theodoratus, D., and LaPena, F., "Wintu Sacred Geography of Northern California," in Carmichael, D., Hubert, J., Reeves, B., and Schance, A., (eds.), *Sacred Sites, Sacred Places: One World Archaeology* 23 (Routledge, London, 1997) pp. 20–31

Thomas, C., "Report on the Mound Explorations of the Bureau of Ethnology," *Twelfth Annual Report of the Bureau of American Ethnology* (Washington, D.C., 1894)

Thomas, E., "Maintaining the Integrity of the Homeland: Recognizing and Re-awakening the Memory of Forgotten Places through Mohegan Archaeology," *Bulletin of the Archaeological Society of Connecticut* 77:41–50 (2015)

Thorson, R. M., *Stone by Stone: The Magnificent History in New England's Stone Walls* (Walker and Company, New York, 2002)

Timreck, T., *The Great Falls: Discovery, Destruction, and Preservation in a Massachusetts Town* (video) (Bullfrog Films, Oley PA, 2012)

Town of Ashland, Massachusetts, Warrant Articles, Information, and Recommendations of the Finance Committee for the November 14, 2017 Special Town Meeting, Ashland High School (2017)

Tylor, E., *Primitive Culture: Research into the Development of Mythology, Philosophy, Religion, Language, Art, and Custom* (John Murray, London, 1871)

United South and Eastern Tribes, Inc., Sacred Landscapes within the Commonwealth of Massachusetts, Resolution 2003:22 (2003); Sacred Ceremonial Stone Landscapes Found in the Ancestral Territories of United South and Eastern Tribes, Inc. Member Tribes, Resolution 2007:32 (2007)

United States Department of Interior, 36 CFR Part 800—Protection of Historic Properties (incorporating amendments effective August 5, 2004) www.achp.gov/regs-rev04.pdf (2004); National Historic Preservation Act of 1966, as amended through 2006 (with annotations), www.achp.gov/docs/nhpa%202008-final.pdf (2006); Determination of Eligibility Notification, The Turners Falls Sacred Ceremonial Hill Site, www.achp.gov/docs/TurnerFallsDOEDecision-Redacted1.pdf (2008)

Vieira, J., Stone Builders, Mound Builders, and the Giants of Ancient North America. TEDx Talk (subsequently withdrawn from the TEDx website—see tedxshelburnefalls.wordpress. com/2012/12/14/jim-vieiras-talk-removed-from-internet/) (2012)

Wagner, G., *Age Determination of Young Rocks and Artifacts: Physical and Chemical Clocks in Quaternary Geology and Archaeology* (Springer Verlag, Berlin, 1995)

Waksman, P., Rockpiles, rockpiles.blogspot.com/ (2009–2016); "A Context for Studying Rock Piles in Massachusetts," *Bulletin of the Massachusetts Archaeological Society* 73(2):68–75 (2012)

Walwer, G., "Stone Piles: A Tale of Two Towns," *Bulletin of the Archaeological Society of Connecticut* 77:111–121 (2015)

Walwer, G., and Walwer, D. N., Phase I Archaeological Reconnaissance Survey Report of the Ridges at Deer Lake Housing Development (Phase III) in the town of Killingworth CT (2003). Manuscript filed with the State Historic Preservation Office, Hartford CT

Wampanoag Tribe, www.wampanoagtribe.net/Pages/index (2017)

Werkheiser, F., and Repsher, D., *Documentary Evidence of Aboriginal Stonework in the American Northeast: A Collection of Documents Referencing Amerindian Stone Building Tradition, Spiritual Expression and Art* (Werkheiser and Repsher, New York, 2005)

Weslager, C. A., *The Delaware Indians: A History* (Rutgers University Press, New Brunswick NJ, 1990 [1946])

Weston, T., *History of the Town of Middleboro Massachusetts* (Houghton and Mifflin, Boston MA and New York, 1906)

Wheeler, M., *Archaeology from the Earth* (Oxford University Press, Oxford, Great Britain, 1954)

White, T. D., Toth, N., Chase, P. G., Clark, G. A., Conrad, N. J., Cook, J., d'Errico, F., Donahue, R. E., Gargett, R. H., Giacobini, G., Pike-Tay, A., and Turner, A., "The Question of Ritual Cannibalism at Grotta Guattari," *Current Anthropology* 32(2):118–138 (1991)

Whitfield, H., *The Light Appearing More and More towards the Perfect Day: Massachusetts Historical Society Collections*, 3rd Series, Vol. 4 (Cambridge, MA, 1814)

Whittall, J., Radiocarbon Dates Associated with Stonework in New England. Work Report, Early Sites Research Society, Rowley MA (1989)

Wilbur, C. K., *The New England Indians*, 2nd ed. (The Globe Pequot Press, Old Saybrook CT, 1996)

Williams, R., *A Key into the Language of America* (Wayne State University Press, Detroit MI, 1935 [1643])

Winter, E., "An Atlantic Phase Mortuary Feature at the Call Site, Billerica, MA," *Bulletin of the Massachusetts Archaeological Society* 67(2):42–47 (2006); "Skug River: The Meaning of a Landscape Name in Andover, Massachusetts," *Bulletin of the Massachusetts Archaeological Society* 71(1):79–87 (2010)

Index

Author and Contributor Biographies

Author's Credentials

Dr. Curtiss Hoffman holds a Ph.D. from Yale University in Near Eastern Languages and Literatures (1974), and since 1973 has directed field operations at numerous archaeological sites in southern New England. He is Full Professor in the Department of Anthropology at Bridgewater State University in Bridgewater, Massachusetts, a position he has held since 1978. He is past president of the Massachusetts Archaeological Society and currently serves as the editor of its *Bulletin*. He is also current president of the Northeastern Anthropological Association. In addition to teaching courses in archaeology since 1973, he has an abiding interest in cognitive anthropology: the study of the ideational world of past and present cultures and the ways in which the members of these cultures represent their world-view in the form of material culture. He frequently teaches courses in this area at Bridgewater State, including myth and culture, anthropology of religion, and culture and consciousness. He is the author of two monographs: *People of the Fresh Water Lake: A Prehistory of Westborough, Massachusetts* (Kluver, 1991) and *The Seven Story Tower: A Mythic Journey through Space and Time* (Perseus Books, 1999); as well as numerous chapters in anthologies and journal articles on both archaeology and cognitive anthropology, and numerous archaeological site reports. He works closely with both antiquarians and indigenous people on projects supporting the preservation of stone monuments.

Commentator Biography

Black-Eagle Sun, also spiritually known as "SUNHEART" is a Nipmuc Turtle Clan Medicine Doctor, devoted husband and father, spiritual counselor, and consultant. Eagle attained his B.A. Degree in political science and special education from the University of Denver in 1962. He attained his M.Sc. in counseling from California State University at Hayward, CA, in 1972. He has been a teacher and counselor in the public school systems in California, Oregon, Idaho, Arizona, and New Mexico. He is presently a behavioral health consultant in Concord, California. Eagle has facilitated workshops and ceremonies in Canada, and the United States, lecturing on the psychology of being indigenous Native American, counseling techniques from an Indigenous Native perspective, and the positive esoteric psychology of the spiritual self. Eagle is a "Sacred Pipe Carrier" with a reverence for Mother Earth and all races of humanity. Eagle embodies all aspects of a true humanitarian servant.